Comparative Public Budgeting

A Global Perspective

Edited by

Charles E. Menifield, PhD

Associate Professor
University of Memphis
Memphis, Tennessee

Visiting Associate Professor
University of Nebraska—Omaha
Omaha, Nebraska

JONES & BARTLETT
LEARNING

World Headquarters
Jones & Bartlett Learning
40 Tall Pine Drive
Sudbury, MA 01776
978-443-5000
info@jblearning.com
www.jblearning.com

Jones & Bartlett Learning
Canada
6339 Ormindale Way
Mississauga, Ontario L5V 1J2
Canada

Jones & Bartlett Learning
International
Barb House, Barb Mews
London W6 7PA
United Kingdom

Jones & Bartlett Learning books and products are available through most bookstores and online booksellers. To contact Jones & Bartlett Learning directly, call 800-832-0034, fax 978-443-8000, or visit our website, www.jblearning.com.

Substantial discounts on bulk quantities of Jones & Bartlett Learning publications are available to corporations, professional associations, and other qualified organizations. For details and specific discount information, contact the special sales department at Jones & Bartlett Learning via the above contact information or send an email to specialsales@jblearning.com.

Production Credits
Publisher: Michael Brown
Associate Editor: Catie Heverling
Editorial Assistant: Teresa Reilly
Production Manager: Tracey Chapman
Associate Production Editor: Kate Stein
Senior Marketing Manager: Sophie Fleck
Manufacturing and Inventory Control Supervisor: Amy Bacus
Composition: DSCS, LLC/Absolute Service, Inc.
Photo Research and Permissions Manager: Kimberly Potvin
Cover Design: Kristin E. Parker
Cover Image: © SVLumagraphica/ShutterStock, Inc.
Printing and Binding: Malloy, Inc.
Cover Printing: Malloy, Inc.

Library of Congress Cataloging-in-Publication Data
Menifield, Charles.
  Comparative public budgeting : a global perspective / Charles E. Menifield.
    p. cm.
  Includes bibliographical references and index.
  ISBN-13: 978-0-7637-8010-4 (pbk.)
  ISBN-10: 0-7637-8010-3 (ibid.)
  1. Budget process. 2. Budget. I. Title.
  HJ2009.M46 2011
  352.4'8—dc22
                    2010010516
6048

Printed in the United States of America
14 13 12 11 10   10 9 8 7 6 5 4 3 2 1

Contents

Part ❷ Asia

Part ❸ Europe

Part ❹ The Middle East

Part ⑤ North America

Part ⑥ South America

Part ⑦ Conclusion

About the Editor

Charles E. Menifield is an associate professor in the Division of Public and Nonprofit Administration at the University of Memphis where he teaches courses in budgeting and financial management, public management information systems, research methods, and public policy statistics. His main research areas are public budgeting and finance and Southern politics. He has authored or edited four books and has written numerous articles for public administration and political science journals. He currently serves on the Executive Council for the Association for Budgeting and Financial Management and the National Association for Schools of Public Affairs and Administration.

Contributors

Bassam ALBassam is an instructor of public administration/public finance and faculty member at the Institute of Public Administration (IPA) in Saudi Arabia. He specializes in public finance, budgeting, and strategic planning, and has participated in many consulting projects for public and private sectors. He is a PhD candidate in public administration at Florida Atlantic University with a concentration in financial management.

Roy Bahl is Regents Professor of Economics and Founding Dean of Andrew Young School of Policy Studies at Georgia State University. Dr. Bahl is internationally known in the field of public finance and fiscal policy and has served widely as a consultant to developing and transitioning economy countries for the International Monetary Fund (IMF), The World Bank, the Asian Development Bank, and various other organizations and governments. In addition to serving several years as a senior staff economist for the IMF and The World Bank, he directed the USAID-funded Jamaican and Guatemalan Tax Reforms and has held numerous positions as chief of party for development projects in several regions of the world. He has published numerous books, including *Urban Public Finance in Developing Countries* (co-authored with J. Linn in 1992 and published by Oxford University Press). In 1991, he was invited to be a special adviser on local government finance issues to the People's Republic of China Finance Ministry, a position that he still holds.

Stephen J. Bailey is a professor of Public Sector Economics at Glasgow Caledonian University. His main research area is public finance and he has published extensively in refereed academic journals. His sole-authored books are *Strategic Public Finance* (2004), *Public Sector Economics: Theory, Policy and Practice* (2nd ed., 2002), and *Local Government Economics: Principles and Practice* (1999), all published by Palgrave Macmillan. He maintains the Local Government Charges section of the Chartered Institute of Public Finance and Accountancy's online Technical Information Service (TISonline).

Cal Clark is the MPA director and a professor of Political Science at Auburn University. He previously taught at the University of Wyoming and New Mexico State University and has been a visiting professor at Chung Yuan Christian University and Tunghai University in Taiwan. His primary research interests concern comparative public policy, economic and political development, and democratization in East Asia. He currently serves on the editorial board of *Journal of Public Affairs Education*. He is the author or editor of 15 books.

Musharraf R. Cyan has worked in government and with international development agencies in the areas of fiscal decentralization and public sector expenditure management and development policy for 15 years. Currently he is a research associate and PhD candidate in Economics at Andrew Young School of Policy Studies, Georgia State University. In addition to his work on intergovernmental sharing of natural resource revenues, he takes part in the ongoing research at the school on tax systems, intergovernmental transfers, and fiscal reform in developing and transition countries. He has authored a number of reports and papers on intergovernmental transfers, development policy, and taxation. He has designed, managed, and implemented training programs for senior and middle level public sector officials. Working for Asian Development Bank (2002–2005), his brief included carrying out a policy dialogue with senior government policy makers in support of fiscal decentralization, design of decentralization instruments for budgeting and public resource management, development of transparent data systems, and capacity building for intergovernmental transfers and local taxation. His work includes studies on subnational taxation in Pakistan (with The World Bank), program evaluation in social sectors, law and justice, fiscal decentralization and structural adjustment (with the Asian Development Bank), and creation of new approaches for public sector training programs for implementation of fiscal decentralization.

Salvador Espinosa P. is an assistant professor at the School of Public Affairs at San Diego State University. He holds a BA in Economics from Universidad Panamericana (Mexico), and an MPA and a PhD in Public Affairs from Indiana University. He specializes in fiscal decentralization, public financial administration, and intergovernmental relations. His current research focuses on the budgetary impact of federal transfers in Mexico. Before starting his doctoral degree, Salvador worked as budget analyst for the City of Bloomington, Indiana; a research associate for the Indiana Fiscal Policy Institute (Indianapolis, IN); and Coordinator of Information and Economic Development for the government of the state of Guanajuato (Mexico). In addition to his scholarly activities, Salvador works as a public finance consultant for state and local governments.

Ronald W. Johnson is senior policy advisor in International Development at RTI International. Previously the executive vice president of the International Development group at RTI, Dr. Johnson specializes in public budgeting and finance and governance reforms in developing countries. In his career at RTI, he has led projects in decentralization strategies, local governance reform, and public sector capital finance in developing countries in all regions of the world. As executive vice president, he was the corporate officer in charge of RTI International Local Governance Program (funded under contract with USAID) in Iraq from the start in 2003 until December 2007, and continues to participate as a governance expert in the program.

Mike Joyce is an adjunct professor at Queen's University's School of Policy Studies in Canada. At Queen's he teaches courses related to government expenditure management and budgeting as well as the program's core public sector management course. His research interests include the impact of recent changes to the federal budgeting process in Canada, government accountability for its overall management of expenditures and the related role of the Canadian Parliament, and the effectiveness of the Treasury Board Secretariat in its expenditure management role. He is a member of the Board of Advisers for the OECD Journal on Budgeting. Previously, Mike was senior assistant secretary responsible for the Canadian Treasury Board Secretariat's Expenditure Management Sector where he was directly responsible for the expenditure management role played by the Treasury Board. He played a lead role in developing and implementing a number of the Secretariat's expenditure management initiatives and served as the Secretariat's representative on the OECD's Senior Budget Officers Working Group. From 1991 to 1993, Mike worked as an assistant secretary in the Australian government's Department of Finance as part of an exchange program with the Treasury Board. During that time, he played a lead role in the Australian government's initiative to commercialize administrative services and to introduce optionality for departments in their real property needs.

Jamil E. Jreisat is professor of public administration and political science in the Department of Government and International Affairs at the University of South Florida. Dr. Jreisat is the author of numerous books and articles on issues in public administration, comparative government, and administrative reform in the Arab world, including *Politics without Process: Administering Development in the Arab World* (Reinner, 1997) and *Comparative Public Administration and Policy* (Westview, 2002). He teaches public budgeting and has chaired an international team to develop performance budgeting for Jordan. Dr. Jreisat serves on the editorial boards of several professional publications, is the associate editor of the *Journal of Asian and African Studies*, and is the recipient of many awards including the University of South Florida's President's Award for Professional Excellence.

Changhoon Jung is an associate professor in the Department of Political Science at Auburn University. He teaches public budgeting and finance, and public financial management. His research interests include public budgeting and finance, public financial management, state and local service delivery, and state and local economic development policy. He currently serves on the editorial board of *International Review of Public Administration* and has published more than 15 journal articles.

Charlotte Kirschner is a PhD candidate at the Trachtenberg School of Public Policy and Public Administration at The George Washington University. Her research focuses on the state and local government financing of homeland security policies and international budgeting practices for disasters in the United States.

Tsuey-ping Lee is an associate professor in the Department of Political Science at National Chung-Cheng University in Taiwan. She received her PhD from SUNY, Albany. Her major areas of research include public finance, public policy with an emphasis on welfare and environmental policy, and system dynamics. She is an author of one book and seven articles in the field of public management.

Deniz Zeynep Leuenberger is an assistant professor of political science/public administration and the Faculty Director of the Institute for Regional Development at Bridgewater State College, Massachusetts. She specializes in public finance and budgeting, sustainable development, and non-governmental organization management. She also teaches courses in the areas of research methods, urban community/economic development, and Middle Eastern government. Dr. Leuenberger has been actively pursuing research and student programming in the United Arab Emirates, focusing on the areas of budgeting reform, nongovernmental organization management, and sustainable development. She is also an active member of ASPA, is the chair of the STPA Executive Committee, and is a member of the ABFM Executive Committee.

Craig S. Maher teaches graduate-level courses in public budgeting and finance, municipal management, research methods, performance management, and policy analysis in the University of Wisconsin–Oshkosh's Masters of Public Administration Program. His primary research interests include public finance with emphases in fiscal federalism, fiscal health, revenue forecasting, and K–12 finance. Professor Maher's work has recently been published in the following journals: *Public Finance Review*, *Public Budgeting and Finance*, *Public Budgeting*, *Accounting and Financial Management*, *Publius*, *International Journal of Public Administration*, *Marquette Law Review*, and the *Korean Journal of Public Policy*.

Christine R. Martell is an associate professor at the University of Colorado Denver's School of Public Affairs. Her fields of interest include public finance and public policy. In particular, her research pertains to the development of credit markets for developing countries, fiscal federalism, budgeting, and debt management. Dr. Martell has a passion for international development issues and has conducted research in countries such as Brazil.

William McCabe is a lecturer of public sector accounting, budgeting, and auditing at Manchester Metropolitan University. He specializes in public sector accounting, budgeting, and auditing. He also conducts consultancy work in developing countries and has worked on a number of projects financed by the European Union, The World Bank, and Department for International Development (DFID) (UK government). The projects have covered public financial management, accruals accounting, and external and internal audit reform. His main research areas are public-private partnerships and best value in local government.

Patrizio Monfardini is research assistant in business administration at University of Siena, Italy. He received a PhD in public sector accounting and management in 2006 at University of Siena. He teaches public sector accounting and management control for public sector at the undergraduate, postgraduate, and master level. His research interests are focused on public sector ethics, sustainable development, and corporate social responsibility.

Riccardo Mussari took up his professorship at the University of Siena, Italy in 1999. He has been a visiting scholar at several US, Australian, and Japanese universities. His doctorate thesis (published in 1990) focused on public management theory. He has published on public sector accounting and management issues, with refereed articles in public administration, public management, and accounting journals. He has been part of major national and international research projects comparing public sector reforms in Italy with various other countries. He is a member of the scientific and editorial boards of several Italian and international scientific journals. His research and teaching interests include public sector management and accounting, knowledge management, program evaluation, and management control in public sector organizations. He also consults, nationally and internationally, on public sector management, management control, performance measurement, and program evaluation. At present, he serves as head of the Department of Business and Social Studies, University of Siena, is a member of the Board of the Italian Academy of Business Administration and Management, is one of the vice presidents of the International Public Management Network, is Chair of EGPA (European Group of Public Administration) Public Financial Management Study Group, and is one of the Italian representatives in the IFSAM (International Federation of Scholarly Association of Management) Council. He is also member of the SICA Committee.

Meili Niu graduated from the School of public administration at the University of Nebraska and is currently an associate professor in the School of Government and a research fellow of the Center for Public Administration Research at Sun Yat-Sen University, China. Dr. Niu does research on public budgeting and financial management and has published in various American and Chinese professional journals. She has done numerous consulting projects for central, provincial, and local Chinese governments and has assisted a number of Chinese local governments in implementing budgetary and legislative reforms. Dr. Niu also serves on the editorial board of *Journal for Public Administration*.

Phuong Nguyen-Hoang is a PhD candidate in public administration at the Maxwell School, Syracuse University. His research interests center on local government finance, particularly education finance in the United States and on public policy issues in developing countries.

Marvin Phaup is a research scholar and professorial lecturer at the Trachtenberg School of Public Policy and Public Administration, the George Washington University, and director of the Federal Budget Reform Initiative for Pew Charitable Trusts. He formerly headed the Financial Studies/Budget Process group at the Congressional Budget Office (CBO), where his work focused on analyses of federal financial policies and institutions, and implications for their budgetary treatment. He also supported the CBO member of the Federal Accounting Standards Advisory Board. He holds a PhD in economics from the University of Virginia and a BA from Roanoke College.

Pasquale Ruggiero is assistant professor in business administration at University of Siena, Italy. He obtained a PhD in public sector accounting and management in 2005 at the University of Siena. He teaches public sector accounting and management control for public sector at the undergraduate, postgraduate, and master level. His research interests are focused on public manager capacities and intellectual capital in public sector organizations.

Hazel Marie A. Sarmiento is a doctoral student at the Public Policy Program at the University of North Carolina at Charlotte. Prior to her doctoral studies, Ms. Sarmiento was a budget and management specialist at the Fiscal Planning Bureau of the Department of Budget and Management (DBM), which is an oversight agency in the government of the Philippines that is in charge of the formulation, implementation, and analysis of the national budget. She has 10 years of experience working with the Philippine government on macroeconomics, fiscal policy, and other public finance issues. She also has extensive academic training on Philippine public policy as well as Asian public policy through the University of the Philippines and the Hitotsubashi University in Tokyo, Japan. Her research interests include budget reforms and measuring efficiency in government spending. She expects to complete her doctoral studies in 2012.

Larry Schroeder is a professor of public administration at the Maxwell School, Syracuse University. His research interests center on local government finance, financial management, and intergovernmental fiscal relations, particularly in developing countries.

Ricardo Silva-Morales has been a Senior Fiscal Policy Advisor onsite in Baghdad, Iraq within the RTI Local Governance Program since 2005. In that capacity, he participates in the US Embassy Budget Reform and Budget Execution advisory team, works closely with Ministry of Finance officials on intergovernmental fiscal relations, and with provincial governors and council members on capital investment budgeting. Prior to his work in Iraq, he worked as an intergovernmental fiscal policy specialist and decentralization advisor in a number of Latin American, Eastern European, and Central Asian countries.

Arwiphawee Srithongrung, assistant professor (DPA, University of Illinois at Springfield), teaches public budgeting, quantitative methods in public administration, the public economy, and introduction to public administration. Her research interests include comparative study in public budgeting, infrastructure management, budgetary institutions, and economic growth. She presented papers at the International Atlantic Economic Society, Asia-Pacific Governance Institute and International Public Management Network, and the Association for Budgeting and Financial Management conferences. Her recent study, which examines impacts of systematic capital management programs on the American state economic growth, appears in *Public Budgeting and Finance*.

LaShonda M. Stewart received her PhD from Mississippi State University in May 2008. Her current research focuses on local governments' unreserved fund balances and those factors that influence the level of savings maintained. She also contributed (with Doug Goodman) a chapter to *The Judicial Branch of State Government: People, Process, and Politics* (2006). She teaches courses in public administration at Southern Illinois University.

Sally Wallace is a professor of Economics at the Andrew Young School. Dr. Wallace is a former senior economist for the United States Department of Treasury, where she was responsible for forecasting the income tax receipts for the administration, and provided policy advice to the executive branch on the tax implications of corporate and individual investment plans, such as the individual retirement account. She is an expert on revenue forecasting and modeling; federal, state, and local income taxes; and intergovernmental fiscal policy. She has consulted widely on fiscal reform and fiscal decentralization issues for The World Bank, USAID, Asian Development Bank, and foreign government ministries in China, the Philippines, Russia, Kazakhstan, Mongolia, Jamaica, Guatemala, Ukraine, the Dominican Republic, and Uzbekistan.

Reviewers

Philip G. Joyce, PhD
Professor, The Trachtenberg School of Public Policy and Public Administration
The George Washington University
Washington, DC

Robert S. Kravchuk, MPA, MBA, PhD
Professor & Chair, Department of Political Science
University of North Carolina–Charlotte
Charlotte, NC

Joseph Wert, PhD
Associate Professor, Department of Political Science
Indiana University, Southeast
New Albany, IN

Chapter 1

An Introduction to Comparative Budgeting

Charles E. Menifield

In order to completely understand the nature and culture of a country, it is necessary to understand the budgeting process. This process not only reveals national policy choices, but it also provides evidence of governance. Hence, as the world becomes more global, it is necessary and feasible to examine how countries engage in the budgeting process from a comparative perspective. In fact, one only needs to look at the changes in Europe and the establishment of the European Union in order to get a glimpse of the changing nature of budgeting at the national level. It is through changes like this that nations learn from the successes and failures of other countries. However, examining budgeting processes throughout the globe is not an easy task given the vast array of cultures, governments, social structures, and economic conditions in the world. Nonetheless, the authors of the various chapters in this text went about the task of describing the budgeting process in a variety of different countries around the globe.

Originally, this book was poised to simply fill a gap in the literature examining budgeting at the national level from a comparative perspective. Hence, the following question was posed: How does public budgeting occur in other countries and can we learn from their successes and failures? In so doing, the authors were initially given a specific set of factors to examine with a bit of latitude to focus on a policy area or other important reform(s) that significantly impacted the budgeting process in the country of interest. The results of their analysis, however, were much more revealing than expected. Analyses of the individual chapters show that there is a great disparity among many countries in terms of pressing issues as well as their budgeting processes. Many countries were found to be very progressive and existing on the cutting edge of budgeting and financial management techniques, while other countries continue to struggle with overt corruption, poor institutional structures, poor (and limited) revenue streams, and other factors that prohibit economic and social advancement.

Framing Comparative Budgeting

Understanding the political and social structure of a country requires an understanding of the budgeting process. Axelrod (1995) refers to it as the "nerve center of government" (p. 1). From one perspective, a budget provides insight into spending on education, health care, social programs, military spending, and a variety of other priorities. Another perspective indicates who will pay for these expenditures. An examination of a budget can also reveal how countries plan, control, and improve accountability in their country.

Over time, the budgeting process has changed dramatically around the world and these changes make it fairly difficult to study. However, we developed and grounded our analysis on two pivotal pieces of research. First, we examine a comparative budgeting model developed by Wildavsky (1975). Second, we focus our attention on a more modern budget decision-making model by Rubin (2010).

WILDAVSKY'S MODEL

Wildavsky (1975) argues that in order to understand the budgeting process of a country, you must first determine the resources available to a country and the level of predictability in the budget process. Only after comprehending these two variables is it feasible to examine other factors. Thus, his foundational model is based on four possible outcomes that focus on the level of *wealth* (rich or poor) in a country and the degree of *predictability* (certain or uncertain) in the budgeting process.[1] In the model, he asserts that, "rich and certain environments lead to incremental budgeting; poverty and predictability generate revenue budgeting; unpredictability combined with poverty generates repetitive budgeting; and riches plus uncertainty produce alternating incremental and repetitive budgeting" or supplemental budgeting (p. 12). Therefore, he expects countries such as the United States and the United Kingdom to produce incremental budgets while countries like Thailand and Ghana are expected to engage in repetitive budgeting. That is, given the lack of resources, government officials in poorer countries find themselves writing and rewriting the budget throughout the year to address the most pressing needs at the time.

In addition to his Five Budgetary Process Model, Wildavsky (1975) goes on to say that it is necessary to compare wealth, taxes, and politics in a nation in order to fully understand the budgeting process. The variables listed below provide a summary of the factors that he viewed as critical when examining the budgeting process in a country:

■ Gross domestic product (GDP),
■ Per capita income,

- Interaction among the various levels of government,
- Revenue structure,
- Expenditure structure,
- Growth rates
- Educational level,
- Political structure and volatility in government, and
- Political culture.

RUBIN'S MODEL

Although written primarily from a US budgeting perspective, Rubin's (2010) model is quite applicable in our study because it hones in on key political processes that affect budgeting from formulation to implementation. In her decision-making model, she posits that the budgeting environment affects the process, individual strategies, and outcomes, and the process affects the outcomes.

The model is based on five decision-making clusters with a number of different actors in each cluster. Hence, the politics of each cluster changes as the number of actors change. Therefore, the outcome is affected by the politics associated with each set of actors. The first cluster is the revenue cluster: Technical data are used to determine how much revenue will be available. Important political questions include, "Will taxes be raised or lowered? Will tax breaks be granted, and if so, to whom, and for what purpose?" "Given the scarcity of resources, revenues are sensitive to the environment because changes in the economy influence revenue level and because the perception of public opinion influences the public officials' willingness to increase taxes" (Rubin, 2010, p. 29).

The budget process is the second cluster and it pertains to how budget decisions will be made. Critical questions include, "Who should participate in the budget deliberations? Should agency heads have power independent of the central budget office? How much power should the legislature have?" (Rubin, 2010, p. 29). Rubin argues that groups jockey for position as well as for power in order to improve their standing in the budget process and for control over the budget process.

The third cluster is the expenditure cluster: Technical data provide estimates of proposed expenditures. Despite the limited discretionary spending available in a budget, issues such as funding levels of existing programs, who will benefit from these programs, etc., are often the source of much competition and trade offs among competing groups.

The balance cluster addresses the basic question of balancing the budget. That is, "does the budget have to be balanced each year with each year's revenue or whether borrowing is allowed to balance the budget?" (Rubin, 2010, p. 30). The answers to these questions are political and are important to citizens because they could see an increase in taxes, a decrease in services, or a combination of the two. Other issues include how to reduce and manage deficits.

Rubin's (2010) last cluster focuses on the politics surrounding budget implementation. Key questions include, "How close should actual expenditures be to the ones planned in the budget? How can one justify variation from the budget plan? Can the budget be remade after it is approved?" (p. 31). Rubin notes that the issue here is implementing the budget as it was written and making changes during the budget year because of changes in the environment.

Rubin's (2010) work really provides us a nice model to work from because the questions that she posits in each cluster really delves into the real issues that we face when comparing budget processes among nations. She notes, by focusing on budgetary actors (microbudgeting), you limit the opportunity for more exploratory analysis of top-down systemic perspectives (macrobudgeting). Many of the countries that we examine are so different that it is difficult to simply compare them by just looking at factors. These and other questions that she has posed allow us to expand our framework by examining the political environment of budget processes.

APPLYING THESE FRAMEWORKS IN A COMPARATIVE SETTING

As noted previously, Wildavsky's (1975) and Rubin's (2010) works serve as the point of departure for our analysis and one does not have to look very far to see the saliency of their models. For example, in Chapter 2, Maher refers to an extensive report by the World Bank that examined financial management in Ghana. One of the findings considered predictability and control in budget execution. More specifically, the report indicated weaknesses in Ghana's management and oversight of control systems. Wildavsky (1975) would argue that management and oversight of control systems in Ghana are tied to the poorly functioning political institutions and revenue structures. Similarly, Bailey and McCabe, in Chapter 10, found that the budget process in the United Kingdom has remained quite predictable despite numerous reforms that have taken place over the last 3 decades. As a result, the budget process remains incremental in nature. Again, Wildavsky would argue that this behavior is a by-product of a rich nation with predictable budget processes.

The authors of the 18 country-specific chapters (Ghana, China, Korea, Philippines, Taiwan, Thailand, Vietnam, Italy, United Kingdom, Iraq, Jordan, Pakistan, Saudi Arabia, United Arab Emirates [UAE], Canada, Mexico, United States, and Brazil) were charged with describing the budgeting process in their respective countries as well as discussing recent reforms that affect the budgeting process. Beyond the descriptive information, several prominent themes and factors are discussed. They include an examination of:

- Transparency in the budget process,
- Improving accountability in the budget process,
- Reforming the budget and financial management systems,
- Managing stable revenue streams,
- Reforming the accounting systems,
- Strong institutional structures with clearly delineated roles,
- Financial dependence on other countries,
- GDP,
- Decentralization,
- Performance budgeting,
- Procurement reform,

- Budget deficits and debt management,
- Improving fiscal stress in regional governments,
- Improving the political systems,
- The World Bank and International Monetary Fund (IMF), and
- Microbudgeting versus macrobudgeting.

Through an examination of these topics, it is the ultimate intention of this book to stimulate thinking and analysis of the practice of budgeting and financial management around the globe. Individually, these chapters do not discuss every single aspect of budgeting and financial management. On the contrary, our main objective is to provide a foundation and framework to an understudied field.

Economic and Country Overviews

Given Wildavsky's (1975) focus on the level of national wealth as a point of departure for comparing budgeting processes around the globe, this section of the chapter provides a brief overview of the economy and economic outlook in each country. Unless noted otherwise, all of the information and data in this section were derived from the subsequent chapters or from various Web sites and scholarly articles.

GHANA

Ghana is one of the few countries in the world that has an abundance of natural resources. It reigns as the most economically stable country in West Africa with roughly twice the per capita output of the poorest country in the region. The domestic economy revolves around agriculture, which accounts for about 35% of GDP and employs about 55% of the workforce. However, the country is quite dependent on international support and technical assistance. In fact, Ghana received funding under the Heavily Indebted Poor Country (HIPC) program in 2002. Priorities under its current Growth and Poverty Reduction Strategy, which also provides the framework for development partner assistance, include human resource development, private sector competitiveness, macroeconomic stability, and good governance and civic responsibility. In 2006, Ghana signed the Millennium Challenge Corporation (MCC) Compact, which aims to assist in transforming Ghana's agricultural sector. Sound macroeconomic management along with high prices for gold and cocoa helped sustain GDP growth in 2007 (Central Intelligence Agency, 2009d; The World Bank, 2006; The World Bank, 2008).

CHINA

China has become a major participant in the global economy during the last quarter century. During this period, the country moved away from a centrally planned economy that focused on domestic markets to a market-based economy. The major economic reforms in China began in the late 1970s, with the phasing out of collectivized agriculture and expanded to include the gradual liberalization of prices, increased autonomy for state enterprises, the foundation of a diversified banking system, the development of stock markets, fiscal decentralization, the rapid growth of the nonstate sector, and the opening to foreign trade and investment. Implementing reforms have been incremental and piecemeal at best. Positive moves include the sale of minority shares in four of China's largest state banks to foreign investors, and refinements in foreign exchange and bond markets in 2005. In July 2005, after keeping its currency tightly linked to the US dollar for years, the country revalued its currency by 2.1% against the US dollar and moved to an exchange rate system that references an array of currencies. GDP has increased more than 10 times since 1978 as a result of restructuring the economy. Measured on a purchasing power parity (PPP) basis, China, in 2007, stood as the second largest economy in the world after the United States, although in per capita terms, the country is still lower middle income. Annual inflows of foreign direct investment in 2007 rose to $75 billion. The Chinese government still faces several economic development challenges: (1) to sustain adequate job growth for tens of millions of workers laid off from state-owned enterprises, migrants, and new entrants to the workforce; (2) to contain environmental damage and social strife related to the economy's rapid transformation; and (3) to reduce corruption and other economic crimes. Despite an aging workforce and a deteriorating environment, China has intensified government efforts to improve environmental conditions by tying the evaluation of local officials to environmental targets, publishing a national climate change policy, and establishing a high-level leading group on climate change, headed by Premier Wen Jiabao. The Chinese government seeks to add energy production capacity from sources other than coal and oil as its double-digit economic growth increases demand (Central Intelligence Agency, 2009c; Economy Watch, 2009c; Li, 2001; Tsui, 1996; Woo, 2008).

SOUTH KOREA

Unlike its neighbor to the north, South Korea has seen unprecedented growth in the integration into the high-tech world economy since the 1960s. Roughly 40 years ago, South Korea's GDP was comparable to those of third-world countries. By 2004, they joined a short list of countries in the trillion dollar club of world economies. In 2004, the GDP was $17,930 compared to $12,850 in Saudi Arabia, and $7,480 in Brazil. Success was achieved with a system of close government/business ties including directed credit, sponsorship of specific industries, import restrictions, and a strong labor effort. The government promoted the import of raw materials and technology at the expense of consumer goods, and encouraged savings and investment over consumption. Longstanding weaknesses in South Korea's development model were exposed during the Asian financial crisis of 1997–1998. This included high debt/equity ratios, massive foreign borrowing, and an undisciplined financial sector. The GDP plunged by 6.9% in 1998, recovered by 9.5% in 1999 and by 8.5% in 2000. Due to the slowing global economy, falling exports, and the perception that much-needed corporate and financial reforms had stalled, growth fell to 3.3% in 2001. Growth in 2002 was an impressive 7%, led by consumer spending and exports despite faint global growth.

Between 2003 and 2007, growth moderated to about 4 to 5% annually. Moderate inflation, low unemployment, and an export surplus in 2007 characterize this solid economy, but inflation and unemployment are increasing in the face of rising oil prices (Central Intelligence Agency, 2009l; Economy Watch, 2009j; Ha, 2004; Koo, 2008; Lee & Lee, 1992).

PHILIPPINES

Higher government spending in the years leading up to 2007, as well as a resilient service sector and large remittances from the millions of Filipinos who work abroad led to GDP growth exceeding 7%. Since 2001, economic growth has averaged 5% since President Macapagal-Arroyo took office. Nonetheless, the Philippine government will need still higher, sustained growth to make progress in alleviating poverty, given its high population growth (30% in 2003) and unequal distribution of income. The president avoided a fiscal crisis by advocating new revenue measures and cutting expenditures. Recent efforts to increase spending on infrastructure and social services, tapering debt and debt service ratios, and declining fiscal deficits have increased the economic outlook for the country. While the general macroeconomic outlook has improved significantly over time, the nation continues to face important obstacles and must continue the reform movement in order to compete with regional competitors, improve employment opportunities, and alleviate poverty. Fiscal stability hinges on sustainable revenue sources, rather than nonrecurring revenues from privatization (Central Intelligence Agency, 2009j; Economy Watch, 2009i; Kwiatkowski, 2005).

TAIWAN

As the government has slowly allowed market forces to drive Taiwan's economy, the country has flourished economically. In fact, the country has privatized some of the large state banks as well as industrial firms. This behavior is the result of a strong export market. The country has a large trade surplus and its foreign reserves are among the largest in the world. Despite economic and political limitations, China is now the largest export market for Taiwan. China is also the island's number one destination for direct foreign investment. Strong trade performance in 2007 pushed Taiwan's GDP growth rate above 5%, unemployment is below 4%, and the poverty rate was less than 1% in 2007 (Central Intelligence Agency, 2009m; Khatkhate, 1977).

THAILAND

Similar to other regional countries, Thailand appears to have recovered from the 1997–1998 Asian Financial Crisis. The country has a well-developed infrastructure, a free-enterprise economy, and generally pro-investment policies. Boosted by strong export growth, the Thai economy grew 4.5% in 2007 and was one of East Asia's best economic performers from 2002 to 2004. This growth was the result of the government's efforts in pursuing preferential trade agreements with an array of partners. By 2007, the tourism sector had largely recovered from the 2004 major tsunami. Following the military coup in September 2006, investment and consumer confidence stagnated due to the uncertain political climate that lasted through the December 2007 elections. Foreign investor sentiment was further tempered by a 30% reserve requirement on capital inflows instituted in December 2006, and discussion of amending Thailand's rules governing foreign-owned businesses. Economic growth in 2007 was due almost entirely to robust export performance. Exports have performed at record levels, rising to 16.7% in 2006 and 12.1% in 2007. Export-oriented manufacturing (especially automobile production) and farm outputs are the driving forces behind these gains (Central Intelligence Agency, 2009n; International Monetary Fund, 2009).

VIETNAM

Vietnam is a densely populated developing country that has had to recover from the ravages of war, the loss of financial support from the former Soviet Union, and the rigidities of a centrally planned economy in the last 3 decades. The country experienced extreme economic stagnation after the reunification from 1975 to 1985. However, in 1986, the congress approved a broad economic reform package that introduced market reforms and set the groundwork for Vietnam's improved investment climate. As a result of these reforms, substantial progress was achieved from 1986 to 1997 in moving forward from an extremely low level of development and significantly reducing poverty (14.7% in 2007). Economic recovery was temporarily halted as a result of the 1997 Asian financial crisis, when opponents of reform were able to highlight the problems in the Vietnamese economy and slow the progress toward a market-oriented economy. Despite the background of the Asian financial crisis and a global recession, GDP growth averaged 6.8% per year from 1997 to 2004. After reaffirming their commitment to economic liberalization and international integration in 2001, government officials have made changes to implement the structural reforms needed to modernize the economy and to produce more competitive, export-driven industries. The economy grew 8.5% in 2007. Other efforts, such as joining the Association of Southeast Asian Nations (ASEAN) Free Trade Area (AFTA) and the entering into a United States–Vietnam Bilateral Trade Agreement in December 2001 have led to more positive economic changes. Vietnam's exports to the United States increased 900% between 2001 and 2007. In 2007, Vietnam joined the World Trade Organization (WTO) after a decade-long negotiation process. Membership in the WTO has provided Vietnam an access point to the global market and reinforced the domestic economic reform process (Beresford, 2008; Bjornestad, 2009; Economy Watch, 2009m; Glewwe, Gragnolati, & Zaman, 2002).

ITALY

Despite boasting a diversified industrial economy with roughly the same total and per capita output as France and the United Kingdom, Italy is in need of further economic reform. Economically, the capitalist country is segregated into two halves. The northern part of the country is well developed from an economic perspective and driven by private companies, whereas the south is less developed, has an agriculturally based economy, is more welfare dependent, and has a higher unemployment rate. The country suffers from a lack of raw materials and energy sources. Hence, most raw materials and more than 75% of the energy supply are imported. Over the last 10 years, Italy has pursued a rigid fiscal policy in order to meet the requirements of the economic and monetary unions and has benefited from lower interest and inflation rates. Several short-term reforms have been enacted to improve competitiveness and long-term growth. However, the country has moved slowly in implementing structural reforms, such as lightening the high tax burden and reforming the labor market and excessively generous pension system. Another economic hurdle for the government is the debt-to-revenue ratio. The official debt is above 100% of GDP, and the government has found it difficult to lower the budget deficit in order to improve the ratio. The economy continues to grow by less than the eurozone average and growth was expected to decelerate from 1.9% in 2006 and 2007 to less than 1.5% in 2008 as the eurozone and world economies continue to slow down (Central Intelligence Agency, 2009f; Economy Watch, 2009f; Helliwell & Putnam, 1995).

UNITED KINGDOM

The United Kingdom is one of the leading economic powers on the globe. The country has continued to distance itself from other European countries by reducing public ownership and dependence of social welfare programs. The country has fairly large coal, natural gas, and oil reserves with primary energy production accounting for roughly 10% of GDP. From an agricultural perspective, the system is highly mechanized with less than 2% of the workforce producing about 60% of the food supply. Banking, insurance, and business services account for the largest percentage of GDP, while industry continues to decline. Since 1992, Britain's economy has enjoyed the longest period of expansion on record; growth has remained in the 2 to 3% range since 2004, outpacing most European countries. The government has also been successful in improving education, health services, and affordable housing at a cost of higher taxes and a growing public deficit (Central Intelligence Agency, 2009o; Economy Watch, 2009l).

IRAQ

Without question, Iraq's economy is dominated by the oil sector, which has historically provided about 95% of foreign exchange earnings. Despite the efforts of many to undermine the rebuilding of the economy through looting, insurgent attacks, and sabotage, economic activity is increasing in areas recently secured by the US military. Currently, oil exports are near the levels seen before Operation Iraqi Freedom, and total government revenues have benefited from high oil prices. Iraq is making some progress in building the institutions needed to implement positive economic policy, despite the political uncertainty, and has negotiated a debt reduction agreement with the Paris Club and a new Stand-By Arrangement with the IMF. Iraq has received more than $33 billion in foreign aid pledges between the years 2004 and 2007. The International Compact with Iraq was established in May 2007 to integrate Iraq into the regional and global economy, and the Iraqi government is seeking to pass laws to strengthen its economy. The Central Bank has also been successful in controlling inflation through appreciation of the dinar against the US dollar. The key to Iraq's success is reducing corruption and implementing structural reforms, such as bank restructuring and developing the private sector (Central Intelligence Agency, 2009e; Economy Watch, 2009e; Vrijer, Kock, & Grigorian, 2008).

JORDAN

Unlike a number of other countries in the region, Jordan has an insufficient amount of water, oil, and other natural resources. In addition, poverty (14.2% in 2002), unemployment, and inflation are fundamental problems that have lingered for years. Nonetheless, the government has been more proactive since 1999 when King Abdallah II assumed the throne. His broad economic reforms have attempted to improve living standards. Since 2002, Amman has continued to follow IMF guidelines by practicing careful monetary policy, improving privatization, and opening the trade regime. Jordan's exports have significantly increased under the free trade accord with the United States and the Jordanian Qualifying Industrial Zones (QIZ), which allow Jordan to export goods tax free to the United States. In 2006, Jordan reduced its debt-to-GDP ratio significantly. These measures have helped improve productivity and have made Jordan more attractive for foreign investment. In the recent past, Jordan imported most of its oil from Iraq. Since 2003, however, Jordan has been more dependent on oil from other Gulf nations. The government ended subsidies for petroleum and other consumer goods in 2008 in an effort to control the budget. Today, the main challenges facing Jordan are reducing dependence on foreign grants, reducing the budget deficit, attracting investments, and creating jobs (Central Intelligence Agency, 2009g; Khaldi, 2008; USAID in Jordan, 2009).

PAKISTAN

Pakistan is an impoverished (24% poverty rate in 2006) and underdeveloped country that has suffered from decades of political disputes, low levels of foreign investment, and a costly and ongoing quarrel with India. The country has, however, begun reforming its economic system. In 2001, the IMF approved the privatization of the banking sector. In addition, the country has been assisted by generous foreign assistance and renewed access to global markets. As a result, the country has had a degree of macroeconomic recovery. GDP growth was in the 6 to 8% range from 2004 to 2007. This was spurred by gains in the industrial and service sectors. In 2007, the fiscal deficit—a result of chronically low tax collection and increased spending—exceeded the government's target of 4% of GDP. Inflation remains the top concern among the public, jumping from 6.9% in 2007 to more than 11% during the first few months of 2008, primarily because of rising world commodity prices (Central Intelligence Agency, 2009i; Economy Watch, 2009h; Khan & Qayyum, 2007).

SAUDI ARABIA

Saudi Arabia controls more than 20% of the world's proven petroleum reserves and leads the world in oil exports. With respect to the budget, the petroleum sector makes up nearly 75% of the budget revenues, 45% of GDP, and 90% of export earnings. About 40% of the GDP comes from the private sector. Recent high oil prices have boosted growth, government revenues, and Saudi ownership of foreign assets. As a result, the country has been able to pay down domestic debt. More recently, the government has been facilitating private sector growth (especially in telecommunications, power generation, natural gas exploration, and petrochemicals) with the objective of decreasing the country's dependence on oil exports and to increase employment opportunities. Unemployment is high, and the large youth population (40% of the total population is younger than 15 years of age) generally lacks the education and technical skills the private sector needs. Hence, the country has substantially boosted spending on job training and education, infrastructure development, as well as government salaries. Saudi Arabia acceded to the WTO in December 2005 after many years of negotiations in order to attract foreign investment and to diversify the economy (Central Intelligence Agency, 2009k).

UNITED ARAB EMIRATES

Since oil was discovered in the country more than 30 years ago, the UAE has developed a prosperous (and open) economy with a high per capita income ($40,000 in 2008) and a large annual trade surplus ($151 billion exports in 2007). Efforts aimed at economic diversity have been successful, but almost 40% of GDP is still based on oil and gas output. Private sector investment has increased as the government has increased spending on job creation and infrastructure expansion. Early in 2004, the country signed a Trade and Investment Framework Agreement with the United States and later in 2004, agreed to undertake negotiations toward a Free Trade Agreement with the United States. Foreign investors have been drawn to the country as a result of the country's Free Trade Zones, which offer 100% foreign ownership and zero taxes. Higher oil revenue, strong liquidity, housing shortages, and cheap credit in the years 2005 to 2007 led to a surge in asset prices (in shares and real estate) and consumer inflation. In addition, rising prices have increased the operating costs for businesses in the UAE and adversely impacted government employees and others on fixed incomes. Diversification and the creation of more opportunities for nationals through improved education and increased private sector employment are a part of the UAE's strategic plan for the next few years (Central Intelligence Agency, 2009p; Economy Watch, 2009d).

CANADA

Following the 1989 United States–Canada Free Trade Agreement (FTA) and the 1994 North American Free Trade Agreement (NAFTA), Canada has seen a dramatic increase in trade and economic integration. The country has a market-based economic system with substantial growth in the manufacturing, mining, and service sectors. In addition, the country has great natural resources, a skilled labor force, and modern capital facilities. As a result of good fiscal management, the country has produced balanced budgets since 1997. However, public debate continues over the equitable distribution of federal funds to the Canadian provinces. Exports account for roughly one third of GDP. Canada has a large trade surplus with its principal trading partner, the United States, which absorbs 80% of Canadian exports each year. Canada is the largest foreign supplier of energy, including oil, gas, uranium, and electric power to the United States. In 2007, Canada enjoyed good economic growth, moderate inflation, and the lowest unemployment rate in more than 30 years (Central Intelligence Agency, 2009b; Economy Watch, 2009b).

MEXICO

Similar to other North American countries, Mexico also has a free market economy in the trillion-dollar group. The economy is dominated by the private sector and focuses mainly on industry and agriculture. More recently, the country has attempted to diversify the economy by expanding into seaports, railroads, telecommunications, electricity generation, natural gas distribution, and airports. Per capita income is $14,200 (2008), about one fourth that of the United States, and the poverty rate was 13.8% in 2006. Also a major beneficiary of NAFTA, trade with the United States and Canada has tripled since 1994. Currently, Mexico has 12 free trade agreements with over 40 countries placing more than 90% of trade under free trade agreements. The government continues to face many obstacles in improving the country's infrastructure, labor force, and energy sector (Central Intelligence Agency, 2009h; Economy Watch, 2009g).

UNITED STATES

In 2008, per capita income in the United States was $47,000, and it operated as the largest and most powerful economy on the globe. The market economy is dominated by the private sector where all levels of government purchase goods and services. Although US business firms enjoy great flexibility in determining their fiscal outlook (expansion of capital plant, laying off surplus workers, and developing new products) when compared to other nations, they also face more obstacles when attempting to compete with home markets. US firms exist on the cutting edge in computer technology, medicine, aerospace engineering, and military equipment. The response to the terrorist attacks of September 11, 2001 showed the resilience of the economy. The war between a US-led coalition and Iraq, and the subsequent occupation of Iraq required major shifts in national resources to the military. The rise in GDP in the years 2004 to 2007 was undergirded by substantial gains in labor productivity. Natural disasters such as Hurricane Katrina caused extensive damage in the Gulf Coast region in August 2005, but had a small impact on overall GDP growth for the year. Soaring oil prices in the years 2005 to 2007 threatened inflation and unemployment, yet the economy continued to grow through year-end 2007. Imported oil accounts for about two thirds of US consumption. Long-term problems include inadequate investment in economic infrastructure, rapidly rising medical and pension costs of an aging population, sizable trade and budget deficits, and stagnation of family income in the lower economic groups. The merchandise trade deficit reached a record $847 billion in 2007. Together, these problems caused a marked reduction in the value and status of the dollar worldwide in 2007 (Banerjee & Marcellino, 2006; Central Intelligence Agency, 2009q; Economy Watch, 2009k).

BRAZIL

Brazil distinguishes itself from all other South American countries with a well-developed agricultural, mining, manufacturing, and service sector. The country has the largest economy on the continent and is making a mark on world markets. Despite the affects of the 2001–2003 financial upheaval, capital inflows are regaining strength and the currency has resumed appreciating. The GDP was $10,100 in 2008. The resilience in the economy stems from commodity-driven current account surpluses and sound macroeconomic policies that have bolstered international reserves to historically high levels, reduced public debt, and allowed a significant decline in real interest rates. A floating exchange rate, an inflation-targeting regime, and a tight fiscal policy are the three pillars of the economic program. Brazil had record trade surpluses from 2003 to 2007 and recorded its first current account surplus since 1992. Productivity gains coupled with high commodity prices contributed to the surge in exports. Brazil improved its debt profile in 2006 by shifting its debt burden toward real denominated and domestically held instruments. President Da Silva restated his commitment to fiscal responsibility by maintaining the country's primary surplus during the 2006 election and announcing a package of further economic reforms to reduce taxes and increase investment in infrastructure following his second inauguration. The government's goal of achieving strong growth while reducing the debt burden is likely to create inflationary pressures (Central Intelligence Agency, 2009a; Economy Watch, 2009a; Guerrero, 2009).

Conclusion

As the preceding information reveals, there is a great variety among the countries considered in this volume in terms of their political systems, economies, and cultures. This data, along with data from the forthcoming chapters, also affords us an opportunity to assess the usefulness of Wildavsky's (1975) primary model. Table 1-1 provides two measures of the level of wealth in a country: per capita income and the poverty rate, along with an assessment of budget predictability as defined by Wildavsky. The data in the table reinforces not only the variety among the countries included in this analysis, but also the great economic disparity among first-, second-, and third-world countries.

More importantly, based on Wildavsky's (1975) definition of predictability, the data in the table shows that the majority of the nonwestern European and North American countries have uncertain budget processes. However, the data in the substantive chapters (Chapters 2 through 19) clearly indicate that some countries, such as the

Table 1-1			
Wildavsky's Model Applied Today			
Country	Per capita income	Poverty rate	Predictability
Brazil	$10,100	31% (2005)	Certain
Canada	$39,300	10.8% (2005)[a]	Certain
China	$6,000	8% (2006 est.)[b]	Uncertain
Ghana	$1,500	28.5% (2007 est.)	Uncertain
Iraq	$4,000	N/A	Uncertain
Italy	$31,000	N/A	Certain
Jordan	$5,000	14.2% (2002)	Uncertain
Korea	$26,000	15% (2003 est.)	Certain
Mexico	$14,200	13.8% (2006)[c]	Uncertain
Pakistan	$2,600	24% (FY 05/06 est.)	Uncertain
Philippines	$3,300	30% (2003 est.)	Uncertain
Saudi Arabia	$20,700	N/A	Uncertain
Taiwan	$31,900	0.95% (2007 est.)	Uncertain
Thailand	$8,500	10% (2004 est.)	Uncertain
United Arab Emirates	$40,000	19.5% (2003)	Certain
United Kingdom	$36,600	14% (2006 est.)	Certain
United States	$47,000	12% (2004 est.)	Certain
Vietnam	$2,800	14.75% (2007 est.)	Uncertain

Adapted from http://siakhenn.tripod.com/exports-total.html. Copyright 2000 by Tong Siak Henn.

[a] This figure is the Low Income Cut-Off (LICO), a calculation that results in higher figures than found in many comparable economies; Canada does not have an official poverty line.
[b] 21.5 million of the rural population live below the official "absolute poverty" line (approximately $90 per year), whereas an additional 35.5 million residents live above that line but below the official "low income" line (approximately $125 per year).
[c] Using the food-based definition of poverty; asset-based poverty amounted to more than 40% of the population.

UAE have made significant strides in changing their budget predictability status. That is, recent reforms and subsequent political behavior are beginning to coincide.

The next 18 chapters will focus on various aspects of public finance and budgeting according to the level of individual expertise and interest of the author. In most cases, the factors examined will coincide with Wildavsky's (1975) and Rubin's (2010) models.

References

Axelrod, D. (1995). *Budgeting for modern government.* New York: St. Martins.
Banerjee, A., & Marcellino, M. (2006). Are there any reliable leading indicators of US inflation and GDP growth? *International Journal of Forecasters, 22*(1), 137–151. Available at: http://dx.doi.org/10.1016/j.ijforecast.2005.03.005. Accessed March 4, 2010.

Beresford, M. (2008). *Doi Moi in review: The challenges of building market socialism in Vietnam. Journal of Contemporary Asia*, 38(2), 221–243.

Bjornestad, L. (2009). Fiscal decentralization, fiscal incentives, and pro-poor outcomes: Evidence from Viet Nam. *ADB Economics Working Paper Series*, 168. Manila, Philippines: Asian Development Bank. Available at: http://www.adb.org/Documents/Working-Papers/2009/Economics-WP168.pdf. Accessed March 4, 2010.

Central Intelligence Agency. (2009a). *Brazil's Economy.* Available at: https://www.cia.gov/library/publications/the-world-factbook/geos/br.html. Accessed on November 25, 2009.

Central Intelligence Agency. (2009b). *Canada's Economy.* Available at: https://www.cia.gov/library/publications/the-world-factbook/geos/ca.html. Accessed on November 25, 2009.

Central Intelligence Agency, (2009c). *The Chinese Economy.* Available at: https://www.cia.gov/library/publications/the-world-factbook/geos/ch.html. Accessed November 25, 2009.

Central Intelligence Agency. (2009d). *Ghana's Economy.* Available at: https://www.cia.gov/library/publications/the-world-factbook/geos/gh.html. Accessed November 25, 2009.

Central Intelligence Agency. (2009e). *Iraq's Economy.* Available at: https://www.cia.gov/library/publications/the-world-factbook/geos/iz.html. Accessed on November 25, 2009.

Central Intelligence Agency. (2009f). *Italy's Economy.* Available at: https://www.cia.gov/library/publications/the-world-factbook/geos/it.html. Accessed on November 25, 2009.

Central Intelligence Agency. (2009g). *Jordan's Economy.* Available at: https://www.cia.gov/library/publications/the-world-factbook/geos/jo.html. Accessed on November 25, 2009.

Central Intelligence Agency. (2009h). *Mexico's Economy.* Available at: https://www.cia.gov/library/publications/the-world-factbook/geos/mx.html. Accessed on November 25, 2009.

Central Intelligence Agency. (2009i). *Pakistan's Economy.* Available at: https://www.cia.gov/library/publications/the-world-factbook/geos/pk.html. Accessed November 25, 2009.

Central Intelligence Agency. (2009j). *Philippine's Economy.* Available at: https://www.cia.gov/library/publications/the-world-factbook/geos/rp.html#. Accessed on November 25, 2009.

Central Intelligence Agency. (2009k). *Saudi Arabia's Economy.* Available at: https://www.cia.gov/library/publications/the-world-factbook/geos/sa.html. Accessed on November 25, 2009.

Central Intelligence Agency. (2009l). *South Korea's Economy.* Available at: https://www.cia.gov/library/publications/the-world-factbook/geos/ks.html. Accessed on November 25, 2009.

Central Intelligence Agency. (2009m). *Taiwan's Economy.* Available at: https://www.cia.gov/library/publications/the-world-factbook/geos/tw.html. Accessed on November 25, 2009.

Central Intelligence Agency. (2009n). *Thailand's Economy.* Available at: https://www.cia.gov/library/publications/the-world-factbook/geos/th.html. Accessed on November 25, 2009.

Central Intelligence Agency. (2009o). *UK's Economy.* Available at: https://www.cia.gov/library/publications/the-world-factbook/geos/uk.html. Accessed November 25, 2009.

Central Intelligence Agency. (2009p). *United Arab Emirate's Economy.* Available at: https://www.cia.gov/library/publications/the-world-factbook/geos/ae.html. Accessed on November 25, 2009.

Central Intelligence Agency. (2009q). *U.S. Economy.* Available at: https://www.cia.gov/library/publications/the-world-factbook/geos/us.html. Accessed on November 25, 2009.

Economy Watch. (2009a). Brazil's Economy. Available at: http://www.economywatch.com/world_economy/brazil/. Accessed on November 25, 2009.

Economy Watch. (2009b). Canada Economy. Available at: http://www.economywatch.com/world_economy/canada/. Accessed on November 25, 2009.

Economy Watch. (2009c). *China Economy China's Economic Profile, The Chinese Economy, Economy of China.* Available at: http://www.economywatch.com/world_economy/china/. Accessed November 25, 2009.

Economy Watch. (2009d). *Dubai Economy.* Available at: http://www.economywatch.com/world_economy/dubai/. Accessed November 25, 2009.

Economy Watch. (2009e). *Iraq's Economy.* Available at: http://www.economywatch.com/world_economy/iraq/. Accessed November 25, 2009.

Economy Watch. (2009f). *Italy Economic Overview.* Available at: http://www.economywatch.com/world_economy/italy/. Accessed on November 25, 2009.

Economy Watch. (2009g). *Mexico's Economy.* Available at: http://www.economywatch.com/world_economy/mexico/. Accessed on November 25, 2009.

Economy Watch. (2009h). *Pakistan Economy.* Available at: http://www.economywatch.com/world_economy/pakistan/. Accessed on November 25, 2009.

Economy Watch. (2009i). *Philippine Economy.* Available at: http://www.economywatch.com/world_economy/philippines/. Accessed on November 25, 2009.

Economy Watch. (2009j). *South Korea's Economy.* Available at: http://www.economywatch.com/world_economy/south-korea/. Accessed November 25, 2009.

Economy Watch. (2009k). *The US Economy.* Available at: http://www.economywatch.com/world_economy/usa/. Accessed on November 25, 2009.

Economy Watch. (2009l). *UK Economy.* Available at: http://www.economywatch.com/world_economy/united-kingdom/. Accessed November 25, 2009.

Economy Watch. (2009m). *Vietnam Economy.* Available at: http://www.economywatch.com/world_economy/vietnam/. Accessed on November 25, 2009.

Glewwe, P., Gragnolati, M., & Zaman, H. (2002). Who gained from Vietnam's boom in the 1990s? *Economic Development and Cultural Change, 50*(4), 773–792.

Guerrero, A. (2009). Emerging Markets: EM roundup Brazil. *Global Finance,* 23(5), 10.

Ha, Y. (2004). Budgetary and financial management reforms in Korea: Financial crisis, new public management, and fiscal administration. *International Review of Administrative Sciences,* 70, 511–525.

Helliwell, P. J. F., & Putnam, R. D. (1995). Economic growth and social capital in Italy. *Eastern Economic Journal,* 21(3), 295–307.

International Monetary Fund (2009). *Thailand: 2009 Article IV consultation—Staff report; staff statement; public information notice on the executive board discussion; and statement by the Executive Director for Thailand.* Washington, DC: Author.

Khaldi, M. D. (2008). Impact of foreign aid on economic development in Jordan (1990–2005). *Journal of Social Sciences,* 4(1), 16–20.

Khan, M. A., & Qayyum, A. (2007). Trade, financial and growth nexus in Pakistan. *Economic Analysis Working Papers,* 6(14). Available at: http://mpra.uni-muenchen.de/6523/. Accessed March 4, 2010.

Khatkhate, D. R. (1977). Evolving open market operations in a developing economy: The Taiwan experience. *Journal of Development Studies,* 13(2), 92–101.

Koo, C. M. (2008). Fiscal sustainability and it implications for fiscal policy in Korea. *The Journal of the Korean Economy,* 9, 497–521.

Kwiatkowski, L. (2005). Globalization, change and diversity in the Philippines. *Urban Anthropology and Studies of Cultural Systems and World Economic Development,* 34(4), 345–359.

Lee, C. H., & Lee. K. (1992). Sustaining economic development in South Korea: Lessons from Japan. *The Pacific Review,* 5, 13–24.

Li, S. M. (2001). Regional development in China: States, globalization, and inequality. *China Review International,* 8, 572–579.

Rubin, I. (2010). *The politics of public budgeting: Getting and spending, borrowing and balancing.* Washington, DC: CQ Press.

The World Bank. (2006). *Ghana—External review of public financial management* (Vol. 1). Available at: http://go.worldbank.org/M2ABLBG3H0. Accessed March 4, 2010.

The World Bank. (2008). *Development of the cities of Ghana: Challenges, priorities and tools* (Africa region working paper series number 110). Available at: http://www.worldbank.org/afr/wps/wp110.htm. Accessed March 4, 2010.

Tsui, K. (1996). Economic reform and interprovincial inequalities in China. *Journal of Development Economics,* 50(2), 353–368.

USAID in Jordan. (2009). *The Jordanian Economy*. Available at: http://jordan.usaid.gov/sectors.cfm?inSector=18. Accessed November 25, 2009.

Vrijer, E., Kock, U., & Grigorian, D. (2008). Iraq makes progress on economic front. *International Monetary Fund*. Available at: http://www.imf.org/external/pubs/ft/survey/so/2008/car021308b.htm. Accessed March 4, 2010.

Wildavsky, A. (1975). *Budgeting: A comparative theory of budgetary processes*. Boston: Little Brown.

Woo, W. T. (2008). Understanding the sources of friction in U.S.–China trade relations: The exchange rate debate diverts attention from optimum adjustment. *Asian Economic Papers, 7*(3), 61–95.

ENDNOTE

1. Wildavsky's model is based on a two-by-two table with five outcomes based on the two variables. There are two possible outcomes for rich nations that are uncertain.

Part 1

Africa

Chapter 2

The Republic of Ghana: A Success Story?

Craig S. Maher

Learning Objectives

- ■ Know and understand how to assess development in a developing country.
- ■ Know and understand fiscal federalism and how it applies to Ghana.
- ■ Know and understand the proliferation of fiscal decentralization and local government reform and its affects on Ghana.
- ■ Know and understanding the elements of good fiscal decentralization.
- ■ Know and understand how to assess the fine line between international loans, expectations, and budget reforms.
- ■ Understand the devolution of power and prosperity.

Introduction

Ghana has often been described as a success story of African independence. According to The World Bank (2009), "Ghana's political rights, civil liberties, and freedom of press rankings are not only amongst the best in Africa, but are compared to those recorded by countries at much higher levels of income."[1] Ghana was the first sub-Saharan colonized country to seize its independence from the United Kingdom on March 6, 1957. While experiencing a series of political and economic ups and downs through its brief history, Ghana is positioning itself to be a leader on the continent. Country assessments put Ghana at the top of the rankings in Africa, and the country's leadership seeks to achieve middle-income status by 2015 (World Bank, 2009).

Despite the optimism surrounding Ghana, concerns about its future remain. The country's future depends on achieving some ambitious goals, including lowering poverty, managing its internal and external debt, oil exploration, fiscal discipline, and continued political stability. Interestingly, many of the country's goals and those that donor organizations have for Ghana are linked to fiscal and political decentralization. What exactly that decentralized model looks like remains to be determined. This chapter begins with an examination of the governing structure and demographic profile of Ghana. Then, I analyze the current and future economic outlook for the country by closely examining World Bank reports. Last, I assess important issues such as budget structure, debt management, fiscal accountability, and decentralization.

Governing Structure

The central government of the Republic of Ghana is a constitutional democracy consisting of an executive (president and cabinet), legislative (unicameral national assembly), and a judicial branch (supreme court). The parliament of Ghana is unicameral and dominated by two parties, the New Patriotic Party and the National Democratic Congress. The most recent presidential election took place in December 2008. One of the more politically stable countries in the region, Ghana's presidential election experienced few problems and in a runoff, John Atta Mills of the National Democratic Congress defeated Akufo-Addo of the New Patriotic Party.

Since 1957, Ghana has operated under four constitutions. The previous three were suspended following military coups. These include military removal of its founding leader, Kwame Nkrumah in 1966 and a military coup in 1979. Approved in 1992, the current constitution has lasted longer than any of the previous three. Now with political and economic stability, Ghana may be poised for the growth envisioned years ago.

Demographics

Ghana's population is 23 million (2007 estimate), many of whom are concentrated along the coast and in the principle cities of Accra (the capital city) and Kumasi (US Department of State, 2010). While the official language is English, Ghanaians speak more than 50 languages and dialects (US Department of State). Some of the larger ethnic groups are the Akans, which consist of the Fantis along the coast and the Ashantis in the forest region north of the coast; the Guans, on the plains of the Volta River; the Ga and Ewe people of the south and southeast; and the Moshi-Dagomba tribes of the northern and upper regions (US Department of State).

One of the concerns expressed in a recent report by the World Bank is the growing urbanization of Ghana and the limited resources available to meet the basic infrastructure needs caused by such an influx (World Bank, 2008). In 1970, Ghana's population was 8.9 million and 29% of the population lived in urban areas (p. 2). By 1990, the country's population nearly doubled to 15.5 million with 36.5% living in urban areas. By 2010, Ghana's population is projected to reach 24.3 million and over half (51.5%) of the population will be living in urban areas (World Bank, 2008). The trend is projected to continue through 2030 when the country is estimated to have 33 million inhabitants, 64.8% of whom will be living in urban areas (World Bank, 2008).

The areas most affected by the urban immigration are and will be Accra and Kumasi. Between 1970 and 2015, the World Bank estimates Kumasi's population will grow from 349,000 to 2.1 million (World Bank, 2008). Similarly, Accra's population is projected to grow from 631,000 to 2.7 million during the same years (World Bank, 2008). These growth rates are putting pressure on these urban areas in terms of land ownership and use, housing, basic infrastructure (e.g., water and garbage collection services), and employment opportunities, among other concerns. As a result, poverty rates, particularly in the urban areas, have become a growing concern (World Bank, 2008).

Economy

Ghana's economy is driven by agriculture and natural resources. Its major exports include cocoa, gold, timber, diamonds, and manganese. Important imports include petroleum, food, industrial raw materials, machinery, and equipment (US Department of State, 2010). Its major trading partners include Nigeria, China, the United States, the United Kingdom, Germany, Togo, France, Netherlands, and Spain (US Department of State). Recent discoveries of petroleum could have a significant impact on Ghana's current trade imbalance.

Ghana's recent economic prosperity is probably the single most important reason it has experienced political stability over the past couple of decades. Since the 1990s, Ghana has sustained real GDP growth of more than 4% and per capita growth of approximately 2% (World Bank, 2009). According to the World Bank (2009):

> Economic growth has averaged over 5% since 2001 and reached 6% in 2005–2006. This strong growth nearly halved the poverty rate in Ghana—the proportion of the population below the country's poverty line—from approximately 52% at the beginning of the 1990s to 28.6% in 2005–2006.

The recent economic growth experienced by Ghana places it among the three strongest, low-income African countries, alongside Tanzania and Uganda (World Bank, 2009). While impressive, concerns about economic development in Ghana remain. According to the World Bank (2009):

> ■ Despite these gains, income inequality across regions and between men and women remains high and has increased during this period of accelerated growth. These inequities remain potent sources of political and social tensions. While all main income groups—from the poorest

to the richest—have benefited from the economic expansion since the beginning of the 1990s, the gains by the poorest were much lower than those of the rest of society. Despite their major role benefiting the society, women continue to earn much less then men, and poor women are the most economically vulnerable. While all regions saw gains in incomes and a reduction in poverty, these gains and poverty reduction were much less pronounced in the north of Ghana.

■ Productivity remains low, especially in agriculture. Ghana's aggregate productivity is improving, but the level remains below the most productive African economies, such as Mauritius and Botswana, and way behind the rapidly growing Asian countries. With irrigation almost nonexistent, Ghana's agriculture still depends largely on weather. Recently, productivity has begun to increase but the use of modern agricultural techniques remains limited. The success stories in Ghana's agriculture, such as cocoa and horticulture (pineapple), provide lessons on how to strengthen the rest of agriculture.

■ While improving, several aspects of the business and investment climate remain weak. These constraints hold back Ghanaian firms from investing, expanding output, and hiring more workers as well as becoming more productive. The most important constraints relate to electricity and access to finance, especially for small and medium-size enterprises.

■ Addressing infrastructure bottlenecks will also help raise productivity in the economy, especially in agriculture. Without water supply and electricity, there is no refrigeration; and without refrigeration, there is no vibrant commercial fishing industry and associated food chains. Productivity is fundamental to long-term growth. Some new technologies, such as cellular and IT offer opportunities to leapfrog into higher and more productive, new economic sectors that offer promises of new jobs, investments, and growth. Additional opportunities beyond infrastructure must be sought to sustainably enhance productivity in sectors important to the well-being of Ghanaians, such as in agriculture. The most important sources of Ghana's future productivity improvements are likely to be through the competitive entry of new and more productive enterprises, as well as the growth of existing firms, and through increasing the available skilled labor. To these ends, policy efforts should focus on:

  ● Eliminating infrastructure bottlenecks and widening the use of technology and ICT.
  ● Transferring to other agriculture sectors the lessons of recent productivity gains in the cocoa sector as a result of disease control, fertilizers, and better product varieties. The last shows that aggressive productivity-enhancing measures on privately owned farms can have major impacts on productivity and output.
  ● Introducing in the public sector a new value-for-money and productivity-enhancing mindset that will lead to better use of resources and wider space for private sector innovation in the new technology-intensive sectors that offer opportunities for leapfrogging.

Ghana's 2008 Budget

Ghana's fiscal year is the same as the calendar year. Their currency is the cedi (¢), which currently exchanges US$1 for approximately GH¢13,800. Marking the country's 50th anniversary, the 2008 budget was named "Brighter Future" by President John Kufuor. Spending in 2008 was estimated at GH¢7.1 billion (see Table 2-1). These expenditures are divided into two broad categories: statutory (GH¢1.7 billion) and

Table 2-1

Ghana's Budget

	2006	2007	2008	2009	2010
Total payments	4,307.5	6,153.8	7,107.2	7,208.4	7,858.7
Statutory payments	1,248.6	1,548.6	1,728.9	1,895.9	2,078.9
External debt service	325.4	354.8	293.2	248.3	218.2
Domestic interest	303.1	242.7	352.3	306.9	292.3
District assembly common fund	104.7	146.2	234.3	277.1	321.8
Transfers to households	236.9	274.8	318.0	437.2	508.2
Pensions	92.6	105.2	127.4	171.1	198.9
Gratuities	46.6	51.2	58.0	95.0	110.5
Social security	97.7	118.5	132.7	171.1	198.9
National Health Fund (NHF)	60.7	255.3	235.4	276.6	324.3
Educational trust fund	106.3	150.5	163.0	195.2	232.8
Road fund	108.6	111.4	129.2	150.6	176.8
Petroleum-related fund	3.0	3.0	3.5	4.1	4.4
Discretionary funds	3,058.8	4,605.2	5,378.2	5,312.5	5,779.7
Ministries	1,859.0	2,217.3	2,811.9	2,702.9	3,142.1
Net lending	0.7	0.2	−2.0	−2.0	−2.0
Foreign-financing investment	527.9	553.2	1,000.2	1,292.7	993.0
Tax refunds	14.1	21.3	37.0	43.1	50.2
Outstanding commitments	48.8	77.7	42.7	0.0	0.0
Utility price subsidies	267.3	21.4	0.0	0.0	0.0
w/o Tema Oil Refinery's under-recovery	177.4	3.7	0.0	0.0	0.0
Other transfers	37.2	104.7	13.4	22.0	22.0
Retention of internally generated funds	0.0	213.9	299.2	368.5	490.1
Safety net for petroleum					
Deregulation	37.2	104.7	13.4	22.0	22.0
Lifeline consumers of electronics	0.0	1.3	10.0	10.0	10.0
Tax expenditures (exemptions)	0.0	339.5	356.6	341.4	405.1
Reserve fund	0.0	160.8	243.7	0.0	0.0
HIPC-financed expenditures	179.2	176.9	127.6	134.2	128.4
MDRI-financed expenditures	124.6	159.9	55.6	59.1	63.7
Repayment of domestic debt	0.0	557.0	382.4	239.6	477.1

Source: Republic of Ghana, Ministry of Finance and Economic Planning.

discretionary (GH¢5.4 billion). Statutory payments consist of external debt service (GH¢293 million), payments to individuals and organizations that purchased government bills (GH¢352.3 million), transfers to the District Assembly Common Fund (GH¢234.3 million), the Ghana Education Trust Fund (GH¢163 million) and the Road Fund (GH¢129 million).

Trends in statutory payments between 2006 and 2010 reveal sizable shifts in the country's priorities. External debt service represents 24.3% of statutory payments in 2006; it is estimated that in 2010, they will drop to 10.5%. Similarly, in 2006, domestic interest payments were 24.3% of statutory payments, and in 2010, they are projected to account for 14.1%. Conversely, funding for local government (DA's Common Fund) will nearly double between 2006 and 2010 as a percent of statutory payments (8.4% to 15.5%). The National Fund experienced a sizable increase in funding between 2006 and 2007, and the support remains in 2010 at about 15%.

Discretionary spending makes up over 70% of Ghana's expenditures. In broad terms, these expenses can be divided into three categories: ministries, foreign-financed investment, transfers and repayment of domestic debt, the sum of which account for approximately 80% of discretionary spending. Ministry expenditures are divided among 38 central government ministries, which are presented in three broad categories: Private Sector Competitiveness, Human Resource Development, and Good Governance. Private Sector Competitiveness consists of 11 ministries, the most sizable (budgetary) in 2008 are the Ministry of Energy (GH¢365 million), Ministry of Transportation (GH¢184 million), and Ministry of Harbors and Railways (GH¢60 million). While only consisting of four ministries, the Human Resources Development category comprises over 40% of total ministry discretionary expenses. The Ministry of Education, Science and Sports, and Ministry of Health assume the bulk of Human Resources Development expenses (GH¢880 million and GH¢269 million). Finally, under the third and final category, Good Governance contains 23 ministries, the largest of which were Ministry of Interior (GH¢156 million), Ministry of Defense (GH¢117 million), and Ministry of Foreign Affairs, Regional Cooperation and NEPAD (GH¢69 million)

Between 2006 and 2010, significant policy shifts are revealed by comparing change in ministry allocations. One of these changes is the sizable drop in funding for the Ministry of Energy from GH¢365 million in 2006, to GH¢10 million in 2010. This is largely attributable to the sizable foreign investment for oil exploration, up from 12% of discretionary spending in 2007, to 26% in 2009.

REVENUES

The central government expected to receive GH¢7.1 million in 2008, GH¢7.2 million in 2009, and GH¢7.9 million in 2010 (see Table 2-2). In general, revenues consist of a combination of taxes (67%), grants (12%), loans (9%), and other receipts (14%). Other receipts include items such as capital market borrowing and Heavily Indebted Poor Countries (HIPC) relief (GH¢77.5 million in 2008).

Tax revenues are divided into five categories: direct (25%), indirect (35%), international trade (17%), national health insurance (5%), and import exemptions (8%).[2]

Table 2-2

Ghana's Revenue Budget

	2007	2008	2009	2010
	Revised budget	Estimated budget	Projected budget	Projected budget
Total receipts				
Total revenue and grants	6,226.0	7,107.2	7,208.5	7,858.7
Total revenue	3,762.6	4,763.2	5,199.9	6.127.8
Tax revenue	3,435.7	4,433.2	4,649.7	6,077.8
Direct taxes	887.7	1,122.4	1,309.7	1,555.0
Personal	382.3	458.8	541.4	644.3
Self-employed	45.4	58.0	68.4	81.4
Companies	382.2	498.0	587.6	699.2
Other direct taxes	77.8	107.7	112.3	130.1
Indirect taxes	1,412.5	1,548.5	1,832.0	2,068.2
Value-added tax	887.6	1,000.1	1,191.9	1,415.1
Domestic	296.3	373.0	439.7	522.1
Imports	591.3	628.1	752.2	893.0
Petroleum	422.6	490.0	571.2	571.2
Excise	102.3	58.3	68.9	81.8
International trade taxes	613.6	746.3	890.0	1053.6
National health				
Insurance levy	182.4	235.4	276.6	324.3
Other revenue measures	0.0	330.0	50.0	50.0
Import exemptions	339.5	356.6	341.4	405.1
Nontax revenue	326.9	424.0	500.2	671.5
Grants	894.5	853.4	1,006.0	826.2
Project	444.8	514.8	613.7	425.0
Program	153.5	201.0	250.7	256.8
HIPC assistance	136.4	81.9	82.4	80.7
Multilateral debt relief				
Initiative	159.9	55.6	59.1	63.7
International Monetary Fund	108.3	0.0	0.0	0.0
World Bank	46.0	49.9	53.1	57.6
African Development Bank	5.5	5.7	6.0	6.1
Loans	598.8	621.5	917.2	824.8
Projected loans	451.9	485.3	780.0	568.0
Program loans	147.0	136.2	137.2	256.8

Source: Republic of Ghana, Ministry of Finance and Economic Planning.

Indirect, particularly value-added import and import duties, and international trade taxes account for roughly half of the county's tax revenues. Direct taxes, personal, self-employed, company and other, comprise approximately 25% of total tax revenues. Between 2007 and 2010, the proportion of tax revenues from these various sources is estimated to change minimally.

Grants received by Ghana's central government account for more than 10% of total revenues and, in 2007, exceeded total direct tax revenue. More than half of the grant funding is for projects, which are generally geared toward infrastructure needs. It is also worth noting that in 2007, nearly GH¢300 million in grant funding went toward debt-relief initiatives sponsored by the International Monetary Fund (IMF), the World Bank, and African Development Bank. These debt relief initiatives are projected to be significantly scaled back in years 2008 through 2010.

Loans account for approximately 10% of total revenues in each of the years 2007 through 2010. As with the grant funds, the lion's share of loans are internationally funded and play a key role in Ghana's poverty reduction efforts. While the totals vary annually, much of the loans funding is for projects related to infrastructure improvements. Also worth noting is that in 2007 and 2008, Ghana generated GH¢350 million and GH¢516 million through capital market borrowing. Their ability to do so reflects a 20-year effort to develop a successful financial market and national banking system.

Fiscal Accountability

Due to the sizable amount of grant and loan funding from international organizations, Ghana's financial reporting and decision making has been closely scrutinized. While there appears to be general approval of the central government's budgeting and accounting practices, expressed concerns are significant. According to the IMF, there remain challenges with the accounting practices for certain central government expenses such as donor flows dispersed directly to ministries and those arising from internally generated funds (International Monetary Fund, 2008b). In addition, it has been difficult to account for spending by extrabudgetary funds. The operations of special funds such as the Ghana Education Trust Fund and District Assemblies Fund (DACF) are not yet covered in fiscal accounts (International Monetary Fund, 2008b, p. 13). Locally, it appears that while government expenses are directly met from budgetary accounts, locally generated revenues from local governments and related spending are not yet covered.

External Review of Public Finance Management

In 2006, an extensive review of Ghana's public finance management objectives and fiscal performance measures was conducted under the auspices of the World Bank. The 2006 Public Expenditure and Financial Accountability (PEFA) assessment was published as a two-volume set in excess of 100 pages. In essence, the report concludes that Ghana has made significant strides since it became eligible for HIPC support in the early 2000s. The assessment is conducted against six core public finance management objectives. The findings for Ghana are as follows:

- *Credibility of the Budget.* Aggregate expenditure and revenue outturns broadly match the budget plans, but credibility is diminished by variance across budget heads, reflecting weaknesses in budget formulation and the treatment of contingencies.
- *Comprehensiveness and Transparency of the Budget.* This has improved considerably over the past two years, through the incorporation of information on internally generated funds, direct donor disbursements, HIPC, and statutory funds on the budget statement. However, in-year reporting is less comprehensive, hampering overall budget scrutiny and management.
- *Policy-Based Budget.* While budgets have become more policy based in recent years, performance is held back by limited ability to cost strategies, the lack of effective wage-bill planning, and the absence of a transparent link between planned and executed budget activities.
- *Predictability and Control in Budget Execution.* The government has improved commitment and other internal controls, but recognizes weaknesses in management and oversight of control systems.
- *Accountability, Recording, and Reporting.* The government still relies predominantly on a paper-based system, resulting in delays and data errors. Analytic and technical capacity constraints hamper the Ministry of Finance and Economic Planning, and departments and agencies' efforts to monitor and analyze budget performance.
- *External Scrutiny and Audit.* There is now more timely completion of accounts and financial statements and submission of audit reports to the legislature, which in turn, is more actively scrutinizing both budget and accounts. Reported progress has been facilitated by the timely submission of the Report and Financial Statements of the Consolidated Fund by Controller and Account General Department (CAGD). However, effective follow-up on audit findings remains a question, and the excessive detail of the budget documents undermines effective parliamentary scrutiny.

Ghana's most challenging recommendations identified in the report are to:

- Expand the coverage and improve the accuracy of CADG monthly budget execution reports by including retained internally generated funds and donor project aid;
- Align better Ghana Growth and Poverty Reduction Strategy for 2006 to 2009 (GPRS II) and the annual budget by strengthening the medium-term expenditure framework (MTEF) and increasing its capacity to reflect the costs of existing and new policies and programs, and thus make the budget more credible; and
- Strengthen the governance framework for state-owned enterprises (SOE) by enforcing the requirement for all SOEs to submit annual financial and operating plans, quarterly implementation reports, and continue to adopt measures to mitigate fiscal risk.

Debt

Ghana currently receives annual payments of approximately US$1 billion in various forms of aid. The IMF, an organization that has a vested interest in Ghana given the amounts loaned, has links to several useful staff reports on its Web site.[3] One of the IMF's primary concerns continues to be Ghana's level of debt. In 2008, Ghana's overall fiscal balance was −10.3% of its GDP. For the same year, the country's total governmental debt was 51.4% of GDP, of which 29.6% was domestic and 26.7% was external (IMF, 2008b, p. 10). The IMF projects debt rising to 60.3% of GDP in 2010, and 80% of GDP in 2028 (IMF, 2008b).

One of the primary drivers of Ghana's fiscal imbalance has been a lack of spending discipline (IMF, 2008b). For instance, recent wage bills were authorized outside of the budgeting process enabling ministries and local agencies to hire significantly more than budgeted. According to the IMF (2008b), "Particular attention is needed to control expenditure commitments; civil service reform needs to resume in earnest, with attracting high-quality labor and reducing public sector employment and fiscal decentralization which can provide efficiency gains."

What might be most concerning is not so much the country's current level of debt, but that debt continues to be an area of focus given its history of debt relief. As early as the 1960s, Ghana was faced with debt problems (Harrington & Younger, 2000). The country's debt woes worsened in the 1970s, peaked in the 1980s, and, because of debt restructuring, steadied in the early 1990s (Osei & Quartey, 2001). According to Osei and Quartey, Ghana's debt service to exports ratio peaked at over 80% in 1982 primarily due to oil price increases, the recession in western countries, and policy mismanagement (Osei & Quartey). In the late 1980s, Ghana was able to restructure their debt, which provided some temporary relief. The relief was, however, short lived as the country was using incoming aid to repay debt. By 1997, Ghana's debt service was exceeding its net aid (Osei & Quartey).

In the early 2000s, Ghana sought and qualified for HIPC assistance. The HIPC initiative is a multinational and multiorganizational effort (principally the IMF, the African Development Fund, and the World Bank) to provide relief for countries overwhelmed by their debt burdens. Eligibility is contingent on several factors, including the creation of a poverty-reduction strategy and fiscal policy reforms. While 41 countries are eligible, Ghana is one of 28 countries that, as of February 18, 2010, have received HIPC assistance (IMF, 2010). According to an African Development Bank Group (2009) report, Ghana has received US$2.2 million in debt relief. The amount of relief was equivalent to a 56.2% reduction in the country's outstanding debt (African Development Bank Group).

What remains to be seen is the extent to which Ghana is able to change past practices of debt growth and meet a principle goal of the HIPC initiative: lowering poverty. Implicit in the HIPC assistance is that public expenditures previously used to service debt will be used to fund programs aimed to benefit those less well off. Lloyd, Morrissey, & Osei (2001), in one of the few available studies, found that the HIPC initiative could produce this intended effect in two ways: economic development spurred by investment and government savings on debt service that would now be spent on social programs.

As previously discussed, Ghana has a dedicated funding source for education, health, roads, and local governments that, in 2008, accounted for 10% of total spending. Those percentages rose to 12.5% in 2009, and 13.4% in 2010. These expenses also do not capture discretionary spending by various ministries, including the Ministry of Transportation; the Ministry of Harbors and Railways; the Ministry of Education, Science, and Sports; and the Ministry of Health.

Just as important, if not more so, is Ghana's debt management strategy. A report by the IMF includes a forecast of Ghana's debt burden under three economic scenarios: a baseline, low growth, and oil exporting (see Table 2-3). The three fiscal stress ratios for 2008 were: net present value (NPV) of debt to GDP (20%), NPV of debt to exports (45%), and debt service to exports (3%). For perspective, Ghana's debt service to exports was 24.9% during the period 1970 to 1983, rose to 44.3% from 1983 to 1989, and fell to 29.8% from 1990 to 1998 (Osei & Quartey, 2001). Similarly, debt to exports was 342.9% from 1970 to 1983, peaked at 443.4% from 1983 to 1998, and dipped to 385.9% from 1990 to 1998 (Osei & Quartey). Finally, external debt to GDP for the same periods were 30.2%, 53.5%, and 81.1%, respectively (Osei & Quartey). Compared to these numbers, Ghana currently appears in a strong position. However, the estimates 10 and 20 years out raise concerns as the ratios worsen. The IMF points to many of the same causes, particularly poor fiscal policy (IMF, 2008b). The discovery of oil reserves could be the nation's salvation, if used primarily to buy down its debt service.

Table 2-3			
Ghana's Debt Ratios			
	2008	2018	2028
	Baseline Scenario		
NPV of debt to GDP ratio	20	35	40
NPV of debt to exports ratio	45	109	150
Debt service to exports ratio	3	11	23
	Low-GDP Scenario		
NPV of debt to GDP ratio	20	38	56
NPV of debt to exports ratio	45	122	185
Debt service to exports ratio	3	12	29
	Oil Exporting Scenario		
NPV of debt to GDP ratio	20	22	9
NPV of debt to exports ratio	45	69	34
Debt service to exports ratio	3	9	7

Source: International Monetary Fund, Debt Sustainability Analysis estimates.

Opportunities: Oil Reserves

In 2007 and 2008, oil reserves were discovered in Ghana by the UK-based Tullow Oil in quantities greater than domestic demand. It is estimated that the current 170 billions of barrels generated in Ghana could reach the 500 to 600 billion barrel mark. The supply is expected to be short-lived, meaning that an analysis by IMF staff predicts that production and exportation could begin in 2011, peak in 2013, and be depleted by 2030 (IMF, 2008b). The same analysis determined that these discoveries could net the government a total of US$20 billion, or 160% of Ghana's 2008 GDP.

Management of the revenues generated from such a discovery has received the attention of international donors. Were Ghana to use all oil revenues to retire debt, the country public service debt would drop from nearly 50% of GDP in 2007 to 19.2% in 2028 (IMF, 2008b, p. 19). According to the IMF (2008a):

> Good international practice suggests that a separate account under the control of the treasury, that clear rules be established for transferring oil revenues into the account and making transfers to the budget to finance the non-oil deficit, that the fund be regulated by the investment strategy supervised by a professionally staffed investment committee, and that arrangements for regular reporting and independent audit of the management and use of oil and gas resources be put in place. (p. 122)

Decentralization: A Panacea for Prosperity?

For all practical purposes, Ghana functions as a highly centralized state. Administratively, the country operates as a unitary state with one level of subnational government comprising five metropolitan assemblies, eight municipal assemblies, and 125 district assemblies. These subnational governments are collectively referred to as MMDAs. In recent years, with the encouragement of lending agencies, the World Bank in particular, there has been a concerted effort by the central government toward greater decentralization. The current framework for intergovernmental fiscal relations is found in the Local Government Act and the 2003 District Assemblies Common Fund (DACF) Act. The Local Government Act (462) of 1993 provides district assemblies with taxing authority, political and administrative authority, and the development of infrastructure.

The District Assemblies (DA) are responsible for preparing and approving an annual budget. Once approved, the budget is submitted to a regional coordinating council for project coordination. In practice, the district assemblies have several limitations, including an inability to generate sufficient own-source revenue, a limited operating budget, and the inability to hire staff or select officials serving on the district assemblies. Regarding the first point, while DAs have the authority to impose property taxes and charge fees for any license or permit, in reality, these account for a small portion of their budget. The majority of DA revenue come from the central government. Only 16% of DA revenues are locally generated. The bulk of their funding comes in the form of grants and intergovernmental aids (see Table 2-4).

Table 2-4

Consolidate Budget for District Assemblies of Ghana

Category	Millions of GH cedis	Average	% of total
Rates	54,420	2,899	3.8
Lands	33,963	1,808	2.4
Fees	68,015	3,620	4.8
Licenses	31,788	1,692	2.2
Rent	11,469		
Investments	7,438		
Miscellaneous	20.003		
Subtotal of internally generated revenues	227,096	12,086	16.0
Transfers salary	115,547	6,150	8.1
Common fund	619,551	32,973	43.5
Donors	138,759	7,385	9.8
HIPC	322,076	17,141	22.6
Total grants	1,195,933	63,649	84.0
Total revenue	1,423,029	75,735	100.0
Expenses			
Personnel	163,708	8,713	11.4
Other current expenditures	149,640	7,964	10.4
Capital expenditures	1,125,003	59,874	78.2
Total expenses	1,438,351	76,551	100.0

Source: The World Bank.

The largest single-source DA revenue source (43.5%) is from the Common Fund. The distributions of aids are generally formula-based, including equality, need (education-related), and population density (World Bank, 2006b). This poses challenges as financing from the Common Fund can only be used to fund projects that are part of the approved development plan for the district. Thus, nearly 80% of DA expenditures are for capital projects.

Not only are the DAs' abilities to make budgetary decisions hampered by revenue and expenditure limitations, so too are their abilities to make personnel decisions. The hiring, firing, and assigning of local staff are currently the responsibility of central government: Ministries, Departments, and Agencies (World Bank, 2008). Thus, the Minister of Local Government and Rural Development, which is responsible for coordinating many local functions, plays an important role in the effectiveness of the DAs.

Exacerbating these fiscal and management limitations, representation on assembly councils consists of a combination of elected and appointed positions. Those appointed are done so by both the central government and president. In addition, the central government (typically the minister of local government) has the power to investigate and even dismiss a council in situations where irregularities have appeared. The central government's role in DA governance has caused resentment by citizens (World Bank, 2008).

The issue of intergovernmental relations has been examined extensively by both the World Bank and the IMF. Areas of concern expressed by both organizations include a lack of local control and blurred lines of responsibilities between the DAs and the central government. According to the World Bank, the result of this relationship has been an inability to provide core services. For instance, water coverage in urban areas has declined from 85% in 1990 to 61% in 2004. Similarly, in 2004, solid waste was collected at a rate of 70%, just as the electricity infrastructure is strained and traffic congestion is problematic.

LOCAL FINANCIAL ACCOUNTING ISSUES

Included in the World Bank's review of Ghana's financial position and management was an assessment of local governments. With respect to intergovernmental fiscal relations, Ghana received a grade of C (World Bank, 2006b). The grade was based on three indicators: transparency and objectivity in the horizontal allocation amongst subnational governments; timeliness and reliability to subnational governments on their allocation; and the extent of consolidation in fiscal data. On the first indicator, Ghana received a grade of A based on the clarity and transparency of criteria. On both the second and third indicators, the government received a D. For the second indicator, the low grade was the result of the distribution formula not being approved until after the subnational governments' fiscal year in 2006. The third and final grade was received because of the different classification systems that prohibit the national and subnational governments from consolidating fiscal data (World Bank, 2006b, p. 16).

The lack of consistency in charts of accounts makes it difficult to assess local fiscal decision making. According to the World Bank, ". . . the lack of up-to-date accounts, lack of a user-friendly accounting system and unfamiliarity with financial control and audit mechanisms . . . limit the ability of residents to participate in DA fiscal decision making" (World Bank, 2006b). In addition, the DAs heavy reliance on transfers, which, historically, have not been reliable in terms of timing and amounts, limits their ability to budget beyond the current year.

Given the previously made points, it should not be surprising that the World Bank has expressed concerns with the level of fiscal discipline by Ghana's DAs. In reference to the DAs, the World Bank (2006b) has stated, that there is "little incentive to control local expenditures as financial oversight and control is primarily done by the central government." The report goes on and states "The implementation of lines of responsibility within the government system leaves much to be desired. Definitions of responsibility are fuzzy at levels control/management and actual delivery. Overlapping responsibilities within the system are considerable." Such a finding is certainly not unique to Ghana. For example, a recent study of fiscal decentralization in Kenya found that local governments that are afforded capital expenditure discretion were, in fact, investing in capital projects that then needed operating funds from the central government due to limited local resources (Bagaka, 2008).

Ghana's Municipal Finance and Management Initiative

Ghana has recently embarked on an effort to enhance local decision making, called the Municipal Finance and Management Initiative (MFMI).[4] In 2007, the Ministry of Local Government and Rural Development, and the Ministry of Finance and Economic Planning organized a 2-day international conference on this initiative in Accra. According to the Cities Alliance, "The main aim of the MFMI is to assist municipal governments achieve the following:

- Significantly increase Internally Generated Funds;
- Identify and find ways of minimizing and finally eliminating financial leakages;
- Significantly improving management and accounting systems;
- Raise necessary funds to meet infrastructural and service delivery requirements;
- Gain public confidence."[5]

The MFMI remains in the development stages and was dealt a serious blow with the recent death of Kwadwo Baah-Wiredu, Ghana's finance minister.[6] However, given the push by the international lending agencies, particularly the World Bank, intergovernmental relations will remain a key focus.

IS FISCAL DECENTRALIZATION THE SOLUTION?

Paul Smoke's work is most useful for the discussion of Ghana's decentralization movement. A key point raised is that there is a serious lack of international comparative work on fiscal decentralization, which limits the ability to define a "best" model (Smoke, 2001). Based on his review of the existing literature and on research on Ethiopia and Uganda, Smoke contends that a good fiscal decentralization program needs, ". . . an adequate enabling environment; assignment of an appropriate set of functions to local governments; the establishment of an adequate intergovernmental fiscal transfer system; and the establishment of adequate access to local governments to development capital" (p. 19).

In terms of environment, it is suggested that not only is it important to have constitutional and statutory definitions of local government roles and responsibilities, but a national will for decentralization (Smoke, 2001). In addition, local government oversight needs consideration. The latter points are particularly worth noting for Ghana. Although Ghana has a history of local governance, recent efforts appear to be more at the desire of the international donor community, the World Bank in particular. Reviews of IMF and World Bank documents consistently reference the need for Ghana to decentralize. Smoke cautions about external pushes for decentralization:

> In spite of current international rhetoric, donors do not always behave in ways that genuinely support gradual and strategic decentralization, institution building and sectoral coordination. Such efforts are time consuming and difficult, and, therefore likely to cause substantial delays in donor efforts move funds. Given common

pressures or programme officers to keep to expenditure schedules, particularly in large lending institutions, substantial funds continue to flow for investment, even if it is clear that recipient governments lack the capacity to ensure that funds will be well spent and that projects being constructed will be well maintained. (p. 29)

Oversight of local governance will also need to be reviewed in Ghana. Smoke (2001) references countries ". . . broad-purpose ministries, such as Local Government, Home Affairs, Finance and Planning . . ." as problematic because the oversight tends to become competitive and disorganized (p. 20). Ghana's Ministry of Local Government and Rural Development, and Ministry of Finance and Economic Planning appear to fit the broad definition of a local government oversight agency warned by Smoke. Each is providing input on the future of Ghana's local government structure and has a stake in the outcome. The outcome could mean a loss of influence with which bureaucrats are not easily willing to part (Smoke). A more desirable oversight model was found in Kenya, which has one ministry (the Ministry of Local Government) whose sole responsibility is oversight of local governments (Smoke). In addition, the ability of Ghana's central government ministries to hire, fire, and place local bureaucrats are an inherent cause for tension and can ultimately weaken local government effectiveness.

The adequacy of an intergovernmental fiscal transfer system lies at the heart of most discussions of fiscal decentralization. The challenges tend to center around balancing the need for local fiscal autonomy with the desire for equity across local areas. The consensus among scholars seems to be that local governments should rely on a few sizable revenue sources—principally property taxes and user fees—that can produce significant returns (Bahl & Linn, 1992; Smoke, 2001). Interestingly, these are currently the primary sources for Ghana's DAs. The administration of property taxes has been problematic for Ghana for a number of reasons, including difficulty in determining property ownership in many cases. Greater use of fees for services by DAs has been as issue pressed by the World Bank and is consistent with the opinions of a number of scholars (Smoke, 2001).

In addition to locally generated revenues, the central government will need to continue to play an important role. As previously discussed, Ghana's DAs currently receive about 80% of their funding from the central government. In addition, those funds are largely restricted for capital projects. While conditional grants are needed in any fiscal decentralization model to encourage spending in particular areas, Ghana also needs to develop unconditional grants. Unconditional grants provide the necessary local flexibility to meet the unique needs of citizens. These grants could be particularly beneficial to Ghana's DAs, as they currently lack resources for general operations.

Somewhat more controversial is the ability of local governments to incur debt for investment capital. Ghana, like most developing countries, receives capital funds from the central government. A key point worthy of consideration is that the ability of local government to access credit markets provides stability when economic fluctuations force central governments to reign in grant funding for such projects (Smoke, 2001). Interestingly, international donors have specifically stated their opposition to Ghana granting local governments the ability to incur debt over fear of abuse. At a minimum, fiscal decentralization models should consist of a range of local government financing options (Smoke).

Conclusion

Ghana's political environment, stability, and civil liberties and freedoms are the envy of most African countries. The country's biggest challenges are fiscal and economic issues. Economically, the discovery of oil reserves will provide a boom over the next 20 years, however, the ability to harness the potential revenues for infrastructure improvements and debt relief will, undoubtedly, be challenged by short-term political gains. Current policies structured toward poverty reduction are positive signs.

Ghana, like many developing countries, is pursuing fiscal decentralization for several reasons, including anticipated economic development opportunities, poverty reduction, fiscal transparency, and international donor prodding. The most recent effort is the MFMI questions. According to the MFMI secretariat,[7] the aims of the initiative are to assist local governments to:

- significantly increase Internally Generated Funds (IGF);
- identify and find ways of minimizing and finally eliminating financial leakages;
- significantly improve management and accounting systems;
- raise necessary funds to meet infrastructural and service delivery requirements; and
- gain public confidence.

Based on the stated goals, the focus is clearly on revenue generation and financial accounting practices. While these are obviously important objectives, they might not be sufficient to ensure success. Basic questions of oversight, local capacity, the appropriate mix of central government grants, representation on municipal councils, and personnel decision making also need consideration.

Discussion Questions

1. Referring back to the chapter's title, is Ghana a success story? What are the bases by which one should evaluate a developing nation's success?
2. Much of the academic literature of fiscal federalism (most common bodies of literature include the "fly-paper effect" and "fiscal illusion") focuses on the United States. Using the Republic of Ghana as an example, how do international studies add to the breadth and/or redefine fiscal federalism literature?
3. According to the World Bank, fiscal decentralization and local government reform have been among the most widespread recent trends in developing countries. Based on this chapter, why is this occurring? Discuss both strengths and weaknesses in this trend.
4. Paul Smoke (2001) wrote that the elements of a good fiscal decentralization include:
   a. An adequate enabling environment;
   b. Assignment of an appropriate set of functions to local governments;
   c. Assignment of an appropriate set of own-source revenues to local governments;

    d. Establishment of an adequate intergovernmental fiscal transfer system; and

    e. Establishment of adequate access of local governments to development capital.

Using these five criteria, evaluate Ghana's fiscal decentralization capacity.

5. The level of debt currently incurred by Ghana and estimated in the upcoming years is substantial. To meet the country's needs, international organizations have loaned money to Ghana. Given this, to what extent should these donor organizations expect Ghana to reform? Discuss this within the context of sovereignty.

6. For all practical purposes, Ghana functions as a highly centralized state yet has been in the process of developing a more decentralized governing structure. From what you have read, is Ghana's decentralization effort a panacea for prosperity?

References

African Development Bank Group. (2009). *Ghana: HIPC Approval Document Completion Point Under the Enhanced Framework.* Available at: http://www.afdb.org/fileadmin/uploads/afdb/Documents/Financial-Information/ADB-BD-WP-2004-124-EN-GHANA-HIPC-APPROVAL-DOCUMENT-COMPLETION-POINT-UNDER-THE-ENHANCED-FRAMEWORK.PDF. Accessed March 16, 2010.

Bagaka, O. (2008, October 23). *Fiscal decentralization in Kenya: The constituency development fund and the growth of government.* Presented at the 20th Annual Conference of the Association for Budgeting and Financial Management, Chicago, IL.

Bahl, R., & Linn, J. (1992). *Urban public finance in developing countries.* New York: Oxford University Press.

Harrington, J., & Younger, S. (2000). Aid, debt and growth. In E. Aryeetey, J. J. Harrigan, & M. Nissanke (Eds.), *Economic reforms in Ghana: The reality and mirage.* London: James Currey.

Lloyd, T., Morrissey, O., & Osei, R. (2001). Aid, Exports and Growth. *Credit Research Paper,* No. 01/01, Nottingham.

International Monetary Fund. (2008a). Ghana aims for firmer fiscal discipline before oil flows. *IMF Survey Magazine,* 37(8), 121–123.

International Monetary Fund. (2008b). *Staff report for the 2008 Article IV consultation.* Washington, DC: Author.

International Monetary Fund. (2010). *Debt relief under the heavily indebted poor countries (HIPC) initiative.* Available at: www.imf.org/external/np/exr/facts/hipc.htm. Accessed March 16, 2010.

Osei, R., & Quartey, P. (2001). *The HIPC and poverty reduction in Ghana: An assessment.* Paper prepared for presentation at the WIDER conference on debt relief, Helsinki, Finland.

Smoke, P. (2001). *Fiscal decentralization in developing countries: A review of current concepts and practice.* Geneva: United Nations Research Institute for Social Development.

US Department of State. (2010). *Background note: Ghana.* Available at: http://www.state.gov/r/pa/ei/bgn/2860.htm. Accessed March 15, 2010.

World Bank, (2006a). *Ghana 2006: External review of public financial management,* (Vol. I). Report Number 36384-GH. Washington, DC: Author.

World Bank. (2006b). *Ghana 2006: Public finance management performance report and performance indicators* (Vol. II). Report Number 36384-GH. Washington, DC: Author.

World Bank. (2008). *Development of the cities of Ghana: Challenges, priorities and tools* (African region walking paper series number 110). Available at: http://go.worldbank.org/QYEG0I8YP0. Accessed March 15, 2010.

World Bank. (2009, March). *Ghana: Overview.* Available at: http://go.worldbank.org/LYKT0D6Z50. Accessed October 16, 2009.

ENDNOTES

1. World Bank. (2009). *Ghana: Country Brief.* Retrieved from http://go.worldbank.org/QAKWTY7640.
2. The percentages do not sum to 100 in 2008 because of a 300 million one-time "other revenues" measure that was not included.
3. International Monetary Fund. (2010). *Ghana and the IMF.* Retrieved from http://www.imf.org/external/country/GHA/index.htm.
4. Cities Alliance. (Accessed April 9, 2010. Retrieved from http://www4.citiesalliance.org/mfmi/mfmi.html
5. Cities Alliance. (Accessed April 9, 2010). Retrieved from http://www4.citiesalliance.org/mfmi/mfmi.html
6. Reuters UK. (2008, September 24). Retrieved from http://uk.reuters.com/article/idUKLO36838120080924.
7. Cities Alliance. (Accessed April 9, 2010). Retrieved from http://www4.citiesalliance.org/mfmi/mfmi.html

Part 2

Asia

Chapter 3

Accountability Building Through Budgetary Reform: China's Experience[1]

Meili Niu

Learning Objectives

- Know and understand the efforts in building budgeting accountability in China.
- Know and understand the role of the legislature in budgeting decision making.
- Know and understand the role of the citizens in the budgetary process.

Introduction

Over the past three decades, China has experienced dramatic economic growth. This growth resulted from efforts to build a strong market economy and restructure the relationship between the state and the market. However, the transition from a planned economy to a market economy eventually changed the relationship between the state and society, and the perspective of the public toward the government. Therefore, instead of an omnipotent and paternalistic government, an accountable government has become a more popular concept in state capacity building. President Hu has proposed a people-centered paradigm that demonstrates a shift away from the previous economy-centered strategy in China. Yang (2001, 2004) argues that the Chinese administrative system has achieved certain institutional accountabilities since the 1980s.

The chapter starts with a brief description of the legal system in China with specific references to the main budgeting institutions. Second, I provide an analysis of a budgeting accountability framework developed by Rubin (1996). The third part of the chapter provides a detailed analysis of a series of reforms since the late 1990s, including departmental budget reform (DBR), treasury management reform (TMR), government procurement reform (GPR), performance-based budgeting reform (PBB), and participatory budgeting reform (PBR). Beyond these endeavors, both the national and subnational congresses have also changed budgeting review and approving procedures to increase transparency and improve budgeting democracy, which further contributes to secure accountability of the executive budgeting system. Finally, the chapter concludes with a discussion of the challenges that China faces in its movements to further enhance accountability.

Background Information

China is a large Asian country with 1.3 billion people. Since the founding of the People's Republic of China in 1974, China has existed as a socialist state. The Constitution of China states that all power of the state belongs to the people (Constitution of the People's Republic of China). And the people exercise their state power through the national and subnational congresses. The National Congress is the highest organ of state power. The president is elected by the National Congress. The State Council is the highest executive organ. The judicial organs are the people's courts. The people's procuratorates are responsible for legal supervisions at all levels of government.

China uses an annual budget cycle and, like many other countries, the budget cycle includes four stages: formulation, approval, execution, and auditing. Based on China's Budget Law of 1994, the fiscal year starts on January 1st and ends on December 31st. However, because China's annual congressional session has a flexible schedule (starting either right before or after the Chinese new year), in practice, a typical fiscal year usually starts in late March. According to the Budget Law, participants in the budget process at the central government include the Ministry of Finance (MOF) (called finance department in subnational governments), the National Congress, the Standing Committee of the Congress, and spending agencies. The communist party is one of the key players as well, although its role is not written in the Budget Law. However, the party's involvement is policy driven, but extensive review is necessary in order to make sure its policy initiatives are funded. Table 3-1 describes the responsibilities of the central government budget participants. Subnational governments apply a similar process.

Table 3-1

Budgeting Participants and Their Responsibilities

Participants	Responsibilities
The National Congress	1. Review the budget requests and executions reports of both the central and the subnational governments; 2. Approve the central government's budget requests and budget execution reports; and 3. Change or abolish inappropriate decisions made by its Standing Committee on the budget requests and final accounts of budget.
The standing committee of the National Congress	1. Supervise budget execution of both the central and subnational governments; 2. Review and approve the central government's budget adjustment; 3. Review and approve the central government's final accounts of budget; 4. Abolish the State Council's inappropriate regulations and orders that are against Constitution and laws; and 5. Abolish inappropriate decisions made by provincial government, autonomous regions, and municipalities directly under the central government on the budget requests and the final accounts of budget.
The State Council	1. Prepare the budget requests and the final accounts of budget; 2. Report both the central and subnational governments' budget requests and execution reports to the National Congress; 3. Consolidate the budget requests from provinces, autonomous regions, and municipalities directly under the central government and file to the Standing Committee of the National Congress; 4. Arrange budget executions of both the central and subnational governments; 5. Decide the use of the central reserve fund; 6. Prepare the central government's budget adjustment; 7. Supervise budget executions of both the central and subnational governments; 8. Change or abolish inappropriate decisions made by the Stand Council or subnational government councils on budget requests and final accounts of budget; and 9. Report both the central and subnational governments' budget executions to the National Congress and the Standing Committee.
The Ministry of Finance (MOF)	1. Prepare the budget requests and execution reports of the central government; 2. Arrange budget executions of both the central and subnational governments; 3. Propose the use of the central reserve fund; 4. Prepare budget adjustment; and 5. Report both the central and subnational governments' budget executions to the State Council periodically.
Spending agencies	1. Prepare departmental budget requests and final accounts of budget; 2. Arrange and supervise departmental budget execution; and 3. Report departmental budget execution to MOF periodically.
The communist party	Review and approve the budget bill before it is sent to legislative review.

Source: Budget Law of the People's Republic of China (1994, March 22). Available at: http://www.npc.gov.cn/wxzl/gongbao/2000-12/05/content_5004614.htm. Accessed on November 1, 2009.

A Framework of Budgeting Accountability

Accountability is a major concern of modern governments. Rubin (1996) argues that besides control, management, and planning, accountability should be one of the major functions of a public budgeting system. According to Rubin, accountability in a modern budgeting system is composed of four dimensions. The first one is bureaucratic accountability, mainly referring to the compliance with laws and statutes. The second dimension relates to government transparency in spending citizens' money. The third dimension of accountability focuses on holding elected officials responsible for budget results and the quality of financial management. And finally, the fourth dimension states that an accountable budgeting system should also secure direct citizen involvement in the budgetary process.

Although Rubin's (1996) definition of budgeting accountability was applied to local governments in the United States, it can also be applied in other countries, including China. First of all, the public budgeting system is created based on bureaucratic authority. China promulgated a new Budget Law in 1994 and its enforcement regulations in 1995. These two statutes provide a legal framework of budgeting decision making and execution. However, China's Budget Law is more like a transitional law, leaving many issues untouched. For example, the Budget Law empowers the People's Congress to review and approve budget requests. However, it does not mention what representatives can do if they disagree on budget requests during legislative review. Enforcement of the Budget Law is also a problem in China. For instance, the Budget Law states that all budget adjustment must be approved by congresses. Unfortunately, it is a common practice that many governments adjust their budgets during the budget year without reporting to the legislature (Ma, Niu, Yue, & Lin, 2008). Therefore, budgetary reform seeks to improve budgeting accountability, improve budget statutes and strengthen enforcement of the Budget Law and relevant regulations.

Second, as a result of market economy reforms, China has transformed into a tax state (Wang, 2007). Under a tax state, the relationship between the state and society has changed; the state is required to respond to citizens' needs because it spends public funds. In addition, open budget information to the public is a fundamental step to build a transparent government. A government is not democratic if it is not transparent (2007). The transparency of China's public budgeting system is considerably low. Before the first round of budgetary reform in the late 1990s, there was very limited information sharing among line agencies, finance departments, or the national and local congresses. Citizens had almost no access to government budget files because all budget documents were classified, and representatives of congresses were only allowed to read a very brief budget report (usually several pages) during the annual congressional session. In order to improve budgeting accountability, recent budgetary reform invested extensively in opening the budgetary process to the public.

Some might argue that the third dimension of holding elected official responsible for budget outcomes in Rubin's definition might not be applicable in China because it is not an electoral regime. Theoretically, holding elected officials responsible is a prerequisite to secure budgeting accountability and the election process could certainly go a long way to that end. However, it is not the only option. Although China currently has limited abilities to improve officials' accountability through the election process, it has changed some institutions to achieve a certain degree of budgeting accountability (Ma, 2009). As a matter of fact, most efforts in the past decade have focused on this dimension.

In the case of direct citizen control on the budgetary process, although it is not popular in practice, participatory budgeting has become a promising approach to create a deliberative dialogue between the government and citizens. Recent budgetary reforms demonstrate evidence of the direct influence of citizen participation in both budget allocation and institutionalizing financial accountability in China's local governments.

The next section provides an analysis of a series of budgetary reforms from these four dimensions. Rubin (1996) argues that the four orientations of budgeting accountability might clash with each other on occasion. However, this is not the case in China. On the contrary, recent budgetary reforms contribute to improvement of multiple dimensions of accountability.

Budgetary Reforms and Accountability: China's Experience

This section starts with a brief introduction to China's budgeting management in the period from 1978 to 1999 prior to reform. It is the key to understanding initiatives of China's budgetary reform in the late 1990s. This section is followed with a detailed description of China's budgetary reforms.

THE BACKGROUND OF CHINA'S BUDGETARY REFORM: FROM 1978 TO 1999

From 1949 to 1978, a planned economy was dominant in China. Resources allocation was highly centralized. Under these circumstances, instead of a finance department, the Planning Commission controlled budget allocation at all levels of government. The finance department was more like a cashier of government accounts rather than an allocator of government resources. The emergence of a market economy in the late 1970s required a transition in the role of government in economic development. The Planning Commission was no longer the dominant player in resource allocation. Instead, the finance department had earned more authority in budgeting and financial management. However, because fiscal administration emphasized the revenue side, China had not built a modern budgeting system in terms of consolidating budget allocation with the decline of the centralized planning system (Ma & Niu, 2006). From 1978 to 1999, budget power was fragmented, because: (1) some spending departments, besides the finance department, such as the Planning Commission, state-owned Assets Supervision and Administration Commission (among others) also had the decisive authority over certain types of expenditures; and, (2) budget power was seen as a way to incentivize agencies to collect and keep miscellaneous fees. Consequently, an extra budget was created and became a large share of the total government budget, but it was not controlled by the finance department and extrabudget revenue was kept within collection departments for their own benefit. More seriously, off-budget items became a popular financing strategy for line agencies in the 1980s; (3) because there was not a well-developed line item budget, the finance department usually allocated a budget to line agencies as a lump sum. In this case, agencies had considerable discretion on their budget allocation.

As might be expected, treasury management was fragmented as well. First, there was not a unified account for cash management. Agencies could open accounts in any commercial bank and deposit their cash into various accounts. Second, because a unified government purchase system did not exist, departments usually directly transferred money from their accounts in commercial banks to suppliers' accounts. As a result, finance departments could hardly monitor department spending. Third, China's government accounting system was composed of three separate parts: administrative institutions accounting, public service institutions accounting, and general budget accounting. Under this system, departments' financial transactions were recorded in different accounting systems, and finance departments could hardly track and supervise agencies' activities (Wang, 2003; Ma & Niu, 2006).

Finally, although both China's constitution and Budget Law empower the People's Congress to review and approve the executive budget, legislative review was still *pro forma*. On the one hand, the executive budget bills submitted to the legislature were fairly brief without detailed departmental budgets. And for a long time, budget bills were classified documents and were not allowed to be disclosed to the public. Even representatives of Congress could access budget information only during the annual congressional session. On the other hand, many representatives of local congresses did not take budget bills seriously and had very little knowledge of how to review budget requests (Ma et al., 2008). Therefore, the congresses did not play a significant role in budget decision making (Ma & Niu, 2006; Yang, 2004).

BUDGET REFORMS SINCE LATE 1990s: ACCOUNTABILITY BUILDING

Since 1999, China has initiated a few budget reforms in the executive budgeting system, including DBR, TMR, GPR, and PBB. These reforms contributed considerably to building an accountable, budgeting system.

Departmental Budget Reform (DBR)

As previously mentioned, in the old system, the finance department assigned each line agency a lump sum budget without requiring a detailed budget proposal for all expenditures. The discretion granted the line agencies made the finance department's budget review process and supervision troublesome. In order to solve the problem, the finance department initiated DBR, addressing three aspects of budgeting management. First, line agencies are required to compile extrabudget revenue requests into their departmental budget requests. In 2002, the State Council issued, *Suggestions on Separation of Revenue from Expenditure* (shou zhi liang tiao xian), requiring all departments to submit all extrabudget revenues to the finance department and budget appropriation to be separate from agencies' revenue contribution. By early 2007, 90% of fees and charges had been incorporated into the departmental budget (MOF, 2007). Second, DBR installs a new budget compilation method. Under the new method, all expenses are classified into three categories: personnel, operating, and program expenditures. The central and many subnational governments applied zero-based budgeting (ZBB) to prepare departmental budget proposals. Both personnel and operating expenses apply a quota approach. The finance department assigns each agency a per capita quota for personnel and operating expenses according to their workload and average operating costs. Program budgets are decided based on priority rankings given the level of importance of the programs.

Niu (2010) argues that target-based budgeting is a more accurate description of China's ZBB system because the finance department still assigns a lump sum budget to each department. However, the innovation of the budget compilation methods did improve the line agencies' bureaucratic accountability. On the one hand, the line agencies are required to prepare detailed budgeting with all expenses so that the finance department can easily monitor the spending departments' activities based on the budgeting and financial management statutes. On the other hand, the finance department has to review departmental budgets based on relevant statutes as well because they provide rigorous explanations to the spending departments on why they cut or raised agencies' budgets.

Third, DBR also streamlines budgetary procedure, the so-called *Two Ups and Two Downs* (TUTD). Figure 3-1 demonstrates the TUTD procedure. TUTD starts with the line agencies' submitting their budget requests to the finance department (the first up). And then, the finance department sends feedback down to line agencies (the first down). The budget target (the lump sum budget) for each agency is then sent to line agencies with feedback over the first down process. After that, line agencies revise their

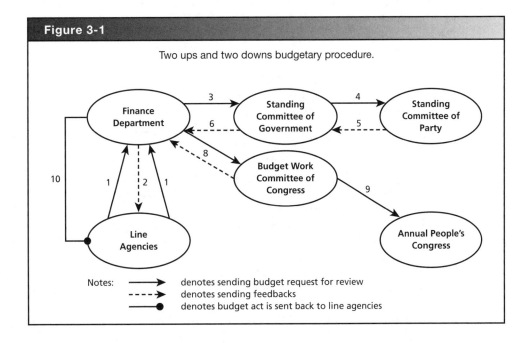

Figure 3-1

Two ups and two downs budgetary procedure.

Notes: ⟶ denotes sending budget request for review
- - -▶ denotes sending feedbacks
●——— denotes budget act is sent back to line agencies

budgets and then submit final budget proposals under the budget target to the finance department (the second up). After receiving all of the departments' budget requests, the finance department incorporates all of the requests into one consolidated budget bill and then sends it to both the government and the communist party's standing committees for approval. Once the party approves the bill, the finance departments will send it to the Congress's Budget Working Committee for initial review. The finance department might need to revise some items of the bill based on the Budget Working Committee's comments before it sends the final budget bill to Congress. Once the Congress approves the budget bill, the budget act will be sent down to line agencies for execution (the second down).

The TUTD procedure improves budgeting accountability in a few ways. First, it requires a longer preparation of departmental budgets. The first up usually occurs in July. Before the reform, agencies did not submit their budgets until December. Before the second up, the finance department must respond to departments' feedbacks. Therefore, TUTD allows agencies to spend more time compiling their budgets based on laws and regulations (Ma et al., 2008). The finance department also has more time to review the budget according to laws and regulations. It creates a rule-based environment for executive budget compilation and review. Second, the TUTD applies a two steps process for legislative review that usually takes a month instead of several days in the old budgeting system, which allows Congress to conduct substantive budget review. Budget transparency has been improved because Congress is able to access detailed departmental budget information. Third, because the finance department must submit the budget bill for the party's approval, it improves the responsibility of budget officials and departments' heads for budget results. Some local governments, such as Hebei province and the City of Tianjin apply a Three Ups and Three Downs procedure by adding another round of up and down before the second up in the TUTD in order to extend budget calculation and negotiation between line agencies and finance department.

Treasury Management Reform (TMR)

Besides reforming budgetary procedure and the preparation method, China also reformed its budget execution by centralizing treasury management. There are three elements to China's TMR (Ma & Niu, 2006). First, China created a unified treasury account system. Line agencies are no longer allowed to open their own accounts in any commercial bank. The unified treasury account is composed of five separate accounts: (1) deposit accounts opened in the central bank; (2) special fiscal accounts in commercial banks to manage extrabudget funds; (3) a finance department's zero-balanced account in a commercial bank for managing direct payment and liquidation; (4) a line agencies' zero-balanced account for delegated payment and liquidation; and, (5) special funds accounts to deal with special revenue and expenditures (Xiang, 2001; Zhang & Teng, 2002).

Second, in order to improve efficiency and enhance monitoring of agency spending activities, TMR also centralized revenue collection and disbursements. On the revenue side, all departments must submit their revenues to the treasury account through either direct submission or pooled submission (Xiang, 2001; Zhang & Teng, 2002). On the disbursement side, according to types of spending, two payment methods were installed in the new treasury management system: direct payment and delegated payment. Direct payment requires the finance department to write a payment command to the treasury so that the treasury could transfer funds to the supplier's account. Delegated payment allows spending agencies to write payment commands themselves and then the treasury transfers the funds through the treasury system as long as they have the finance department's authorization.

The central government agencies started experimenting with the new treasury systems in 2001. By the end of 2005, 30 provinces, over 200 cities, and more than 500 counties adopted a similar system. By the end of 2006, it applied to all central agencies (MOF, 2006).

Under the centralized treasury management system, the finance department strengthened its external control and monitoring of departments' financial activities. Line agencies have to follow timelines strictly in their budget proposals to complete their transactions. Meanwhile, because of application of zero-balanced accounts, cash management has been improved (MOF, 2006). More importantly, TMR contributes in curbing corruption in the public sector (Ma & Niu, 2006).

Government Procurement Reform (GPR)

Along with TMR, China also reformed its government purchase system. The purpose of China's GPR is to improve financial management efficiency and prevent corruption. In 1995, Shanghai started experimenting with GPR. Compared with TMR, GPR is more complicated since it involves regulating the activities of both the public and the private sectors. In 1998, the MOF created a procurement branch under its budget bureau, and later became a separate agency under the MOF. Meanwhile, in order to improve organizational capacity, the finance department also created staff training programs at all levels of government. In 1999, the MOF promulgated a series of regulations to define principles and standards of government purchasing, clarified requirements and procedures of contracting and bidding, and enhanced supervision of procurement. In 2003, China issued the Government Procurement Law that created a legislative foundation for procurement and its supervision (Xiang, 2001).

With the GPR, the finance department centralized its control over agencies' purchasing. Line agencies are required to prepare a separate procurement budget incorporated within their departmental budgets for the finance department's review. The procurement center created by the finance department is in charge of all government purchases. In order to reduce costs and prevent corruption, open and competitive bidding is the fundamental rule of government procurement (Ma & Ni, 2008). Although there are two procurement approaches, pooled and decentralized procurement, the former approach is applied more frequently. According to Ma and Niu (2006), over 60% of products and services were pooled purchased.

The three reforms discussed, DBR, TMR, and GPR, were all initiated by the MOF and the finance department. Even though these reforms target different aspects of budgeting and financial management, the goal is to create new institutions through approaches and procedural innovation to improve bureaucratic accountability of spending departments. In China, the finance department plays a more significant role than Congress in fiscal policy making. Therefore, compliance with regulations initiated by the finance department became a major aspect of bureaucratic accountability in recent budgetary reforms. Through these three reforms, the finance department has centralized its authority in budgeting management.

However, there are still two remaining issues that these three reforms were not able to solve. One is that innovations in budgetary procedure, approaches, fiscal transaction, and procurement do not perfectly secure accountability. In other words, compliance with these new rules does not necessarily produce responsible outcomes.

For example, the innovation on budget compilation enhanced the finance department's control on expenditure. However, it did not necessarily create the incentives for good results. Second, the increased authority of the finance department raises concerns about balancing budget power between the finance department and other participants. The finance department exercises extensive supervision over line agencies. This leads to the challenge of overseeing the finance department. In the next section, I explore how recent transitions to performance-based budgeting, legislative reform, and participatory budgeting contribute to solve these two problems.

Performance-Based Budgeting (PBB)

In 2004, China's local government started experimenting with PBB. Similar to other budgetary reforms, the finance department initiated the reform. As a result of implementing the DBR, the finance department was granted more authority. However, setting budget priority has become a challenging issue. On the one hand, spending departments complain that budget officials do not have enough knowledge of various public programs and department operations, thus they cannot make the best decisions on budget allocation. On the other hand, due to increasing budget transparency, the Congress and the public have become more concerned about public budgeting decisions; they always criticize the finance department's budget allocations if they are not satisfied with the outcomes. Under such pressure, the finance department decided to install PBB to create an outcome-oriented budgeting system.

Based on recent observations, rich and poor regions applied PBB for different purposes (Niu & Ma, in press). Due to the limited budget, the competition for budget resources in poor localities is relatively severe. Cutting a department's budget requests is a big challenge for the finance department because a reasonable and confirmative explanation must be given to spending departments, and sometimes, to key politicians. Under this situation, PBB provides a practical tool to the finance department because it requires allocating budget resources based on a program's performance. On the contrary, in a wealthy area, although it is unlikely that each agency would get everything it requests, many line agencies with abundant budgets do not take their budgets seriously. For example, many departments with considerably larger appropriations sometimes do not spend all of their budgets by the end of the fiscal year. In such a case, the finance department uses PBB to force spending departments to use the requested budget and produce certain outcomes.

Improving budgeting accountability is the major goal of PBB implementation in China. However, China's PBB distinguishes itself from the western concept because most agencies only apply program performance evaluation after budget execution, which means there is no strong tie between program performance and budgeting decision making. Spending departments do not have to include program performance objectives in their budget requests and the finance department actually conducts ex post performance evaluations in most cases. During the evaluation, spending departments submit their self-evaluation reports with detailed program information to the finance department. Then the finance department invites outsiders, such as accounting or financial agents and experts in various fields, such as engineers, professors, accountants, to evaluate program performance. The finance department creates the rules regulating evaluation and arranges the evaluation process instead of directly involving program evaluation.

Few agencies use a comprehensive PBB that requires departments to provide prospective performance information, the so-called ex ante evaluation, in their annual budget requests allowing the finance department to use performance information to make allocation decisions. In some comprehensive implementation cases, for example, the finance department of Sanshui County in Guangdong province, required to evaluate both intermediate and final outcomes. In order to create incentives, besides program performance measures, the finance department also added indicators of departments' arrangements of PBB implementation into their evaluation index, such as whether a spending department creates a working committee of PBB implementation, whether a department assigns staff to be in charge of PBB implementation, and whether a department submits performance evaluation reports on time. These nonfinancial indicators instruct departmental PBB implementation and also raise the pressure on spending departments to implement PBB because the evaluation of organizational arrangements account for up to 50% of the total credit of a department's PBB implementation.

There is no evidence showing a direct link between program performance and a departments' budget appropriation in ex post performance evaluation in China. However, PBB implementation enhances budgeting accountability in several ways. First, in comprehensive PBB implementation cases (applying both ex ante and ex post evaluations to link performance evaluation information with budgeting decision making), although the departments' lump sum budget is not decided based on performance, program priority ranking in a department can change, which means PBB improves allocation efficiency within individual spending departments. Second, it increases budget transparency because the finance department, outside agents and experts need access to detailed financial information to evaluate performance. Third, it forces departments to consider budget outcomes when they apply their budgets. For instance, in Sanshui County, a comprehensive PBB implementation case, budget requests dramatically reduced after PBB was adopted. This is the most significant achievement in the application of PBB in Sanshui. Fourth, PBB improves the quality of budget reports because departments are required to provide detailed and substantive analysis on program performance to defend their budget requests.

The Rise of Legislative Power

DBR not only solidifies the finance department's authority in budgeting management, but also provides an opportunity window for the People's Congress to enhance its budget power (Ma & Niu, 2008). First, DBR requires departments to compile detailed budgets so that the Congress could require the finance department to submit detailed budgets for legislative review. Second, DBR allows the Congress to extend legislative review from a week to a month. These two changes allow both the Standing Committee and representatives of the Congress to conduct substantive review.

In 1999, the Standing Committee of the National People's Congress promulgated *The Decisions on Enhancing Review on Central Government Budget*. After that, many subnational governments had their own legislations on budget review and supervisions (Ma et al., 2008). In order to improve effectiveness of legislative budget review, the Congress developed several strategies (Ma et al.). Because there is very limited time for budget review during the annual congressional session, the Congress first focuses on the initial review occurring before the congressional session. The Budget Working Committee usually has a month instead of a week to review the draft of the budget bill.

Second, instead of reviewing all of the details of the budget bill, the Budget Working Committee only reviews selective agencies' or program budgets. The local congress' Budget Working Committees usually have only four to five staff. It is impossible for them to review all budgets in detail. Therefore, it is very common that in each year, the committee chooses certain programs or departments to conduct substantive review. Generally, those are the programs or departments that draw more public attention or consume a large amount of the budget.

Third, borrowing expertise from outsiders is a common practice during legislative review. Meanwhile, since public programs are largely diverse, the Budget Working Committee invites members from other legislative special committees and experts from those that practice in relative fields to review departmental budgets.

Moreover, besides improving the budget review, many localities enhance legislative supervision of budget execution. So far, most provinces and city congresses have promulgated *Ordinances on Budget Review and Supervision* to provide a legislative base for budget review and supervision. Because the Budget Working Committee has upgraded to one of the working committees in Congress, it has the power of investigation which allows it to organize representatives to visit and investigate agencies and the finance department during the adjournment of the annual congressional session. In Guangdong province, the Budget Working Committee uses electronic real time supervision. By so doing, the Budget Working Committee connects its system to the Treasury Department's operation database. As a result, each transaction made through the treasury is automatically shown on the Budget Working Committee's internal Web site.

Meanwhile, Congress also tried to improve its organizational capacity. In 1998, the National People's Congress created the Budget Working Committee, increasing Congress' authority for both budget review and supervision. After that, subnational congresses established their counterparts. Moreover, besides creating a new organ and hiring more competent budget officials, both national and subnational congresses also train representatives on how to review budget bills and supervise budget execution. The rise of legislative power extensively improves accountability for both the finance department and the spending agencies.

PARTICIPATORY BUDGETING

Citizen participation in public affairs is not unfamiliar in China. Chairman Mao's mass line emphasizes the importance of citizens' input on policy making. However, citizen participation in a budgetary process, as a new mode of democracy, is quite a new experience for the Chinese. Beginning in 2005, China's local governments began experimenting with citizen participation in the budget process. Theoretically, there is no big difference between China's participatory budgeting and other countries' experiences: The public is directly involved in budgeting decision making in several ways, such as participating in town meetings or public hearings, and their comments are reflected in the budget bill. However, in practice, due to the diversity in localities, China has used a variety of different modes of citizen participation.

First, who participates in the budgetary process? China's Budget Law does not mention the role of citizens in budgeting decision making. Some localities, such as the Xinhe Town, amended its budget statutes to legalize citizen participation in the budgetary process before they applied participatory budgeting. According to Xinhe's *Regulations on Budgeting Deliberative Discussion* (2006), the public can attend the initial budget review hosted by the congress without an official invitation from the government. The Zeguo Township uses random selection to choose a certain number of citizens to participate in deliberative discussion of projects budget. In 2005, 275 citizens were selected from 275 households among a total of about 120,000 residents. In some cases, only invited citizens or departments participate, such as in the Daoli District in the City of Harbin.

Second, what is the nature of the discussion when citizens are present? The Xinhe Town allows citizens to discuss all of the government budgets. A common practice in other cases is to choose certain project budgets to discuss. For example, the Zeguo Township selected 30 infrastructure projects that cost over RMB 100 million yuan. However, the town only had RMB 40 million yuan for the infrastructure budget. The purpose of citizen participation was to prioritize the 30 projects. By the end of two meetings, 12 projects were selected by the citizens. The city of Wuxi applied a different strategy; although they only discussed certain projects, citizens were encouraged to choose which projects they wanted to discuss.

The third question is how do citizens participate? In most cases, participants vote for favorable projects. This usually occurs after extensive deliberation and discussion among the participants. Discussion can occur in groups and larger town hall styled discussions between citizens and government, and among citizen groups according to either their career or the electorate they represent. Public officials, such as mayors, budget officers, and department heads, also attend and answer questions addressed by participants. Xinhe's case is unique because it is incorporated with the legislative budget review. During this stage of the initial review, the Budget Working Committee broadly invited citizens to discuss the budget requests and then reported participant's comments at the annual congressional session. Representatives spent a fair amount of time discussing and debating the budget bill during the congressional session. Some of them also proposed budget revision bills. As a result of citizen participation, 8.9% of total budget was revised in Xinhe in 2006 (Niu, 2007).

The last and, presumably, the most important question is, How influential is citizen participation on budget allocation? In Wuxi, Zeguo, Daoli, and the City of Acheng, citizens participate during budget formulation. Their votes are final because line agencies prepare the budget based on citizen vote without reservation. Xinhe's case is different because it occurs during the legislative review. Therefore, all comments from citizens during the initial review are reported in the congressional session. Whether these comments are written in the final budget bill depends on whether the representatives vote to amend the budget bill.

Conclusions

Accountability has been a major concern for China in building a modern budgeting system. Although reformers use various terms to highlight their initiatives, such as efficiency, effectiveness, and budgeting democracy, building accountability is a core goal reflected in all reforms if Rubin's (1996) definition is applied. First, most reform efforts focused on improving bureaucratic accountability. The finance department is the driving force of this orientation. On the one hand, the finance department institutionalized the budgetary process, redefined the roles of budget participants, and modified budget compilation methods by issuing new statutes. On the other hand, the finance department stressed compliance among the spending departments by issuing these new statutes and by enhancing supervision both through budget preparation and execution. DBR, TMR, and GPR contribute to this direction extensively.

Second, PBB was adopted to improve budget results. Spending departments are required to report both intermediate and final program performance, which force budgeting decision makers to request accountable budgets and improve program management in order to achieve designed results. Although most efforts have been invested in ex post performance evaluation thus far and performance reports are not open to the public or to Congress, spending departments have to budget toward results because the finance department uses performance information to set up the priorities of future programs for each department.

Third, compared with other reforms that focus on innovative techniques or budgeting and financial management, citizen participation is more influential on budget allocation. Most citizens are not professionals in government budgeting. Therefore, instead of reviewing details of the government budget, participants spent more time in discussing budget results. Their comments are outcome driven, which further forces those involved in budgeting decision making and execution to innovate their managerial skills and to improve budget results.

Although current reforms improve accountability, there are still some challenges that China is facing in building an accountable budgeting system. First, there is a need to improve budgeting law making and enhance its enforcement. Bureaucratic accountability requires budget participants to comply with statutes. China has issued many new laws and regulations during recent reforms. However, some statutes are not enforceable. For instance, the Budget Law states that the fiscal year starts on January 1 and ends on December 31, whereas the budget execution generally starts in late March. The

Enforcement Regulations of the Budget Law requires a separate state-owned operation budget and social security budget, but it was never enforced. Moreover, there are also some legal vacuums needed to be filled. For example, both China's Constitution and Budget Laws empower the People's Congress to review and approve budget bills. However, neither the Budget Law nor its enforcement regulations address the procedure of how to revise budget bills. Therefore, besides enhancing the supervision of compliance with statutes, China also needs to improve its laws and regulations in order to provide a legal base for building accountability.

Second, the transparency of the public budgeting system needs to be further improved. The public should have access to public budget information in detail because they contribute revenue in the form of taxes. However, how to deliver this information is a technical issue. It is well-known in China that budget reports are very technical and complicated. Therefore, beyond opening all data to the public, a more important question is how to make this information transparent and understandable to the public. That is to say, the budgeting document should provide the public budget information in a comprehensible way.

Third, holding elected officials accountable for budget outcomes under a nonelectoral regime is a big challenge. However, Ma (2009) argues that accountability building does not necessarily involve a competitive election. Institutional building is also an option. China's experience in reforming its executive budgeting system indicates there is a lot of room to institutionalize the budget process and innovate approaches of budget compilation, review, and supervision in order to make budgeting decision makers responsible for budget results. The Audit Department and the Disciplines and Inspection Commission have started some experimentation in evaluating officials' performance. However, in order to extensively increase officials' accountability for budget outcomes, those individual officials' performance evaluation must be incorporated into programs' performance evaluation.

Last, citizen participation is not a popular practice in the budgetary process in China. However, it is the most efficient approach because it produces direct influence on budget allocation. Furthermore, it also provides an educational opportunity for the public to understand the procedures of public policy making and implementation. Given the diversity of localities, China developed different models of citizen participation. However, most cases are towns, districts, or small cities. In the next step of the budgetary reform, China needs to adopt citizen participation in larger cities. It will be more complicated and require various innovations, but it is a promising venue to improve budgeting accountability.

Discussion Questions

1. Describe the budgetary process in China.
2. How does the Chinese government compile its departmental budget requests?
3. What is the role of the Chinese congress in the budgetary process?
4. Describe the different methods of citizen participation in the budgetary process in China.

References

Constitution of the Peoples Republic of China, Art. 2.

Ma, J. (2009). The dilemma of developing financial accountability without election: A study of China's recent budget reforms. *Australian Journal of Public Administration, 68*(1),62–72.

Ma, J., & Ni, X. (2008). Toward a clean government in China: Does the budget reform provide a hope? *Crime, Law & Social Change, 49*(2), 119–138.

Ma, J., & Niu, M. (2006). Modernizing public budgeting and financial management in China. In H. A. Frank (Ed.), *Public financial management* (pp. 691–736). New York: Taylor & Francis.

Ma, J., & Niu, M. (2008). Restructuring China's budgeting system: Power and relations. *China Development Observer, 2*, 13–16.

Ma, J., Niu, M., Yue, J., & Lin, M. (2008). *Public budgeting reader.* Beijing, P. R. China: China Development Press.

Ministry of Finance of China (MOF). (2006). *Guidelines for preparing central agencies budget (2007).* Beijing, P. R.China: China Financial & Economic Publishing House.

Ministry of Finance of China (MOF). (2007). *Guidelines for preparing central agencies budget 2008.* Beijing, P. R. China: China Financial & Economic Publishing House.

Niu, M. (2007). Budgeting democracy: Opportunities and challenges toward good governance. *Journal of Huazhong Normal University (Humanities and Social Sciences), 1*, 14–20.

Niu, M. (2010). *Zero-based budgeting in China's local government.* Beijing, P. R. China: Central Compilation & Translation Press.

Niu, M., & Ma, J. (in press). *Performance-based budgeting in Chinese local governments: Accomplishment and challenges.* Shanghai: Truth & Wisdom Press.

Rubin, I. S. (1996). Budgeting for accountability: Municipal budgeting for the 1990s. *Public Budgeting & Finance, 16*, 112–132.

Wang, S. (2007). From a tax state to a budget state. *Dushu, 10*, 3–13.

Wang, Y. (2003). Restructuring treasury system and fiscal administration reform. *Journal of Central University of Finance and Economics, 4*, 112–132.

Xiang, H. (2001). *China's fiscal management.* Beijing, P. R. China: China Financial & Economic Publishing House.

Xinhe People's Congress. (2006). *Regulations on budgeting deliberative discussion.*

Yang, D. (2001). Rationalized the Chinese state. In C. Chao & B. J. Dickson (Eds.) *Remaking the Chinese state* (pp. 19–45). New York: Routledge.

Yang, D. (2004). *Remaking the Chinese leviathan: Market transition and the politics of governance in China.* Stanford: Stanford University Press.

Zhang, T., & Teng, X. (2002). Causes, achievements, and future of reforming China's fiscal treasury management system. *Fiscal Studies, 9*, 2–9.

ENDNOTE

1. This research is funded by the State Social Science Foundation, China (Project ID: 08CZZ020). Budgetary reform and accountability building.

Chapter 4

Budgetary and Financial Management Reforms in Korea

Changhoon Jung and Cal Clark

Learning Objectives

- Know and understand South Korea's development strategy and its impact upon the nation's budgetary system.
- Know and understand the major stages in the budgetary process and how they are related to each other.
- Know and understand the major institutions in the budgetary process.
- Know and understand the major problems associated with special accounts and public funds and the shortcomings of the current attempts to reform them.
- Know and understand the other reforms in the Korean budgetary system and why they appear to be more successful.

Introduction

Korea, having seen the rapid industrialization of the 1960s and 1970s turn into rapid, sustained economic growth, is now the world's 12th largest economy. The early reliance upon government-promoted industrial policy required centralized budgetary processes and policies. Unfortunately, this strong centralization was shown to be limited in both efficiency and effectiveness during the move toward full democratization, local autonomy, and globalization that characterized the 1980s and 1990s. The financial crisis that swept the country in late 1997 provided an opportunity to reconsider the efficacy and efficiency of the financial management and budgeting systems in place at the time (Ha, 2004). To create more efficient and adaptable budgetary and financial management systems, the Korean government introduced a series of budget and financial management reforms following the financial crisis of 1997. As of early 2009, the government has adopted most of those elements considered key to the reform of budgeting and financial management systems.

We begin this chapter by outlining the evolution of Korea's fiscal and economic policy. The second section describes the country's budgetary institutions and process. Finally, we provide a brief overview the latest budget reform initiatives, such as the implementation of top-down budgeting, program budgeting, and full accrual basis accounting.

The Evolution of Korea's Economic and Fiscal Policies

The modern history of the Republic of Korea begins in 1945, when Allied forces liberated the nation from the 36 years of Japanese colonial rule. After a brief period of rule by US occupational forces (1945–1947), the general elections of 1948 gave birth to the Republic of Korea, also known as South Korea. Backed by the Soviet Union and China, North Korea remained firmly under the control of the communist party. In 1950, after US occupational forces left the Republic, the Soviet Union instigated the invasion of South Korea by North Korea, and the two Koreas suffered through three years of internecine slaughter until a truce was reached in July 1953. After the civil war, the young Republic, poor in natural resources, faced the daunting tasks of nation building and economic development, hampered by vicious cycles of poverty, weak leadership, and political instability. In 1961, General Chung-Hee Park used the chaos to assume leadership in a military coup.

After a brief period of military rule, the authoritarian and politically repressive General Park was elected president in the general election of 1962, ruling the country until his assassination in 1979. To legitimize his coup and gain popular support for his government, Park focused on building a strong economic base for the poverty-stricken young nation, initiating a series of ambitious 5-year economic development plans designed to create the industrial base necessary for sustained growth and self-sufficiency, taking advantage of the one resource Korea had in abundance: labor (Rhee, 1992). These 5-year plans were instrumental in effectively allocating scarce resources to Korea's most productive sectors, and their effect on Korea's economy far outlasted Park's rule. By progressively shifting the focus of these plans, Korea effectively implemented many of the best aspects of an export-oriented growth model. The first plan (1962–1966) and second plan (1967–1971) focused on rapid, export-oriented industrialization, progressing into skill-intensive, chemical, and heavy industries during the third 5-year plan (1972–1976). Equity in both income distribution and regional development became the focus of the fourth plan (1977–1981), leading to the beginnings of economic stabilization policies and a continuation of export-oriented industrialization during the fifth (1982–1986) and sixth (1987–1991) 5-year economic development plans (Rhee, 1992; Shin & Ha, 1996).

The Economic Planning Board (EPB), created in 1961, was staffed with competent officials who planned and executed Park's 5-year plans. With Park's full support, the EPB possessed the authority to coordinate the economic and fiscal policies for the nation, making it Korea's most powerful economic policy-making agency during its 33-year life span (1961–1995). The EPB used the nation's banking and financial systems as its strongest tools for development, setting low interest rates, targeting loans to those industries engaged in governmental priorities, controlling foreign direct investment (FDI), setting policies for the government guarantee of foreign loans, and serving as an intermediary between foreign and domestic capital. These roles enabled the EPB to monitor and control the specific investment decisions of the private sector (Shin & Ha, 1996).

This focus on export-oriented development, combined with the favorable postwar international trade environment, allowed for a remarkable growth in GDP under the Park administration that averaged 7% annually. It is important to note that, as in many countries relying on export-oriented growth, the "visible hand of the state" guided Korea's rapid industrialization and growth, rather than the "invisible hand of the market" (Rhee, 1992; Shin & Ha, 1996). This state-level focus on industrialization, combined with fiscal policies designed by the EPB to direct private investment toward business conglomerates (*chaebol*), not only facilitated Korea's rapid growth and industrialization, but also had lasting effects on the nation's budgetary system.

To promote Korea's industrialization and ensure proper allocation of scarce resources, the budget process was heavily centralized. Channeling funds to specific economic development projects led to the creation of numerous special accounts and extrabudgetary (off-budget), unconventional funds comprised of public funds and other funds. The majority of these extrabudgetary funds were out of legislative control, which led to occasional double funding of certain projects (Ha, 2004; Ko, 2000). Tax and expenditure policies promoting export-oriented industrialization made for poor redistributive policies and heavily regressive indirect taxation, generous incentives for private sector investment by big businesses, and low levels of the provision of welfare services and other public goods characterized Korea's fiscal policy until the financial crisis of 1997 (Ha, 2004).

While creating strong economic growth, the Park administration's focus on the development of the chemical and heavy industries in the 1970s was not without its flaws. The oil shock of the early 1970s and the international recession that followed highlighted problems of overcapacity and overinvestment in the heavy industrial sector. Excessive competition, underutilization of nonindustrial resources, and the inefficiency bred of centralized control of budgetary and fiscal policy led to high levels of inflation and foreign debt (Rhee, 1992; Shin & Ha, 1996).

Faced with these weaknesses, the Doo-Hwan Chun administration (1980–1987), which took power with a military coup after the assassination of Park, focused on a program of economic liberalization designed to encourage domestic competition and induce foreign direct investment through a more liberal banking and financial environment. While maintaining some level of industrial development, Chun's reforms led the groundwork for the future reform efforts of the Tae-Woo Roh (1988–1992) and Young-Sam Kim (1993–1997) administrations.

Both the Roh and Kim administrations engaged in several reform efforts, including the democratization of administrative procedures, political decentralization, moves toward a smaller and more efficient government, restructuring of government–business relations, market-oriented economic management, and performance-oriented management. Credit policy in Korea provides an excellent example of the liberalization of the economy as a whole. The export-oriented policies of the 1960s and 1970s, which often extended credit and other support to firms that would not have otherwise been competitive, gave way to a focus on removing noncompetitive firms and promoting competitive ones. The financial and industrial restructuring of the 1980s continued into the 1990s, with greater attention paid to research and development and the promotion of small and medium-sized companies through more liberal financial policies. In contrast to the overregulated, highly distorted economies of the 1960s and 1970s, in recent decades the Korean economy has been characterized by diminishing intervention in most spheres of economic activity, with noticeably less economic distortion (Shin & Ha, 1996). Nonetheless, these reform efforts were not enough to dismantle a highly centralized and inefficient system of government and public sector controls before the outbreak of the Asian financial crisis in 1997, as the government could not respond to the competing forces of pluralism, democratization, and globalization rising in Korea. These liberalization and stabilization measures taken by the Chun, Roh, and Kim administrations were far from being coherent and a systematic method of addressing the problems associated with developmental states (Lee, Rhee, & Sung, 2006; Shin & Ha, 1996).

The financial crisis of 1997, precipitated by a dramatic drop in Korea's foreign currency reserves, forced Korea to turn to the International Monetary Fund (IMF) for a rescue loan in November 1997. As a part of the IMF's restructuring conditions, Korea found itself required to reform aspects of its fiscal, monetary, and governmental policies, which had been quite difficult without an external impetus. Korea was required to restructure its financial sector, business and industry sectors, public sector interaction with the private sector, and government-labor relations (Kim, 2000). The IMF determined that the government's history of widespread involvement in economic and regulatory matters had weakened private sector competitiveness in the international market and thereby accelerated the economic crisis (Ha, 2004; Kim, 2000).

The IMF also found that government inefficiency had grown to staggering proportions, further eroding the country's economic competitiveness. The Dae-jung Kim administration (1998–2002), accepted this critique and introduced many of the themes of the New Public Management (NPM), which had been implemented to great effect in New Zealand, the United Kingdom, and several other countries of the Organisation for Economic Co-operation and Development (OECD). Basically, the core of NPM is the application of market principles such as privatization and deregulation to government operations (Ha, 2004). While the Kim and Roh administrations have enacted numerous reforms to renovate the Korean government, particularly the unnecessary complexity of the budget structure owing to the explosion of unconventional expenditures, some problems remain.

Budgetary Institutions and Process

Reforms to the budgetary institutions and processes have been made over time, but the basic budget actors and the process remain relatively intact. As in most democracies, the budget process involves both the executive and legislative branches of government and follows the typical budget stages of executive preparation, legislative review, execution, and audit and program evaluation. However, the legislature can only reduce the executive budget. It has no power to increase the total size of or add new expenditure items to the budget without the consent of the executive branch, thus giving the executive branch much greater power over the budget in Korea.

BUDGETARY INSTITUTIONS (ACTORS)

The three major actors involved in the politics and processes of Korean budgeting are the Budget Office within the Ministry of Strategy and Finance (MOSF), the National Assembly (legislative branch), and the Board of Audit and Inspection (audit office).

The Office of Budget in the Ministry of Strategy and Finance (MOSF)

The MOSF is the Executive Budget Office in a system weighted heavily toward the executive branch, giving it a great deal of power in the budgeting process. It has not been a static entity however, and a brief history of the MOSF is in order. As mentioned previously, the EPB was the arm of the chief executive budget office during Korea's rapid, sustained growth from 1961 to 1995, charged with budget formulation and execution and the preparation and implementation of economic development plans. In 1995, the Young-Sam Kim administration merged the EPB and the Ministry of Finance (that had jurisdiction over taxation and part of budget execution) into the Ministry of Finance and Economy. Under the Dae-jung Kim administration (1998–2002), the function of the central budget office was moved from the Ministry of Finance and Economy to the Ministry of Planning and Budget. However, the Myong-Bak Lee administration (2008 to present at time of press) reconsolidated executive budget authority by creating the MOSF, a merger of the Ministry of Finance and Economy with the Ministry of Planning and Budget. Within this central ministry, the Budget Office plays a pivotal role in the budgetary process.

Adhering to both the presidential agenda and the year's economic forecast provided by the Economic Policy Bureau (also within the MOSF), the Budget Office issues budget guidance to individual agencies, reviews and adjusts those agency requests, compiles the individual agency budgets into a comprehensive budget, and presents this budget to the Cabinet. Once the Cabinet passes the budget, it is sent to the president, after whose review the budget document is sent to the National Assembly for review. Once the budget is passed in the National Assembly, various agencies within the MOSF, including the Budget Office, are responsible for budget execution and control.

The National Assembly

The unicameral National Assembly has the right to deliberate upon and approve the budget proposal submitted by the executive branch and to authorize the closing of revenue and expenditure accounts submitted by the Board of Audit and Inspection (analogous to the Government Accountability Office in the United States). One of the major powers of the National Assembly is the inspection of government activity prior to deliberation upon the executive budget proposal. However, unlike the US Congress, the National Assembly of Korea has no authority to increase the total size of the budget or to add any new expenditure items to the budget. To reflect constituent demands and further its own agenda, the ruling party usually consults with the administration (specifically, the central budget office) prior to the president's budget proposal, ensuring that their priorities are present in the budget document (He, 2003; Ko, 2000). The result is a situation unusual in industrialized nations, with lobbying focused on the central budget office and the individual line ministries and agencies within the administration or the ruling party itself rather than on the legislative body.

It should come as no surprise that legislative review has resulted in negligible amounts of budget cuts, or that the budget has never been a core issue in the National Assembly (Ha, 1997; Kim, 1995; Kim & Kang, 1983). The structure of the legislature also contributes to a minimal role in tax and expenditure policy. Considering the relative insignificance of the National Assembly to the budgetary process, the opposition parties have had to link the budget with other political issues in their attempts to block passage of a budget proposal (Ha, 1997).

Prior to 2004, the National Assembly had no independent agency charged with the collection and analysis of economic or other data to inform their budget decisions. Hence, the legislature was entirely reliant upon the executive branch for any relevant information, such as revenue and expenditure forecasts, which severely constrained their capacity for budget review. The National Assembly did not have a standing committee responsible for budget review until the creation of the Special Committee on Budget and Accounts in 2004. Furthermore, committee members usually lack the expertise necessary to review a budget proposal thoroughly since most of the committee members are first-term legislators with only a 1-year tenure on the committee. Combining this with the facts that the time allotted for budget review is usually less than 2 weeks of the 90-day regular session and that the heads of line ministries can, without approval from the National Assembly, increase outlays of public funds by up to 30% (remember, these are unconventional budgetary accounts), the National Assembly is a relatively weak player in the budgetary process. This subordination of the legislature has allowed the executive branch to dominate the budgeting process, allocating resources and furthering its agendas with ease. The power of nonelected bureaucrats within the administration (especially the central budget office) has been, and continues to be, a problem even after the numerous administrative reforms of the last 20 years (Ha, 1997; Kim, 1995; Kim, 2000; Nam & Jones, 2003).

In 2004, to enhance the legislative review function of the executive budget proposal and fiscal policy, the National Assembly installed the National Assembly Budget Office (NABO). The mission of the NABO is to serve the members of the National Assembly by providing them with research and analysis on budget and fiscal policies. It is a nonpartisan legislative support agency, which is modeled after the Congressional Budget Office (CBO) in the United States. While the NABO has increased the capacity of the National Assembly to comprehend, review, and challenge executive budget proposals, the National Assembly's lack of authority to increase the budget and the short time horizon for budget review ensures that the executive branch still dominates Korea's budgetary process (Ha, 2004; Yoon, 2006).

Board of Audit and Inspection

The Board of Audit and Inspection is a functionally and constitutionally independent agency, although it is located directly under the president. The board inspects the closing of accounts of revenues and expenditures at the end of the fiscal year, presenting the results to the president and National Assembly in the following year. Much like the General Accountability Office in the United States, it also reviews the work performed, services provided, and the duties of government agencies and their employees, recommending improvements in their efficiency and effectiveness.

THE BUDGETARY PROCESS

In Korea, the fiscal and calendar years coincide, beginning on January 1st and ending on December 31st of the same year. The principle of fiscal year separation applies, wherein all spending during a fiscal year must be funded by revenue raised during the same fiscal year. Unlike in the United States, the executive budget office must prepare both revenue and expenditure budgets. Moreover, the National Assembly passes the executive budget proposal as a budget document rather than as a comprehensive budget bill.

Formally, the Korean budget document consists of five parts: the general provision, revenues and expenditures, multiyear expenses, authorized carryover, and contract authorization. The general provision applies to the entire budget, and it specifies the totals for the General Account and Special Accounts of the budget, defines limits on government bond issuance and borrowing, and also includes directives for budget execution, such as allowances for fund transfers between budget items (Koo, 2002; 2006). Providing comprehensive revenue and expenditure plans by line ministries and agencies and accounts (and funds), the revenue and expenditure portion is the core of the budget document, with additional spending details provided by function and characteristic in the case of the expenditures budget.

Multiyear capital projects such as large-scale construction or research and development projects are the major exception to the principle of fiscal separation between fiscal years. As funding and expenditures for such projects are much more efficiently done with multiyear plans, the National Assembly can approve multiyear expenditure plans accounting for both the total expense of and annual expenditures on such projects (He, 2003). The National Assembly may also explicitly authorize carryover, or funding allowed to be made in the following fiscal year.

The government is allowed to incur future liabilities relating to large-scale fiscal or construction projects authorized in the current year but for which spending begins in the following year. Contract authorization is the approval of these liabilities by the National Assembly, required before the government can contract to incur those liabilities. Contract authorization is not required when the government is allowed by law to incur liabilities, or in the case of authorized multiyear expenditures. Contract authorizations are included in the following year's expenditure budget rather than the current year's revenue and expenditure budget (Koo, 2006).

Executive Preparation

The executive budget proposal is the initial phase of the budget process, involving all administrative agencies. Line ministries and agency heads must submit their expected expenditures for the coming year's new and ongoing projects to the Budget Office no later than the end of February each year. By compiling these investment plans for all agencies, the Budget Office creates a comprehensive picture of expenditure requirements for the coming year. Working in conjunction with the Office of Tax and Customs and the Bureau of Economic Policy (both in the MOSF), the Budget Office determines revenue forecasts, assumptions of economic health for the coming year, and the possible necessity of bond issuance.

By considering the estimates of revenues and expenditures, midterm financial planning, and national policy priorities, the Office of Budget sets the overall expenditure ceiling and subceilings for each line ministry and agency and delegates detailed resource allocation decisions to the line ministries. This top-down budget (which is a variation of target-based budgeting) was introduced in 2004 to provide management flexibility and efficient resource allocation to line ministries while controlling the budget deficit (Kim & Park, 2006). Ministries must submit their budget requests no later than the end of May of each year. These requests will follow the guidelines provided by the Budget Office and include the ministries' own spending requirements as well as the requirements of their subsidiary agencies. The Budget Office prepares an initial draft of the budget proposal by mid-August, after which it spends a month renegotiating budget requests with both government ministries and agencies and any other parties with a stake in the budget. The Constitution states that the final executive budget proposal must be submitted to the National Assembly by October 2nd (Koo, 2002; 2006). Details of the public funds must be submitted no later than October 12th.

Legislative Review and Approval

Once the budget is submitted to the National Assembly, it is sent piecemeal to one of the 17 standing committees with jurisdiction over relevant portions. After committee review, the document is submitted to the Special Committee on Budget and Accounts, which performs a detailed review of each agency's budget requests. The Adjustments Subcommittee within the Special Committee then makes the necessary changes to the budget, submitting this revised proposal back to the Special Committee for passage. The budget proposal is then presented for a vote to a plenary session of the National Assembly. The Special Committee on Budget and Accounts plays a vital role in the overall budget process, as its final resolution is usually passed, and the president cannot veto the budget passed by the National Assembly.

The Korean Constitution mandates that the budget be approved by December 2nd, which is 30 days before the beginning of the relevant fiscal year. If the National Assembly does not pass the executive budget proposal before the start of the new fiscal year, line ministries are allowed a continuing resolution, automatically spending up to the amount of the last year's actual expenditures in the same period until passage of the budget proposal. If necessary, the central budget office may request a supplemental appropriation from the National Assembly in the middle of the fiscal year (Ha, 1997).

Execution

Once the budget proposals are passed in the National Assembly, quarterly allotment plans are drawn up by the Budget Office prior to the start of the fiscal year. The plan is reviewed by the Cabinet and finalized with presidential approval. Timing of the allotments is often set so as to accommodate favorable or to counter sluggish economic cycles. By mid-January, agencies are provided with guidelines for budget execution, which give direction, set standards, and provide a reference for the Board of Audit and Inspection during their annual reviews. Actual allotment is performed by the Treasury Bureau (which is currently under the MOSF), guided by both scheduled disbursement and the current state of the treasury. Agencies must submit their budget settlements to the Budget Office no later than the end of February in the subsequent fiscal year.

Audit and Evaluation

Once individual settling reports have been submitted, the Budget Office compiles a comprehensive settling report and presents it to the Cabinet and president for approval. Assuming their approval, the Budget Office submits the report to the Board of Audit and Inspection (audit office) no later than June 10th. The audit office then presents its evaluation of the settling report to the head of the MOSF no later than August 20th, who must then provide the National Assembly with the final settlement report by September 2nd, which is 120 days before the start of the subsequent fiscal year. Once approved by the National Assembly, no further political responsibility for budget execution will accrue upon the administration.

Recent Budgetary and Financial Management Reform Initiatives

Historically, the major problems with the budgetary and financial management system in Korea have been overly rigid central control, the enormous complexity in the budget structure created by special accounts and public funds, lack of transparency, lack of accountability, and a low level of efficiency in the management of financial resources (Ha, 2004).

President Dae-jung Kim introduced measures to improve Korea's financial management system as part of the IMF's requirements for organizational restructuring in the public sector following the crisis of 1997. Understanding the problems presented by increasing public debt and spending on necessary but expensive social welfare programs, the Kim administration set down a map of the budgetary and financial management reforms and the necessary policy measures for current and future years (Kim & Park, 2007). The subsequent administration followed the basic tenets and directions of the Kim administration and eventually implemented most of its reform agenda. After more than 10 years of reform efforts, Korea currently implements most of the advanced budgeting and financial management systems and techniques (such as top-down budgeting, performance-based systems, program budgeting, medium-year and multiyear resource allocation frameworks, and accrual accounting) recognized as best practices and widely used throughout OECD countries. In its attempt to achieve autonomy and flexibility while maintaining agency accountability, Korea has followed the lead of countries such as New Zealand and Australia, front-runners in market-oriented budgeting and financial management reform.

The goals of budgetary reform for the Kim and Roh administrations were to provide Korea with a transparent, efficient, results-oriented budget process in which proper agencies and individual were held accountable (Ha, 2004). To achieve these goals, the government set forth four major fiscal reforms: (1) to establish a medium-term expenditure framework (National Fiscal Management Plan) and multiyear budgeting; (2) to introduce top-down budgeting; (3) to establish a performance management system; and (4) to build a digital budget information system (including a transition from the line-item budget to a program budget structure and the introduction of accrual accounting). These reforms became law in January 2007 as the National Financial Management Law (Kim & Park, 2007). Some of the major components of these reforms follow.

REFORM OF UNCONVENTIONAL EXPENDITURES

Korea's budget system has been challenged by the rapid proliferation of unconventional expenditures, such as special accounts and extrabudgetary funds (public funds and other funds). Special accounts rely on earmarked revenue, which is used for specific purposes, requiring that they be managed apart from general revenue and expenditures (Ha, 1997; Ko, 2000; Nam & Jones, 2003). When policy objectives dictate stable long-term financing of, or a certain amount of administrative discretion over spending on a project, that project may be funded under a public fund. Public funds often have dedicated revenue sources and include what would be considered trust funds in other countries (Ko; Nam & Jones). Line ministries have historically preferred public funds for their flexibility and the low level of detail required in their operational plans relative to general and special accounts (Ha, 1997; He, 2003; Ko). Prior to 2003, the Korean government had established other funds that pertained to the private sector but were managed by line ministries. Financial information of their operations was not provided to the National Assembly, nor were these funds subject to National Assembly approval, although the National Assembly did have some control over these funds as ministry officials often received appointments as board members (Ha, 2004).

In 2007, there were 22 special accounts and 57 public funds that constituted 40% of all outlays (Ministry of Strategy and Finance, 2009), creating fragmentation and opacity in the budget structure (Ha, 2004; Ko, 2000). These problems made effective, accountable management of financial resources almost impossible and seriously constrained the administration's ability to prioritize strategic goals and improve allocation efficiency. More than three decades of unchecked growth in unconventional accounts and funds necessitated one of the most important budgeting reforms of the Kim administration: streamlining the extrabudgetary funds. Prior to the reform, extrabudgetary funds could be established whenever there was a need to operate specific funds in areas functionally independent from the national budget, and these funds had no clear-cut accountability controls. In 2002, the Kim administration merged the other funds category into public funds, subjecting them to review by the National Assembly. Obsolete funds were eliminated and redundant funds were consolidated as well.

The streamlining of funds and the subjection of all public funds to review by the legislature were seen as a major victory for the forces of public accountability, but the victory was not complete (Ha, 2004). After the reform, there were 57 public funds, including 10 financial funds. This number increased during the next administration and stands at 61 public funds as of 2007, accounting for 40% of total consolidated expenditures. Line ministers still have the right to increase outlays of public funds by up to 30% without approval by the National Assembly, although this is a reduction from 50% prior to the reforms. The 10 financial funds are still excluded from the national debt, and the National Health Insurance Fund is still extrabudgetary, while all other social security funds are included in the budget as public funds (Nam & Jones, 2003). This creates a situation where a significant portion of national expenditures remain outside the oversight capacity of the National Assembly, a situation at odds with the government's professed desire for transparency and accountability.

In addition to an incomplete reform of public funds, the Kim administration failed to streamline the special accounts and eliminate earmarked taxes (the major revenues source for numerous special accounts) or simplify the budget structure by consolidating other special accounts, although all of these reforms had been proposed (Ha, 2004; Nam & Jones, 2003). For example, the number of special accounts before the reform was 23 in 2000 and only dropped to 21 in 2002 following the reform. The proportion of special accounts to total consolidated expenditures rose throughout the 1990s, peaking at 32.9% in 1999. Kim's effort to streamline special accounts contributed to the decline of their relative share to 24.2% by 2003 and 14.4% in 2004. However, the primary reason for this decrease in the relative share of special accounts is actually the dramatic increase of public funds created by the conversion of massive sums of government debt guarantees into public funds in 2003.

Korea's difficulty with the simplification of the special accounts highlights a difficulty inherent in many budgetary reform efforts: The elimination of earmarked taxes should be pursued simultaneously, which necessitates an overhaul of the tax system. Fundamentally, the simplification and consolidation of the budget structure is not just an attempt to simplify the financial structure; it is an effort to enhance the government's ability to coordinate societal interests and prioritize policy directions, which is no easy task (Ha, 2004).

REFORM IN THE ACCOUNTING AND BUDGETING SYSTEMS

Accrual Accounting

Accrual accounting and performance budgeting form the core of market-oriented budgetary reform (Ha, 2004; Robinson, 2002; Schick, 1997; Shand, 1998). Although debate continues concerning the efficacy of accrual accounting in the public sector, accrual accounting facilitates strategic planning and greatly improves accountability and transparency, a hallmark of democratic principles (Kravchuk & Voorhees, 2001). Led by New Zealand, Australia, and the United Kingdom, an increasing number of OECD countries are adopting accrual accounting and performance budgeting to improve transparency, accountability, and responsiveness (Matheson, 2002).

Prior to 2009, the Korean government employed a cash accounting basis and single-entry bookkeeping for financial reporting, while commercial special accounts and public funds employed accrual accounting and double-entry bookkeeping. The Dae-jung Kim administration originally planned for all local governments to adopt double-entry bookkeeping by 2003, but it took several years of preparation for the switch to the new accounting system (as is the case in most countries), pushing the implementation of accrual accounting by local governments to 2007 under the Roh administration, and the central government implemented the pilot program starting January 2009. The central government is scheduled to fully implement accrual accounting beginning 2011.

Performance-based Management and Performance Budgeting

During the years 2000 to 2002, the Korean government implemented an experimental pilot performance-based system. After following a phased-in set of steps for the implementation of the performance-based system, a full blown version was implemented beginning in 2007. To solidify the system and to implement the 2006 National Financial Management Law effectively required all ministries and agencies to submit annual performance plans to the Central Budget Office. The Central Budget Office took the lead in designing performance measures and is considering using the results in its budgeting and planning (Kim & Park, 2007). Based on the Program Assessment Rating Tool (PART) used in the United States, the Self-Assessment of the Budgetary Program (SABP) was implemented in 2005 to evaluate agency performance. Line agencies are responsible for answering questionnaires concerning program design and planning, management, and the actual performance of government programs.

The central budget office performs a watchdog function over line ministries' performance, providing the self-evaluation results to the National Assembly for consideration during resource allocation and the authorization or reauthorization of individual programs. Ideally, this will improve resource allocation by line agencies, and some agencies are developing their own evaluation system as more feedback becomes available. Although performance evaluations are not yet linked directly to budget allocations, the Budget Office is considering it as the system matures (Ministry of Strategy and Finance, 2009). Continuous improvement in the development of accurate and reliable performance indicators and the active linking between an agency's performance and budget allocation will be necessary to make Korea's investment in performance measurement worthwhile.

Program Budgeting

Line item budgeting and cash accounting obscure the relationship between program inputs and outputs. To take full advantage of its performance-based system, the Korean government began using a program budget as the basis for resource allocation beginning in 2008 after a pilot program. Prior to the adoption of the program budget, a budget item could be identified in a chain of eight levels of appropriation in a budget document. However, the government streamlined the appropriation levels from eight to five. The five levels include: (1) function (e.g. environmental protection), (2) subfunction (e.g. air), (3) program (e.g. air quality of the Seoul area), (4) activity (e.g. natural gas buses), and (5) object (e.g. personnel expenses). This allows the government to manage resource allocation by program. It also enables stakeholders to understand the budget document based on the linkage (relations) between program inputs and outputs (and outcomes). This system manages all budget processes for all fiscal programs from preparation to audit, providing easily understood reports concerning program status, results, and performance in real-time, with the expectation that this will improve the transparency and accessibility of the budget (Yoon, 2006).

FLEXIBLE FINANCIAL MANAGEMENT ARRANGEMENTS

The Kim and Roh administrations introduced a series of reform measures designed to increase financial management flexibility in order to improve the efficiency of public spending. These reforms included a medium-term expenditure framework (MTEF) and multiyear budgeting, feasibility studies, total operational expense systems (top-down budgeting), and carry-over provisions and incentive schemes for budget savings.

Single-year planning in the annual budget process is often associated with inefficiencies in public investment. Since the 1980s, the central budget office used medium-term fiscal plans for internal use only (Nam & Jones, 2003). The financial crisis of 1997 provided the government with a reason to explore medium-term fiscal analysis. Since 1999, the government has publicly announced its midterm fiscal plan and has taken steps to ensure that annual budgets comply with the broader spending framework laid out in the plan. In 2007, the National Fiscal Management Plan was incorporated into the National Financial Law establishing the requirement for a 5-year mid- to long-term national fiscal management plan reflective of the national policy agenda and investment plans. These plans guide annual expenditure limits in the budget document and provide direction for the long-term management of spending and priorities. This ensures some measure of continuity and coherence in the government's fiscal policy, especially concerning the national debt. Under this system, the central budget management system develops a fiscal management plan for the government, after which individual agencies prepare their budget requests. The central budget office reviews agency requests by comparing information regarding program execution status, performance, and feasibility, and approving the agency requests if they meet the overall expenditure ceilings and agenda priorities (Ministry of Strategy and Finance, 2009).

Preliminary feasibility studies have been mandated for large construction projects (50 billion won or higher) since 1999. This analysis by impartial review ensures that only projects of demonstrable benefit are implemented. The feasibility studies are necessary for a medium-term expenditure framework (MTEF) to be effective, and multiyear budgeting is rationalized as the most effective way to suppress the large annual increases in project budgets that had become customary.

The use of a total budget allocation system (top-down budgeting) for autonomous spending enables each ministry to draw up its own budget plan, within the spending limits set by the national fiscal management plan and allows audit agencies to find information concerning program evaluations, actual versus budgeted expenditures, and so forth easily (Kim & Park, 2007). Since the introduction of the total allocation system in 2004, more funds have been designated as general running cost, which allows line ministries to use those funds at their discretion. The system provides agency heads with a great deal of operational autonomy and discretion.

Carry over provisions allow agencies to transfer up to 5% of unused operating funds from the current fiscal year to the following fiscal year. Previously, unused appropriations almost certainly resulted in a reduction of the agency budget in the following year, providing no incentives for agencies to pursue cost-effective measures. By allowing agencies to retain their savings, the government hopes to halt the long tradition of the year-end spending spree, providing a more efficient and effective use of public funds (Ha, 2004).

Personal and institutional incentives for ideas and measures that either save money or increase revenue are also being implemented. A portion of the savings will be paid directly to the individual or institution, and this program has expanded to include the private sector as well (Ha, 2004; Ministry of Strategy and Finance, 2009).

A DIGITAL BUDGET AND SYSTEM INTEGRATION (REAL-TIME SYSTEMS)

Prior to 2007, the central and local government fiscal information systems were segregated, often using different and incompatible operation protocols. This made the provision of budget and account settlement information to the Budget Office haphazard and inefficient which, in turn, made the effective allocation of national resources difficult. After consultation with relevant government agencies and private sector experts, the Korean government launched the Digital Budget & Accounting System (DBAS) in 2007. The motivation behind DBAS was the development of an information system capable of providing a stable yet innovative financial system (Ministry of Strategy and Finance, 2009; Yoon, 2006). DBAS fully supports the four major fiscal innovations discussed previously, allowing the operation of all budgeting and accounting activities in one system (Ministry of Strategy and Finance, 2009). This integration provides the government with the tools to make effective policy decisions through statistical analysis at various levels including sector, ministry, and function, as well as to obtain varied and accurate analytic data on past performance, current status, and future forecast. It could also be used to provide detailed information to the public in a transparent manner, as well as integrating and streamlining managerial processes throughout the public sector.

While it is too early to evaluate the efficacy of Korea's recent budgetary reforms, it is expected that by implementing most of the current advanced budget techniques and systems, the efficiency and effectiveness of budgeting and financial management will increase greatly.

Conclusions

The authoritarian regimes of the 1960s and 1970s effectively spurred rapid industrial growth in Korea by selectively channeling the nation's scarce resources into the industrial and chemical sectors. The excessive involvement of the government in budgetary and fiscal policy was not without its downside, as this strong centralization resulted in a fragmented, opaque, and absurdly complex national financial structure, creating an environment of inefficiency at best and outright graft at worst. Until the Asian fiscal crisis hit in 1997, the government had been unable to overhaul the outdated and inefficient budgeting and financial management system, but the requirements of IMF aid ensured that such reforms would be made.

Alarmed by soaring public debt and increasing spending on social welfare programs in the wake of the financial crisis, the Dae-jung Kim administration provided a roadmap for the future of Korea's budgetary and financial management system based on the themes of the New Public Management. This market-oriented approach taken by the Kim and Roh administrations included measures such as results-oriented budgeting, improvement of budget efficiency, and enhancement of transparency and accountability (Ha, 2004). In achieving these policy goals, the Korean government gradually implemented: (1) a MTEF and multiyear budgeting; (2) top-down budgeting; (3) a performance management system and program budget; (4) a digital budget information system; and (5) accrual accounting. After more than 10 years of reform efforts, Korea now utilizes most of the advanced budgeting and financial management systems and techniques considered best practices by national and international economic and financial organizations. As in those countries that were front-runners in the implementation of New Public Management reform themes, Korea's ultimate goals are to provide autonomy and flexibility at the agency level while holding agencies accountable for results and efficiency.

The Korean case demonstrates that budgeting and fiscal policy can be effectively used as an important policy instrument, channeling scarce resources for rapid economic development, especially in less developed countries under an authoritarian regime. However, such centralized budgetary and fiscal policy eventually results in a nontransparent, unaccountable, and inefficient system. Finally, it demonstrates that budget reform is a key for administrative reform, yet it is very difficult to achieve due to the political nature of the budgeting processes.

Discussion Questions

1. What was the government's role in promoting rapid economic development in Korea and what were the primary effects on the nation's budget system? How does this suggest that a seemingly good economic strategy can have bad unintended consequences?
2. What are the major institutions involved in Korea's budget processes? What special features of the budget process limit the role of the legislature in budget decisions? Do you think that this is good, or bad?

3. What are the major stages in the Korean budget process? How well integrated are they? Overall, how well do you think the budget processes operate?
4. How can you explain the large role that special accounts and public funds have in Korea's budget? What problems has this created for the overall national budget?
5. What are the basic policy goals of the New Public Management? How are they reflected in the Korean reforms of the last decade? What do you think are the strengths and weaknesses of this approach?

References

Ha, Y. (1997). Public finance and budgeting in Korea under democracy: A critical appraisal. *Public Budgeting & Finance, 17*, 56–73.

Ha, Y. (2004). Budgetary and financial management reforms in Korea: Financial crisis, new public management, and fiscal administration. *International Review of Administrative Sciences, 70*, 511–525.

He, D. (2003). *Budget formulation and implementation in Korea: A macroeconomic perspective* [MPRA paper no. 9576]. New York: International Monetary Fund.

Kim, D., & Kang, I. J. (1983). The budget system and structure in Korea. *Public Budgeting & Finance, 3*(4), 85–96.

Kim, J. M., & Park, C. K. (2006). Top-down budgeting as a tool for central resource management. *OECD Journal of Budgeting, 6*, 87–125.

Kim, J. M., & Park, N. (2007). Performance budgeting in Korea. *OECD Journal on Budgeting, 7*(4), 91–101.

Kim, P. S. (2000). Administrative reform in the Korean central government: A case study of the Dae-jung Kim's administration. *Asian Review of Public Administration, 12*(2), 81–95.

Kim, S. (1995). Budgetary process and bureaucratic control: How to control bureaucracy through the budgetary process in Korea. *International Review of Administrative Sciences, 61*, 270–294.

Ko, Y. S. (2000). *Budget structure, budget process, and fiscal consolidation in Korea.* Seoul: Korea Development Institute.

Koo, C. M. (2002). *Assessing fiscal sustainability in Korea after the currency crisis in 1997.* Paper presented to the 58th Congress of the International Institute of Public Finance, Helsinki.

Koo, C. M. (2006). Public expenditures and fiscal policy in Korea. PowerPoint project presented at the UNESCAP 2nd Regional Policy Dialogue, Beijing.

Kravchuk, R. S., & Voorhees, W. R. (2001). The new governmental financial reporting model under GASB (Statement no. 34: An emphasis on accountability). *Public Budgeting and Finance, 21*(3), 1-30.

Lee, Y., Rhee, C., & Sung, T. (2006). Fiscal policy in Korea: Before and after the financial crisis. *International Tax Public Finance, 13*, 509–531.

Matheson, A. (2002). Better public sector governance: The rationale for budgeting and accounting reform in western nations. *OECD Journal of Budgeting, 2* (Supplement 1), 37–49.

Ministry of Strategy and Finance (MOSF). (2009). *Digital budget and accounting system.* Available at: http://unpar1.un.org/intradoc/groups/public/documents/ungc/unpan038068.pdf. Accessed March 23, 2010.

Nam, Y. S., & Jones, R. S. (2003). Reforming the public expenditure system in Korea. *OECD Economics Department Working Papers, N. 377.* Paris: Organization for Economic Co-operation and Development (OECD).

Rhee, P. W. (1992). Public finance and economic development. In K. Choi, D. K. Kim, T. Kwack, & K. Y. Yun (Eds.), *Public finance in Korea* (pp. 76–105). Seoul: Seoul National University Press.

Robinson, M. (2002). Output-purchase funding and budgeting system in the public sector. *Public Budgeting & Finance, 22*(4), 17–33.

Schick, A. (1997). *Modern budgeting*. Paris: Organization for Economic Co-operation and Development (OECD).

Shand, D. (1998). Budgetary reforms in OECD member countries. *Journal of Public Budgeting, Accounting, and Financial Management, 10*, 63–88.

Shin, R. W., & Ha, Y. (1996). Political economy of policy reform in Korea: Review and analysis. *Policy Studies Review, 16*(2), 65–97.

Yoon, Y. J. (2006). *Sae chaemoo hangjunghak* [Public financial management. (3rd ed.)]. Seoul: Daeyoung Press.

Chapter 5

Budgeting for Results: Enhancing the Budget Process in the Philippines Through Reforms

Hazel Marie A. Sarmiento

Learning Objectives

- Understand the role of budget reforms in the Philippines' budget process in addressing basic weaknesses which has inhibited the budget from being an effective tool for fiscal management.
- Describe the history and the existing budget process in the Philippines.
- Describe key budget reforms currently implemented in the Philippines.
- Identify key revenue and sectoral dimensions of the national budget.
- Identify the next steps in improving the existing budgetary process toward results-based budgeting.

Introduction

The budgetary practices in the Philippines have evolved from improving planning and budget programming links in the 1970s and 1980s to implementing budget enhancements in 1990s. Building on these past budget reforms, results-based budgeting has become the primary goal for public budgeting in the succeeding years up to the present. The Department of Budget and Management (DBM) continues to spearhead budget reform initiatives, with the support of other oversight agencies, in an effort to maintain fiscal discipline and achieve efficiency. Through government efforts, public expenditure management reforms have helped promote better expenditure planning and performance-based budgeting in the Philippines.

Budgetary reforms have been in place to address basic weaknesses that have inhibited the budget from being an effective tool for fiscal management. In the 1970s and 1980s, the budget was not structured according to socioeconomic priorities. In addition, the budget was formulated without considering the availability of revenue funds to support programs and activities. Aside from these issues, there was also a proliferation of special funds earmarked from revenues with specific purposes, which prevented the government from identifying the total government spending as authorized by different finance laws. Finally, the line-item approach to budgeting persisted despite the intent to use a performance budget approach. Hence, it was difficult to determine which programs and activities were achieving results under the previous budgeting practices (Yoingco & Guevara, 1984).

In the 1990s, the DBM continued to address these gaps in expenditure management with a series of budget process enhancements on allotment programming and cash programming. The government also pursued different types of reforms on the management of accounts payables, contingency planning, and accountability monitoring during the period. However, strategic allocation of resources continued to be a challenge, with the proliferation of unfunded mandates and agency flexibility issues in expenditure management. Even with accountability mechanisms in place, there is lack of a cohesive and integrated set of public sector financial reforms that enabled the government to determine the level of efficiency in government service delivery (Boncodin, 1998).

An understanding of the budgeting system of the Philippines lays the groundwork for analyzing the importance of budget reforms and its impact on achieving desired budgetary outcomes. This chapter provides a comprehensive review of the government budgeting system, historic and legal basis, and the institutional mechanisms that are currently in place in the Philippine budgeting system. Key budget reforms will also be discussed in a separate section to provide a chronology of the government's effort to modernize the budget process. Finally, the impact of these reform initiatives in terms of different dimensions in the budget will be discussed together with some relevant budgetary issues and challenges in achieving results-based budgeting in the Philippines.

Government Budgeting in the Philippines

The annual preparation and administration of the national budget is one of the twin functions of the DBM, the primary agency in charge of expenditure management in the Philippines. Together with its management and oversight function, the DBM facilitates the task of expenditure control on the institutional and manpower structure, and incentive and management systems of the government (Boncodin, 1998). The department's budget function was established as early as 1902, under the Philippine Bill, which mandated that "no money shall be paid out of the Treasury except in pursuance of an appropriation by law" (57th Congress of the United States of America, 1902). With the establishment of the Philippine legislature under the Philippine Autonomy Act in 1916, a budget of receipts and expenditures is required to be submitted by the then governor-general to the Philippine Senate and the House of Representatives (64th Congress of the United States of America, 1916). Consequently, the budget system was established in 1917, with the Council of State in charge of preparing the budget for the governor-general (Diamonon, 1920, p. 106).

Budget policy and procedures were also established under the 1935 Constitution, which required the president to submit the budget to Congress at the opening of each regular session to form the basis for the General Appropriations Bill (GAB). Accordingly, the Budget Commission was established (Executive Order No. 25, 1936) and was later transformed as the Ministry of Budget and Management under the Office of the President (Presidential Decree No. 1405, 1978). Under the 1973 Constitution, following a change in the form of government from presidential to parliamentary, the prime minister was then required to submit the budget to the National Assembly within 30 days from the opening of its regular sessions. Among the key policies introduced during the period include the adoption of the line-item framework for government budgeting and the concept of a balanced budget, which matches proposed expenditures with existing revenues (Commonwealth Act No. 246, 1937). Performance budgeting was also introduced under the Revised Budget Act (Republic Act No. 992, 1954), which was later amended to include specific guidelines on the budget laws and procedures and the adoption and application of management information systems (Presidential Decree No. 999, 1976).

In accordance with the mandates of the 1973 Constitution and with the establishment of the New Society, the Budget Decree of 1977 was enacted (Presidential Decree No. 1177, 1977) in an effort to modernize the budgeting system. The decree outlined the specific guidelines for a national budget policy and strategy, the budget process, and the operational guidelines for the use of appropriated funds. With the national budget declared as an instrument for national development, the decree mandated the implementation of several strategies, including the establishment of planning and budgeting linkages, the national resource budget, as well as regional and long-term budgeting. The importance of development projects were also highlighted along with the use of performance and financial reviews, compensation and position classification, and treatment of contingent liabilities (Presidential Decree No. 1177, Sec. 3–11).

The budget decree also specified the procedures for the budget process, beginning with guidelines for budget preparation to the process of budget authorization. As the budget is passed into law, budget execution guidelines were also mandated in the decree, with the whole process culminating on the budget accountability stage (Presidential Decree No. 1177, 1977, Sec. 12–63). Furthermore, the use of appropriated funds is governed by restrictive guidelines in the decree on contractual arrangements, compensation of government officials and employees, maintenance and other operating expenses, as well as misuse of government funds and property (Presidential Decree No. 1177, Sec. 64–88). In 1978, the decree was amended to improve the budget process in accordance with the Philippines' parliamentary practices (Presidential Decree No. 1421, 1978).

Following another change in the country's government structure in 1986 from parliamentary to presidential form, a provisional constitution was enacted with the president exercising legislative powers until a new constitution is adopted (Proclamation No. 3, 1986). The ratification of the 1987 Constitution established new mandates, including budget policies and guidelines that became the basis for current budgetary practices. In addition, the implementation of the new Administrative Code established the mandates and functions of the DBM, along with current guidelines of the national government budgeting system including constitutional policies on the budget, the budget process, and operational guidelines on the use of appropriated funds (Executive Order No. 292, 1987, Books IV & VI). Under the code, DBM is responsible for the formulation and implementation of the national budget and for the efficient and sound utilization of government resources in achieving the country's development objectives (Boncodin, 1998).

The Budget Process

The budget process is characterized by four phases: budget preparation, budget authorization, budget execution, and budget accountability (see Figure 5-1). The preparation of the annual budget starts with the issuance of the macroeconomic and fiscal parameters by the Development Budget Coordination Committee (DBCC). This committee is a top-level interagency fiscal policy and coordination body composed of the heads of oversight agencies, each in charge of specific functions in fiscal and economic policy making. The DBM, as chair of the committee, is in charge of resource allocation and management, while the Department of Finance (DOF) provides the oversight on resource generation and debt management. The National Economic Development Authority (NEDA) is responsible for the overall economic policy, while the *Bangko Sentral ng Pilipinas* (BSP) provides guidance on monetary measures and policies. Finally, the Office of the President (OP) provides the presidential oversight (Executive Order No. 232, 1970). At this level, the proposed budget aggregates as well as the fiscal and macroeconomic targets are set, consistent with the development objectives of the government and its medium-term development plan. Upon agreement by the DBCC of the budget parameters, the Budget Call is issued (DBM, 2000).

The Budget Call is a document that defines the budget framework, the economic and fiscal targets over the medium-term, and priority programs and aggregate budget levels for the year (see National Budget Memorandum No. 101 [2008] for the latest budget call). The Budget Call also outlines the guidelines, procedures, technical instructions, and the budget calendar. Agencies are requested to submit their respective budget proposals to DBM in accordance with the guidelines in the Budget Call. DBM, in turn, conducts technical budget hearings for each agency and reviews each budget proposal. After each review, DBM consolidates a proposed expenditure program to be confirmed by department and agency heads. The proposed budget levels are then presented to the DBCC for approval. With the DBCC's approval, the proposed budget is submitted to the president and the Cabinet members for review. After it has been approved and reviewed by the president, the budget is submitted to the Congress within 30 days from the opening of its regular session (DBM, 2000).

Figure 5-1

The national budget process.

Budget Preparation

- Issuance of the macroeconomic and fiscal parameters by the DBCC
- Issuance of the budget call by the DBM
- Submission of budget proposals by national agencies to DBM
- Technical budget reviews by the DBM
- DBM prepares the proposed expenditure program
- Department and agency heads confirm the proposed expenditure program
- Approval of the proposed expenditure program by the DBCC
- Submission of the proposed expenditure program to the president and the cabinet members for review
- Approval of the Proposed Budget by the president
- Submission of the president's budget to Congress

Budget Accountability

- Submission of midyear and annual physical and financial performance reports by agencies to the DBM and to COA
- Preparation of audit reports and recommendations by the COA
- Publication of the agency's physical and financial performance for the year
- Performance reports are used as a basis for budget preparation for the next fiscal year

Budget Authorization

- Submission of the president's budget and supporting documents to Congress
- Conduct of Agency Budget Hearings by the House of Representatives
- Approval by the House panel of the proposed budget as the General Appropriations Bill
- Conduct of Agency Budget Hearings by the Senate
- Approval of the proposed budget by the Senate
- Consolidation of the House and Senate versions of the General Appropriations Bill through a Bicameral Conference Committee
- Approval of amendments to the General Appropriations Bill by the Bicameral Conference Committee
- Submission of the General Appropriations Bill to the president
- Ratification of the General Appropriations Act by the president

Budget Execution

- Formulation of the cash budget and allotment release programs
- Preparation of the Agency Budget Matrix
- Issuance of the General Allotment Release Order (GARO), the Special Allotment Release Order (SARO) and the Notice of Cash Allocation (NCA)
- Agencies implement programs, projects, and activities as authorized by the national budget

Along with the president's budget, supporting budget documents are also submitted to Congress. The Budget of Expenditures and Sources of Financing (BESF) and the National Expenditure Program (NEP) provides details of the proposed expenditures. The president's budget message is also submitted, which summarizes the budget policy directions and priorities for the year. The House of Representatives, through its Committee on Appropriations, conducts reviews and agency budget hearings on the proposed budget. An amended budget proposal is then presented to the House panel for approval as a GAB. This revised budget is then submitted to the Philippine Senate, through the Senate Finance Committee, for their review and amendments, after which, the budget will be submitted to the Senate floor, through a plenary session, for approval. The House and the Senate versions of the GAB are consolidated under the Bicameral Conference Committee. This committee finalizes the amendments and changes made to the GAB. As an agreement is reached and as both the House and the Senate approves the budget, the GAB is submitted to the president for signing into law. The approved and ratified budget is then known as the General Appropriations Act, which provides the legislative authorization for budget appropriations for each department and agencies to implement programs, activities, and projects of government agencies for the year (DBM, 2000).

The budget execution phase starts with the formulation of the cash budget and the allotment release programs immediately after the budget was signed into law. The cash budget and the allotment release programs prescribe guidelines on the available cash requirements of the budget and the prioritization of fund releases, respectively. An agency budget matrix (ABM) is also prepared by the DBM in consultation with agencies to reflect the work and financial schedules for each of the expenditure categories in the agency's budget. The ABM serves as a basis for determining the timing, compositions, and the magnitude of the release of authorized funds in the budget. With the cash budget program, the allotment release program, and the ABM, the General Allotment Release Order (GARO) and the Special Allotment Release Order (SARO) are issued to authorize government agencies to spend for their expenditure obligations. The DBM also issues the Notice of Cash Allocation (NCA) on a monthly or quarterly basis, which provides for the maximum amount of withdrawal that an agency can make from a government bank. This document gives agencies with the maximum flexibility to use their cash allocations provided that their authorized allotments do not exceed their agency allocations. Consequently, the Bureau of Treasury is tasked to replenish funds on a daily basis to government servicing banks with cash funds for the agencies' financial requirements. Agency programs, projects, and activities are then implemented as agency funds become available (DBM, 2000).

Agency budget performance is monitored and evaluated under the budget accountability phase. Agencies are required to submit their actual physical and financial performance during their midyear and year-end evaluation with the Commission on Audit (COA). The COA is assigned to conduct audits on the legality, propriety, and accuracy of government financial transactions. The assessment of the agencies' physical and financial performance is conducted with the use of performance indicators to measure agency outcomes, outputs, processes, and client satisfaction. Trial balance reports are also submitted by the agencies to the DBM and COA to identify each agency's cash management performance. On the basis of its review, COA prepares its audit reports and publishes an annual report that includes their recommendations for the agency's physical and financial performance for the year (DBM, 2000).

While each phase in the budget process is distinct, each stage overlaps when implemented during a budget year. Budget preparation for the next budget year starts in the first quarter of the fiscal year while government agencies are implementing their respective programs, projects, and activities for the current year. The budget accountability stage for the previous fiscal year is also conducted during the budget execution period of the present budget year, with the monitoring and evaluation of agency budget operations and performance (DBM, 2000). As each stage of the budget process is implemented, the national budget becomes an action plan, a financial plan, and a strategic agency guide to achieve the government's national development goals. To enhance and strengthen the budgeting process, reforms are being put into place to monitor the efficiency of fund utilization in government, assess agency performance, and provide sound management information in resource allocation.

Key Budget Reforms

Various reforms that have been initiated in the past continue to define and improve the current budgeting system. Table 5-1 presents a summary of major budget reforms in the Philippines from the 1970s to present. In the 1970s and the 1980s, key reforms

Table 5-1

Major Budget Reforms in the Philippines, 1970s to Present

Budget reforms	Legal basis and sources	Implementation year
Coordination of development and tax planning (Creation of the DBCC)	Presidential Decree No. 1177	1977
One-fund concept in budgeting	Presidential Decree No. 75	1975
Regional budgeting	Presidential Decree No. 1177	1977
Zero-based budgeting	Presidential Decree No. 1177	1977
Nationwide implementation of performance-based budgeting	Presidential Decree No. 1177	1977
Redefining the mandate of the DBM and the national government budgeting system guidelines	The 1987 Constitution; Executive Order No. 292	1987
Synchronized planning–programming–budgeting system	Memorandum Order No. 295	1990
Accountability reporting	National Budget Circular No. 422	1991
Baseline budgeting scheme	DBM Issuances	1994
Regional budgeting allocation scheme	DBM Issuances	1994
Simplified fund release system	DBM Issuances	1995
Budget enhancements	DBM Issuances	1994 and onward
Medium-term expenditure framework	DBM Issuances	1993 to present
Organizational performance indicator framework	DBM Issuances	1998; 2005 and onward

Sources: Yoingco & Guevara, 1984; Boncodin, 1998; DBM, 2000.

include improving the planning and budgeting linkages, establishing the national resource budget, and introducing regional budgeting. The one-fund concept in budgeting was also introduced together with the use of the zero-base approach and later with the adoption of performance budgeting (Yoingco & Guevara, 1984). Improving planning and budgeting linkages entails the use of the budget as a tool to achieve targets in the country's development plans. It also involves tax planning and the use of available revenue information in formulating fiscal targets for the year.

The national resource budget, on the other hand, was established to support the formulation of the budget based on the totality of revenues, expenditures, and borrowings of all levels of government and government corporations. Regional budgeting was implemented to promote "countryside" development by developing agency budgets in accordance with regional plans and involving regional offices in budget preparation. The one-fund concept in budgeting subjects all income and revenues of government to accrue to the General Fund and be subject to appropriations and the budgeting process. Zero-base budgeting was also introduced to identify, evaluate, and rank the new and existing activities of the government according to their importance. Finally, as a response to the disadvantages of using line-item budgeting, performance budgeting was adopted, wherein items in the budget are matched with their corresponding outputs.

Budget enhancements were also implemented in 1990s to include the baseline budgeting scheme, improved program presentation of the General Appropriations Act, and the implementation of the Simplified Fund Release System. Regional budgeting was also enhanced during this period with the implementation of the Regional Budgeting Allocation Scheme and the regionalization of lump-sum appropriations, where funds are released directly to the regional offices. In addition, budget functions were also decentralized to the regions, including fund releases and addressing the budgeting concerns of local agencies and the local government units. Certain budget powers have also been devolved to agencies, including the granting of honoraria for projects, authorized incentives, amelioration, and hazard pay. Finally, automation and information technology were also used to improve budget preparation, budget execution and tracking, and the management of government manpower and expenditures. Key projects that were introduced include the Budget Preparation and Management System (BPMS), the Budget Execution and Accountability Tracking System (BEAT), the Government Manpower Information System (GMIS), and the Manpower Management and Information System (MMIS) (Boncodin, 1998). These systems are still being utilized within the DBM throughout the budget process along with other automated processes on government procurement, cash management, and accounting.

The idea of a multiyear budgeting system was also introduced as a key budget reform that will link budgeting decisions to future spending constraints. The Medium-Term Expenditure Framework (MTEF) and the Organizational Performance Indicator Framework (OPIF) were introduced to pursue strategic policy-based approaches to budget preparation and identify agency budgetary outcomes. The MTEF and the OPIF focus on improving aggregate fiscal discipline, improving budget allocation to strategic priorities and promoting high-quality services at least cost. Both reforms are also being pursued and adopted in the current planning, programming, and budgeting system (National Budget Memorandum No. 101, 2008).

The MTEF is a top-down and bottom-up multiyear budgeting approach to budget preparation that allows government spending to be driven by policy priorities and revenue constraints. The approach is defined by aggregate projections of government revenue, spending, and borrowing over the medium term, as well as estimates on the cost of existing policies. The aggregate projections comprise the medium-term fiscal program, which the estimates of the future cost of existing programs and policies are referred to as forward estimates. As the DBCC decides on the macroeconomic and fiscal targets for budget preparation, these aggregates are then included in the budget strategy paper that is submitted to the president prior to the issuance of the Budget Call. This budget innovation includes the president in decision making in setting budget parameters and strategic allocation of resources (DBM, 2006).

The OPIF, on the other hand, is an approach to expenditure management that directs resources toward results by measuring agency performance using key performance indicators. The OPIF adopts an analytic approach based on a logical framework that links societal and sectoral goals with organizational outcomes and major final outputs. Departments and agencies formulated their respective log frames, major outputs, and key performance indicators and linked these items to agency programs, activities, and projects that are specified in their budget (DBM, 2007b). As agencies undergo physical and financial performance review in the budget process, this framework enables agencies, such as the DBM and the COA to identify achievements in service delivery and agency performance in terms of their organizational outcomes.

As reforms are being mainstreamed to the current budgeting system, there will always be opportunities for improvement and innovation. The budget process will continue to be improved as reforms are initiated to adapt to changes in government structure, budget policies, agency fiscal behavior, and best practices. In all current budget activities, the MTEF and the OPIF are implemented and remains the primary approach for achieving efficiency in government.

Revenues and Sectoral Dimensions of the National Budget

Recent expenditure trends show the shifting priorities of government from debt servicing programs to economic and social programs. Incidentally, the MTEF and OPIF were put in place during the formulation of the 2007 budget. Figure 5-2 shows the increasing trends in economic services and social services, and a decreasing trend for payment of government debt from 2007 onward. At the aggregate level, economic services include spending for agriculture, environment and natural resources, trade and industry, tourism, communication, and transportation. Program expenditures for this sector increased from 21.2% in 2006 to around 25% in 2007 and onward. Social services, on the other hand, comprise spending for health, education, social security and welfare, housing, community development, and land distribution. Spending for this sector also increased from 27% in 2006 to roughly about 28 to 30% in 2007 and onward (DBM, 2007a; 2008; 2009).

General public services spending for general administration and public order and safety remained relatively the same, with around 17% of total government spending from

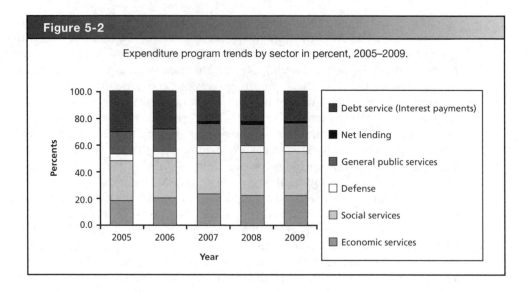

Figure 5-2

Expenditure program trends by sector in percent, 2005–2009.

the years 2006 to 2009. Defense spending and net lending to corporations also remained relatively the same since 2005, with defense comprising around 5% of the budget and net lending to roughly less than 1% of the budget (DBM, 2007a; 2008; 2009).

Debt service payments have declined significantly, from roughly 30% of total expenditures in 2006 to around 23% in 2007, and roughly 22% in 2008 to 2009 (DBM, 2007a; 2008; 2009). The shift in priorities from debt servicing to economic and social programs has signaled the government's commitment to strategic allocation of resources. Through the implementation of budget reforms, resources are directed toward outcome-oriented spending and achieving efficiency in service delivery.

Figure 5-3 shows the percentage composition of revenue sources that support the national budget for each fiscal year. The bulk of revenue sources come from tax revenues, from 86.5% in 2005 to 91.8% in 2009. Tax revenues comprise taxes on net income and profits, property taxes, taxes on domestic goods and services, and taxes on international trade and transactions. Nontax revenues include fees and charges, income from the Bureau of Treasury, privatization proceeds, and foreign grants. In 2005, nontax revenues are 13.5% of the total revenue program and continued to decrease at around 8.2% by 2009 (DBM, 2007a; 2008; 2009).

Next Steps in the Budgeting Process

A crucial next step to results-based budgeting is the rollout of these budget innovations to implementing agencies and enhance capacity building. The MTEF and the use of the OPIF approach to budgeting needs to be institutionalized to harness its potential to achieve key budgetary outcomes. Both reforms have been mainstreamed in the national budget process and will need to be used to map out multiyear requirements of spending decisions. The estimation of the forward estimates will enable agencies to

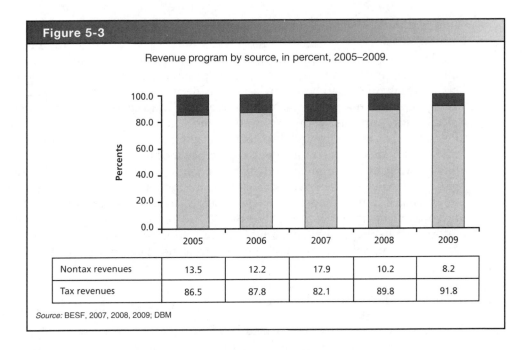

Figure 5-3

Revenue program by source, in percent, 2005–2009.

	2005	2006	2007	2008	2009
Nontax revenues	13.5	12.2	17.9	10.2	8.2
Tax revenues	86.5	87.8	82.1	89.8	91.8

Source: BESF, 2007, 2008, 2009; DBM

determine available fiscal space or available resources in the medium-term expenditure program to provide leeway for new program and project proposals.

The budget strategy paper, which is submitted to the president prior to the issuance of the budget preparation guidelines, can be enhanced to make government budgeting process a policy-oriented exercise. The strategy paper can be used to identify budget pressures brought by unfunded mandates and pending obligations of unfinished programs and projects. Furthermore, the linkages between the country's medium-term development plan with the budget can be enhanced through the formulation of the budget strategy paper.

The OPIF approach to budgeting still needs to be expanded to cover all government agencies. The approach was initially implemented in key departments and agencies and is expected to be rolled to Congress, other government agencies, and government-owned and controlled corporations. There is also room for improvement in refining the performance indicators and measures to identify agency outcomes, outputs, and targets. As most budget outcomes are not easily quantifiable, measures need to be formulated to improve the monitoring and evaluation of agency performance.

Another relevant challenge for improving the budget process includes the timely submission of the president's budget proposal to Congress at the opening of the legislative sessions. This entails a possible restructuring of the existing budget calendar for the DBCC to set its budget parameters for the next year at the start of the current fiscal year. In addition, the formulation of the budget strategy paper also needs to be incorporated in the budget preparation process to allow ample time for the president and the policy makers to decide on strategic allocation of resources in the budget.

Conclusion

Through the years, the implementation of key budget reforms and the adoption of budget innovations have transformed the budget process from being an accounting and bookkeeping exercise to becoming a strategic decision-making tool for development. The government budgeting system has successfully adapted to the changing dynamics of the budget process, with best practices and emerging budget innovations in the fields of public budgeting and finance. From an initial budget perspective of spending based on available resources and deficit reduction, the budget is now also more focused on achieving fiscal discipline, and allocation and operational efficiency. These budgetary outcomes are the driving force of key budget reforms that are currently being implemented in the Philippines. As new ways of achieving and measuring efficiency in government are developed, policy makers are hoping that the implementation of reforms will enhance and strengthen the budgeting process as a policy-driven and results-oriented approach to public policy formulation and implementation.

Discussion Questions

1. Based on your basic understanding of the budget process in the Philippines, has the country been successful in addressing the basic weaknesses that has inhibited the budget as an effective fiscal management tool? Why or why not?
2. Is the use of an MTEF approach appropriate for addressing multiyear expenditure gaps? Why or why not?
3. Will identifying specific agency goals and outcomes through the OPIF approach enable agencies to get funding for programs that lead towards these goals and outcomes?
4. How extensive should the budget strategy paper be in terms of enabling the decision makers (such as the president and the legislature) in making the budgeting process a policy-oriented exercise?
5. Provide proposals on how existing available resources can be divided into agency budgets that is both efficient and/or equitable.

References

Boncodin, E. (1998). The department of budget and management under the Ramos presidency and administration: Record and legacy. In J. V. Abueva & E. R. Roman (Eds.), *The Ramos presidency and administration: Record and legacy* (1992–1998). Quezon City: University of the Philippines Press.

Commonwealth Act No. 246. (1937). *General Appropriations Act of 1936.*

Department of Budget and Management (DBM). (2000). *Primer on government budgeting.* Manila, Philippines: Author.

Department of Budget and Management (DBM). (2006, May 12). *Budget framework and fiscal targets.* Presented at the FY 2007 Budget Forum at the University of the Philippines, Diliman, Quezon City.

Department of Budget and Management (DBM). (2007a). *Budget of expenditures and sources of financing.* Manila, Philippines: Author.

Department of Budget and Management (DBM). (2007b). *Organizational performance indicator framework: Reforming Philippine expenditure management*. Manila, Philippines: Author.

Department of Budget and Management (DBM). (2008). *Budget of expenditures and sources of financing*. Manila, Philippines: Author.

Department of Budget and Management (DBM). (2009). *Budget of expenditures and sources of financing*. Manila, Philippines: Author.

Diamonon, V. D. (1920). *The development of self-government in the Philippine Islands*. Iowa City: University of Iowa.

Executive Order No. 25. (1936). *Creation of the budget commission*.

Executive Order No. 232. (1970). *Creation of the development budget and coordination committee*.

Executive Order No. 292. (1987). *Instituting the administrative code of 1987*.

Fifty-Seventh Congress of the United States of America. (1902). *An act temporarily to provide for the administration of the affairs of civil government in the Philippine Islands, and for other purposes* [Philippine Bill of 1902]. Washington, DC.

National Budget Memorandum No. 101. (2008). *Policy guidelines and procedures in the preparation of the 2009 budget proposals*.

Presidential Decree No. 999. (1976). *Amending republic act numbered nine hundred and ninety-two, known as the revised budget act*.

Presidential Decree No. 1177. (1977). *Revising the budget process in order to institutionalize the budgetary innovations of the New Society*.

Presidential Decree No. 1405. (1978). *Converting the budget commission and the national science development board into ministries*.

Presidential Decree No. 1421. (1978). *Amending presidential decree No. 1177, Known as the budget reform decree of 1977*.

Proclamation No. 3. (1986). *Declaring a national policy to implement the reforms mandated by the people, protecting their basic rights, adopting a provisional constitution, and providing for an orderly transition to a government under a new constitution* (Also known as The 1986 Provisional "Freedom" Constitution of the Republic of the Philippines).

Republic Act No. 992. (1954). *An act to provide for a budget system for the national government*.

Sixty-Fourth Congress of the United States of America. (1916). *An act to declare the purpose of the people of the United States as to the future political status of the people of the Philippine Islands, and to provide a more autonomous government for those islands* [Jones Law]. Manila, Philippines: Bureau of Printing.

Yoingco, A. Q., & Guevara, M. M. (1984). Budgetary practices and developments in the Philippines. *Public Budgeting and Finance, 4*(2), 99–115.

Chapter 6

The Limits of Budget Reform in Taiwan

Tsuey-ping Lee and Cal Clark

Learning Objectives

- Know and understand the major historical and political legacies in Taiwan that have shaped the nation's budgetary system.
- Know and understand the major institutions in the budgetary process.
- Know and understand the major stages in the budgetary process and the problems associated with each stage.
- Know and understand the fiscal crisis facing local governments in Taiwan and why this calls for budgetary reforms.
- Know and understand the basic difference in the budgets of the Lee Teng-hui and Chen Shui-bian administrations and how they reflect the philosophic divide between the Kuomintang and the Democratic Progressive Party.

Introduction

Taiwan inherited the government and constitution of the Republic of China when Chiang Kai-shek's Nationalist Party or Kuomintang (KMT), which had ruled China since 1928, lost the Chinese Civil War to Mao Zedong's Chinese Communists in 1949 and evacuated to Taiwan. This produced several somewhat contradictory institutional heritages. On the one hand, the Constitution was, on paper, a democratic one, reflecting the ideology of the KMT's founder Sun Yat-sen (who died before the party gained power) and was designed for a huge continental nation. On the other hand, the KMT ruled through a quasi-Leninist party-state based on the organizational advice of Soviet advisors in the 1920s (Botjer, 1979; Eastman, 1974; Wilbur, 1983). Once in Taiwan, the KMT continued to rule in a strongly authoritarian manner. It did promote a very successful industrialization project, though, that was being termed an "economic miracle" by the 1980s (Clark, 1989; Wade, 1990). Political development was delayed, however, until a successful democratization in the late 1980s and early 1990s (Rigger, 1999; Tien, 1996).

These legacies had several implications for budgeting in Taiwan during the postwar period. First, the process has been quite centralized. For example, the Directorate-General of Budgeting, Accounting, and Statistics (DGBAS) issues the *Instructions and Guidelines on the Preparation of Central and Local Government Budgets* (DGBAS, 2009b), which is binding on local governments and state corporations, as well as on national government agencies. Consequently, while local governments prepare their own budgets that are reviewed by their city and county councils, the financial autonomy of local government is very limited (Hsu, 2001; Wang, 2007), as is discussed in more detail in the second part of this chapter. Second, until Taiwan's democratization, the national Legislative Yuan was fairly powerless and, consequently, did not develop the professionalism, sophistication, and care in reviewing and shaping budgets that usually marks the legislative process in developed democracies (Copper, 2009). Third, this combination of centralization and limited parliamentary participation results in many aspects of budget politics being much less salient and transparent than in other nations (Hsu, 2005; Su, 2002). Finally (and unfortunately), democratization did not bring the expected improvement in the legislative budgeting process. Rather, in Taiwan's hypercompetitive political environment, legislators focused on gaining publicity rather than professionalism (Rigger, 1999).

This chapter on Taiwan's public budgeting system begins with a description of the four stages in the national budgeting process and a discussion of some of the problems associated with the budgeting process. The second part of the chapter considers two more specific topics. First, we analyze how the current system has failed in its attempt to reform and improve local government finance; and then we examine the differences between the national budgets of the last KMT administration under President Lee Teng-hui and the first administration of the previously opposition Democratic Progressive Party (DPP) under President Chen Shui-bian. Overall, our analysis suggests that the budget process in Taiwan needs significant reform in order to overcome some of the institutional legacies of the authoritarian era but that major reform efforts have been quite limited.

The Budget Process in Taiwan

The budget process in Taiwan is similar to most other countries in that it involves the preparation and formulation of the national budget by the executive, approval by the legislature, and implementation and audit by the executive. The actual political institutions in Taiwan are distinct, if not unique, though. There is an elected president and Legislative Yuan. However, the executive or Executive Yuan (which is in charge of the budget) is headed by a premier who is selected by the president without the consent of the legislature but is also, at least in theory, responsible to the Legislative Yuan that can force him or her to resign by a vote of no confidence, although this would open the legislature to being dissolved by the president. Consequently, even when the Executive and Legislative Yuans are controlled by different parties, as they were from March 2001 to March 2009, the Legislative Yuan is very hesitant to remove the premier (who is not a legislator). Furthermore, over the last two decades when Taiwan has been a democracy, the relationships between the president and premier have varied considerably, introducing further complexity into Taiwanese politics (Copper, 2009).

The overall budget process is divided into four stages: (1) budget preparation, (2) budget proposal review, (3) budget execution, and (4) budget audit. The fiscal year in Taiwan extends from January 1st through December 31st. The budget preparation occurs during the first 8 months (January to August) of the preceding year. The Legislative Yuan must complete its budget review 1 month before the new fiscal year so that this stage is effectively set for September through November. The president then must promulgate the budget 15 days before the start of the fiscal year or December 15th. Obviously, budget execution and implementation are conducted throughout the fiscal year by individual agencies and authorities. Finally, the Ministry of Audit (MOA) reviews and audits the budget both during the fiscal year and following its close and prepares a report for the Legislative Yuan.

BUDGET PREPARATION

Each year, the DGBAS in the Executive Yuan prepares and coordinates the Central Government General Budget (DGBAS, 2009c). It begins by issuing the *Instructions and Guidelines on the Preparation of the Central and Local Government Budget* (DGBAS, 2009b) to guide the central and local governments in preparing their annual budget estimates. In addition, DGBAS is responsible for stipulating an annual expenditure limit for each authority and agency based on the *National Medium-Term* (4-year) *Plan* created by the Executive Yuan. This medium-term plan includes details about expenditure limits for the entire 4 years, along with policy priorities and resource allocations. The Executive Yuan also constitutes an Annual Programs and Budget Screening Council for screening budget proposals. According to the most recent *Regulation for Preparing the Central Government General Budget of FY 2009* (DGBAS, 2009c), the budget preparation process includes three distinct stages: (1) preparing budget estimates, (2) reviewing budget estimates, and (3) preparing the final budget proposal.

The various governmental agencies and authorities are responsible for developing their initial budget estimates. However, their budget preparation occurs under fairly tight constraints. For example, each authority has to use estimated revenue data from DGBAS and the Ministry of Finance (MOF) to define its resources. Moreover, it has to allocate its expenditures based on task priorities set by *National Medium-Term* (4-year) *Plan* and by the *Instructions and Guidelines on the Preparation of the Central and Local Government Budget.* In particular, its projected annual expenditures must not exceed the limit set by DGBAS.

Once all the individual proposals are submitted to the Executive Yuan, DGBAS initiates a two-stage review process. In the first stage, DGBAS checks to make sure that the annual expenditures of each authority have not exceeded its assigned limit. If they do, the budget estimates will be rejected and returned for reworking. Second, after the levels or amounts of the proposals have been vetted, DGBAS will invite budget-related authorities and agencies to give the estimated annual expenditure a preliminary review. The preliminary review results are then submitted to the Annual Programs and Budget Screening Council for evaluation. The screening results include each authority's amount of annual revenue, annual expenditure limit, subsidy to local government, and so forth. They are then integrated by DGBAS for submission to the Executive Yuan. After that, the Executive Yuan formally informs the central authorities and local governments about all these detailed data for preparing their final budget proposals.

Finally, the formal budget proposal is prepared for legislative review. All the authorities have to submit budget proposals with an annual plan, expected objectives, and performance measurement indicators to DGBAS. DGBAS then combines all the budget proposals and submits them to the Executive Yuan for final review. After this review, the Executive Yuan submits the Central Government General Budget Proposal to the Legislative Yuan for review.

Several important problems are easy to identify with the budget preparation process in Taiwan. First, it clearly utilizes top-down processes. The flexibility of each authority is very limited, as its revenues and even expenditure priorities are defined by central plans and regulations. Second, departmentalism can often be a problem. Each authority develops its own plan under expenditure limits set by DGBAS. There is not much connection and integration among different authorities. Therefore, the public services provided by different authorities may be redundant; or some services might be slighted when different agencies assume that somebody else is taking care of them. Finally, there are no predictions of long-term revenues and expenditures. Consequently, rational program development is inhibited.

BUDGET PROPOSAL REVIEW

Taiwan has a unicameral Legislative Yuan. Before the nation's democratization in the early 1990s, the powers and activities of this legislature were quite circumscribed. Democratization brought more robust parliamentary politics, but significant criticisms of legislators emerged as well. The Legislative Yuan became infamous for its raucous politics and occasional brawls; legislative interpellations of executive officials, one of the few methods for promoting accountability during the authoritarian era, often became nasty and contemptuous; and many legislators were seen as being much more interested in publicity-seeking and grandstanding than in making informed policy decisions. These untoward trends were seemingly exacerbated by Taiwan's electoral system of the "single nontransferable vote" or SNTV (i.e., citizens cast just one vote in large multimember districts) because legislative candidates could win office with only small minorities, leading to the election of criminals and extremists (Copper, 2009; Rigger, 1999).

This nature of legislative politics, which has not been noticeably altered by a recent change in electoral systems, is obviously quite relevant to the budgetary process. The legislative process for reviewing the government's budget proposals appears fairly standard with a First Reading and assignment to a substantive committee, committee deliberations that culminate in the Second Reading that sets off discussion by the full Legislative Yuan, and final approval of the Third Reading (The Legislative Yuan of the Republic of China, 2010). Yet, the special nature of the Legislative Yuan creates significant problems for the budgetary process and suggests the need for budgetary reform.

Government-proposed bills are listed on the bill agenda for report to the Legislative Yuan. All the titles of the bills are read out loud to the legislature in what is called the First Reading. After the First Reading, the proposed bills are referred to appropriate committees for consideration and committee action. In the case of the budget proposal, however, the premier, the minister of Finance, and the minister of DGBAS must report on the annual administrative plan and budget formulation in person to the Legislative Yuan and answer interpellations from individual legislators before the budget proposal is referred to committee.

Once this stage of the process is completed, the budget proposal is broken up by subject matter and referred to one of the eight substantive committees: Internal Affairs; Foreign Affairs and National Defense; Economic Affairs; Finance; Education and Cultural Affairs; Transportation; Justice and Legal Affairs; and Social Welfare and Environmental Hygiene. These committees parallel the eight major ministries closely, but not quite exactly (there are separate Ministries of Defense and Foreign Affairs but no Ministry of Social Welfare). During their deliberations on the budget bills, the committees may invite relevant government employees to attend committee meetings, to present oral explanations about the budget, to answer interpellations, and to provide information for the committee members' reference. When the committees finish working on the budget, they submit their results to the Finance Committee for integration in a report to the Legislative Yuan as a whole in the Second Reading.

At the Second Reading, the proposed budget is subjected to both general discussion and article-by-article discussion. At this stage, the legislators can decide upon revision, reexamination, revocation, or withdrawal. Once the proposed budget bill has completed the Second Reading, it proceeds to the Third Reading in the subsequent Sitting of the Legislative Yuan. Only rephrasing can be made in the Third Reading unless a bill is found to be self-contradictory, unconstitutional, or in conflict with other laws.

The budgetary bills that have completed the Third Reading are sent to the Executive Yuan and to the president for promulgation. The president must promulgate these bills within 10 days after receiving them. If the Executive Yuan objects to part of or the entire budgetary bill, the budget can be returned to the Legislative Yuan for reconsideration in accordance with the procedures stipulated in Article 3 of the Additional Articles of the Constitution.

The nature of the Legislative Yuan creates significant problems for the budget process. First, until the very recent reform of the electoral system, legislators were subjected to fierce competition not just from candidates from other parties but from their own party as well (Copper, 2009; Rigger, 1999). Consequently, the individual members of the Legislative Yuan were often highly particularistic or antagonistic because of their concern with reelection, emphasizing specific constituent district interests or grandstanding about emotional issues. Second, many legislators do not possess the professional skills and knowledge for reviewing the complicated budget proposals. The assistants of the legislators are generally not professional enough to help the legislators to do their jobs either. Third, legislators compete strongly for gaining membership of the committees with greater budgetary powers (e.g., the Foreign Affairs and National Defense Committee). In contrast, they are not interested in committees with relatively low budget limits (e.g., the Transportation Committee); so that their budgets receive little attention and analysis. Finally, the Budget Center is supposed to be a research institute which compiles objective research results for the use of the legislators. However, the insufficient personnel and limited functions of the Budget Center cause legislators, their assistants, and the public to generally disregard its data and reports. In short, major reforms bringing greater professionalism to the Legislative Yuan appear to be vital to improving the budgetary process in Taiwan.

BUDGET EXECUTION

According to the *Instructions and Guidelines on the Budget Execution of Central Government Agencies* (DGBAS, 2009a), budget execution by the individual agencies and authorities includes distributing budget expenditures, exercising budget control, asking for supplementary budget support if necessary, and completing a performance evaluation of budgetary activities. At the beginning of the fiscal year, the head of each authority or agency has to distribute its budget to each subordinate agency or unit in allocations for each month or some other specific time period. Budget control means that each unit, agency, and authority should not expend more funds than their monthly or time-period limit. Conversely, delays in budget spending or execution are not allowed either, and administrative units with budget backlogs or delayed expenditures will encounter problems at the last stage of the budget audit. When an administrative unit, agency, or authority feels that its budget is insufficient, it can ask for supplementary funds. However, based on the Budget Act, a supplementary budget request can only be initiated under fairly limited circumstances, and the supplementary budget has to go through the same complex process as the formal budget proposal does. Finally, the budget performance evaluation is used to ensure that each unit executes its budget as planned. Each month, every unit, agency, and authority has to fill out a form reporting its revenues and expenditures for that very month to DGBAS, MOF, and the MOA.

It is easy to identify several important problems that occur in this stage of budget execution. First, there is very little flexibility once the budget has been set and promulgated. Thus, it is very hard to switch funds among budget categories in the face of problems and contingencies that inevitably arise during the fiscal year. Second, the analysis of budget performance evaluates just the amount of money expended rather than seeking to measure the real performance of a unit or agency. Third, if the budget funds are not expended as planned, a unit will face possible budget cuts for the next year. Therefore, government agencies try their best to spend all their budget money, even if it is not necessary. This system certainly does not provide any incentive for an administrative unit to perform more efficiently and effectively to save money.

BUDGET AUDIT

According to the Audit Act, each authority must submit a report on the percentage completion of its budget plan in terms of revenues and expenditures to the MOA every month or for each specific time period if its budget is not monthly. When the fiscal year comes to the end, each authority has to submit an overall financial statement with a full performance report to the MOA for the final audit. Based on these reports, the MOA scrutinizes whether the revenues and expenditures were executed as planned and whether the budget was balanced. If the budget was not executed as planned or if the revenues and expenditures were not balanced, the MOA determines and analyzes the reasons causing these problems. In addition, the MOA has to examine if the pattern of revenues and expenditures is consistent with the national administrative plan set by the Executive Yuan. If any inappropriate budget execution is found, the MOA is responsible for notifying the upper level of government, as well as the Control Yuan (which acts as a watchdog guarding against governmental abuses). At the end of the process, the Auditor-General has to prepare and submit the annual Audit Report to the Legislative Yuan.

There are several significant problems in the budget audit stage in Taiwan. First, the system is limited to an annual audit rather than auditing long-term spending. Therefore, for the performance or budget execution for long-term projects, such as public infrastructure projects, the budget audits are fairly inadequate. Second and more broadly, the audit of the performance of any unit really is incomplete because performance measurement has not been very well developed. Therefore, the audit emphasizes money flows rather than the performance or policy outputs in terms of expenditures rather than policy outcomes and impacts. Third, the annual Audit Report submitted to the Legislative Yuan is supposed to be a reference for legislators when they deliberate on subsequent budget proposals and a feedback to administrative agencies. However, the Audit Report does not appear to be valued or used very much by legislators, administrative agencies, or the general public.

Issues in Public Budgeting

This part of our discussion of public budgeting in Taiwan examines two more specific issues. The first concerns the budgetary stress on local governments that the current centralized system has produced, and the second compares the macro budgets of the last two presidents, Lee Teng-hui of the KMT and Chen Shui-bian of the DPP, to see whether partisan differences were reflected in the budgets of their administrations. These two discussions produce quite differing conclusions about the need for budgetary reform. The daunting fiscal problems of Taiwanese local governments suggest a strong need for reform. In contrast, the significant differences in the Lee and Chen budgets do indicate that national administrations have the flexibility to respond to their constituencies.

FISCAL STRESS AND LOCAL GOVERNMENTS

In the past decade, Taiwan's annual revenue grew very slowly, creating serious fiscal challenges for both central and local governments (Lu, 2003; Shan, 1996). As part of Taiwan's democratization, the central government has been trying to reform the local election system and make local government more self-governing. However, the regulations about local self-governing are not well designed, and the local legislative and administrative authority (competence) are not well constructed either. In particular, regarding fiscal matters, local governments remain quite financially dependent on the central government, thereby creating a fairly high degree of central government control. Theoretically, then, there is no local financial crisis in Taiwan because the financial and administrative autonomy of local governments are limited. There is only a national financial crisis in Taiwan because everything is under the control of the central government (Hsu, 2001; Wang, 2007). In this section, we will discuss the financial problems encountered by local governments from three aspects: (1) institutional, (2) political, and (3) economic.

Institutional Problems

The strong centralization of Taiwan's fiscal system creates major institutional problems for its cities and counties. This is certainly the case for governmental revenues. The categories of local tax, tax base, tax rate, as well as fees and fines are all regulated by the central government, so that local governments cannot change them even if there are local financial needs (Lu, 2003; Yeh, 2003). The tax share between the central and local governments is also regulated by the national government. Based on the controversial *Allocation of Government Revenues and Expenditures Act*, the income tax, excise tax, and business tax are all categorized as national taxes, meaning that the central government has full control over the use of these tax revenues. For example, the central government grants 10% of the income and excise taxes to counties and cities and allocates these tax shares proportionally among local governments based on a fixed formula.

For some local governments, a significant proportion of their annual revenue comes in the form of a subsidy from the central government. These subsidies are divided into general grants and project grants. General grants are allocated based on a fixed formula. Local governments have to compete for project grants and initiate their own applications. It is obvious that project grants are not necessarily based upon local needs but might depend more upon the central government's preference. This subsidy system causes the following problems. First, there is competition among local governments for the grants. In terms of Taiwan's political realities, this means that local governments that have good contacts and relations (*guanxi*) with the central government can develop local projects that are preferred by the central government, thereby always obtaining project grants. Cities and counties that lack this *guanxi*, however, might not be able to get project grants even though they are in need (Chang, 2003; Lu, 2003). Second, this subsidy system gives local governments the incentive to develop local projects that meet the central government's preferences rather than local needs. Third, the availability of subsidies lessens the incentives for local governments to work on their budget balance or to use existing resources efficiently (Lu, p. 122; Yeh, 2003).

Fourth, and more broadly, the subsidy system increases the central government's control over local decision and policy making.

A considerable portion of local spending is also fixed or mandated by the central government, similarly to what are called unfunded mandates in the United States. According to the *Allocation of Government Revenues and Expenditures Act*, local police expenditures, education expenditures, and civil servant retirement pensions must be paid from local revenue. Accordingly, a significant amount of local spending is fixed. For example, more than 60% of local annual spending is for personnel. In addition, a local government is responsible for several social welfare expenditures regulated by the central government. Consequently, these fixed expenditures occupy so much of their annual budgets that local governments do not have much flexibility to develop projects customized for their localities (Chao & Liu, 2006; Wang, 2007; Yeh, 2003).

Another serious structural problem is that local governments have strong incentives to be less than totally honest in their budgeting, leading to very significant budget deficits. In order to balance their budget proposals, local governments have become very good at overestimating revenues to justify greater estimated expenditures. Based on the theory of public choice, bureaucrats prefer to maximize budgets because higher budgets mean more power. In addition, higher budgets allow Taiwan's cities and counties to respond to citizen demands for local development and public services. Thus, overestimating revenues make budget proposals look feasible and easier to pass the budget review by the city or county council (Chao & Liu, 2006; Wang, 2007). The following numbers show the story. Based upon local government financial statements for fiscal year 2007, 22 out of 25 local governments had their estimated revenues higher than real revenue. The gap between estimated and real revenue was NT$9.1 billion (about US $280 million) in Taipei County alone (Ministry of Audit, 2009).

Political Problems
Political dynamics also create problems for local government budgeting. City or county mayors are elected officials who do not want to alienate voters (Shan, 1996). This means that imposing a higher rate of a local tax will not be considered because whoever proposes higher taxes will almost certainly lose votes in the next election. Accordingly, local governments follow the less risky strategies of applying for more grants and asking for more subsidies from the central government, or even getting loans from banks (Wang, 2007). Furthermore, local politicians like to promise citizens some policies that are financially infeasible to gain electoral support. This makes annual spending increase without enough revenue to pay for it (Lu, 2003). The rivalry of political parties makes the situation even worse. Political benefit becomes the first priority when elected officials prepare the budget plan. Whatever policy that can earn more electoral support will be on the top of the budget priority list. Realistic budgeting and keeping the budget in balance, therefore, are often ignored under these circumstances.

Economic Problems
Two important economic problems facing local governments in Taiwan are that their revenue sources are quite constrained and that many face imposing debt burdens. Some

local governments are very limited in their own source revenues. The national average ratio of own source revenue

([total revenues − grants and subsidies from the central government]/total expenditures)

for local governments in fiscal year 2007 was only 55.57%. Moreover, there is a huge variation among local governments on this figure. Among all of the 25 local governments, this ratio ranged from 22% (in Lien-Chiang County) to 113% (in Taipei City). For 12 of the 25 local governments, the ratio of their own sources of revenue was less than 50%. Only five local governments had ratios over 70% (Taiwan National Statistics, 2009). These numbers certainly show the insufficiency of local governments' own sources of revenues. The limited own source revenues of local governments are, in addition, vulnerable to economic downturns. This is because property-related taxes (including the land value increment tax, land value tax, house tax, and deed tax) form the major financial source for local government. In economic downturns, the value of land drops, and there are fewer property transactions. Consequently, property-related tax revenues decrease, thereby increasing the fiscal stress on local governments.

The outstanding public debts of local governments have been rising dramatically in the past decade. According to the statistics on local public debts for fiscal year 2007, the highest three local governments with long-term (more than 1 year) outstanding debts are Tainan County, Hsin-Chu County, and Tainan City. The ratio of outstanding long-term debt to annual expenditures for them was 44.97%, 44.80%, and 43.43%, respectively. This almost reached the upper limit of 45% allowed by the Public Debt Act. For the ratio of outstanding short-term debt to annual expenditures, the three local government with the highest ratios were Taipei County, Hsin-Chu County, and Tainan County. These ratios were 30.04%, 29.91%, and 29.08%, respectively, which almost reached the upper limit of 30%. For local governments like Tainan County and Hsin-Chu County, the ratio of total public debt to annual expenditures was almost 75% (National Treasury Agency, 2009). These figures demonstrate that these local governments are under tremendous financial pressure.

THE BUDGET PRIORITIES OF THE DPP AND KMT

Taiwan's two major political parties, the KMT and DPP, are fiercely competitive, but because of historic circumstances politics in Taiwan revolve around somewhat different cleavages than in most other industrialized democracies. The KMT government, which Chiang Kai-shek installed when the KMT evacuated to Taiwan, was dominated by mainlanders who came with him, while many islanders (long-time residents of Taiwan who also were almost all ethnically Han Chinese) felt excluded from the government and treated as second-class citizens. The KMT strongly emphasized national security and reconquering China, promoted economic development, and did little to develop social welfare programs. Consequently, the political opposition, which became formalized in the DPP in 1986, emphasized democratization (which was also advocated by KMT reformers), ethnic justice, antimilitarism, and KMT corruption in their political appeals, while economic policy was not really that controversial. Social welfare policy was subject to a more complex evolution. During the 1980s, social movements (rather than political parties) became the leading advocates of reform and expansion, the DPP assumed a much more supportive position in the early 1990s, and when this appeared to benefit them politically, the KMT co-opted their more popular issues by the end of the decade. The DPP's winning control of government in 2001 also changed the partisan mix a little. The KMT became more liberal on social welfare, in part to embarrass the government which was facing strong budget constraints. In contrast, President Chen's assertive policy toward China made the DPP much more conscious of security policy and led the KMT-controlled legislature to reject large arms sales from the United States (Clark, 2002).

In terms of western ideology, the DPP would be considered the more liberal party in Taiwan, and the KMT is the more conservative. This section explores whether these ideological differences can be seen in the budget policies of Presidents Lee Teng-hui of the KMT and Chen Shui-bian of the DPP late in their administrations (1998 and 2006, respectively). As a first cut, we examined data on the overall budgets for Taiwan's national government in Table 6-1. There is certainly evidence that Chen pursued more liberal budgetary policies in even these aggregate data. First, total public spending grew by 42.6% in current New Taiwan dollars from NT$1.1 trillion to NT$1.6 trillion during this 8-year period. Second and probably more importantly, the growth rate in expenditures was almost double that of revenues at 23.8% from NT$1.1 trillion to NT$1.4 trillion. The spending increases under Chen clearly outstripped revenue growth by a considerable extent. This created a third characteristic of liberal government: the explosion of the government's budget deficit, which skyrocketed from a small surplus of NT$13 billion in 1998 to a huge deficit of NT$195 billion in 2006 that constituted 13.9% of the national government's revenues. Consequently, the deficit has now become a very significant problem.

Table 6-1

Total Revenues and Expenditures of the National Government, FY 1998 and 2006

	1998	2006	% Increase
Revenues	1,134,399,069[a]	1,403,822,810	23.8
Expenditures	1,121,386,536[b]	1,599,560,424	42.6
Balance	+13,012,533	−195,737,614	
Balance (% Revenues)	+1.1	−13.9	

Unit: thousands of NTD

Source: DGBAS Government Budget. Available at: http://www.dgbas.gov.tw/ct.asp?xItem=3374&CtNode=1690. Accessed February 26, 2009.

[a] The original amount of revenues for FY 1998 is 1,225,264,656 (in thousands of NTD). However, a very significant difference in revenues between FY 1998 and 2006 is that the debt revenues are included in 1998 revenue figure but not in the amount for 2006. To make the figures directly comparable, the debt revenues in 1998 (90,865,587 in thousands of NTD) were subtracted from the 1998 original revenues figure.

[b] The original amount of expenditures for FY 1998 is 1,225,264,656 (in thousands of NTD). However, a very significant difference in expenditures between FY 1998 and 2006 is that the expenditures for debt paydown were included in 1998 expenditures figure but not in the 2006 ones. To make the figures directly comparable, the expenditures for debt paydown in 1998 (103,878,120 in thousands of NTD) were subtracted from the 1998 original expenditures figure.

Table 6-2

The Revenue Sources of the National Government, FY 1998 & 2006

	1998		2006	
	Revenue	%	Revenue	%
Tax and monopoly	847,033,000	74.6	989,752,000	70.5
Fees and fines	33,728,419	3.0	74,880,478	5.3
Public properties	54,095,172	4.8	65,368,899	4.7
Surplus of public enterprises	184,492,556	16.3	257,490,778	18.3
Other	15,049,922	1.3	16,330,655	1.2
Total	1,134,399,069	100.0	1,403,822,810	100.0

Source: DGBAS Government Budget. Available at: http://www.dgbas.gov.tw/ct.asp?xItem=3374&CtNode=1690. Accessed March 25, 2010.

The more detailed breakdown of revenue sources in Table 6-2 indicates that the Chen administration was fairly constrained in increasing taxes and other sources of government income since the structure of Taiwan's public revenues only changed at the margins between 1998 and 2006. While liberal governments supposedly want to tax and spend, the share of taxes in total revenues actually dropped significantly by four percentage points from 74.6% to 70.5%, demonstrating that the DPP administration was not able to fund an expansion of social services through increased taxation. The use of fees increased very substantially, more than doubling from NT$34 billion to NT$75 billion. However, this was still only 5.3% of the budget in 2006. The other source of increased revenue came from the surpluses of state corporations, which jumped by 40% from NT$184 billion to NT$257 billion, representing an increase in the share of public revenues from 16.3% to 18.3%. Squeezing state corporations harder would normally be a conservative strategy, but their long association with the KMT administration has generated suspicion on the part of the DPP. Thus, a survey of the change in the revenues of the national government between the Lee and Chen presidencies implies less a change in ideology than an apparent inelasticity of the government's revenue system.

Generally, government spending patterns are considered to be the best reflection of an administration's political priorities. Table 6-3, which presents data on the budget shares of the major items in the central government's budget for 1998 and 2006, constitutes fairly strong evidence that the Chen administration was markedly more liberal than the preceding Lee one. This can be seen in categories whose priorities both rose and fell. First, Chen Shui-bian cut spending in two important areas. One was national defense, which is normally championed by conservatives. Despite the DPP's more aggressive policy toward China, the defense budget actually fell slightly in terms of current NT dollars from $257 to $254 billion over the 8 years under analysis. Since overall expenditures rose rapidly during this period (see Table 6-1), the share or priority of defense in the national budget dropped by nearly a third from 23 to 16%. Expenditures for pensions suffered an even more drastic cut, as they fell from NT$153 billion in 1998 to NT$134 billion in 2006, which resulted in their share

Table 6-3				

Expenditure Categories of the National Government, FY 1998 and 2006				
	1998		**2006**	
	Expenditure	%	Expenditure	%
General affairs	110,398,410	9.8	173,682,879	10.9
National defense	257,481,060	23.0	253,787,490	15.9
Education, science, and culture	187,148,032	16.7	323,775,686	20.2
Economic development	128,426,059	11.5	204,358,910	12.8
Social welfare	157,703,109	14.1	296,567,413	18.5
Community development and environmental protection	16,557,881	1.5	21,207,003	1.3
Retirement payment and pensions	152,954,952	13.6	134,047,495	8.4
Debt interest payment and administration	71,544,368	6.3	139,514,167	8.7
General subsidy and others	39,172,665	3.5	52,619,381	3.3
Total	1,121,386,536	100.0	1,599,560,424	100.0

Source: DGBAS Government Budget. Available at: http://www.dgbas.gov.tw/ct.asp?xItem=3374&CtNode=1690. Accessed March 25, 2010.

of the budget plummeting from 13.6% to 8.4%. Normally, liberals would oppose and conservatives would support reducing the benefits and pensions of public employees. In Taiwan, though, the DPP is suspicious of many long-time civil servants, including old soldiers, because they worked for the KMT during the authoritarian era.

In contrast to these cuts, the Chen administration considerably expanded spending in two liberal budget categories. Spending on social welfare almost doubled from NT$158 billion to NT$297 billion between fiscal years 1998 and 2006, causing its share of the overall budget to jump from 14.1% to 18.5%. Likewise, spending for education, science, and culture rose almost as much from NT$187 billion to NT$324 billion, as its share of the budget increased from 16.7% to 20.2%. The Chen administration was clearly able, therefore, to shift the central government's budget in a more liberal direction. However, another previously noted liberal aspect of his budgeting, the burgeoning payments for debt service, which approximately doubled from NT$71.5 billion to NT$139.5 billion, will almost certainly constrain Taiwan's budgetary choices in the future. Thus, ironically, liberal budget practices in the past might well promote the conservative objective of limited government in the future, as well as suggesting that both conservatives and liberals should have an interest in budget reform in Taiwan.

Conclusions

The description of the overall system of public finance in Taiwan in the first part of this chapter certainly demonstrates that there is a strong need for very substantial reform in Taiwan's budget process. Regarding the executive branch, the budgets are far too centralized, rigid, and short-term in focus, as well as lacking mechanisms to promote horizontal coordination and cooperation among different agencies and authorities. For its part, the Legislative Yuan suffers from a lack of professionalization and intense politicization, both of which undercut rational budget making. Moreover, whereas the four stages of the overall budget process (preparation, review, execution, and audit) should be strongly connected and integrated, each of them seems very isolated and disconnected from the others in Taiwan's budgeting process. The two case studies of specific issues in the second part present a more mixed picture. If anything, there is more need for drastic reform for local government finance than for the national budgeting system. In contrast, there were enough differences in the budgets of the Lee Teng-hui and Chen Shui-bian administrations to demonstrate a very significant degree of flexibility, although even here, growing deficits and public debt indicate the need for remedial action. Despite the strong need for reform, however, the political realities of contemporary Taiwan make significant reform fairly unlikely.

Discussion Questions

1. What are the primary historical legacies of Taiwan's political system and how do they affect the country's budget system?
2. What are the major stages in the budget process? How well integrated are they? What reforms do you think should be implemented to make the budget system operate more smoothly and effectively?
3. How important are legislative politics for budget making in Taiwan? Do you think that this helps or hurts effective budgeting? What could be done to enhance the legislature's contribution to budget making?
4. What are the major problems facing local governments in the budget area? Do you think that they should be given more or less autonomy? Overall, what reforms would you suggest to reduce the fiscal stress on Taiwanese local governments?
5. How different were the budgets of the KMT's Lee Teng-hui and the DPP's Chen Shui-bian? What does this imply about budgetary politics in Taiwan?

References

Botjer, G. F. (1979). *A short history of nationalist China, 1919–1949*. New York: Putnam.

Chang, S. S. (2003). Current fiscal problems and the outlook for fiscal reform in Taiwan. *Journal of Contemporary Accounting, 3*, 123–142.

Chao, Y-C., & Liu, H-S. (2006). Analysis of local finance. *National policy forum*. Available at: http://www.npf .org.tw/post/2/3671. Accessed March 24, 2010.

Clark, C. (1989). *Taiwan's development: Implications for contending political economy paradigms*. Westport, CT: Greenwood.

Clark, C. (2002). Democratization and the evolving nature of parties, issues, and constituencies in the ROC. In P. C. Y. Chow (Ed.), *Taiwan's modernization in global perspective* (pp. 135–159). Westport, CT: Praeger.

Copper, J. F. (2009). *Taiwan: Nation-state or province?* (5th ed.). Boulder, CO: Westview.

Directorate-General of Budgeting, Accounting and Statistics (DGBAS). (2009a). *Instructions and guidelines on the budget execution of central government agencies.* Taipei: Author.

Directorate-General of Budgeting, Accounting and Statistics (DGBAS). (2009b). *Instructions and guidelines on the preparation of the central and local government budget.* Taipei: Author.

Directorate-General of Budgeting, Accounting and Statistics (DGBAS). (2009c). *Regulation for preparing the central government general budget of fy 2009.* Taipei: Author.

Eastman, L. E. (1974). *The abortive revolution: China under nationalist rule, 1927–1937.* Cambridge: Harvard University Press.

Hsu, J-H. (2001). The study of local governments' budgetary decision making of expenditures. *Journal of Public Administration, 5,* 1–17.

Hsu, J-H. (2005). The study of Taiwan's fiscal transparency. *Public Finance Review, 37*(4), 15–23.

The Legislative Yuan of the Republic of China (2010). *Legislative Procedures.* Available at: http://www.ly.gov.tw/ly/en/01_introduce/01_introduce_10.jsp?ItemNO=EN080000. Accessed April 5, 2010.

Lu, B-Y. (2003). The central-local fiscal legal system: Taiwanese legislators' perspective. *Public Administration & Policy, 36,* 119–154.

Ministry of Audit (MOA). (2009). *2007 Annual report of financial statements of local governments.* Available at: http://www.audit.gov.tw/Public/Doc. Accessed March 24, 2010.

National Treasury Agency. (2009). *Local government public debt statistics of FY 2007.* Available at: http://www.nta.gov.tw/files. Accessed March 24, 2010.

Rigger, S. (1999). *Politics in Taiwan:Voting for democracy.* London: Routledge.

Shan, C. C. (1996). To inaugurate a new local finance situation. *The Chinese Public Administration Review, 3,* 123–142.

Su, T. T. (2002). The fiscal transparency of local finance. *Journal of Chinese Local Self-Governance, 55*(7), 25–31.

Taiwan National Statistics. (2009). *Index of local finance.* Available at: http://61.60.106.82/pxweb/Dialog/varval.asp?ma=CS2501A1A&ti=&path=../database/CountyStatistics/&lang=9. Accessed March 24, 2010.

Tien, H. M. (Ed.) (1996). *Taiwan's electoral politics and democratic transition: Riding the third wave.* Armonk, NY: M. E. Sharpe.

Wade, R. (1990). *Governing the market: Economic theory and the role of government in East Asian industrialization.* Princeton: Princeton University Press.

Wang, Y. K. (2007). The fiscal research of local government. *Journal of Business, 15,* 1–19.

Wilbur, M. (1983). *The nationalist revolution in China, 1923–1928.* Cambridge: Cambridge University Press.

Yeh, C. N. (2003). The amendments of the law governing the allocation of government revenues and expenditures as well as the future of local governments finance. *The Chinese Public Administration Review, 12*(4), 205–228.

Chapter 7

Public Budgeting and Financial Management Performance in Thailand

Arwiphawee Srithongrung

Learning Objectives

- Distinguish the budgeting process in Thailand from your country of origin.
- Distinguish the financial management approaches in Thailand from other approaches.
- Examine the various measurements of financial management outcomes.
- Know and understand how the central government budgetary structure is organized.
- Examine how budget reforms have affected the Thai budget process.

Introduction

The Kingdom of Thailand is an ancient unitary state that has existed for about 800 years. Under the democratic regime introduced in 1933, the country's budget preparation and budget document, as well as the financial management system, was developed to become relatively more sophisticated than in the previous period. By 1958, the Thailand Bureau of Budget (BOB) was promoted to be an executive department for the review, analysis, and consolidation of agency requests under an ideologic view that budget and spending policies were tools to develop the country economically and socially (Thailand Development Research Institution, 2004). This view was adopted based on the recommendation of the Public Administration Service Committee in the 1950s (Veerakul, 2005). This fundamental value reflects the core ideology of the budgetary function viewed through the country's leading public officials, that the budget should be the main blueprint in planning the country's economy and society through allocation efficiency derived from systematic approaches, such as management analysis. Judging from the message in the budget documents, this view was used as the major rationale for budget reforms throughout the democratic period, from 1959 to 2007.

At present, Thailand is executing a performance-based budget (PBB), in which the country's master plan is incorporated into budget preparation, the adoption of an accrual accounting basis to complement the country's strategic budget, and the utilization of an information technology system to enhance the preauditing capacity of the Comptroller General's Department. Based on the fundamental principle of the Thai government in using budgeting and financial management as the country's policy planning and public management tool, this chapter describes the country's most recent budgeting process and financial management, analyzes the likely impacts of the country's financial management practices on the country's macroeconomy, and offers recommendations for future practices.

The following section describes the country's budgeting process in the present period. The third section evaluates financial performance during the 1990s and 2000s. The fourth section outlines the country's budget reforms experienced through the democratic period, focusing on the most recent reform, performance-based budgeting. The last section provides a summary and conclusions.

The Budgeting Process in Thailand

Constitutionally, the Thai government is a dual system, comprising central and local governments. The central government is comprised of 19 ministries,[1] the Office of the Prime Minister (OPM), and eight independent organizations.[2] Although the Thai government is considered a dual government system, in practice, it has a unitary system.[3] Public service decentralization has actually been limited due to the limited income of local communities (especially for those in rural areas), lack of technical and personnel expertise in financial management, and disagreement on the part of local groups that possess informal power regarding public management at the local level (Trakarnsirinont, 2006).

The Thai government structure is comprised of three branches: the legislature, the executive, and the judiciary. The legislature, or Parliament, is also called the National Assembly. There are 630 elected and appointed members in the two chambers: the Thailand House of Representatives and the Senate of Thailand. Of the 480 MPs in the House of Representatives, 400 are elected through provincial constituency voting (76 provinces).[4] The Senate is comprised of 76 elected senators from 76 provinces, and 74 senators are nominated by the Senate Selection Committee. The total elected and appointed members in the Senate is 150. The House and Senate members undertake 4 and 6 years terms, respectively. For the executive branch, the prime minister is the head of the government. The premier minister (PM) is the leader of the major party in the House of Representatives and is elected by the MPs in the lower chamber. The prime minister appoints cabinet members, which can be elected officials in the lower house or nonelected officials from outside the lower house (e.g., career civil servants). As of December 2008, the Thai cabinet had 19 ministries, 3 deputy prime ministers, and 11 deputy ministers. The judiciary of Thailand is comprised of the Judiciary Court, Administrative Court, and Constitutional Court. All judges are appointed by His Majesty the King.

Figure 7-1 shows the organizations involved in central government budgeting and financial management. The organizations under the executive branch, including the BOB, the Office of the National Social and Economic Development Board (NSEDB), the Ministry of Finance (MOF), and an independent agency, the Bank of Thailand (BOT), are the four major actors in the budget preparation and execution stages. These four actors are known as the Gang of Four in the international budgeting literature, given that they play a highly centralized role in designating strategic public management policies, annual budgeting and financial management policies, and setting up macroeconomic policy (e.g., fiscal and monetary policies). The National Assembly makes decisions regarding appropriation approvals in the budget decision stage. The Comptroller's General Department is an independent organization, and the Office of the Auditor General of Thailand conduct financial and performance audits in the budget evaluation stage. The Constitutional Court involves budget decisions when there are grievances and appeals in the voting process. The country's fiscal year ranges from October 1st through September 30th of the following calendar year. The Thai budget process consists of a budget preparation, legislative decision, execution, and audit phase. The phases are as follows.

PHASE 1: BUDGET PREPARATION

Annual budget preparation lasts from January to June of each calendar year. Three other activities, including administrative and policy planning, national budget policy establishment, and budget consolidation are conducted during this phase. First, the BOB and the Civil Services Commission study the country's 5-year Master Plan, known as the National Social and Economic Development Plan (NSEDP), before preparing the Government Administrative Plans (GAP). This plan lasts 4 years as it is meant to coincide with the electoral term of the government (Blondal & Kim, 2006). The GAP is revised annually by the BOB and Civil Service Commissions to be responsive to the political, administrative, and economic changes that often occur during each administration.[5] The BOB uses the GAP as the main strategic guidance in its budget allocation decisions and recommendations. By law, the GAP established at this stage must be approved by the cabinets before the departments (i.e., operating agencies) in each ministry and state enterprises can begin to develop their own individual short- and long-term administrative and policy plans, which last 1 year and 4 years, respectively. These individual agencies' plans must be responsive to

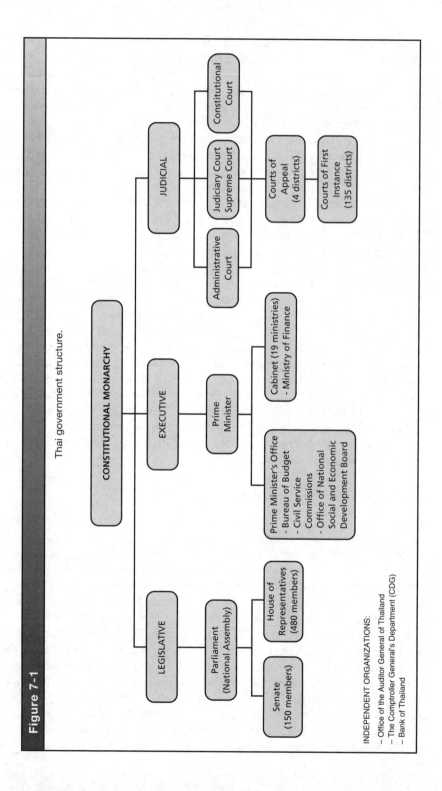

Figure 7-1

Thai government structure.

INDEPENDENT ORGANIZATIONS:

– Office of the Auditor General of Thailand
– The Comptroller General's Department (CDG)
– Bank of Thailand

the country's central plan. At the same time, the MOF forecasts the country's annual total revenue within a 2-year time frame and transmits revenue estimation to the BOB. This task takes about 7 weeks in total, ranging from the first week of January to the third week of February.

Next, each bureau and organization prepares their individual budget requests based on their own short- and long-term plans. The BOB prepares its baseline budget using forecasted revenue, economic performance predictions, and debt levels obtained from the MOF for further use in establishing the Annual Budget Policy Proposal, which is used as a guideline in budget allocation. Meanwhile, the MOF, the BOB, the BOT, and the NSEDB participate in a series of meetings to mutually estimate total revenue during the 2-year time frame, determine total expenditure in the coming fiscal year, designate the budget format of the budget document for the coming fiscal year, as well as establish the country's spending policy structures (e.g., a combination of programs and projects in each of the seven service functions, and spending levels for each spending type, such as current and investment expenditures). In general, the seven service functions include education, national defense, economic development, public welfare, general administration, public safety, among others. As a result of the meeting process, the BOB issues the Annual Budget Policy Proposal, which describes the annual strategic budget plan, targeted spending on specific policy and program areas, total expenditure, and total functional spending. This annual budget policy is considered as a blueprint in accomplishing the goals stated in the 4-year administration and policy plan. After the BOB, BOT, MOF, and NSEDB have endorsed the proposal, the BOB submits the proposal to the cabinet and the PM for approval. After the approval, the BOB issues budget request forms, instructions, and guidelines, including the central government's policy priorities, the strategic budget plan, and targeted goals in each public service function to all bureaus and agencies in each of the ministries as well as the state enterprises. This activity takes 2 weeks in total, ranging from the end of February to the beginning of March.

Concurrently, agencies, as well as state enterprises, submit their budget requests in both summary and detailed forms, as well as their estimated total revenue, to their ministry heads for approval. The ministries then consolidate budget requests and transmit them to the BOB. This submission must be completed by the second week of March. In this first round of submissions, spending usually exceeds ceiling limits set by the Annual Budget Policy Proposal. After the Annual Budget Policy Proposal is approved by the PM, the ministries submit their requests to the BOB that meet the BOB's ceiling for the second round. During this round, the ministries actually do not reallocate funds across programs or projects in practice (Blondal & Kim, 2006). This means that final program and project spending at the lower level in Thailand are based on fair shares according to revenue limits and expenditure ceilings, rather than the merits of the programs or projects in terms of maximizing social benefits to public expenditure that should result from the ministry's systematic project-ranking process. The BOB then consolidates the country's annual budget and prepares the national budget document.

At present, the national budget document is comprised of four main elements: (1) a budget message which describes economic outlooks, the annual budget policy, budget structure, budget allocation based on national administrative and policy strategic plans, and total spending by types of expenditure; (2) estimated revenue by types of revenue sources, collection departments (i.e., The Revenue Department, The Excise Department, The Custom's Departments, State Enterprises, and others), ministries, and the country's regions (Bangkok, North, Northeast, Central, and South); (3) budget expenditure classified by programs and functions; and (4) government finance, which includes the treasury account balance, outstanding debts, and foreign aid. The third and fourth elements resulted from the 2006 statutory requirement that the annual budget document transmitted to Parliament must list programs and projects under each service function, along with program goals, objectives, strategies, and estimated spending, and provide financial information to aid parliamentary decisions regarding budget approvals. The budget document is then transmitted to the cabinets for revision and suggestions. Once the budget document is revised and approved by the cabinet, the BOB issues the draft of the fiscal year budget bill, which must be approved again by the cabinet before being transmitted to the National Assembly for budget decisions and bill approval during the decision-making phase (Thailand Bureau of Budget, 2009).

This preparation process suggests three things. First, the central budget preparation is relatively solid in terms of adhering to fundamental principles suggested by the strategic budgeting literature. These technical activities range from the Gang of Four's establishment of the 4-year GAP, which logically reflects the country's 5-year master plan; the NSEDP; the development of the Annual Budget Policy Proposal, which is based on a systematic baseline budget; the macroeconomic policy set by the MOF and BOT; and the MOF's revenue forecast, as well as the annual strategies identified in the GAP. This process suggests that the Thai budget process during this phase is systematic. Second, budget preparation is highly centralized. As mentioned, the GAP and the Annual Budget Policy Proposal are established in a closed-door system, where only senior officers from the Gang of Four participate. Ministerial and departmental officers that are close to public service clients do not participate in this national policy decision process. Furthermore, public participation is limited, given that budget hearings do not occur. The National Assembly's policy priorities are not incorporated in such a process. Third, although the GAP and the Annual Budget Policy Proposal are solidly established based on technical steps; however, in practice, they might not help tailor effective resource allocation because the GAP encompasses all activities necessary to accomplish strategic goals (Blondal & Kim, 2006), which are usually categorized into six or seven areas, reflecting all functional spending specified in the budget documents.[6] Since the GAP is used as a reference for the Annual Budget Policy Proposal, all programs and projects proposed by ministries and agencies are qualified to be funded, given that they will fit at least one of the strategic goals set in the GAP. This practice, when combined with broad criteria used by the BOB to evaluate budget requests, results in incremental spending, given that all programs are funded as long as they pass the BOB criteria.

PHASE 2: LEGISLATIVE APPROPRIATION

This phase takes about 3 months, ranging from the end of June to the end of September. The legislative decision-making process begins after the PM transmits the budget document to Parliament. There are three periods in the house budget decision process. The first period includes budget consideration by the MPs and the Budget Bill Drafting Committees (appointed by the MPs). The MPs vote for the budget document through a simple majority voting rule (this is known as a parliamentary vote-of-confidence). If the MPs vote of support is less than 50%, the PM must resign, the Parliament must be dissolved, and a national election will take place. During this period, the drafters can veto portions of the budget by deleting some spending categories, which is limited to only debt principal and interest payment and prior appropriation, but they cannot insert any new spending into the budget. If the PM wins a vote of confidence, the Scrutiny Committee, which is appointed by the PM and led by the MOF head, will examine the budget.

The second period involves the Scrutiny Committees' consideration and decisions. The Scrutiny Committees are divided into several subcommittees responsible for examining program spending within each service function. The decision-making process is conducted through a series of meetings among Scrutiny Committees, subcommittees, and ministry heads in a closed office (Blondal & Kim, 2006). At this point, the MPs must vote to amend individual program spending or suggest changes in the PM's budget if they disagree with the drafters. But in practice, changes affect the PM's budget only at a marginal level—that is, the total spending levels and functional spending ceiling are the same, while some programs might be shuffled within each function, given that the amendments must be approved by the PM. During the final period, the House votes for the entire budget through a simple majority rule and transmits the budget to the Senate. The House approval process must be completed within 105 days after the budget document is transmitted from the PM; otherwise, the budget document is automatically approved by the House and moved on to the Senate. The Senate then has 14 days to vote for the budget bill through a simple majority voting rule. The Senate's failure to comply with this timeline results in automatic bill approval by the Senate. The bill that receives more than a 50% vote in the Senate will then be signed by the King and the budget bill is effective for the coming fiscal year. In the case that the bill does not pass in the Senate, but it does pass in the House, the House has the ability to override the Senate with a simple majority vote. Hence, the role of the Senate is nullified and the bill moves forward in the process. Should 10% of the members in each chamber appeal the voting process based on a lack of due processes, the dispute shall be resolved by the Constitutional Court within 7 days. If the budget bill process is not completed by the end of September, the previous year's budget is used for the coming fiscal year.

The legislative budget process described suggests that the Thai budgeting process is executively dominated based on three facts: the country's political regime, constitutional restrictions on Parliament's roles, and the budget formulation process in practice. First, as described by Fred Riggs (1966; 1981), the Thai political system is considered a bureaucratic polity, where the state bureaucracy, which is filled with elite-class senior civil servants[7] and military officers, monopolize power rather than sharing it with Parliament. As a result, a check and balance system is not effective, relatively, compared to other democratic regimes. This situation is exasperated by local beliefs that political officers are self-interested and tend to be corrupt. Political party fighting and indistinctive partisan ideologies also weaken the role of Parliament. Thus, for a bureaucratic polity state like Thailand, senior civil servants have both political and administrative power regarding public policy and management, including the national budget.

Second, the state constitution restricts the parliamentary role in the sense that the MP's vote for amendment, must be approved by the PM, the amendment must be approved by all members from the same political party, and the House is only allowed to reduce spending instead of reducing and adding new spending. Third, given that the House and Senate do not participate in reviewing budget requests at the preparation stage, nor directly provide advice to agencies' heads, inputs from elected officials based on constituencies' needs and interests are not thoroughly considered. The 105 days for the House and 14 days for Senate decisions, as well as the failures to comply with this timeline (resulting in automatic yes votes) suggest that the budget process does not support Parliament's roles.

PHASE 3: BUDGET EXECUTION

The budget execution phase ranges from October to September during the following year. Operating units, including departments and state enterprises, prepare their annual work plan for programs and projects and fill out the BOB's form for the annual spending plan, which must be aligned with the activities and operation phases stated in its work plans. By mid-November, the BOB approves the proposed spending plans. All appropriations, including personnel and operating expenses, subsidies, and investments, except debt authorization, are disbursed two times during a fiscal year. The first period is in the third week of November, and the total disbursement amount covers the operating units' work plan during November and April. The second period releases the rest of the total appropriation scheduled to be used in the second week of April through September of the following calendar year. Operating units may adjust their annual work plan and spending plan during the fiscal year; the adjustment, including transferring funds from one type of appropriation to another, must be submitted to the BOB by the end of April, along with a demonstration that all of the programs are executed as identified in the appropriation bills. For debt authorization, the Policy and Strategic Planning Department of the BOB submits the total aggregated debt amount to the ministry cabinet for approval by the end of November. The operation units can incur authorized debt after the cabinet's approval, around the second week of April. Debt amount and authorizations can be adjusted through official requests by operating units and if approved by the cabinet, the new debt is authorized during the second week of August. Unspent appropriations cannot roll over to the next fiscal year; however, obligation can be forwarded to the next fiscal year.

Since fiscal year 1998, the Thai government has used Government Fiscal Management Information Systems (GFMIS) to disburse appropriations to the operating units. This information technology system reduces paperwork and thus streamlines the bureaucratic processes and establishes systematic, tractable, and transparent spending records. Departments and bureaus file appropriation disbursement schedules in information networks called ZSUB_ AG_ MASTER, which is accessible during the entire fiscal year by the BOB and the Comptroller General's Department (CGD). The CGD is fully responsible for ensuring that the appropriation is expended in a correct manner country-wide. After all, units complete their disbursement schedule filing process, the CGD establishes a disbursement database and issues numeric codes for the final budget spenders listed by the bureaus and departments authorized for appropriations. The final spenders of each authorized department include other government units at the same level or at lower levels, suppliers, or contractors. Spending is recorded in the database whenever the appropriations are cashed by either the authorized spending units or final spenders. This information technology system thus significantly enhances the CGD's preauditing capacity and performance. The CGD updates and reviews the budget status every month.

An internal financial audit is conducted by the operating units (e.g., agencies). The operating units submit a budget execution report which contains implementation results, including outputs and outcomes, as well as financial transaction records, to the BOB quarterly. By the end of November, the operating unit submits its annual performance report, especially the program's goal accomplishments, outputs, and outcomes, which are aligned with the goals of each individual supervising ministry, program progress, and barriers to success, to the BOB. The BOB consolidates the performance and fiscal reports of the executive agencies and releases a summary document for each quarter. The BOB's performance and fiscal report are available for a 10-year period through the bureau's Web site (www.bb.go.th/bbhomeeng).

PHASE 4: BUDGET EVALUATION

This phase involves financial and performance audits of the external government. The CGD is responsible for controlling revenue receipts and budget disbursements during the budget execution phase, maintaining government accounting, and auditing and preparing an annual governmental financial statement during the evaluation phase. To be responsive to the new budget reform, Thailand has used a modified accrual accounting since fiscal year 2001, 2 years after the country officially adopted a PBB. According to the Public Sector Accounting Policies and Principles (CGD, 2001), a modified accrual account, which reports government expenditure when obligation occurs and government revenue when total amount is known, is adopted by the Thai government at all levels to support the country's results-oriented management reform, in that it provides useful accounting information for budget planning and evaluation of the country's entire economy. The CGD, which is a department in the Office of the Auditor General (OAG), audits and endorses the national financial statements. The country's annual financial report, which includes a Statement of Receipts and Payments, a Statement of Financial Status, a Currency Reserve Account, and Notes, is prepared by the CGD and submitted to the prime minister and Parliament.

The auditing officers in the CGD and OAG audit both program and financial performance, focusing on compliance with laws, appropriation bills, and the country's policy statements and regulations. They, however, focus more on detecting financial waste and frauds in public spending rather than program efficiency and effectiveness. The heads of the OAG and the CGD are appointed by the PM, approved by the Parliament, and endorsed by His Majesty the King. The auditors are not independent enough to execute investigations, given that they are in executive agencies, but this limitation is compromised by their responsibilities to report to the Parliament. The State Audit Act of BE 2522 grants the OAG the authority to summon audited officers or agencies to submit evidence and to testify as witnesses (Henry & Attavikamtorn, 1999). This adds a greater degree of independence regarding program and financial examinations to the OAG.

Since 1996, each government operating unit under the executive branch, including departments, independent agencies, state enterprises, and local governments has been required to prepare its own balance sheet and financial statement and submit its report to the OAG within 3 months after the fiscal year ends. The CGD examines the operating unit's financial report without endorsement (Henry & Attavikamtorn, 1999). The time frame for the annual financial report is October 1st to September 30th.

Financial Management Performance

This section describes the size and growth of the central government expenditures, finance, and budget structure. Table 7-1 presents the path of government spending in Thailand from 1993 to 2007. Similar to the private sector, government spending contributes to a country's national income and product account measured through gross domestic product (GDP). According to Mikesell (2006), there are two types of government spending that affect a macroeconomy, current expenditure and investment. Current government expenditures include government purchases and transfer payments. Government purchases occur when a government buys production inputs that last for 1 year (e.g., materials and labor from the private sector for service production and delivery). A transfer payment is a resource redistributed to some specific group or groups of people entitled by constitutions (e.g., people that live below the poverty line).

Both spending types occur every year. Government purchases are further divided into two types: consumption and investment. Consumption includes buying materials and labor lasting for 1 year, while the investment includes public infrastructure that has a long useful life for more than 1 year (Mikesell, 2006).

As shown in Table 7-1, from 1993 to 2007, current expenditure was at about 9% to 12% of Thailand's GDP. Government size is relatively small compared to that in Organisation for Economic Co-operation and Development (OECD) countries, which range from around 14% to 24% (OECD, 2005). Current expenditure has grown from baht 292 billion in 1993, which is about 9.4% of GDP to baht 491 billion, approximately 12% in real 1988 baht value. During the 14-year period, Thailand's current expenditure has grown approximately 5% per year on average. This growth rate has mainly resulted from increasing transfer payments, whose annual average growth rate is about 13% per year. However, given that the transfer payment size is only about 0.3% and 1.3% in relation to the country's GDP, from 1993 to 2007, respectively, this spending was relatively small.

TABLE 7-1

General Government Spending in the National Income and Product Account

	1994	1996	1998	2000	2002	2004	2006	2007	Average annual growth rate across 15-year period
Current Expenditures	**243.4**	**281.8**	**290.4**	**334.2**	**361.6**	**399**	**452.5**	**491.4**	**5%**
Consumptions	220.9	260.5	263	277.1	286.1	309.9	353.2	385.6	4%
Employee compensation	128.9	149.5	173.3	180.3	192.2	200.6	219	234.6	4%
Purchases from enterprises and abroad	92	111	89.7	96.9	93.8	109.2	134.3	151	5%
Transfer payments	7.1	14.9	16.1	23.1	31.1	42	48.5	53.7	13%
Current transfers to households	6.6	14.4	15.7	22.4	30.7	41.2	48	52.9	14%
Current transfers to the rest of the world	0.5	0.5	0.4	0.7	0.4	0.8	0.5	0.9	4%
Interest on the public debt	15.3	6.4	11.3	34	44.4	47.2	50.8	52	7%
Consumption and gross investment	**399.5**	**505.7**	**461.3**	**428.3**	**425.1**	**449.3**	**508.1**	**549.8**	**3%**
Consumption expenditure	220.9	260.5	263	277.1	286.1	309.9	353.2	385.6	4%
Central government	206.4	237.1	241.5	249.8	254	266.9	299.8	325.9	4%
Local authority	14.6	23.4	21.5	27.3	32.1	43	53.4	59.8	11%
Gross investment	178.6	245.2	198.3	151.2	139	139.4	154.9	164.1	1%
Residential	9.3	13.2	8.6	7.3	4.6	7.5	19.7	24.6	9%
Nonresidential	50.9	62.2	44.4	25.4	21.1	17.1	19.4	24.7	–2%
Other construction	118.4	169.9	145.4	118.6	113.3	114.8	115.8	114.8	1%
Comparison data									
Wage and salaries of general government employees	106.8	125.7	147.2	155.7	165.7	171.8	189.8	204.3	5%
GDP at 1988 prices (in billions of baht)	2693	3115.3	2749.7	3008.4	3237	3688.2	4059.6	4259.6	4%
Gross fixed capital formation (GFCF) at 1988 prices (in billions of baht)	1111.1	1323	585.3	597.4	643.8	816.4	937.4	949.3	0%
Growth rate of GDP at 1988 prices (%)	9	5.9	–10.5	4.8	5.3	6.3	5.2	4.9	5%
Implicit GDP deflator 1988 = 100	134.8	148	168.3	163.6	168.4	176	193.2	199.9	3%
Population (in millions; as of July 1)	58.7	60	61.2	62.2	63.1	64.2	65.2	65.8	1%

Sources: Office of the National Economic and Social Development Board. Available at: http://www.nesdb.go.th/Default.aspx?tabid=94. Accessed March 25, 2010.

This current expenditure size and growth rate is a spending benchmark set by the BOT and the MOF based on the country's fiscal conservative policy. The country's fiscal conservative policy was characterized by its balanced-budget law and revenue surplus throughout the entire period of the 1980s and 2000s, except during the years 1997 to 2002, when overall revenue surplus was not achieved, although public expenditure was cut to about 10% from 1997 to 1998, from baht 932 billion in 1997 to baht 843 billion in 1998 (see Total Expenditure row in Table 7-1). This overall deficit was due to the country's use of a cash balance to maintain a national reserve fund to recover the country's low credits, coupled with total revenue decline at about 15% from baht 848 billion in 1997 to baht 718 billion in 1998 (see Total Revenue, Overall Surplus/Deficit, and Financing rows in Table 7-1). This situation is a result of the country's 1997 economic crisis, when the Thai baht was depreciated in the world capital market due to the fixed exchange rate the country adopted in the 1970s. As a result, the country's reserve funds declined and revenue bases dramatically eroded due to the bankruptcy of private businesses. Historically, Thailand's fiscal policy has been conservative since it focuses on savings rather than using deficit finances during poor economic periods. However, this practice brought in an overwhelming supply of money from foreign investors and eventually led the country into a fiscal crisis when foreign debts were high and beyond the private sector's capacity (Veerakul, 2005). This crisis resulted in the floated exchange rate of the Thai baht and catalyzed the new budget reform, which was expected to produce fiscal policies (tax and spending levels) that could revitalize the economy after the crisis (Veerakul).

According to Nidhiprabha (2003), the country's chronic surplus may obstruct the country's growth, given that the macroeconomic policies of the country have aimed at having its economy rely more on the export business and private sector outputs rather than government spending. This might result in an unstable economy, especially when the money exchange rate is floated and the agricultural export sector is the country's economic base. As a result of the perennial revenue surplus, income taxes and tariff taxes have been gradually cut (Nidhiprabha). According to Nidhiprabha, expansionary polices, including deficit public capital investment, reducing interest rates to increase money supplies, and price inflation increases to reduce the unemployment rate, should be adopted at the optimal level, especially after 1999, when the country was able to recover from the 1997 fiscal crisis. As shown in the Long Term Debt Interest row in Table 7-1, debt payment was about 0.8% of GDP in 1993 to 1.2% of GDP in 2007, a size that equaled transfer payment. The growth rate of the country's debt cost is about 7% per year, which is higher than the country's GDP growth (4% per year).

As shown in Table 7-1, the country's total government purchase, including consumption and gross investment (excluding transfer payment), ranged from B348 billion in 1993 to B549 billion in 2007. This amount was about 55% of government spending in 1993 to 60% of total government spending in 2007. This amount corresponded with that in the OECD countries. The growth rate for total government consumption and investment is about 3% per year on average, a rate that is slower than the country's productivity (or GDP). As shown in Table 7-1, this relatively slow growth rate is due to a slow gross investment rate, which was about 1% per year on average from 1993 to 2007. The Thai government's long-term investment started at B144 billion in 1993 and ended at B164 billion in 2007 in the real 1988 baht value. This was about 5.8% of the GDP in 1993 and 3.9% of the total GDP in 2007. Thus, the country's public investment, from B144 billion in 1993 to B164 billion in 2007, declined about 14% over the 14-year period.

The above findings are consistent with the country's Gross Fixed Capital Formulation (GFCF). As presented in Table 7-1, one can see that the GFCF was 40.4% of the country's GDP at the beginning of the period (1993) and plunged to about 20% of the GDP after the fiscal crisis in 1999, 2000, and 2001 (19.7%, 19.9%, and 19.9% respectively) before jumping up to about 22.3% of the country's total GDP. This fluctuation and decline trend contributed to the growth rate at about 0% per year of the country's GFCF on average over the 14-year period. Combining the gross investment spending and GFCF data, it is expected that Thailand will sooner or later face a serious infrastructure shortage due to infrastructure depreciation and productivity growth. The low capital stock growth rate (0% per year) also implies that the country's saving's rate is lower than the population rate (1% per year).

Local government spending ranges from 12.6% to 59.8% of the country's total spending. Spending grew at about 11% per year on average over the entire period. This indicates that the central government has attempted to decentralize the public service authority to local governments. The local government size increased significantly given that the share of local government spending to total GDP was about 3.9% in 1993 and 10.9% in 2007. Wages and salaries of Thai government employees have slightly declined from 45% of current consumption to 41% of current consumption. As mentioned in the budget process section, the GAP aims to cut wage and salaries from 45% to 35% of total current spending. However, the ratio of salaries and wages to total expenditure calculated from the data in Table 7-1 shows that the attempt has not yet been successful. The country's inflation rate is about 3% per year. Again, compared to the GDP growth rate, this annual average growth rate of the inflation confirms that the country has adopted a conservative approach to stabilize its macroeconomy.

Figure 7-2 presents information on the Thai central government's financial trend and ratios, using data from the MOF and Asian Development Bank's (ADB), Key Indicators for Asia and Pacific 2008. As previously described, the Thai government maintained an overall surplus throughout the 14-year period from 1990 to 2003, except during the financial crisis and recovery period of 1997 to 2002, where total expenditure exceeded total revenue. As shown in Figures 7-2a and 7-2c, the size and trend of total expenditure coincided with those of total revenue, which increased constantly from 1990 to 1996 and dropped sharply during 1997 to 1998 before slowly increasing during 1999 to 2003. As shown in Figure 7-2b, the sudden drop in revenue from 1997 to 1998 was due to the sharp decline in tax revenue sources during the same period. Tax revenue is the major total revenue source for the central government budget, contributing about 88% to 93% of total revenue for the entire period. This tax revenue source, however, has increased about 132% from 1990 to 2003 partly due to the expanding economy. During the fiscal crisis period, the proportion of tax to total revenue reduced to about 85% of total revenue in 1997 to 88% in 1998, while nontax revenue soared to about 14% of tax revenue in 1997 and 15% in 1998.

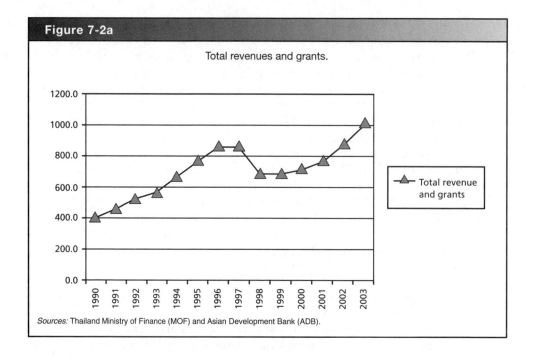

Figure 7-2a

Total revenues and grants.

Sources: Thailand Ministry of Finance (MOF) and Asian Development Bank (ADB).

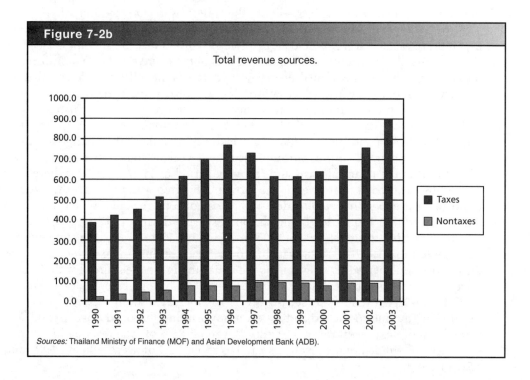

Figure 7-2b

Total revenue sources.

Sources: Thailand Ministry of Finance (MOF) and Asian Development Bank (ADB).

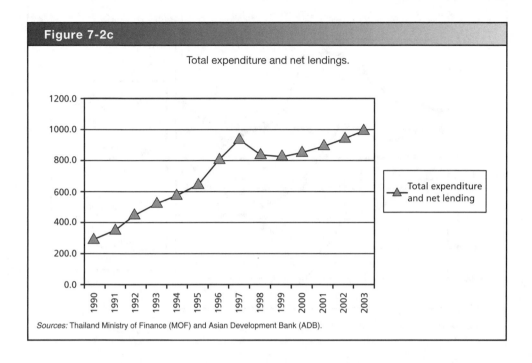

Figure 7-2c

Total expenditure and net lendings.

Sources: Thailand Ministry of Finance (MOF) and Asian Development Bank (ADB).

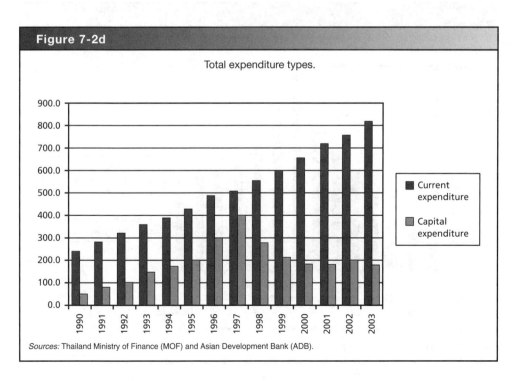

Figure 7-2d

Total expenditure types.

Sources: Thailand Ministry of Finance (MOF) and Asian Development Bank (ADB).

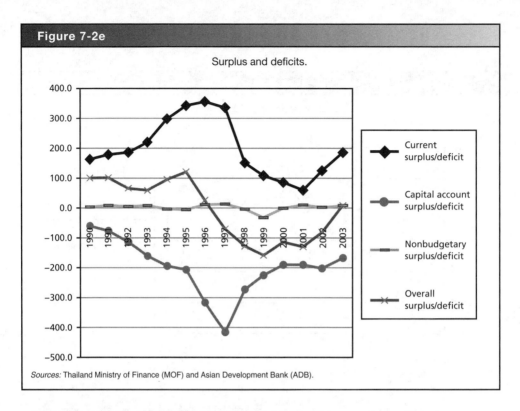

Figure 7-2e

Surplus and deficits.

Sources: Thailand Ministry of Finance (MOF) and Asian Development Bank (ADB).

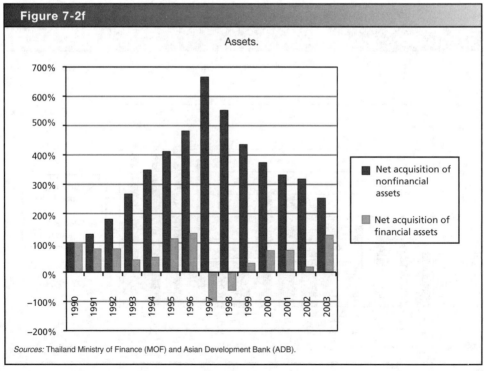

Figure 7-2f

Assets.

Sources: Thailand Ministry of Finance (MOF) and Asian Development Bank (ADB).

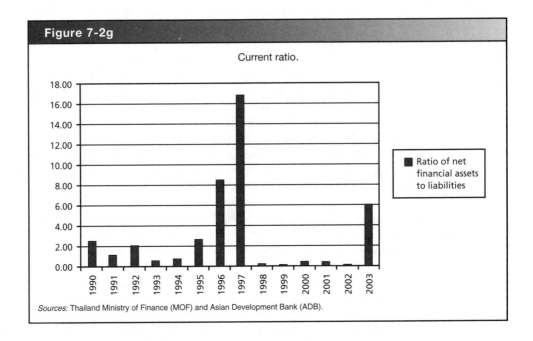

Figure 7-2g

Current ratio.

Legend: Ratio of net financial assets to liabilities

Sources: Thailand Ministry of Finance (MOF) and Asian Development Bank (ADB).

Figure 7-2d presents the ratio of capital to current expenditures and their trends. As seen in the figure, capital expenditure ranged from 25% of the current expenditure in the early period (1990 to 1992), 50% from 1993 to 1996, and 75 to 85% from 1997 to 1998, before declining to 25% from 1999 to 2003, the rate which the BOB and MOF set as a benchmark for the Thai government in general. Capital expenditure soared to 82% of current expenditure in 1997. Current expenditures increase steadily throughout the 14-year period. Overall, the trends in Figure 7-2d show that current expenditures steadily increased at about 232% from 1990 to 2003 (which might be uncontrollable expenditure), while capital expenditure fluctuated and increased at about 206% according to capital needs and infrastructure life cycles. Current and capital expenditure grow faster than tax revenue collection (i.e., 232% for current expenditure, 202% for capital expenditure, and 132% for tax revenue). When this data is combined with the GFCF data in Table 7-1, capital investment is increasing, but not sufficiently enough to catch up with depreciation. A plausible approach is to increase tax revenue to achieve a higher proportion of capital investment to consumption and to gain a more stable investment rate than during the years 1990 to 2006.

The central government finance data retrieved from ADB (2009) and Thailand Ministry of Finance (2009) indicate that the overall deficits from 1997 to 2002 were due to three factors: (1) steady increases in current expenditure, (2) rising capital expenditure, and (3) slow growth of tax revenue. Figure 7-2e indicates that the main cause of overall deficits is the capital account deficits, given that current expenditure surplus occurs throughout the period. Thus, judging from the data and trends, the Thai government has used its current expenditure surplus to reduce its overall deficits due to the capital deficits during the entire period. This trend suggests that Thailand has faced serious capital formation during the years 1997 to 2003 and this situation will likely continue, and there is a need to prevent a sudden drop of revenue in the future. The data sources from MOF indicate that Thai government's spending is cyclical and that tax revenue collection is highly resilient to the economy; thus, deficits tend to occur when revenue drops, and capital expenditure tends to fluctuate due to the life cycle of infrastructure and the country's funding capacity.

Net asset refers to the differences between total assets and total liabilities. Net asset is comprised both of nonfinancial and financial accounts. Figure 7-2f presents the trends of the country's wealth measured through the annual percentage change of financial and nonfinancial assets. As seen in the figure, during the years 1990 to 1997, nonfinancial assets increased from 143% from 1990 to 1991 to 665% from 1996 to 1997 and declined during the years 1998 to 2003. Financial assets fluctuated throughout the entire period, ranging from -103% changes from 1996 to 1997 to a 137% change in net wealth from 1995 to 1996, indicating high volatility in the country's working capital. Part of this is again due to the 1997 fiscal crisis.

Figure 7-2g presents the current ratio, which is the ratio of financial assets to liability. A current ratio that is lower than 2:1 indicates that the government has low liquidation capacity in that period; however, a high current ratio means that wealth accumulation is too large, causing less consumption (Hiranrassmi, Piyawan, & Tummanon, 2006). As seen in Figure 7-2g, the Thai government liquidation capacity is relatively low for the entire period, except in the years 1990, 1995, 1997, and 2003. The ratio of 17:1 in 1997 suggests that the Thai government was trying to restore the country's wealth to a high degree due to the country's financial crisis. According to Netiniyom (2008), the national reserve used for the 1997 fiscal crisis recovery and the country's wealth accumulation mainly came from foreign debt used to balance cash during the fiscal year.

Table 7-2 presents the central government's budget structure from 1990 to 2007. In 1990, total revenue was about B411 billion (US$12 billion); by 2000, the total revenue was about B788 billion (US$23 billion), and by 2007, the total revenue was B1,683 billion (US$50 billion). From 1990 to 2007, total revenue grew at about 8.1% per year on average. In 1990, total expenditure was about B297 billion (US$8.76 billion), by 2000, the total expenditure was about B858 billion (US$25 billion), and by 2007, the total expenditure was B1,606 billion (US$47.2 billion). From 1990 to 2007, total expenditure grew at about 9.8% per year, on average. This indicates that total expenditures grew faster than total revenue by about 1.7% per year. Thailand has long faced revenue collection problems, given that there are tax loopholes (Trakarnsirinont, 2006) and uneven tax structures (a declining income tax rate and increasing sales tax rate) in the country's revenue collection system.

Tax revenue is the main source of total revenue, contributing about 90% in 1990, 83% in 2000, and 81% in 2007 to total revenue. The second main revenue source is other revenue, which contributes about 8% in 1990, 13% in 2000, and 14% in 2007. The third significant revenue source contributed about 1.6% in 1990, 0.6% in 2000, and 0.1% in 2007. As shown by the data in Table 7-2, tax revenue grew at about 7.5% per year, a rate that is slower than that of total revenue, while other revenue grew at about 12% per year, a rate that is faster than total revenue growth. This indicates that tax

Table 7-2

Central Government Budgetary Structure

	1990	1992	1994	1996	1998	2000	2002	2004	2006	2007
TOTAL REVENUE	502,710	502,710	671,163	876,024	757,304	788,812	937,639	1,275,147	1,580,045	1,683,398
Taxes										
Taxes on income, profits, and capital gains	97,725	137,219	199,403	277,671	214,892	235,421	279,326	407,871	576,667	606,369
Taxes on payroll and workforce	0	0	0	0	0	0	0	0	0	0
Taxes on property	13,387	11,397	16,087	13,530	5,119	3,572	276	383	149	0
Taxes on goods and services	164,840	204,342	256,045	351,544	357,301	328,129	396,081	510,833	633,065	660,958
Taxes on international trade and transactions	89,366	83,506	115,170	127,693	67,757	87,231	97,487	107,121	97,845	91,602
Other taxes	3,861	4,926	4,866	5,425	3,189	3,544	4,009	6,734	9,551	7,295
Social contributions	441	5,138	9,272	11,993	8,968	27,073	30,210	61,999	74,009	79,809
Social security contributions	441	5,138	9,272	11,993	8,968	27,073	30,210	57,817	74,009	79,809
Other social contributions	0	0	0	0	0	0	0	4,182	0	0
Grants	6,605	3,472	3,856	3,146	4,485	4,341	3,095	2,238	1,687	1,687
From foreign governments	6,605	3,472	3,856	3,146	4,485	4,341	3,095	2,238	1,687	1,687
From international organizations	0	0	0	0	0	0	0	0	0	0
From other general government units	0	0	0	0	0	0	0	0	0	0
Other Revenue	34,912	52,710	66,464	85,022	95,593	99,501	127,153	177,967	187,073	235,677
Property income	23,321	38,026	51,108	62,404	66,951	58,356	72,249	88,234	138,464	147,928
Sales of goods and services	5,486	7,218	8,442	7,490	8,321	19,319	37,519	61,414	36,440	31,417
Fines, penalties, and forfeits	2,952	2,955	4,271	5,950	7,939	7,607	6,856	6,242	5,567	6,474
Voluntary transfers other than grants	0	0	0	0	0	0	15	1,424	3,691	1,791
Miscellaneous/unidentified revenue	3,153	4,227	2,643	9,178	12,382	14,219	10,515	20,654	2,911	48,066

(continues)

Table 7-2 *(continued)*

Central Government Budgetary Structure

	1990	1992	1994	1996	1998	2000	2002	2004	2006	2007
TOTAL OUTLAYS	297,960	419,975	578,331	739,756	1,035,046	857,899	1,311,411	1,196,762	1,450,298	1,606,915
General public services										
Public debt transactions	40,211	29,636	21,332	10,150	8,686	58,265	68,227	84,355	95,038	90,888
Transfers of between levels of government	0	0	0	0	0	0	0	206,970	296,930	359,762
Defense	53,264	73,200	87,507	95,601	88,327	73,571	79,394	81,037	89,657	42,513
Public order and safety	15,884	23,200	35,038	46,615	52,281	54,261	57,829	67,843	82,401	136,471
Economic affairs	58,668	106,000	154,157	218,594	435,130	209,440	230,325	242,724	261,903	278,944
Environmental protection	0	0	0	0	0	0	1,651	10,953	35,399	4,339
Housing and community amenities	6,665	11,500	24,292	40,734	40,612	39,642	54,326	9,465	35,423	10,137
Health	20,672	32,600	42,224	55,254	70,129	65,039	88,370	102,062	108,406	255,231
Recreation, culture, and religion	1,109	2,500	6,532	7,694	13,459	8,495	7,224	7,377	16,566	14,350
Education	61,730	89,600	126,858	159,023	196,411	198,396	226,503	262,975	276,490	331,991
Social protection	10,930	16,300	19,634	26,845	32,880	47,995	81,326	132,484	110,785	7,330

Sources: Thailand Ministry of Finance. Available at: http://dw.mof.go.th/foc/gfs/c.asp. Accessed March 25, 2010.

revenue collection is declining, while other revenue collection (i.e., user fees and user charges in terms of sales of government goods services and licenses) is increasing rapidly. This shift in revenue sources suggests that vertical equity in the society is reducing, given that user fees and user charges are not collected according to one's ability to pay. As shown in the table, tax sources in Thailand include income, payroll, property, sales, and tariff taxes. The largest tax source is the sales tax, which contributed 45% in 1990, 50% in 2000, and 48% in 2007 to total tax revenue. The second largest tax source is the income tax, which contributed 26% in 1990, 36% in 2000, and 44% in 2007 to total tax revenue. The third largest tax source is the tariff tax, which contributed 24% in 1990, 13% in 2000, and 7% in 2007 to total tax revenue. Sales tax grows at about 8% per year, the same rate as that of total tax revenue, while income tax grows at about 10% per year, a rate that is faster than that of total tax revenue. The slow growth rate of total tax revenue is due to the constant growth rate of the sales tax, which is the first main tax source. Because sales taxes are the major tax source, Thailand may face revenue volatility, given that sales taxes are highly sensitive to the country's economy as well as to vertical inequity and sales taxes are relatively regressive compared to income taxes, which are collected at a progressive rate.

Expenditure structure shifted during the 1990 to 2007 period. In 1990, general public service was the largest service function, consuming about 33% of total expenditure, followed by education, consuming about 20% of total expenditure. The third largest expenditure was economic affairs, consuming at about 17% of total expenditure. In 2000, economic affairs ranked as the first major spending function, consuming about 34% of total expenditure, followed by education and general administration at about 21% and 11%, respectively. In 2007, the expenditure structure reverted to reflect the structure that existed in 1990; that is, general administration ranked as the first major spending function, consuming at about 23%, followed by education and economic affairs at about 21% and 23% respectively.

Recent Budget Reform

From 1959 to 2008, the Thai budget experienced three reforms: the line-item budget, the planning-programming budgeting system (PPBS), and the strategic PBB. The line-item budget was used during the years from 1959 to 1981. The annual budget documents during this period report service inputs by departments under the view that the appropriation law should be an effective tool to control agencies' spending. Owning to the disadvantages of the line-item budget, for example, a lack of agency flexibility and an inability to aid the country's economic-oriented resource allocation, the Thai government adopted the PPBS in 1982 with the main goal of using the new budget to rank functional appropriations in a way that would enhance the country's traditional goal of social and economic development (TDRI, 2004). Based on the experience of the Thai government, one can see that in theory, the PPBS was to link resource allocations with the country's overall goals. However, in practice, one finds that the agencies' missions and service goals are not well-coordinated with service strategies because they are redundant and lack meaningful connections across departments (TDRI, 2004). This situation results in an incremental resource allocation process in which decisions are fragmented and rely mainly on negotiations among ministry heads (TDRI, 2004).

Thailand adopted a PPB system in 1997. The unique characteristic of the budget in Thailand is that it focuses on strategic management in order to achieve full benefits of performance measurement data, both in terms of holding public agencies accountable and also in aiding executives' decisions on resource allocation, in which national policy priorities are officially identified and tied with the expected outcomes of the agencies' budget requests (Thailand Bureau of Budget, 2007). Thailand has been careful in implementing PBB. In 1997, the PBB was implemented as a pilot project within two agencies. In 2001, the PBB was fully adopted throughout the government through the public law requirement that all ministries plan and submit their budgets according to PBB frameworks (Veerakul, 2005). According to the TDRI study of 1998, the strategic PBB is expected to reduce fragmentation in the decision-making process, especially at the legislative consideration stage. The fragmentation is due to "the country's political system in which the ministers are largely parliamentarians from various provinces who think locally rather than nationally" (Christensen, 1992; Kao Sa-Ad, 1998, p. 6). The strategic PBB was adopted officially in 2001 with full knowledge of the failures of PPBS and incremental budget practices (in terms of supporting strategic resource allocation), along with the government's readiness to implement strategic planning and performance measurements, given that the accrual accounting system and the GAP were successfully established during the period after 1997. At the micromanagement level, the reform demanded that the BOB identify agencies' goals that are responsive to the national master plan (NSEDP) and the GAP. The NSEDP of 1997 called for analysis, consolidation, and preparation of the executive budget according to its ranked policy priorities. Due to the budget reform during this period, the BOB has restructured its budget preparation and evaluation process at the macromanagement level, as mentioned in the budget process section, since 1997.

Under the official PBB beginning in 2001, the process of linking the national master plan with the resource allocation strategy is summarized as follows. The country's overall strategic goal, which corresponds to the national economic and social development plan, is used as a common guide by every ministry to identify his or her individual strategic plans (TDRI, 2004). At the planning level, the Public Service Agreement (PSA), which identifies key indicators to measure the ministry's budget performance (in terms of output or outcome), is regarded as a performance contract between the prime minister and individual ministries. Then, the ministries' PSAs are translated into a Service Delivery Agreement (SDA) for each agency within each individual ministry to further guide program planning, budgeting, and operations. The SDA, which contains key indicators to measure an agency's budget performance, indicates how each agency contributes to the ministry's strategic goal accomplishment. At the technical level, agencies plan their programs and budgets according to their ministry's strategic goal and propose a budget according to cost analysis and program evaluation. The BOB is responsible for evaluating agency performance by comparing targeted goals with actual outcomes identified by the indicators in the PSA and SDA. The BOB's performance measurement results are used to allocate resources through various ministries and agencies, and motivate agencies to accomplish targeted outcomes (Interview with Kulalpaijit, N., 2008; Na Songkla, 2007).

For the results of PBB implementation at the early assessment, Kao Sa-Ad (1998) found that the national plan does not set priorities or strategic plans or take annual budget constraints into consideration. Further, the plan was found to be too broad to be translated into an operational level without a central coordinator, such as the BOB. As a result, all ministers tend to include as many ideas and projects as possible, assuming that the proposed projects will be considered as responsive to the national plan; thus, ministers hope to receive a reasonable share in the national annual budget (Kao Sa-Ad). This situation is previously described in the budget process section of this chapter. Based on interview data with the BOB planning officials in the summer of 2007 and 2008, performance measurement had not been officially used to aid the decision-making process. Given that the GAP is too broad and embraces all strategic activities necessary to accomplish all public management goals identified in the NSDEP without priority ranking, the PBB has not yet accomplished its function in linking budgeting with macromanagement planning at this time. This conclusion is derived from the recent interview data that indicate that ministries and agencies view budget requests submitted to the BOB as a bid for government funding and comply with the ministries' spending ceiling set by the BOB. Consequently, they cut spending across the programs instead of ranking the projects (Blondal & Kim, 2006). This traditional practice, coupled with the BOB's project evaluating criteria, which are relatively less restricted in terms of priority ranking, tend to obstruct the functions of the PBB and thus restructure the BOB's budget evaluating criteria; additionally, the ministries' systematic budgeting practices might be needed in the future.

Conclusions

This chapter described Thailand's central government budgeting process, its financial management performance, and recent budget reforms. The analytic impacts of these practices on the economy are provided, along with the descriptive data, given that the management ideology of the central government is to use budgeting and financial management practices as a planning tool to improve its economic and social well-being. The budgeting process in Thailand is highly centralized. The four organizations, including the BOB, BOT, MOF, and NSEDB, have strong power in setting the country's master plan, the long-term public management plan, known as GAP, and the annual budget policy proposal. The MOF and BOT set benchmarks on public spending levels that correspond to conservative fiscal and monetary policies. Parliament has a weak role in the checks and balances system due to its political instability. Public budgeting hearings are not open to the public via media, and citizen participation rarely occurred before 1997. The executive agencies tend to lack systematic budgeting practices in priority ranking, resulting in their limited participation in setting the country's budget policies.

Overall, the country's budgeting and financial management practices are considered technically oriented, as described in the budgeting process section. This solid process results in good fiscal discipline, as can be seen through the budget surplus throughout the years 1990 to 2007, except during the economic crisis period of 1997 to 1998. However, the solid budgeting and financial management budgeting process alone might not help the country utilize its resources to achieve its ultimate goal of enhancing economic well-being at the utmost level. As described in the financial management performance section, the perennial centralized and conservative practices result in a chronic budget surplus, a relatively small current expenditure, and unstable capital investment. Tax revenues grew at a slower pace than expenditures during the period studied due to cuts in the progressive income tax rate, and revenue sources shifted from income tax to sales taxes. Given that the economy relies heavily on exports and private sector outputs, and that the economy expanded at about 7% of GDP during the recent period of 2005 to 2008, public expenditure, including consumption and investment, could be raised to support private sector development in terms of long-term capital and human stock investment. These centralized and conservative practices might be appropriate at a time when the economy is contracting, but when the economy is expanding, surplus spending could hinder growth.

The PBB budget reform, during the early evaluation period, tended to be limited in terms of its ability to enhance resource allocation in a way that corresponded to the national master plan, although the BOB practice is technically solid in terms of strategic planning and budgeting steps. This is likely a result of the central focus on change at the macromanagement level without empowering lower management (i.e., ministerial agencies and local agencies ranking their program and project spending based on public service clients' interests that they know better than the BOB). Empowering agencies' budget planning and implementation could be a promising approach for true budget reform in Thailand.

Discussion Questions

1. Describe Thailand's budget process. Include in your response a discussion of the main activities and actors in each of the four budget phases. What impacts, in terms of resource allocation, are likely to occur given that Thailand's budget process is relatively centralized and executively dominated?

2. Describe the main characteristics of Thailand's fiscal management policy. What are the major advantages and disadvantages of such a policy? Since Thailand is a developing country, what would you change, in terms of fiscal management, to help enhance the country's macroeconomy, including budget deficits and infrastructure investment levels?

3. Describe how accrual accounting would facilitate or obstruct the country's recent budget reform (i.e., PBB).

4. Discuss whether PBB is appropriate to Thailand's budgeting process and fiscal management. What practices would you recommend to improve the budget process (e.g., a better performance measurement system or more budget authority should be granted to the lower-level public managers)? Give specific examples.

5. After examining the country's central budget structure, briefly describe the main sources of revenue and expenditures. Then, determine whether the budget structure will likely generate:
   a. Stable revenue (i.e., will the total revenue be highly sensitive to the country's macroeconomy?);
   b. Equity across citizens in different income groups; and
   c. Efficiency (i.e., will the tax structure distort private investment, consumption, and saving levels? How much such tax structure likely to distort the economy? And compared to the benefits of Thailand's major government spending, will such distortion be appropriate?)
6. What are your recommendations to improve Thailand's central budget structure based on the assessment obtained from question 5?

References

Asian Development Bank,(ADB). (2009). *Key Indicators for Asia and Pacific 2008. Available at* http://www.adb.org/statistics/ Accessed May 30, 2009

Blondal, J., & Kim, S. (2006). Budgeting in Thailand. *OECD Journal on Budgeting, 5*(3), 7–36.

Christensen, S. (1992). The public policy process and political change in Thailand: A summary of observation. *TDRI Quarterly Review, 13*(1), 3–11.

Comptroller General's Department (CGD). (2001). *Public Sector Accounting Policies and Principles.* Available at: http://www.cgd.go.th/index.asp. Accessed March 24, 2010.

Henry, L., & Attavikamtorn, P. (1999). Government accounting and auditing in Thailand: An overview and some suggestions for improvement. *International Journal of Accounting, 34*(3), 439–454.

Hiranrassmi, T., Piyawan, P., & Tummanon, W. (2006). *Basic accounting principles.* Bangkok: Wayapat Publisher, Inc.

Kao Sa-Ad, M. (1998). Economic development and institutional failures in Thailand. *TDRI Quarterly Review, 13*(1), 3–11.

Kulalpaijit, N. (2008). Interview by A. Srithongrung. Thailand Bureau of Budget, Bangkok, Thailand. The interviewing results are available by the author upon request and interviewee permission.

Mikesell, J. L. (2006). *Fiscal administration: Analysis and applications in the public sector* (7th ed.). Belmont, CA: Thomson/Wadsworth.

Na Songkla, D. (2007). Interview by A. Srithongrung. Thailand Bureau of Budget, Bangkok, Thailand. The interviewing results are available by the author upon request and interviewee permission.

Netiniyom, P. (2008). International Finance. Union Ultraviolet Publisher, Co.Ltd. (In Thai language), Bangkok, Thailand.

Nidhiprabha, B. (2003). Thailand's macroeconomic policy after July 1997. *Asian Economic Papers, 2*(1), 158–168.

Organisation for Economic Co-operation and Development (OECD). (2005). *Statistics on member countries.* Available at: http://www.oecd.org/countrieslist/0,3351,en_33873108_33844430_1_1_1_1_1,00.html. Accessed March 24, 2010.

Riggs, F. (1966). *Thailand: The modernization of a bureaucratic polity.* Honolulu: University of Hawaii Press.

Riggs, F. (1981). Cabinet ministries and coup group: The case of Thailand. *International Political Sciences Review, 2,* 159–188.

Thailand Bureau of Budget. (2007, June 10). *Strategic performance-based budget* [Presentation to Bhutan government]. Bangkok, Thailand.

Thailand Bureau of Budget. (2009). *Strategic budgeting practices for FY 2010* [Internal Memo]. Available at: http://www.bb.go.th/bbhomeeng/. Accessed on May 30, 2009.

Kaosa-ard, M. (1998). Economic development and institutional failures in Thailand. *Thailand Develeopment Research Institution (TDRI) Quarterly Review,* 13(1), 3–11.

Thailand Development Research Institution (TDRI). (2004). *A study report of new budgeting system*. Available at: http://www.bb.go.th/bbhome/index.asp. Accessed March 25, 2010.

Thailand Ministry of Finance (MOF). (2009). *Thailand Public Finance Data*. Available at http://dw.mof.go.th/foc/gfs/c.asp. Accessed May 30, 2009.

Trakarnsirinont, P. (2006). *Public finance*. Chang Mai, Thailand: Chang Mai University Press.

Veerakul, K. (2005). *Cost calculation in strategic budgeting system. Thailand bureau of budget internal study report*. Bangkok: Bureau of Budget.

ENDNOTES

1. As of June 2009, these ministries include: the Ministry of Defense, the Ministry of Finance, the Ministry of Foreign Affairs, the Ministry of Tourism and Sports, the Ministry of Social Development and Human Security, the Ministry of Agriculture and Cooperatives, the Ministry of Transport, the Ministry of Natural Resources and Environment, the Ministry of Information and Communication Technology, the Ministry of Commerce, the Ministry of Interior, the Ministry of Justice, the Ministry of Labor, the Ministry of Culture, the Ministry of Science and Technology, the Ministry of Education, the Ministry of Public Health, and the Ministry of Industry.

2. Independent public agencies include the Auditor General of Thailand Office, the Bangkok Metropolitan Administration, the Bank of Thailand, the Bureau of the Crowd Property, the Bureau of the Royal Household, His Majesty's Principal Private Secretary Office, the Royal Institute, and the Secretariat of National Assembly.

3. In brief, Thai local governments include provincial, municipal, and district units, as well as special districts (i.e., Bangkok and Pattaya). Local revenue comes from locally levied taxes on properties and business operations as well as fees for local school administration, business operations, and gas and fuel usages. Surcharge taxes, which are collected by both central and local governments on general and special sales, are also important revenue sources at local the level. The last source is a shared tax, which is public revenue transferred from the central government to the local governments according to population numbers. Local expenditure includes current expenditure for routine operations of public services and special expenditure whose funds are created specifically for specific spending, such as local commercial development activities.

4. The 80 MPs are elected through the voting process in which the 76 provinces were combined and organized to be 10 electoral party-list districts whose elected representatives (10 for each of the nine districts and six for the last district) are from the lists of the political party, that wins the popular vote in these districts. The party-list system is meant to reduce intracompetition among political candidates from the same party and thus encourage the electorate to focus more on partisan campaign platforms rather than individual platforms.

5. The country has chronic political instability, such as coups d'état, as well as a relatively small economic system that relies heavily on global trade, international finances, and money exchanging rates.

6. For example, in fiscal year 2005, there are seven strategic goals identified by GAP and 27 strategic plans identified in Annual Budget Policy Proposal. The 27 strategic plans are sorted through the seven goals according to their relevancy. As found in fiscal year 2005 budget document, the seven goals include poverty reduction and rural economic development, social and human capital development, stabilizing macroeconomy, sustainable development and natural resource preservation, energy efficiency, national security and good governance, and public administration improvement.

7. The elite-class senior civil servants are systematically recruited through education, nationality, social and economic networks, and loyalty to His Majesty the King.

Chapter 8

Budgeting in Vietnam: Decentralized Decision Making in a Unitary Budget Environment

Phuong Nguyen-Hoang and Larry Schroeder

Learning Objectives

- Know and understand how Vietnam's budgeting environment and its recent developments unraveled.
- Know the roles of key players in the current budget process.
- Know and understand the degree of fiscal autonomy empowered on subnational governments in Vietnam.
- Determine the revenue and expenditure assignments at the subnational level of government.
- Distinguish potential perverse incentives created by the current law for subnational governments.

Introduction

Relative to most developing and transition economies, Vietnam is known as one of the most successful since it emerged from many decades of internal conflicts in the 1980s. Indeed, some have considered the nation a success story for its deliberate and cautious market-oriented reforms and strong encouragement of private enterprise (Schmidt, 2004) in spite of its status as a one-party communist state.[1] The reforms stem from the so-called *doi moi* policy articulated at the Communist Party's Sixth National Congress in 1986, whereby a "market-oriented socialist economy under state guidance" was adopted in lieu of the central planning model of socialism (Beresford, 2008).

Although Vietnam's economic policy reforms and their outcomes are quite unique, so is the public budgeting system used in the country. The single-party, unitary state utilizes a single state budget for public revenues and expenditures; however, the budget process is also constructed so as to rely heavily on decentralized decision making with provincial governments given considerable flexibility in making public expenditure and revenue allocation decisions.

The intent of this chapter is to review the overall budgetary framework and process used in Vietnam along with a brief history of how the current process came into being. The second half of the chapter focuses on the decentralized aspects of the budget process. The implications of the process of interest are relevant not only for the subnational level, but also for the outcome of the overall process. A brief summary concludes the chapter.

The Budget and Budgeting Environment of the Socialist Republic of Vietnam

To appreciate the budget process in Vietnam, it is useful to first understand the political environment in which it is formulated. After that discussion, we turn to a review of the history and legal basis for the budget and its formulation process, including some of the recent policy initiatives that are linked to the budget system. This section then discusses the salient features of the budget process and the fiscal system that it controls, and provides a breakdown of the allocation of revenues and expenditures.

GOVERNMENT STRUCTURE AND POLITICAL ENVIRONMENT

Vietnam has a one-party political system with a 15-strong[2] politburo as the supreme leading body. Although not directly involved in the budget-making process, the politburo, with its members chosen from plenums of the Party Central Committee, is de facto the country's highest decision-making body (Abuza, 2001). The politburo membership always includes the president as the ceremonial head of state representing Vietnam in domestic and foreign affairs and prime minister (PM) as the head of the executive branch. Both the president and the PM are elected for terms of 5 years by the unicameral National Assembly. The National Assembly deputies are popularly elected and also serve 5-year terms. Nearly all of the more than 490 deputies are party members and recommended for election by the Vietnamese Fatherland Front (VFF), a mass organization closely affiliated with the Communist Party.

The executive branch consists of 18 ministries. The principal budget-making ministries are the Ministry of Finance (MOF) and the Ministry of Planning and Investment (MPI). It is the former that oversees the administration of the state budget with its

State Budget Department serving as the primary oversight body for the day-to-day implementation of the budget. The MOF also includes the Taxation Department and Customs Department as the primary revenue-raising departments and the State Treasury Department, which has the task of managing state funds and mobilizing capital. The MPI has the responsibility for developing economic policies, including assisting in the formulation of the capital portion of the budget.

Below the central government are three levels of government: 58 provinces and five provincial-level cities[3] under the direct jurisdiction of the central government, 690 districts, and more than 10,000 communes. Each level of government has a popularly elected legislative body called the People's Council,[4] and an executive authority, the People's Committee, which is appointed by the People's Council. The committees and councils often have overlapping membership. Residents of each jurisdiction directly elect the People's Council members; however, the candidates for those positions are usually nominated by the VFF and approved by the next higher-level administrative unit.

EVOLUTION OF THE BUDGETING ENVIRONMENT

With the end of military fighting and the unification of the country in 1975, Vietnam had a centrally planned economy of its own style[5] with agriculture based on collective farms (Carlsson, Nam, Linde-Rahr, & Martinsson, 2007) and all industry and trade considered state property (Norlund, 1984). The administrative subunits (provinces, districts, and communes) continued to be in place, but the budgeting process was highly centralized in keeping with the centrally planned economy. As Rao (2003) states, "The fiscal system was rigid and highly centralized, with little room for local initiative in providing public services" (p. 49) since fiscal arrangements were based on orders emanating from the PM.

The budgeting process has become increasingly decentralized over time. The greater authority of local governments in the budget process was represented in the Council of Government's 1978 Resolution 10-CP, and later, in the Council of Ministers' 1983 Resolution 138/HDBT. These legal documents officially recognized the budgets of local governments as an integral component of the state budget. A substantial improvement in the process manifested itself in the 1990 enactment of the Council of Ministers' 186/HDBT on *Fiscal decentralization to local governments* as part of the *doi moi* policy. The resulting budget process was, however, somewhat convoluted. Provincial People's Committees submitted their estimated budgets to the Council of Ministers, who then decided on budget targets for the provinces. Based on these targets, the People's Committees revised their estimated budgets and had to get the approval from the People's Councils. Despite its lack of sophistication, the resolution served as a foundation for later developments in budget laws and regulations.

The budget legislation was altered again in 1997 in the form of the State Budget Law, which was further amended in 1998 to include provision for the newly adopted value-added tax (VAT). This version of the budget law defined the roles to be played by the actors engaged in the preparation of the budget, as well as the roles of the line ministries and subnational levels of government in its implementation.[6] The 1997 law also defined the responsibilities and sources of revenues for the various levels of government. In practice, however, not all commune expenditures were included in the state budget (The World Bank, 2000).

The current law governing the budget process in Vietnam is the 2002 Law on the State Budget, which serves as the organic law on budgeting for the country.[7] As suggested previously, the law specifies that there is a single, unified public sector budget that must ultimately be ratified by the National Assembly. There are several features of the law which are of interest. First, it is extremely broad in its coverage (which is not uncommon in organic budget laws). Its chapters include (among others) specifications of the powers and duties of various state organizations (e.g., the National Assembly and several of its standing committees, the State Bank, MOF, MPI, and People's Councils and People's Committees at the subnational level); lists of the various revenue sources and expenditures for both the central and provincial levels; and details regarding how the budget is to be drafted and implemented.

Second, the law gives more power to the National Assembly. Whereas the allocation norms from the central to local governments were previously established in MOF circulars, they are now submitted to the standing committee of the National Assembly and are made public to sector ministries and provinces, thereby improving the transparency of the budgeting process (Socialist Republic of Vietnam & The World Bank, 2005). The National Assembly has the final say in the sharing rates of shared revenues between provinces and the central government and in the duration of a budget stability period. Also, unlike previously, the National Assembly approves not only total estimated and budgeted revenues, expenditures, and intergovernmental transfers, but also their composition. Similar powers are now also granted to the provincial People's Councils, which can decide on the province's overall budget, budget norms, and revenue allocations among the three tiers of local government. This suggests a move to a broader representative-based budget process in spite of the single-party state.

Third, the law differentiates between regular, or recurrent, spending and development investment spending, and stipulates that the regular portion must be balanced (and not be financed by debt). It also states that mandated spending imposed on lower level jurisdictions by high level ones should be fully financed by the latter (i.e., no unfunded mandates). The law specifies that draft budgets at all levels must include allocations of 2 to 5% of total spending to contingencies so as to be prepared to meet unplanned spending needs and also provide for creation of reserve funds into which unspent closing balances are transferred at the conclusion of the fiscal year.

Finally, the first paragraph of Article 13, followed upon by the Decision 192/2004/QD-TTg on Fiscal Transparency, states "Drafting, final accounts, and audit of final accounts of the State budget and budgets of various levels, budget drafting units and organizations supported by the State budget must be publicly disclosed." In spite of this legal provision, recent evaluations by the International Budget Project of the Center on Budget and Policy Priorities (CBPP) have given Vietnam extremely low scores on its Open Budget Index. In 2006, the only key budget document available to the public was the year-end report. The budget proposal, in-year reviews, and the auditor's report were not accessible, resulting in a paltry score of 2% on the CBPP's index. The situation improved slightly in the 2008 index when the score was raised to 9% with the publication of both the enacted budget and in-year reviews in addition to the year-end report.[8] This lack of transparency can be attributed to Vietnam's traditional state budgeting system not being geared for public accountability (Painter, 2003).

Since the promulgation of the 2002 law, there have been several additional policy developments related to the budget process. These policies are linked to externally financed projects, particularly The World Bank's Public Financial Management Reform Project, which included the development of a Medium-Term Expenditure Framework (MTEF) and an integrated treasury and budget management information system.[9] In addition, there has been some progress made on developing an accrual-based accounting system to replace the current cash-based system.[10]

BUDGET CYCLE AND OUTCOMES

Chapter IV of the 2002 law outlines the steps of the budget cycle with details of the process specified in the Decree No. 60/2003/ND-CP *Detailing and Guiding the Implementation of the State Budget Law.* The budget process is initiated by the PM by May 31st prior to the fiscal year (the fiscal year in Vietnam coincides with the calendar year) who provides a broad outline of the socioeconomic development plan and an overall budget estimate. By June 10th, the MOF is to issue a circular that contains details on how the regular portion of the budget is to be prepared by the various budget offices. The MPI also prepares a circular focused on development investment plans.

The circulars are distributed to all budget units that are required to make estimates of revenues and expenditures and, in a bottom-up approach, send them to their immediate managing agencies. Finally, by July 20th, all agencies submit their proposed budgets to the MOF and MPI. (Procedures for subnational governments are discussed in the next section.) For capital, planning agencies in each budget unit also draw up plans for investment spending, but coordinate those plans with the recurrent side of the proposed budget within the budget unit. By September 10th, the MPI synthesizes those plans and submits them to the Finance Ministry.

The law does not specify an exact date by which the MOF is to submit the proposed draft budget to the National Assembly; instead, Article 43 requires that it be submitted "10 days at the latest before the opening of the year-end session." The assembly finalizes the budget by November 15th. This provides adequate time to inform subnational governments of what was ultimately decided by the National Assembly and gives local governments time to finalize their specific plans prior to the start of the fiscal year. The law also provides for revisions in the budget during the course of the fiscal year in the event of major changes to the economy or other emergencies. Available evidence suggests that this time schedule is generally followed in practice.

The Treasury Department of the MOF oversees the financial aspects of budget implementation. It maintains offices in all provinces and in each of the 690 districts. Those offices maintain accounts for both subnational governments as well as for local offices linked to national ministries. Revenue collecting agencies are to deposit funds in government bank accounts and report such deposits to the Treasury Department, which then credits the appropriate account (e.g., the provincial account for revenues assigned to provinces). There is an electronic accounting system used by the Treasury Department, which permits daily determination of the cash position of the government and its subnational governmental entities.

Once the fiscal year is complete, the State Treasury certifies the closed accounts. Of the positive closing balances in the central or local budgets, 50% are transferred to their respective reserve funds, with the remaining 50% being carried over into the next budget year. The reserve funds are intended to provide financial cushions to meet unexpected spending needs or to provide liquidity in the event of cash flow shortfalls. The Budget Law stipulates that the fund is to be replenished after having been drawn upon; at the same time, the government sets a maximum size of the reserve funds for each level of government. If, at the end of the fiscal year, that maximum is already met, the entire closing balance is transferred to the following year's budget. Thus, unlike some countries with a unitary budget, subnational governments in Vietnam are not required to give back unspent local funds.

The government also has a State Audit Office, which audits the final accounts. Its reports are provided to the National Assembly, which can also request specific special audits. When it was originally created, the State Audit Office was directly under the PM; however, in 2005 the assembly passed the law that made the State Audit Office subordinate to the National Assembly and stating that it should perform independently of the government.

In summary, the law on the state budget is broad and comprehensive and is in keeping with most budget norms. At the same time, of course, there can be major differences between the statutes and actual practice. Unfortunately, we are not aware of studies that document the degree to which the budget process, as practiced, differs from the statute.

Table 8-1 provides a breakdown of the actual revenues and expenditures for fiscal year 2006 (which are the most recent disaggregated data available) and reflects the split between the central and subnational governments. The largest revenue source is from business-related activities that include the VAT on both exports and imports and business related revenues that are shared between the central and subnational levels. These constitute about 27% of total revenues and are only slightly larger than the 24% of aggregate revenues obtained from taxes on the extraction of oil and natural gas. As in most countries, the bulk of all taxes and fees are reserved by the central government; however, once transfers were netted out, as the table reveals, subnational government revenues exceeded those retained by the center, from 186 trillion Vietnamese dong (VND) to about VND 165 trillion.[11] Excluding shared taxes, explicit transfers from the center to the subnational level constituted about 31% of subnational government revenues. Nonrefundable aids (primarily development assistance grants) are channeled mostly to the central government (VND 7,344 billion to the center and VND 554 billion to subnational levels).

Recurrent expenditures represent nearly 53% of the total spending mandated by the National Assembly. Also, subnational governments spend nearly seven times more on education and training than the central government. This spending pattern corresponds with levels of educational responsibilities. While responsibility for tertiary education

Table 8-1

Actual Revenues and Expenditures at Central and Subnational Level, Fiscal Year 2006

	Central	Shared	Local
Revenues	**164,739**		**186,105**
Current revenue	189,965		89,508
Taxes, fees, and other current revenues	182,621		88,954
Revenues assigned 100% to central level			
Revenues from gasoline and oil	83,346		
Export and import duties	26,260		
Value-added taxes on exports and imports	16,545		
Other fees and charges	4,986		
Revenues assigned 100% to subnational level			
Taxes on land and housing			594
Taxes on use of agricultural land			111
Taxes on transfers of land-use rights			5,251
Land rent			16,697
Sales of state-owned houses			1,993
Registration fees			3,363
Lotteries			6,142
Other			6,845
Shared revenue			
(central and local shares not available)			
Business-related revenues		94,273	
Income taxes on high income earners		5,179	
Gasoline and oil Fees		4,986	
Non-refundable grants	7,344		554
Transfers from financial reserve funds	113		13
Investment mobilization			9,572
Carryover balance from 2005 budgets			10,934
Carryover revenues: salary reform and staff streamlining	17,682		2,000
Carryover revenues for other mandated items	14,638		16,419
Transfers from the central to subnational governments	−57,659		57,659
Balancing transfers	−22,362		22,362
Targeted transfers	−35,297		35,297

	Central	Local
Expenditures (and items carried forward to 2007)	**213,351**	**172,315**
Financed by budgeted revenues	161,353	146,705
Capital expenditures	32,061	56,280
Debt repayment	40,764	7,427
Recurrent expenditures	78,989	82,863
Education and training	4,748	32,584
Science and technology	1,920	620

(continues)

Table 8-1 *(continued)*

Actual Revenues and Expenditures at Central and Subnational Level, Fiscal Year 2006

	Central	Local
Transfers to financial reserve funds		135
Subsidies to oil companies	9,539	
Items carried forward for salary reform and staff streamlining in 2007	26,987	
Other items carried forward to 2007	25,012	25,610
Balance	**−48,613**	**13,789**
Borrowing to cover budget deficits	48,613	
Domestic borrowing	35,864	
Foreign borrowing	12,749	
Other Self-financed expenditures (outside state budget)	**20,356**	**12,288**
Expenditures financed by government bonds, fees on roads, bridges and ports, tuition, and hospital fees	12,596	12,288
Expenditures financed by foreign aid	7,760	

Source: Constructed by authors from data by the Ministry of Finance of the Socialist Republic of Vietnam. Available at: http://www.mof.gov.vn. Accessed April 7, 2010.

Note: Amounts given in billions of VND.

and vocation training lies with the central government, subnational governments are in charge of general education.[12] In contrast to education, spending on science and technology is still highly centralized with VND 1,920 billion spent centrally and only VND 620 billion spent at the subnational level. Table 8-1 also shows that subnational governments oversee a greater level of capital spending than does the central government.

The final panel of expenditure portion of Table 8-1 brings to light an issue associated with the budget process in Vietnam, namely, off-budget spending. The amounts are large, with off-budget expenditures in 2006, at about 8% of expenditures that flowed from the budget process. At least two issues arise from this type of spending. One relates to its macroeconomic implications since, as mentioned in Table 8-1, at least some of this off-budget spending is financed with bonds. As noted in the report of the Socialist Republic of Vietnam and The World Bank (2005), the interest on those bonds will ultimately be on budget and could add to the already substantial public deficits.

A second aspect of the off-budget items is that at least some are related to fees and charges for services with neither the fee revenues nor the spending of those fees incorporated into the state budget. Although these transactions can be considered a quid pro quo exchange, the fact that they are off budget likely means that neither the fees imposed nor how they were spent face the same level of scrutiny as do on-budget items. Painter (2003) states, "Much of this off-budget revenue is used to supplement salaries" (p. 265) and goes on to quote a Government of Vietnam report that acknowledged lack of government control over capricious behavior by bureaucrats. Even though that report was from analysis of the situation in the late 1990s, the 2006 data in Table 8-1 suggest that the problem was unlikely to have been fully solved.

Subnational Budgeting in a Single State Budget Environment

As suggested, there is a hierarchic link between subnational governments with the provinces (and major cities, which are treated equivalent to provinces) at the apex with districts and communes following them.[13] For example, candidates for elected office at a lower level must be approved by the next higher level. That same hierarchic structure carries through to the budget process. Indeed, many observers characterize the process similar to a nested or "Matruska doll" model (Martinez-Vazquez & Gomez, 2005).

At the same time, budgeting at the subnational level in Vietnam has characteristics that differentiate it from most other countries with a single state budget. The law gives provinces considerable latitude in how each allocates revenues and arranges for spending by the districts and communes within its territory. Here we first detail the structure of revenues reserved for subnational governments followed by a discussion of the arrangements for the provision of public services. We then turn to the budgeting process used at the subnational levels with special emphasis on the decentralized nature of the process.

REVENUES AND EXPENDITURES OF SUBNATIONAL GOVERNMENTS

The 2002 law specifies the revenues dedicated to subnational governments; however, the tax rates are set by the central government and are uniform throughout the country. As such, it cannot be concluded that there is any real fiscal decentralization of revenues. The list of dedicated local revenues includes taxes on land and housing, natural resources (excluding petroleum), license tax, transfer of land-use rights, tax on use of agricultural land, fee on land use, land rent, revenue from leasing and sale of dwelling houses owned by the state, registration fees, revenues from state-run lotteries, as well as fees and charges. Table 8-1 reveals that these revenues accounted for only about 22% of total subnational government revenues (inclusive of transfers). The law also specifies that the following taxes are to be shared between the central government and local governments[14]: the VAT (other than the VAT on imported goods), corporate income tax (other than on corporations with a "whole-unit" accounting system),[15] income taxes on high-income earners, taxes on profits remitted abroad (but not on companies earning profits in the petroleum industry), the special consumption tax on domestic goods and services, and gasoline fees. The sharing system applies to taxes where the domicile of the taxpayer can be identified since the sharing is done on the basis of the site of collection of the tax. The tax department of the MOF maintains offices throughout the country (even at the commune level), which serves as the tax collecting unit for all tax revenues (including those dedicated to subnational governments).

One interesting feature of the sharing system is that the shared percentages are not uniform across provinces. Instead, the central government sets differential rates depending on its estimate of provincial-level spending needs (based on nationally uniform norms) and an estimate of tax capacity. According to MOF's Table 02/CKTC-NSNN for 2006, 49 provinces were allocated 100% of the shared taxes whereas Ho Chi Minh City was to retain 29%; Ha Noi, 32%; Ba Ria–Vung Tau, 42%; Binh Duong, 44%; and Dong Nai, 49%. These five are the urbanized and more economically active areas in the country with considerably more tax capacity than the other provinces.

A second interesting aspect of the tax sharing system is that, once in place, the shares are to remain intact for a period of 3 to 5 years (known as the "budget stability period") as determined by the National Assembly. Prior to 2004, sharing rates could change from year to year. For example, the rate for Ho Chi Minh City rose from 24% in 2002 to 33% in 2003 (the 2002 State Budget Law did not become effective until 2004). This unique feature means that subnational governments can be reasonably sure of their sharing proportion, which should lead to less uncertainty in the budgeting process.

A third interesting aspect of the law concerning tax sharing is that each province has flexibility to determine how the various centrally shared taxes, as well as some of those assigned fully to local government, are to be distributed to the districts and communes within the province. This means that intraprovincial sharing rates can differ across provinces. For example, whereas all rental fees of land and water are retained at the provincial level in the Hai Duong Province, the fees paid in Lang Son Province are credited to the jurisdiction (commune, district, or province) in which the tax office where the payments are made is located.[16] Registration fees collected in Lang Son Province are entirely credited to the districts, whereas in Hai Duong Province, any fees collected within the city of Hai Duong is shared between the province and district, but outside the city, all collections are retained by the communes. The sharing rates of a revenue source may even vary among districts within a province. In 2005, while the two commercial districts (districts 1 and 5) in Ho Chi Minh City retained 15 and 16% of corporate income taxes respectively, 29% of those revenues were retained in most other districts. Interestingly, the sharing rates are not always set as prescribed in the law. It specifies that a minimum of 70% of the tax on transfers of land-use rights, land and housing taxes, registration fees, and several others are to be retained by communes in which the property is located. We discovered that in at least one province, all registration fees are credited to the districts.

Locally assigned and shared taxes are not the only revenues of subnational governments. Given the substantial interprovincial disparities in economic levels in Vietnam (Hill, 2002), there are also two types of transfer programs in place. One consists of conditional or targeted transfers to support the implementation of nationally targeted programs to reduce poverty or to provide for specific services, such as housing or vaccinations. The provinces also receive intergovernmental transfers to address consequences of unexpected national disasters or adverse socioeconomic events (Martinez-Vazquez & Gomez, 2005). The second type of transfer is unconditional balancing transfers intended to yield greater horizontal fiscal equity by balancing the differences between provinces' own-source and shared revenues with their overall expenditure needs.[17] These transfers flow to the provinces with no earmarking for districts and communes;

the provincial government has the autonomy to determine the portions passed through to the districts and communes within its boundaries. Spending norms are used to determine spending requirements in the various sectors. Prior to 2004, these norms were uniform throughout the country; however, the 2002 State Budget Law gives provinces autonomy in setting the norms (Socialist Republic of Vietnam & The World Bank, 2005). There is no explicit system for capital transfers; instead, the balancing transfer program can include money intended to improve infrastructure facilities (but is not earmarked for this purpose).

The State Budget Law also permits local government to borrow with the provision that the borrowing be from domestic sources and that the total outstanding debt cannot exceed 30% of the capital spending of a province.[18] Since the regular portion of the budget is to be balanced, the proceeds of this borrowing is expected to be dedicated to capital investment projects.

In summary, the revenue side of the subnational government budgets remains highly centralized; thus, at least for revenues, one cannot conclude that there is any significant fiscal decentralization. The rates and definitions of the bases of taxes, both shared and exclusive to the subnational government, are determined centrally and the tax department of the MOF collects those levies. The only revenue autonomy enjoyed at the subnational level is in the hands of the province, which does have some leeway in determining how tax revenues will be shared among the provinces, districts, and communes within its boundaries.

The law also provides a listing of spending tasks (Article 33) associated with local budgets; however, the list is long and quite vague. For example, on the capital development side, the list includes activities such as investment in state enterprises, state economic organizations, and state financial institutions. For regular spending, the functional areas include education and training, health care, culture, information, arts, science, environment and "other locally managed nonproductive activities." But the law also includes tasks associated with national defense and security if assigned by the center, support of the Communist Party of Vietnam, and support for local political, social, and professional organizations.

This relatively long list of functional assignments has both advantages and disadvantages. It does permit subnational government the flexibility to respond to differential needs unique to that area rather than a highly centralized and uniform supply of services. Furthermore, it means that each province has the freedom to determine which level (province, district, or commune) is most appropriate to take on spending responsibilities in a functional area. However, since the law (Article 31) lists identical activities (e.g., education and training, health care, etc.) for both the central and subnational governments, the resulting overlapping responsibilities (Yeung, 2007) create the possibilities for duplications in spending or that services may not be provided by neither level under the assumption that the other is carrying out the tasks. The single political party environment may, however, decrease the likelihood of these possible outcomes.

THE SUBNATIONAL BUDGET PROCESS

The budget process at the subnational level is somewhat more complex than for ministries and government agencies directly linked to the central government. This is due to the fact that the process is decentralized yet its outcomes must ultimately become a part of the state budget. Adding to the complexity is that budgets of lower levels are viewed and may be altered by the next higher level of government (Fforde, 2003).

Although none of the subnational governments have much revenue autonomy, the budget process begins with estimates of budget year revenues by the various agencies authorized to collect taxes and other revenues. One interesting feature of the 2002 law is that it contains an incentive for revenue collecting agencies to collect all that is due since a portion of the revenues actually collected that are in excess of the estimated amounts are retained locally. While this provides a strong incentive for local leaders to encourage tax compliance, it also creates the potential for underestimation of future tax revenues since this can result in windfall revenues, the spending of which is less likely to be closely scrutinized by other authorities. In 20 provinces, for which data on both budgeted and actual revenues for 2005 are available, the median underestimate of revenues was 25%. This suggests either a strong conservative bias on the part of revenue estimators or, more likely, a recognition that collections in excess of estimated amounts will reflect positively on revenue collectors (who also make the initial revenue estimates) and provide additional revenues to the subnational governments who approve the initial estimates.

Based on estimates of revenues, together with instructions received from the center (via the province and district), the People's Committee at the commune level prepares a budget that it submits for approval to the communal People's Council. Once approved, this budget is passed on to the district People's Committee, which examines it and can ask the commune-level People's Council to adjust the estimates. A similar pattern is applied by the People's Committee and Council at the district level, which passes its approved budget to the province. Ultimately, the province compiles the budgets of its own and all subsidiary governments and, once approved by the provincial People's Council, it is submitted to the center. Finally, as explained previously, once the National Assembly authorizes the final state budget, the resulting budgets for all subnational governments are made available to the respective local governments and also to the treasury department offices located around the country, which serve as the agency that records revenues and expenditures of the local bodies located within its service area.

Unfortunately, due to lack of full disclosure, it is not possible to report on detailed allocation of spending items by subnational governments in a disaggregated fashion. The MOF Web site contains data for some, but not all provinces; furthermore, the degree of disaggregation on the spending side is no more detailed than what is illustrated in Table 8-1. Finally, we stress that the previous description constitutes a summary of how the system is supposed to work; we are not aware of detailed analyses of the degree to which the process adheres to the norms stated in the 2002 law.

In fact, various analysts have argued that the outcomes of the budgetary process still leave much to be desired. Fritzen (2006) contends that the greater decentralization inherent in the law can worsen fiscal capacities of poorer provinces and reinforce regional disparities; and Beresford (2008) states that local revenue raising is highly regressive. Apparently some provincial and district officials believe that officials at the commune level have insufficient skills and, therefore, give them little budgetary discretion; but, as Fritzen (2005) argues, this may lead to disappointing implementation of community-based infrastructure programs. It has also been asserted that provincial autonomy under the 2002 law can lead to a reduction in income of the poor (Nguyen, 2008) or poor coordination in policy implementation (Martinez-Vazquez, 2005). Clarke (2007), in his review of the MTEF exercise in the Ministry of Education, observed a lack of interaction between the policy-making ministry and negotiations between the MOF and provinces. This silo-management orientation can, therefore, lead to a substantial disconnect between nationwide policies and expenditure implementation on the ground.

Conclusions

As a one-party country, Vietnam also maintains a unitary budget system. This budgeting system is, however, geared towards giving increasingly greater budget powers to subnational governments.[19] Decentralization in Vietnam has intensified since the introduction of the *doi moi* in 1986 and culminated in the 2002 State Budget Law that still governs the budget process in the country. The law has put Vietnam's fiscal decentralization on par with other quite decentralized countries such as the United States and India (Klump, 2007), at least in terms of expenditure autonomy.

Under this law, provinces in Vietnam enjoy substantial autonomy over the allocation of expenditures, and, although they have no freedom in setting tax rates or defining their base, they do have independence in assigning revenues among their constituent subnational entities. As long as the government retains the unitary budget framework, the potential of full fiscal decentralization (including decentralization of revenue powers) is unlikely to be possible. And although the budgeting system used in the country has seemingly performed adequately, there are still weaknesses, particularly ones associated with the quality and quantity of public services delivered to the poor and with coordination of policies.

Discussion Questions

1. How have changes in the budgeting environment in Vietnam coincided with the liberalization of its economy? Why might this be more than a coincidence?
2. What are some of the prominent features of the 2002 State Budget Law? How do they play out in the budget process?
3. How would you characterize the degree of fiscal autonomy enjoyed by provincial governments in Vietnam? How does it compare with another developing or developed countries?
4. Explain how some subnational governments fail to comply with legal mandates in their budgeting process.
5. What are potential perverse incentives that the 2002 law creates for subnational governments?

References

Abuza, Z. (2001). Debating the future: Vietnamese politics and the US trade deal. *Problems of Post Communism*, 48(1), 3–15.

Beresford, M. (2008). Doi moi in review: The challenges of building market socialism in Vietnam. *Journal of Contemporary Asia*, 38(2), 221–243.

Carlsson, F., Nam, P. K., Linde-Rahr, M., & Martinsson, P. (2007). Are Vietnamese farmers concerned with their relative position in society? *Journal of Development Studies*, 43(7), 1177–1188.

Clarke, G. (2007). *Developing an MTEF for the education and training sector: The experience of Vietnam*. Bangkok, Thailand. Available at: http://cms.unescobkk.org/fileadmin/user_upload/epr/MTEF/04Financial_Planning/03MTEF_for_Education_Sector/04030300/Clarke%20Grayson%20(2007).doc. Accessed March 29, 2010.

Economist Intelligence Unit. (2008). *Vietnam: Country report*. London, UK: The Economist.

Fforde, A. (2003). *Decentralisation in Vietnam—Working effectively at provincial and local government level—A comparative analysis of Long An and Quang Ngai provinces* (Policy report). Available at: http://www.ausaid.gov.au/publications/pdf/decentralisation_vietnam.pdf. Accessed April 7, 2010.

Fforde, A., & De Vylder, S. (1988). *Vietnam: An economy in transition*. Stockholm: Swedish International Development Authority.

Fritzen, S. (2005). The 'misery' of implementation: Governance, institutions, and anticorruption in Vietnam. In N. Tarling (Ed.), *Corruption and good governance in Asia* (pp. 98–120). New York: Routledge.

Fritzen, S. A. (2006). Probing system limits: Decentralisation and local political accountability in Vietnam. *Asia-Pacific Journal of Public Administration*, 28(1), 1–24.

Gainsborough, M. (2003). Corruption and the politics of economic decentralisation in Vietnam. *Journal of Contemporary Asia*, 33(1), 69–84.

Hill, H. (2002). Spatial disparities in developing East Asia: A survey. *Asian-Pacific Economic Literature*, 16(1), 10–35.

Irvin, G. (1995). Vietnam: Assessing the achievements of Doi Moi. *Journal of Development Studies*, 31(5), 725–750.

Klump, R. (2007). Pro-poor growth in Vietnam: Miracle or model? In T. Besley & L. J. Cord (Eds.), *Delivering on the promise of pro-poor growth: Insights and lessons from country experiences* (pp. 119–146). Washington, DC: Palgrave Macmillan and The World Bank.

Martinez-Vazquez, J. (2005). Making fiscal decentralization work in Vietnam (Working paper). Atlanta, GA: Andrew Young School of Policy Studies.

Martinez-Vazquez, J., & Gomez, J. L. (2005). Effective fiscal decentralization in Vietnam. *Proceedings of the Annual Conference on Taxation*, 356–361.

Nguyen, H. P. (2008). What is in it for the poor? Evidence from fiscal decentralization in Vietnam. *Journal of Public and International Affairs*, 19.

Norlund, I. (1984). The role of industry in Vietnam's development strategy. *Journal of Contemporary Asia*, 14(1), 94–107.

Painter, M. (2003). Public administration reform in Vietnam: Problems and prospects. *Public Administration and Development*, 23(3), 259–271.

Rao, M. G. (2000). Fiscal decentralization in Vietnam: Emerging issues. *Hitotsubashi Journal of Economics*, 41(2), 163–178.

Rao, M. G. (2003). Challenges of fiscal decentralization in developing and transitional economies: An Asian perspective. In J. Martinez-Vazquez & J. Alm (Eds.), *Public finance in developing and transitional countries: Essays in honor of Richard Bird* (pp. 35–62). Cheltenham, UK: Edward Elgar.

Schmidt, U. (2004). Vietnam's integration into the global economy: Achievements and challenges. *Asia Europe Journal*, 2(1), 63–83.

Socialist Republic of Vietnam, & The World Bank. (2005). *Vietnam—Managing public expenditure for poverty reduction and growth* (Vol. 1). Available at: http://www-wds.worldbank.org/external/default/ WDSContentServer/WDSP/IB/2005/06/13/000011823_20050613154301/Rendered/PDF/ 300350vol101100vietnamese.pdf. Accessed April 7, 2010.

The World Bank. (2000). *Vietnam—Managing public resources better: Public expenditure review* (Economic Report, Vol. 1). Washington, DC: Author.

Yeung, Y. (2007). Vietnam: Two decades of urban development. *Eurasian Geography and Economics, 48*(3), 269–288.

ENDNOTES

1. Admittedly, as this chapter is being written, the Vietnamese economy is encountering major challenges (not unlike many countries throughout the world in 2009) with slowing international trade and declines in foreign direct investment after having experienced extremely rapid inflation in 2008, which was estimated to have been in excess of the 20%.

2. The number of politburo members can change because it is not specified in the Charter of the Communist Party.

3. The five cities considered administratively equivalent to provinces (and not overlapping provinces) are Can Tho, Da Nang, Ha Noi, Hai Phong, and Ho Chi Minh City.

4. Removal of People's Councils has been piloted in some districts and urban communes since February 2009.

5. This style is dubbed as the Democratic Republic of Vietnam (DRV) model (Fforde & De Vylder, 1988). As Irvin (1995) notes, it is different from the Soviet central planning model on two important counts. First, most state enterprise was managed at the subnational level in Vietnam, and, second, there was a large informal economy alongside the state sector.

6. More details on the budget process under the 1997 law are provided in Rao (2000).

7. The full text of the Law (Law No. 01/2002/QH11) as well as of the decree detailing the implementation of the law (Decree No. 60/2003/ND-CP) can be found at http://www1.worldbank .org/publicsector/pe/countrybudgetlaws.cfm.

8. See http://openbudgetindex.org/files/CountrySummaryViet Nam.pdf for the 2006 report and http://openbudgetindex.org/files/cs_Viet Nam.pdf for the 2008 report. On the subject of transparency, it should be noted that as late as 2007, the government was still undertaking efforts to implement a functional budget classification system in accord with the standards established in the International Monetary Fund's *Government Finance Statistics*. Thus detailed comparisons of Vietnam with other countries can suffer from lack of comparability. Another limitation to the use of these data is the fact that the country was first included in the GFS in 1999.

9. For a discussion of the experience in developing the MTEF in the education and training sector, see Clarke (2007).

10. The International Federation of Accountants reported that in 2007, the government of Vietnam had a process in place (with The World Bank's support) to adopt the International Public Sector Accounting Standards, which includes accrual accounting. See http://homepage.test.ifac.org/PublicSector/ Downloads/IPSAS_Adoption_Governments.pdf.

11. In 2006, US$1 could be exchanged for approximately VND 16,000 (Economist Intelligence Unit, 2008).

12. The relative lack of transparency is also reflected in Table 8-1. Even though nearly VND 79 trillion was spent by the central government on recurrent expenditures, published data permit disaggregation only into the two very small categories: education and training, and science and technology. All other spending is not explicitly accounted for.

13.   Major cities attempt to gain unique power-making autonomy. For instance, under Decision 93/2001/ND-DP, Ho Chi Minh City's autonomy in investment and urban planning has been expanded.

14.   In fact, this aspect of the intergovernmental fiscal system was put in place in the 1996 budget law and retained in the 2002 version.

15.   The current list of such corporations includes eight electric companies, six official banks, Vietnam Airlines, Vietnam Railways, Vietnam Post and Telecom, and Vietnam Insurance Corporation (Martinez-Vazquez, 2005).

16.   As specified in Decisions 25/2006/QD-UBND and 44/2006/QD-UBND issued by Lang Son and Hai Duong provinces respectively on December 22, 2006.

17.   A few provinces with sufficient own-source revenue do not receive balancing transfers. According to data provided by Vietnam's Ministry of Finance, while all provinces received some balancing transfers in 2002, 15 out of 64 provinces did not get the transfers in 2005. However, the eligibility of these 15 provinces for targeted transfers stayed unchanged.

18.   Apparently, cities have been known to borrow and use a unique debt financing mechanism. Each public employee in the city is "expected" to buy a locally issued bond where the price of the bond is deducted from the employee's pay. Each bond is in small denominations to make it affordable, but the bond also carries a long duration to maturity.

19.   Gainsborough (2003) reports that the central government had attempted to recentralize on several occasions even before adoption of the 2002 State Budget Law.

Part **3**

Europe

Chapter 9

Italian Central Government Budgeting: Future Hopes and Past Disappointments

Riccardo Mussari, Pasquale Ruggiero, and

Patrizio Monfardini

Learning Objectives

- Understanding the budget reform processes in Italy over the last 30 years.
- Understand the adoption of the financial based budget and the accrual budget.
- Understand the power structure and responsibilities of both politicians and managers in the budgetary process.
- Understand who manages the resources, how resources are used, and the objectives to be reached.

Introduction

Like many Organisation for Economic Co-operation and Development (OECD) countries, Italy has been reforming its public administration in recent decades. With an emphasis on "New Public Management," the reform process has redesigned the institutional and organizational structure of the public administration. The start-up of intricate reforms based on a complex set of new laws was basically triggered by overwhelming dissatisfaction with the performance of the Italian public administration, both from a macroeconomic and a social perspective. Against a dynamic and developing socioeconomic backdrop, the Italian public administration wallowed in difficulty, with the most evident symptoms of its problems being the expansion of diseconomies, a mounting public debt, and its virtual incapacity to become a factor in the nation's development.

The European unification process and the changes mentioned in the socioeconomic backdrop have fostered a broad reform process aimed at overcoming bureaucratic organizational models, and a situation in which the respect of the formal rules represented the sole criterion for assessing the actions of public officials (i.e., a situation in which the role of the citizens and the fact that satisfaction of the citizens' needs is the reason for the existence of the public administration were overlooked). Central government budgeting and accounting reforms have been part of the whole picture considered necessary to modernize the state.

State Structure and Administrative Structure

The Italian Constitution states, "The Republic is composed of municipalities, provinces, metropolitan cities, regions and the State. The municipalities, provinces, metropolitan cities and regions are autonomous authorities with their own statutes, powers and functions according to the principles established by the constitution" (Article 114). The state territory is currently subdivided into 20 regions, 110 provinces, and 8101 municipalities.

Despite a series of privatizations since the early 1990s, the public sector in Italy still plays an important role in the country's economy and employs a considerable amount of financial and human resources. In order to evaluate the impact of the public sector (as broadly defined) on Italy's economic system, an Enlarged Public Sector Account was developed in the mid-1970s on a modified cash basis. The account included organizations that then had the legal status of autonomous firms (i.e., Italian State Railways, Italian Post Office, the State Telecommunications Company [SIP, now Telecom Italia S.p.A.], and other state monopolies), municipal companies or special enterprises for the supply of local public services (transport, electricity, and gas and water supply), port authorities, and Enel, the state-controlled monopolist producer and distributor of electrical energy.

As a result of the privatization policies originating from the Amato Law, the majority of aforementioned organizations lost their status as public bodies, including from a legal point of view, from 1992 onward. More specifically (and leaving aside the permanent transfer of property, only part of which has been completed), both the autonomous firms (Italian State Railways, monopolies, and the State Telecommunications Company) and Enel, the Italian Post Office and the companies in which the state held an equity interest (Iri and Eni) have been transformed into joint-stock companies. Therefore, the public sector account no longer refers to what was previously the enlarged public sector, and today it differs from the public administration account in that it includes a few public bodies not comprised in the latter, and some financial items in relation to transfers between bodies, which are not included in the public administration account (drawn up based on the accrual accounting principle).

The central administration has had its functional and organizational system redesigned. The most important functional change was initiated in 2001, with the formation of the new legislature; the change was triggered by Decree-Laws No. 300/99 and No. 303/99, which respectively addressed the organization of the government and the presidency of the Italian Cabinet.

The decree reorganizing the central administration sanctioned:

- The reduction of the number of ministries from 18 to 12; and the consequent extension of the area of political responsibility of a minister (and his upper echelon) to what are mostly standard functional fields (e.g., the institution of a welfare minister has vested with a single minister the responsibility for social, employment, and health policies);
- The narrowing of operational responsibility in favor of a centralized government's role in political tasks, via the definition of strategies and the coordination and supervision of their implementation;
- The introduction of new offices for directly collaborating with the ministries (and the secretaries) as a new structure to support the political upper echelon in policy development, and in assigning resources and objectives to department head (the direct collaboration offices take the place of traditional legislative offices); and
- The identification of the department as a first-level organizational unit that becomes a liaison between the political upper echelon of the ministry and the technical and operational system. Normally, the department is vested with responsibility for assuring standardized and integrated practices of the functions, carrying out objective tasks concerning large areas of standard matters, and the related instrumental tasks, including those related to the direction and coordination of the units into which the functions are divided (organizational units and units with instrumental, financial, and human resource management attributed to them).

The operational reforms of Decree-Laws No. 300/99 and No. 303/99 identified two fundamental organization models: one based on departments and one based on a general secretariat and general administrative offices. Additionally, an attempt was made to streamline the administrative structure of each ministry, not only to limit its costs and to reflect the process of functional devolution to regional and local government, but also to better distinguish the tasks of supporting the political function, strategic direction and control (assigned to the ministry and handled by minister's staff), and operational or technical/specialist tasks attributed to various structures (departments, agencies, corporations, and independent authorities) to which the specific pursuit of each policy is attributed. In addition, Decree-Law No. 300/99 introduced, for the first time, a unitary discipline (with some differentiation) for government agencies; some new agencies were created, and were to be managed by a general director supported by a steering committee, both appointed by the central government. Decree-Law No. 303/99 reinforced the role of coordination carried out by the presidency of the cabinet and streamlined its responsibilities, which had become stratified over time and included a big mix of functions (civil protection, tourism, urban areas, publishing, copyrights, social affairs, civil service, disability pensions, to name a few) that were then assigned to the sector functions of the ministries that have responsibility for the matters.

Central Government Budgeting

In order to understand the central government's budgeting, it is fundamental to refer to Article 81 of the Italian Constitution, which defines the roles regarding the constitutional bodies on this subject and some of the rules about the budgeting process in general:

> 1. Every year the Chambers approve the budget and the annual accounts presented by the government. 2. The provisional running of the budget cannot be granted if not by law and for a period not longer than four months. 3. With the law approving the budget, neither new taxes nor new expenditures can be established. 4. Any other law that entails new or higher expenditures must indicate the means for covering them.

The first point establishes the duties of the government and Parliament in matters of public accounting: the former has the role of proposing and, therefore, preparing the budget (with the input of departments and agencies), and the latter is in charge of examining and approving the budget document. Obviously, Parliament has the power to amend the text presented by the government, thereby contributing to the creation of the state budget, the Italian central government's main accounting document. The distinction of roles is important because it is through the approval of the budget that the two chambers (Parliament) authorize the government (i.e., the executive power) to tap resources from the community and to expend those resources within the limits of Parliament's authorization; furthermore, this authorization is the legal foundation on which the system of accounting controls is based.

The provisional running of the budget referenced in point 2 of Article 81 is a situation applicable to all entities that are subject to government accounting whenever the budget is not approved before the beginning of the fiscal year. This provision is aimed at guaranteeing the continuity of the central government's action and avoiding dangerous gaps in budget management: It lasts for a maximum of 4 months and is conferred only by law.

The prohibition in point 3 refers to the need for Parliament to carefully consider the forecast of new revenues and new expenditures; the budget law is, per se, an extremely broad and varied document and its complexity could impede an accurate evaluation of all of its implications. For this reason, the introduction of new revenue or expenditure may occur only through the approval of specific laws.

On the other hand, the budget document has a planning function, meaning it is the focal point for planning revenue and expenditure. Recognizing that it may be necessary to amend the revenue and expenditure forecasts (appropriations) within the budget, and that this cannot occur because of the limits imposed by point 3 of Article 81 of the Italian Constitution, Law No. 468 of 1978 introduced the so-called Finance Law (*Legge Finanziaria*) as the instrument to remedy this problem.

Finally, point 4 of Article 81 of the Italian Constitution is designed to maintain a balance between revenues and expenditures; the obligation includes not only the current financial period, but all of the financial periods included in the multiyear budget, and applies both in the case of new laws that produce expenditures and in the quantification of the budgeted charges planned (*oneri a regime*) for the permanent expenditures.

Articles 100 and 103 of the Italian Constitution are also relevant to the subject of budgeting. Article 100 identifies the State Audit Court (*Corte dei Conti*) as the accounting control body, with two types of duties: (1) the ex-post control over the management of the central government budget, and (2) the control over the financial management of the institutions to which the government assigns resources in an ordinary way. As a consequence, the State Audit Court is autonomous and independent from the executive power, and it reports directly to Parliament. Article 103 then qualifies the State Audit Court as the jurisdictional body in matters of public accounting.

Constitutional principles are flanked by those of the European Union (EU): Article 104 of the Treaty of Amsterdam prohibits excessive public deficits, although it is the Maastricht Treaty that outlines the concrete limits to be respected by member states (Maastricht criteria). In addition, Articles 246, 247, and 248 of the Treaty on EU vested a function of financial control with the European Audit Office; such control is focused on the utilization of resources appropriated at both the EU and national levels, in order to ensure pursuit of objectives that are common to all of the EU member states.

Functions and Principles

From the standpoint of the administration of Italy's public accounts, the central government budget has a key role in addition to forecasting the financial consequences of future management with public accounts. The main functions of the central government's budget are:

1. Political function: The political function refers to the consideration that the budget preparation and approval process represents a time when different social interests are mediated by elected representatives, and when social aims and the ways in which they will be pursued are determined. Budget approval by the Parliament is the manifestation of a traditional basis of democracy, the right to budget, in that it quantifies the resources that Parliament allows the government to withdraw from citizens and then to assign to public aims.

2. Steering and programming function: The steering and programming function refers to forecasting the means needed to reach the objectives (quantifying and assigning resources and activities with respect to the various administrations). Even though the emphasis is on resource control, the budget reports only monetary figures (appropriations), and contains no information about operating results (outputs) and social effects (outcomes). The information about the

purposes of the spending can only be obtained from the budget reclassification by functions objectives, affected by considering the economic destination of expenditures.

3. Authorization and limit function: The authorization and limit function is the most typical function of government budgets. Constraints apply not only with respect to aggregate amounts of revenues and expenditures (which are more related to the political function or the economic policy function), but also with regard to the amount and specific purposes of each appropriation. In other words, appropriations approved by Parliament (voting units) set the limits for the administrations (and their managers) in charge of spending them.

4. Economic (cyclical) policy function: The economic policy function refers to the substantial weight and influence of government within the national economy; moreover, some measures (transfers, infrastructure investment, incentives to industries, and social welfare initiatives) are clearly designed to have an effect on the economic cycle. Finally, managing the huge flows of money connected with public expenditures and revenues is an important aspect of monetary policy.

Laws regulating national government budgeting contain complex rules, but do not explicitly indicate the principles to be followed. However, as theory traditionally suggests, annual budgets and multiyear budgets should be prepared with respect to the following principles: annualize, unity, specificity, universality, integrity, financial balance, transparency to the public, truthfulness, and clarity.

As previously mentioned, Parliament's approval of the budget respects the principle of the right to budget, which is specific to all democracies and in Italy is regulated by its constitution. The approval essentially identifies the limits of the (financial) resources that the government can use in carrying out its own policies during the next financial period, and, correspondingly, the resources that can be collected from the national community. This obligation is conceived and expressed in terms of spending limitations, and not in terms of limits on the consumption of resources and, consequently, the accounting and assignment criteria for the various transactions during the financial year is obligation and cash based, and not accrual based.

For this reason, the collection and payment procedures are complex and are organized into several phases, and it is possible to exercise control over them in relationship to each of these phases. The fundamental distinction, in any case, is between (1) the legal phase, in which the governmental body's obligation to pay (spending commitment) or the right to cash (revenue assessment) is finalized, and (2) the material or factual phase, in which the cash settlement (collection and payment) is made. When Italian Law No. 468/78 went into effect, both phases became important, and thus the budget and, consequently, the relative reporting were divided into:

- Management of obligations (*gestione di competenza*) with regard to revenue assessment and spending commitments; and
- Management of cash (*gestione di cassa*) with regard to revenue collection and payment for expenditures.

Considering the State Treasury materially manages the revenues and expenditures for the central government, a report detailing each single expenditure and revenue item, information about the management of obligations (contained in accounting records of the departmental and nondepartmental bodies of the central government), and information about the management of cash (obtainable from the Treasury) is possible only if the classification of the items is identical and has the same degree of detail in both systems.

The budget appropriations establish limits for the operations of each administration, but the limits take on significance for the balances of the public accounts overall. From this point of view, the key data can be taken from the balances reported in the General Summary (*Quadro generale riassuntivo*) of the Italian central government budget, according to Article 6 of the Law No. 468/78 (Table 9-1). In this document the balances are calculated with respect to both obligations and cash flows. The differential result between total tax and nontax revenues and total current expenditures is the state savings (*Risparmio pubblico*). The balance between all revenues and expenditures, excluding transactions involving shareholdings, grants, loans, and loan reimbursements, yields the net indebtedness (*indebitamento netto*), or (if positive), net growth (*accrescimento netto*) of public capital due to ordinary management.

The difference between final revenues and final expenditures derived from ordinary current and capital management of the budget is the net balance to be financed (*saldo netto da finanziare*), if negative, or the net balance to be invested (*saldo netto da impiegare*), if positive. This final balance, calculated with reference to obligations, expresses the effects on the state's financial position of the transactions whose obligations originate in the financial period to which the budget refers.

Table 9-1

Balances from General Summary of the Central Government Budget

Tax and nontax revenues	340,179	Current expenditures	276,817
+		State savings	63,362
Other current revenues	28,977	+ Other ordinary expenditures	48,627
Total revenues	369,156	Ordinary operating expenditures	325,444
		Net financial balance	43,712
		+ Contributions for shareholdings and concession of credit	76,475
		Total expenditures (except loan reimbursements)	496,478
Net indebtedness	−32,763		
		+ Loan reimbursements	174,839
		Total expenditures	576,758
(Maximum) Recourse to the market	207,602		

Source: Ministry of Economy and Finance. Available at: http://www.rgs.mef.gov.it/ENGLISH-VE/index.asp. Accessed April 21, 2010.

Note: Amounts given in billions of euro.

Considering the effect of loans to be reimbursed or renewed coming due during the budget period, and adding this amount to the previous net financial balance will yield the aggregate recourse to the market (*ricorso al mercato*), namely, the amount of the entire financial shortfall that needs to be financed by the market. Because the budget appropriations are operating limits and considering that such amounts must be specifically indicated (and, therefore, authorized) in the finance law, the final financial shortfall is also referred to as the maximum recourse to the market (*ricorso massimo al mercato*).

FORM AND CONTENT OF BUDGET DOCUMENTS

The Law No. 94/97 and the Decree-Law No. 279/97 introduced numerous changes to the Italian central government accounting system with regard to the structure of both the state budget and the annual financial statement, as well as the single Treasury system (*sistema di tesoreria unica*) for the public sector. First of all, the classifications of revenue and expenditure accounts were profoundly changed.

The annual budget is composed of several sections and outlines, attached to the budget law. The main figures (public finance balances) are in the law approving the budget. Exhibits to the budget law include:

- A list of voting units or basic budget units (*unità previsionali di base*) of revenues and expenditures;
- A list of functions and objectives, for each ministry;
- A single statement for revenues;
- A statement of expenditures for each ministry; and
- A general summary outline.

Revenues

A single forecast statement (*stato di previsione*) is prepared for the central government's revenue, and is organized on the basis of the nature of the revenue even though the revenues of each ministry are indicated. The classification is thus by basic budget units (*unità previsionali di base*), headings (*titoli*), categories (*categorie*), and items and subitems (*capitoli* and *articoli*). In this classification, the fundamental unit of the budget is the voting unit to which Parliament's decisions apply. Compared with the former system, when the voting unit was the item, the decision is now centered on a higher level of aggregation, the budget unit. As a consequence, in the budget for the year 2000, there were around 150 basic budget units for revenues and around 1250 for expenditures, compared to nearly 7000 items (that remain the fundamental unit for management and reporting). The subdivision of basic budget units into items is carried out by special decree of the Ministry of Economy and Finance, immediately after the approval of the budget. In parliamentary practice, the parts of the budget regarding revenues and the net financial balance are debated and approved first, with the limits for all forecasted expenditures established thereafter. Once the revenue section of the budget is approved, the amendments proposed for the single items (basic budget unit) of expenditure must also indicate the means for covering possible higher expenditures involved.

As for classifications of items, currently, Article 6, Paragraph 1 of Law No. 468/78 (as substituted by Article 4 of Law No. 94/97) and Article 1, Paragraph 2 of Decree-Law No. 279/97 state that the revenues should be subdivided into:

- Headings (*Titoli*)—according to the origin: fiscal or nonfiscal nature, derived from the sales of properties, from credit collection, or obtaining loans;
- Basic budget units (*Unità previsionali di base*)—for parliamentary approval and administrative assessment; in the case of tax revenues only, the basic budget units are to be further subdivided according to the revenues derived from ordinary management activity or from tax assessment and control activity of financial offices;
- Categories (*Categorie*)—according to the nature of the revenues; (this reclassification is shown only in the general summary of the budget; for example, Heading I—Tax revenues, subdivided into: Category I—income and property tax; Category II—business taxes and duties;
- Items (*Capitoli*) and Subitems (*Articoli*)—according to the respective object, only for management and reporting purposes (this classification is not important for the approval of the budget). For each revenue and expenditure, the budget indicates: (1) the forecast assessment or commitment, and (2) the forecast cash inflow or outflow. Actually, the basic budget unit has three or four sublevels, only the highest of which corresponds to a responsibility center.

A further subdivision is shown in Table 9-2.

For management and reporting purposes, a decree of the Ministry of Economy and Finance can divide each basic budget unit into more items, which can then be divided into subitems (but not necessarily; for example, income tax corresponds to a single item). The division in items is carried out in agreement with the administrations involved, and is almost simultaneous to the approval of the budget. This is possible since this division into items closely reflects the contents of the technical exhibits

---

Table 9-2

Further Subdivision of the Basic Budget Unit–Tax Revenues

1. Responsibility center (1st level)
  1.1. Heading (tax revenues) (2nd level)
    1.1.1. Nature of revenue (name of the tax) (3rd level)
      1.1.1.1. Revenues from ordinary management (4th level)
      1.1.1.2. Revenues derived from tax assessment and control activity (4th level)
    1.1.2. Nature of the revenue (name of the tax) (3rd level)
      1.1.2.1. Revenues from ordinary management (4th level)
      1.1.2.2. Revenues derived from tax assessment and control activity (4th level)

Source: Ministry of Economy and Finance. Available at: http://www.rgs.mef.gov.it/ENGLISH-VE/index.asp. Accessed April 8, 2010.

(*allegati tecnici*) that supplement each forecast statement, as adopted by the Council of Ministries during the presentation of the budget in Parliament and updated with the notes of variations (*note di variazione*) during the debate. Because these exhibits are prepared by the single administrations involved, with the coordination of the government, the agreement required by the law is automatic and the adoption of the decree can occur quickly.

Expenditures

The appropriations of expenditures are contained in forecast statements (*stati di previsione*) for each of the ministries. The classification of expenditures is based on: (1) functional analysis, and (2) basic budget units (relevant within the budget) and for management and reporting only, with further subdivision into items (according to economic and functional content). The procedure for subdividing the expenditure related basic budget units into items is the same that for revenue related basic budget units.

As shown in Table 9-3, the basic budget units are allotted to responsibility centers within the central government administration, with offices directed by a general director (senior manager). Each basic budget unit can be associated with only one responsibility center. Accordingly, the reform intended to reflect, via the accounting plan, greater autonomy and responsibility in public management. Indeed, the managers are responsible for achieving objectives, while they also have the authority to commit the amounts assigned in the budget and are generally responsible for the efficient use of the financial, human, and material resources that are assigned to them. In the system of accrual budget and cost accounting by cost centers, the organizational units associated with the basic budget units also are the top-level responsibility centers to which the ministerial directives for planning administrative activity assign the managerial objectives. These units are also the cost centers for carrying out economic analyses of a central government accrual budget and a central government cost report (*rilevazione dei costi dello stato*).

As in the case of revenues, the expenditure-related basic budget unit is not a single level of classifications, but refers to four levels, with the highest of them corresponding to a responsibility center under a senior manager, as shown in Table 9-3.

Another criterion for the classification of expenditures introduced by Law No. 94/97 is the function of the expenditures, which is intended to make the budget understandable in terms of the sector policies and services offered to the public. In a special exhibit to the budget, the expenditures of each ministry are therefore divided into target functions, identified, as consistent with the classifications for national accounting on the basis of the classifications of the functions of government (COFOG), that have been adopted by the EU and OECD countries. The COFOG functional classification is organized on the basis of three levels (ten divisions, subdivided into groups, and further subdivided into classes). However, in order to adapt the classification to Italy's administrative structure and to provide better representation of the institutional power of each ministry, a fourth level of classification was established, in collaboration with the State Audit Court and each ministerial administration, and it includes around 400 subclasses.

Table 9-3

Further Subdivision of the Basic Budget Unit of Expenditure

1. Responsibility center	
1.1. Current expenditure	(1st level)
1.1.1. Working expenditure	(2nd level)
1.1.1.1. (Personnel)	(3rd level)
1.1.1.2. (Other specifications)	(4th level)
. . .	
1.1.2. Interventions	(3rd level)
1.1.2.1. (Specifications)	(4th level)
1.1.2.2. (Specifications)	(4th level)
. . .	
1.1.3. Compensations for retirement	(3rd level)
1.1.4. Public debt burdens	(3rd level)
1.1.5. Common expenditures	(4th level)
1.1.5.1. (Specifications)	(4th level)
1.1.5.2. (Specifications)	(2nd level)
1.2. Capital expenditures	(3rd level)
1.2.1. Investments	(4th level)
1.2.1.1. (Specifications)	(4th level)
1.2.1.2. (Specifications)	
. . .	
1.2.2. Common expenditures	(3rd level)
1.2.2.1. (Specifications)	(4th level)
1.2.2.2. (Specifications)	(4th level)
. . .	
1.2.3. Other expenditures	(3rd level)
1.3. Reimbursement of loans	(2nd level)

Source: Ministry of Economy and Finance. Available at: http://www.rgs.mef.gov.it/ENGLISH-VE/index.asp. Accessed April 8, 2010.

This reclassification needs to be facilitated by another subdivision of expenditure items into subitems, according to the objective contained in special exhibits to the expenditure forecasts pursuant to Article 6, Paragraph 6 of Law No. 468/78.

The draft of the budget bill must indicate for each basic budget unit of revenue or expenditure:

- The presumed amount of uncollected assessments (revenue) and unpaid commitments (expenditure) at the end of the financial year preceding that to which the budget refers (such amounts are obviously not those to be approved by Parliament, inasmuch as they refer only to amounts presumed at the time when the budget is debated and approved);

■ The forecasts of revenue assessments and of spending commitments; and

■ The forecasts of revenues to be collected and expenditures to be paid (without distinction, however, between current-year obligations and transactions regarding uncollected assessments and unpaid commitments from the previous financial year). In order to be counted, the sums have to have been paid to the State Treasury, and not only to collection agents, whereas the payments refer to those sums actually paid by the Treasury. Therefore, the system assumes and requires the uniformity of classification between the items in the budget and those used by the Treasury.

BUDGETING PROCESS

The decision making that leads to the preparation of the Italian central government's economic and financial planning process is complex, and it entails several phases, corresponding to which specific administrative and legislative acts are adopted and which correlated accounting documents are drafted by the government and Parliament. The procedure of planning and approving the central government budget (i.e., the programming component of public finance) is carried out over a period of around 9 months, from March of the year prior to the financial year referenced in the budget, when a special circular is issued by the Ministry of Economy and Finance, up until the last 10 days of December when parliamentary procedure is usually concluded, and the documents having the rank of state law are approved. The main steps of the process are illustrated in Table 9-4.

THE GOVERNMENT ACCRUAL BUDGET

One of the main new changes in central government budgeting and accounting at the end of the 1990s was the introduction of a cost-budgeting process and a cost center accounting system, based on analytic forecast and actual data. In line with the principles that redefined the delegation of managerial responsibility (starting with Decree-Law No. 29/93), the cost-budgeting process and a cost center accounting system adopted by the central government aim to disclose information for qualifying one of the areas for which this responsibility is vested: the value of consumed resources. In other words, the information aims to determine if the assigned objectives within the organizational unit of which the managers are in charge have been reached.

Two summary accounting documents originate from the cost-budgeting process and cost center accounting system: a forecast document known as the central government accrual budget (which now only includes cost data and no revenues), and a document providing actual data known as a central government cost statement. These are administrative documents prepared for information purposes and are not subject to any parliamentary or governmental approval. Since the cost-budgeting process and cost center accounting system are intended to produce cost information, they should be based on accrual basis. In effect, both in the circular that instituted the procedures

Table 9-4

Timetable for the Process of Drafting and Approving for Central Government Budget Documents

Bodies	Formal acts	Documents	Deadlines
General Accountancy Office (Ministry of Economy and Finance)	Basic circular for formulating the budget	Contains the principles and general criteria on which forecasts are based.	March
Government	Economic and Financial Planning Document and presentation to the Chambers	The Economic and Financial Planning Documents identifies the percentages of variation for revenues and expenditures compatible with the planned state sector borrowing requirement and the net indebtedness of the public administration.	June 30th
Government	Presentation to the Chambers of the draft bill for the approval of the previous year financial statement	The Annual Account is organized as a Profit and Loss Statement and a Statement of Assets and Liabilities.	June 30th
Government	Presentation to the Chambers of the draft of the budget for the current year	Contains the definitive forecasts both in terms of assessments and commitments, and cash flows; it must be approved by law, the same as the document that it modifies.	June 30th
Ministries and other administrations	Proposed forecast of expenditures	Compiling of the budget schedules (schede di bilancio) on the basis of unchanged legislation and of the basic circular	Within the limits indicated in the basic circular
Parliament	Voting on a resolution	The resolution indicates for each year covered by the Economic and Financial Planning Document the net amount to be financed, the recourse to the market, and the criteria of variation of revenues and expenditures.	Within 30 days of the presentation of the Economic and Financial Planning Documents
Ministries/General Accountancy Offices/Government	Elaboration of the annual and multiyear budget based on unchanged legislation (bilancio a legislazione vigente), debate and approval by the cabinet	Budget without varying the financial legislation in force (It is the result of the basic circular: The quantification of the revenue and expenditure items contained in it is based on the expected trends of macroeconomic variables, but founded on laws already in effect.)	September 30th
Government	Presentation to the Chambers of draft bill of annual and multiyear budget based on current legislation	Beyond the actual budget, it contains a series of documents that together form the so-called financial maneuver, a revenue/expenditure package; not all of the documents are subject to parliamentary approval.	September 30th
Ministry of Economy and Finance	Presentation to Parliament of the Forecasting and Planning Report (RPP–Relazione Previsionale e Programmatica)	This is not an accounting document, but it delineates government's objectives in relationship to the forecast economic framework.	September 30th
Parliament	Approval of finance law and annual and multiyear budgets	The annual and multiyear budgets are approved.	December 31st

Source: Ministry of Economy and Finance. Available at: http://www.rgs.mef.gov.it/ENGLISH-VE/index.asp. Accessed April 8, 2010.

and in the successive basis circulars, the definition of cost that has been adopted and the informative purposes that have been pursued are perfectly in line with an accrual approach.

The process of developing the accrual budget follows and reflects the process for approving budget with reference to obligations. Nevertheless, with the accrual budget being an administrative document, and not requiring any type of political, parliamentary, or governmental approval, its preparation does not pose, per se, the need to involve the existing numerous decision-making levels. Indeed, every individual administration, with the coordination of the General Accounting Office, prepares its own forecasts and updates them for keeping track of the changes in the draft cash/obligation budget progressively approved in Parliament. As long as the preparation of the cost budget follows that of the budget prepared with regard to obligations and cash flows, it means that the political decisions regarding the use of public resources will be centered on cash flows or obligations, namely, financial measures (appropriation of monetary resources) and not the economic measures (use of resources). The preparation of the cost budget is closely linked to the cost center accounting system.

The cost centers (*centri di costo*) serving as one of the bases for the organization of the accrual system, together with the Chart of Accounts (*Piano dei Conti*) and the list of Services Supplied (*elenco dei Servizi Erogati*) are appropriately identified with the system of the responsibility centers for each administration. In particular, as previously noted, the top-level cost centers coincide with the top-level responsibility centers (general departments or directions) relevant for the definition of the basic budget units for the budget with reference to obligations.

The accrual budget and the chart of the accounts were updated by Ministerial Decree No. 34558 dated March 25, 2002, by the Ministry of Economy and Finance. Similarly, the services supplied are classified according to target functions (COFOG classification, extended to the fourth level for identifying the institutional missions of each responsibility center) in relation to the objectives of the state budget. The whole system is aimed at the construction of a budget by cost centers, which defines the objectives to be reached in terms of functions to be pursued, services to be supplied, and activity to be put into place, compared with the value of the resources (financial, human, and instrumental) to be used by and assigned to the managers responsible for a center.

However, the accrual budgeting process and the accounting system, although involving both forecast and actual data, have limited their objectives to cost information, ignoring the concept of matching costs to revenues for the financial year. The process of preparing the central government's accrual budget starts in March of the year prior to the one to which the forecasts refer, with the issuing of a basic circulahr by the Ministry of Economy and Finance (starting with the forecasts for 2003, unified with the circular that starts the budget process). It involves a dialogue and exchange of information, mainly between the administrations and the General Accounting Office, as the approval of Parliament or of any other constitutional body is not required. The calendar and the process of preparation for the accrual budget for 2003 are summarized in Table 9-5.

Table 9-5

Timetable for the Preparation of the State Accrual Budget, Fiscal Year 2003

Bodies	Acts	Documents	Deadlines
Each central administration	Electronic transmission of budget charts to Central Offices of the Budget	Budget charts and other attachments (personnel, illustrative notes, cost centers summaries, etc.)	June 12th
Central Offices of the Budget (Central State Accounting Office)	Electronic transmission to General Inspectorate for Budget Policies—Service of Analyses of Costs and Staff Efficiency	Data to be verified and validated by the Central Offices of the Budget	June 19th
Each central administration	Electronic transmission of variations to the Central Offices of the Budget	Variations of costs following the budget variations made by July 31st	September 9th
Central Office of the Budget	Electronic transmission to General Inspectorate for Budget Policies—Service of Analyses of Costs and Staff Efficiency	Data verified and validated by the Central Offices of the Budget	September 13th
Central administrations and Services of Analyses of Costs and Staff Efficiency	Further revisions	During the procedure of approval of the budget, the adaptation of cost forecasts continues.	In conjunction with the budget procedure

Source: Circular No. 16/2002 of the Ministry of Economy and Finance.

The structure of the accrual budget document is very similar and is not dictated by the law, but it generally includes:

- Summary tables and graphs of costs by type of cost and by administrations (distinctly for the two dimensions and crossing them);
- Analyses of operating costs and of depreciation, in relation to the administrations that generate them;
- A reconciliation between the cost budget and the budget with reference to obligations; and
- Accrual budgets of the individual central administrations (ministries and related bodies), by organizational structure (cost centers), and type of cost (cost of personnel, other operating costs, depreciation, taxes, disputed expenditure). Transfers to other bodies, included in the general summarizing tables of the central government, are obviously not considered to be costs for the single administration that allocates them.

BUDGET VARIATIONS AND MANAGEMENT

The central government budget is the basis for budgetary control: The activities for realizing the forecasts included in the budget (in substance, the activity of managing revenues and expenditures) are known as "budget execution." On the basis of the description provided earlier, the budget forecasts seem to be absolutely rigid and unable to be modified. Unforeseen expenditures are not admitted, and no expenditure can exceed the allotment in the relative basic budget unit, even if it appears to be necessary and opportune; also in the case of revenues, it would be impossible to record items (type of revenue) that did not have a budget classification. In order to get around this rigidity, the following provisions have been made for making the budget more flexible: reserve funds and budget amendments.

Reserve Funds

Reserve funds are general spending items that cannot be utilized as such, but can feed the specific expenditure items during the budget execution period. The mechanism used is that of a reversing entry to the reserve fund and a transfer to the item for which the increase of the financial appropriation is needed. The use of reserve funds responds to the need to simplify budget execution, without having to secure the approval of Parliament (that is, the same body that approved the budget) for certain types of amendments. The use of a reserve fund and the reverse entry are administrative steps, although notably important, and generally are sanctioned by a decree of the minister of economy and finance. The main reserve funds are included in the forecasting statement of the Ministry of Economy and Finance:

- The reserve fund for obligatory expenditures and memorandum accounts, (*fondo di riserva per le spese obbligatorie e d'ordine*); the sums reversed from it can be assigned to: (1) the payment of unpaid commitment, eliminated from the budget via administrative quashing (*perenzione amministrativa*), after a specific number of years, but not yet prescribed on the basis of the private law, in the event of the request by the person entitled, (2) expenditures recognized as obligatory, as they are included in a special list attached to the budget forecast statement of the ministry of economy and finance, or (3) expenditure connected to revenue assessment and collection (e.g., commissions paid to collection agents or tax collector fees).
- The reserve fund for unexpected expenditures (*fondo di riserva per le spese impreviste*), whose types are included in a list approved with a special article of the budget law. This fund may only be tapped by order of a decree by the president of the Republic of Italy as proposed by the minister of economy and finance and registered at the State Audit Court.
- The special funds for draft bills in the course of approval (*fondi speciali per i provvedimenti normativi in corso di approvazione*), appropriated for expenditures derived from bills that are expected to be passed during the financial period of the multiyear budget. If not used (for example, because the law is not approved), the amount allocated to these funds constitutes budget savings. Because the approval of new laws can also achieve reductions in expenditures or increased revenues, by the same logic, some negative appropriations (*accantonamenti di segno negativo*) can be included in the budget and are identified with a letter of the alphabet, which are then correlated to positive appropriations (indicated with the same letter) for new or

higher expenditures. These positive appropriations can only be used if the regulation that provides the revenues indicated in the negative appropriation enters in force.

Administrative Variations

For certain basic budget units listed in a table attached to the central government budget, the minister of economy and finance is authorized to carry out reverse entries. With the same provision, that is, the increase of one or more items must be exactly offset by a decrease in other items belonging to a basic budget unit included in the list. This is not an exception to the principle according to which the modifications can be carried out only by the same body that approves an act (for the budget, the approving body would be Parliament).

An administrative-type act is also sufficient for revenue variations. As already noted, no specific provision is needed for incremental revenues because the revenue forecast does not have a limiting or authorizing function, and the administrations must assess and collect the credit of the state as it becomes payable. However, for new revenues, that is, those that cannot be attributed to one of the existing revenue items, a new item must be created, formalized with a decree by the minister of economy and finance, on the proposal of the General Accounting Office.

Adjusted Budget (Bilancio di assestamento)

With the exceptions of the cases noted previously, in order to change the forecasts of expenditure, a legislative act is necessary, of the same nature and with the same limitations (Article 81, Paragraph 3 of the Italian Constitution: it is prohibited to institute new taxes and new expenditures) as for that approving the budget. In light of the results of the previous year and the course of the current period, provided that the obligation of balancing the budget is respected, the appropriations of the budget can be adapted in the adjusted budget to new or unexpected needs, as presented by the minister of economy and finance to Parliament, and to the exact quantification of the uncollected assessments and unpaid commitments of the preceding financial period, as reported in the financial statement. To this end, the presentation of the bill for the approval of the adjusted budget must occur by June 30th, according to Article 17 of Law No. 468/78, in connection with the presentation of the financial statement for the preceding financial period. The law covering the adjustment can therefore authorize offsetting between different basic budget units, but further variations can be made, with specific adjustment laws, if presented to Parliament by October 31st. Often, the variations in the budget are not sufficient for guaranteeing the balancing of public accounts: In this case, more substantial measures can be approved through ordinary laws, capable of instituting new revenue and new expenditures, defined as public-finance maneuvers, which, obviously, will also be followed by the consequent changes in the budget.

Because there is no strict deadline for approving the budget adjustment bill, the approval is often not particularly prompt (for example, the bill for adjusting the 2001 budget was approved with Law No. 419 of November 29, 2001). This late date of approval for adjustments causes one to suppose that it is mostly a ratification of irreversible tendencies or of changes already made by administrations, made on the basis of provisional data supplied by the Treasury, in order to facilitate the approval of the financial report.

The adjusted budget includes a list of basic budget units and target functions that have been changed, and an exposition of all the variations, for each ministry or related body. The adjusted budget law is also followed by a decree of the minister of economy and finance that subdivides the basic budget units into items.

(Re)Starting the Reform Process

As a part of the public sector reform process aimed at both balancing public accounts and achieving economic and social growth for Italy, a new structure of the central government budget was defined in 2007 with respect to the 2008 budget. The adoption of a new structure for the budget was mainly aimed at establishing a direct causal link between the resources appropriated by the budget and the actions or activities to be carried out. The new budget is a tool available to Parliament and the government that is potentially suitable for achieving greater awareness and a broader understanding of the decision-making processes regarding financial and economic planning at the central government level. As a consequence, it should be possible to allocate resources more efficiently and more effectively to the different sectors of activity.

This new budget is more transparent and it is thus easier for citizens to get a better understanding of public decisions in terms of quantitative appropriateness and the correlation of those decisions with the government's program. In these terms, the structure of the 2008 budget provides a clearer definition of the functions carried out by the central government, and consequently, a better understanding of the expenditure process.

The previous legislation (Law No. 94/97 reforming some rules provided by the Law No. 468/78), first applied for the 1998 Annual Budget, provided a structure for the budget that was based on forecast statements, responsibility centers (*centri di responsabilità*) (from an organizational standpoint), the basic budget unit (from an accounting standpoint), and target functions (from a functional perspective). After 10 years, the government was aiming to use the 2008 Annual Budget to give new life to the budget reform process started in 1997, and was specifically interested in developing a management by objective (MBO) culture.

Consistent with the current legislation, reform of the budget structure aims at shifting the focus of the budget from the organizational structure of the central government (that manages the resources) to the functions fulfilled (how resources are used) and the objectives to be reached.

The new structure of the budget, on the expenditure side, is based on two new levels of aggregation: missions (*missioni*) and programs (*programmi*). Expenditures set out in the forecast statements are allocated to 34 missions, which are divided into 165 programs, as shown in Table 9-6.

Table 9-6

An Example of Missions and Progams

Mission code	Missions	Program code	Program	Ministries
1	Constitutional bodies, bodies having constitutional relevance, and presidency of the cabinet	1	Constitutional bodies	Ministry of Economy and Finance
		2	Bodies having constitutional relevance	Ministry of Economy and Finance
		3	Presidency of the cabinet	Ministry of Economy and Finance
2	General administration and support for the central government and state representation on the territory	1	Central government and state representation on the territory	Ministry of the Interior
3	Financial relations with territorial administrations	1	Financial provisions to territorial administrations for sector initiatives	Ministry of Economy and Finance
		2	Services and support for territorial administrations	Ministry of the Interior
		3	Financial transfers to local public administrations for general purposes	Ministry of the Interior
		4	Federalism	Ministry of Economy and Finance
		5	Accounting regulation and other financial transfers to regions with special autonomy	Ministry of Economy and Finance
		6	Contribution of the central government to health expenses	Ministry of Economy and Finance

Source: Ministry of Economy and Finance. Available at: http://www.rgs.mef.gov.it/ENGLISH-VE/index.asp. Accessed April 8, 2010.

Missions represent the main functions and the strategic objectives to be reached by public expenditures. Many ministries are involved in different missions, and some of the missions are jointly in charge of multiple ministries. Two transversal missions are in the forecast statements of all ministries:

- Funds to be allocated (*Fondi da ripartire*), which incorporate the reserve funds and the special funds which will be allocated during the financial year; and
- Institutional and general services (*servizi istituzionali e generali*), which cover the common expenditures not attributable to any specific mission.

Programs are uniform aggregations of activities carried out within a ministry in order to reach the objectives planned for the specified mission. Each ministry participates in two transversal programs, contained in the mission named institutional

Table 9-7

Basic Budget Units (Macroaggregates)

Current expenditures	Capital expenses	Loan reimbursement
Operating expenditures	Investments	Public debt reimbursement
Intervention	Other capital expenses	
Public debt expenses	Common expenses	
Common expenses		

Source: Ministry of Economy and Finance. Available at: http://www.rgs.mef.gov.it/ENGLISH-VE/index.asp. Accessed April 8, 2010.

and general services. This program covers all indirect expenses not ascribed during the budgeting process to the different program and all expenses related to policy management.

The programs themselves are subdivided into macroaggregates (*macroaggregati*), which refer to the different types of expenses and are the new basic budget units to be discussed and approved by the Parliament. In the forecast statements, the macroaggregates are contained in three headings: current expenses, capital expenses, and loans reimbursement, as shown in Table 9-7.

Furthermore, each macroaggregate is subdivided in responsibility centers that are ministerial organizational units in charge of the financial resources (see Figure 9-1).

Figure 9-1

New structure of the budget: expenditure classification.

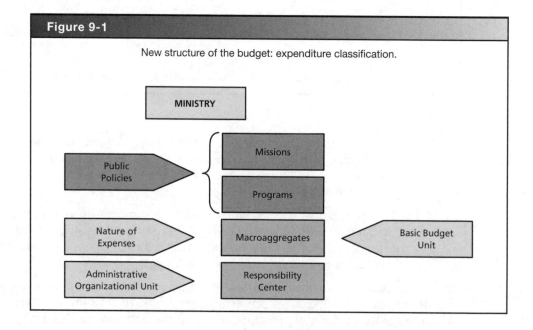

This new classification has also been adopted for the aforementioned accrual budget so that the documents are more comparable, even if having a different basis (accrual versus financial). The classification has also been changed on the revenue side, with four levels of aggregation: At the first level, the headings have been confirmed: (1) tax revenues; (2) nontax revenues; (3) income derived from sales and depreciation of fixed assets and revenues derived from credit drawing; and (4) revenue derived from loans. At the second level, a distinction has been made between current revenues and noncurrent revenues.

At the third level, the type of revenues is highlighted. For example, the tax revenues heading's most important components are the income tax, VAT, and aggregation of other taxes having the same features. In the other headings, the revenues are classified according to content (e.g., income for services provided by the organization, etc.).

At the fourth level, the classification is "revenues derived from ordinary management" and "revenues derived from tax assessment and control activity of financial offices." The new classification of revenues and expenses make it possible to reduce the number of basic budget units to be discussed and approved by Parliament from 1656 in 2007 to 690 in 2008 (see Table 9-8). Finally, for managerial purposes, the macroaggregates are subdivided in items and subitems in each ministry's forecast statement.

The latest regulation is the Law No. 196/2009. At the end of the 2009, an important new regulation on state budgeting and accounting was issued in Italy. In the following section, information is provided with reference to the main novelties introduced by the Law No. 196/2009 with reference both to the documents and the budgeting and accounting process. The Law No. 196/2009 introduces several important novelties that will come into force as of 2011.

Firstly, the new law is going to modify the budgeting cycle, as shown in Table 9-9.

The most important novelties involve the report on economy and public sector finance, the public finance decision, and the stability law proposal.

The timing of the report on economy and public sector finance has been postponed, as have all the budgeting and accounting documents, to the 15th of April. It contains the following information.

- The analysis of the national economic trend and of the economic and cash accounts of public administrations at the end of the previous year by comparing them with the forecasts included in the public finance decision.
- The update of the macroeconomic forecasts, of resource accounts of public administrations, and of their cash balance. In addition, in case of budget variance, adjustment actions that will be applied by the government are shown.
- The cash balance of the central government and the relative financial backing.

Furthermore, the report on economy and public sector finance shows detailed information both on the accounts and the budgets referring to the main expenditure areas: public employment, social care, and health care. Detailed information on public debt is also provided.

Table 9-8

Basic Budget Units in the Annual Budget, Fiscal Years 2007 and 2008

Ministry	Mission	Program	Basic budget units		
			2007	2008	Difference
Revenues	—	—	164	60	−104
Economy and Finance	25	45	295	115	−180
Economic Development	7	16	84	46	−38
Labor and Social Security	5	9	60	26	−34
Justice	3	7	39	16	−23
Foreign Affairs	3	10	85	26	−59
Public Education	5	14	201	44	−157
Interior	7	15	67	47	−20
Environment, Territory, and Sea	4	10	61	30	−31
Infrastructures	4	13	67	31	−36
Communications	5	8	54	20	−34
Defence	4	11	81	26	−55
Agriculture, Food, and Forestry	7	12	59	34	−25
Arts and Culture	5	11			
Health	4	10	55	25	−30
Transport	5	12	65	40	−25
University and Research	5	9	34	30	−4
Welfare	5	10	37	26	−11
International Trade	3	6	40	14	−26
Total			**1,656**	**690**	**−966**

Source: Ministry of Economy and Finance. Available at: http://www.rgs.mef.gov.it/ENGLISH-VE/index.asp. Accessed April 8, 2010.

Note: Amounts given in billions of euro.

Another important budgeting document is the public finance decision. It replaces the economic and financial planning document and has to be submitted to the parliament by the 15th of September. In summary, the public finance decision:

- Contains the updated budget forecasts of the current financial year;
- Shows the variances among the forecasts contained in the last planning documents and the current macroeconomic situation;
- Contains the general objectives of the economic policy and a 3-year forecast of public finance;
- Defines the objectives per sector with reference to the central government, the local government, and the national insurance bodies;

Table 9-9

Comparing the Old and the New Law on Public Budgeting and Accounting

Law No. 468/1978	Law No. 196/2009
Report on economy and public sector finance (by 28th of February)	Report on economy and public sector finance (by 15th of April)
General annual financial statement (by 30th of June)	General annual financial statement (by 30th of June)
Adjusted budget proposal (by 30th of June)	Adjusted budget proposal (by 30th of June)
Economic and financial planning document (by 30th of June)	Public finance decision (by 15th of September)
Forecasting and planning report (by 30th of September)	Canceled
Finance law proposal (by 30th of September)	Stability law proposal and technical notes (by 15th of October)
Annual budget law proposal (by 30th of September)	Annual budget law proposal (by 15th of October)
Other legislative measures related to the finance law (by 15th of November)	Other legislative measures related to the finance law (by 28th of February)
n.a.	Stability pact updates (european timesheet)
n.a.	Other public sector organizations planning and budgeting documents

Source: Ministry of Economy and Finance. Available at: www.rgs.mef.gov.it. Accessed April 22, 2010.
n.a., not available.

■ Defines the maneuvers to be carried out in order to reach the aforesaid objectives; and
■ Contains several forecasts among which the most important regards the gross domestic product (GDP) and the structural indicators of the income statement of the public administrations both at the central and the local level.

On the basis of the public finance decision, the 3-year maneuver of public finance is prepared. It is composed of the annual budget law and the stability law. This latter contains the qualitative and quantitative measures necessary to reach the objectives defined in the public finance decision.

Other main novelties contained in Law No.196/2009 are (Figure 9-2):

1. Accounting systems and schemes will be harmonized through a governmental regulation in the following years according with COFOG schemes;
2. Accrual-based accounting and performance indicators will be added to the existing modified cash-based accounting system;
3. Whole of government accounts will be prepared;
4. An unique database for public sector organizations' accountings will be created at the Ministry of Economy and Finance; and
5. The voting unit of the annual budget of the central government is moved up from BBU (basic budgeting unit) to the programs level; every program is assigned to a single responsibility unit.

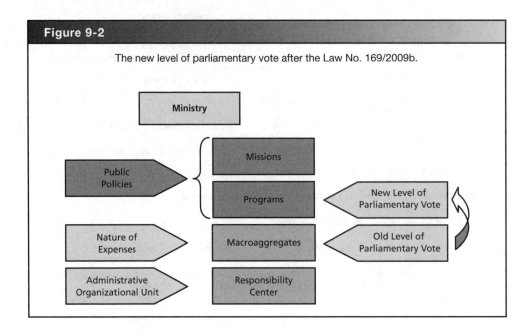

Figure 9-2

The new level of parliamentary vote after the Law No. 169/2009b.

Therefore, the public budgeting and accounting system is still in flux in Italy. During 2010, the Italian government passed several decrees, in coherence with the Law No. 196/2009, in order to redefine it both at the central and at the local level.

Discussions Questions

1. What are the main functions of the central government budget?
2. What are the main phases of the central government budgeting process?
3. Why does the central government budget contain reserve funds?
4. What is the function of the adjusted budget in the budgeting process?
5. What is a basic budgetary unit and what is its function in the parliamentary approval procedure?
6. What is the general summarized outline and what results does it contain?

Suggested Readings

Borgonovi, E. (1995). *Il controllo della spesa pubblica: aspetti istituzionali di politica economica e sistemi contabili* [The control of public expenditure: Economic policy and institutional aspects of accounting systems]. Milan: Egea.

Borgonovi, E. (2002). *Principi e sistemi aziendali per le amministrazioni pubbliche* [Principles and business systems for government]. Milan: Egea.

Caperchione, E., & Mussari, R. (Eds.). (2000). *Comparative issues in local government accounting.* Boston: Kluwer Academic.

Casini Benvenutti, S. (2000). *Il nuovo sistema dei conti economici nazionali e regionali SEC 1995* [The new system of national accounts and regional ESA 1995]. Milan: Franco Angeli.

Chan, J. L. (2003). Government accounting: An assessment of theory, purposes and standards. *Public Money & Management,* 1, 13–20.

De Ioanna, P. (2000, May). *Riforma del bilancio e riforma dell'amministrazione* [Reform of the budget and reform of the administration]. Paper presented at the XVIII Convention of Public Accounting—The New Budget of the State, Teramo, Italy: University of Teramo.

Fazio, G., & Fazio, M. (2000). *Il nuovo Bilancio Statale nel sistema finanziario italiano* [The new state budget of the Italian financial system]. Milan: Giuffré.

Giovanelli, L. (2000). *Modelli contabili e di bilancio in uno Stato che cambia* [Accounting and budget models in a state that changes]. Milan: Giuffré.

Guarini, A. (1971). *Le aziende pubbliche di erogazione* [Public distribution companies]. Venice: Libreria Universitaria Editrice.

Luder, K. (1994). The contingency model reconsidered: Experiences from Italy, Japan and Spain. In E. Buschor & K. Schedler (Eds.), *Perspectives on performance measurement and public sector accounting* (pp. 1–15). Bern: Haupt.

Luder, K. (2002). I sistemi di contabilità economico-patrimoniale delle amministrazioni centrali in Europa: Situazione attuale e sviluppi future [The economic-patrimonial accounting methods of the central administrations in Europe: Their effects and future developments. In R. Mussari (Ed.), *Il controllo di gestione nelle amministrazioni centrali* [The control of management in central administrations] (pp. 33–41). Soveria Mannelli: Rubbettino.

Monorchio, A., & Mottura, L. G. (2008). *Compendio di contabilità di Stato* [Compendium of state accounting]. Bari: Cacucci.

Mussari, R. (2003). Italy. In K. Luder & R. Jones (Eds.), *Reforming governmental accounting and budgeting in Europe.* Frankfurt: Fachverlag Moderne Wirtschaft.

Mussari, R. (2005). Il sistema di contabilità e bilancio dello Stato in Italia [The accounting method and budget of the state of Italy. In R. Mussari (Ed.), *I sistemi di contabilità e bilancio dello Stato nell'europa comunitaria* [The accounting methods and budgets of the states of Europe] (pp. 87–134). Milan: Giuffré.

Pavan, A., & Reginato, E. (2004). *Programmazione e controllo nello Stato e nelle altre amministrazioni pubbliche* [Programming and control in the state and other public administrations]. Milan: Giuffré.

Perticone, F. (2000). *La riforma del bilancio dello Stato tra modifiche recenti e nuove applicazioni* [The reform of the state budget from recent modifications to new applications]. Naples: Simone.

Pitzalis, A. (2001). Le nuove prospettive economico-aziendali nell'evoluzione del Bilancio dello Stato [The new economic-business perspective in the evolution of the state budget]. *Rivista Italiana di ragioneria e di economia aziendale* [Italian Review of Accounting and Busines Economy], 5, 280–294.

ADDITIONAL RESOURCES

Central State Accounting Office: www.rgs.mef.gov.it
Department for Civil Service: www.funzionepubblica.it
Italian Central Government: www.governo.it
Italian Parliament: www.parlamento.it
Ministry of Economy and Finance: www.mef.gov.it
Supreme Audit Institution: www.corteconti.it

Public Sector Budgeting in the United Kingdom: Devolution of Powers and Responsibilities

Stephen J. Bailey and William McCabe

Learning Objectives

- Understand the budgetary structure and processes of the UK public sector.
- Appreciate the constitutional and procedural foundations of UK public sector budgeting.
- Recognize and understand the ongoing evolution of UK public sector budgeting.
- Understand the influence of international protocols and procedures on UK public sector budgeting practices.
- Understand the ways in which standardization of accounting practice across the component parts of the UK public sector can help improve financial transparency, facilitate devolution of budgetary responsibility, and safeguard fiscal rectitude.
- Appreciate the impact of the 2007–2009 Global Credit Crunch on the UK public sector budgets.

Introduction

This chapter examines the history of public sector budgeting in the United Kingdom's (UK) unitary state and outlines the present 3-year budgeting cycle. The legal foundations of budgets are described and the changing relations between central, regional, and local government are considered. Particular reference is made to the impact of the devolution of budgetary powers to UK territorial governments in 1999.

Recent reforms are considered in detail, including the recent introduction of the prudential borrowing framework (PBF) for local governments, resource accounting and budgeting (RAB), and whole of government accounts (WGA). The implications of the 2007–2009 Global Credit Crunch are considered for the UK central government's observance of the European Union's (EU) Stability and Growth Pact (SGP), for its own fiscal rules and for prudential borrowing.

Budgetary Structure of the UK Public Sector

Within the UK National Accounts, the public sector comprises the central government (its departments, agencies, arm's-length bodies, and National Health Service [NHS] trusts), local government (including police and fire authorities), and public corporations (government-controlled companies and quasi-corporations). In 2006/2007 (prior to the credit crunch), the central government accounted for 73% of public sector spending, while the local governments accounted for 26%, and 1% for public corporations (The Chartered Institute of Public Finance and Accountancy [CIPFA], 2006).

Control of the central government's budget is via the UK Parliament in London, exercised by the House of Commons through the supply process when Parliament is asked to approve the appropriation of funds to deliver the UK central government's spending plans. The UK chancellor of the exchequer sets out the government's priorities and spending plans in biennial spending reviews and its associated proposals for taxation are set out in the annual budget.

The supply estimates detail the resources and cash (net of anticipated receipts) required to deliver the government's activities for the year in question. Parliament provides funding from the Consolidated Fund through the Supply Process. Her Majesty's (HM) Treasury approves the allocation of resources to departmental programs, delegates management of those resources to government departments and provides advice on the way they and their agencies should manage their resources. HM Treasury retains overriding responsibility for control of expenditure.

Government departments allocate resources to meet strategic priorities and deliver Public Service Agreement outcomes. They also allocate resources to other public, private, and voluntary organizations in the service delivery chain. They remain responsible for day-to-day control of expenditure.

Nearly 90% of public spending in the UK is financed from taxes. The rates of personal income tax, corporation tax (on company profits), and national insurance (a form of social security tax) require parliamentary approval each year; these three taxes account for more than half of government revenue. The remainder comes from "permanent" taxes, which include all indirect taxes (on spending), taxes on capital (wealth), and petroleum revenue tax. Parliamentary approval is only required for changes in the rates of permanent taxes. The chancellor of the exchequer presents the UK government's tax proposals to Parliament in the spring budget and they are enacted through the annual finance bill.

Supply estimates exclude about 30% of total managed expenditure (TME), being funded directly from the National Insurance Fund and the self-financed expenditures of agencies and arm's-length bodies. The UK Treasury monitors departmental spending against both the control totals and fiscal rules (further explanation follows).

Separate budgets are determined for England, Northern Ireland, Scotland, and Wales, of which the last three UK territories are paid block grants by the UK government. Those three territorial governments, established in 1999, are free to determine the budgetary breakdown of their block grants, to which they all add (relatively minor) revenues from fees and charges. Only Scotland has powers to raise a territorial tax but it had not done so at the time of writing.

UK territorial budgets are largely developed on an incremental basis by making adjustments at the margin to existing budgets. However, this approach to budgeting will not be suitable for the soon-to-be severely restrained public finances made necessary to deal with the adverse effects of the credit crunch.

For example, in its report on Scotland's public finances, Audit Scotland (2009) argues the case for better activity, cost, and performance information to enable the Scottish Parliament to scrutinize more effectively the Scottish government's expenditure plans, and better informed choices between competing priorities. This approach should encourage greater efficiency and productivity.

UK local governments receive block grants from their territorial governments, to which they add revenues from both fees and charges and their own council tax. They are also largely free to determine the budgetary balance between services, albeit subject to considerable central and territorial government influence.

The Evolution of Central Government Budgeting

UK central government budgetary policies during the 1980s, 1990s, and 2000s became increasingly focused on limiting the share of public spending in national income (gross domestic product [GDP])and seeking more value for money. Spending was increasingly restructured toward investments in human and physical capital. These policies had significant implications for public sector budgets.

Public expenditure rose from just more than 30% of GDP in the early-to-mid 1960s, to almost 50% in the mid-1970s, thereafter falling to just below 40% in the late 1980s and again in the late 1990s, then rising back above 40% by 2009. However, even though expenditures were rising in real terms, it was often claimed that they were still falling when judged against rising expenditure needs created by demographic change (e.g., more elderly people) and the cost implications of advances in medical technology.

A UK central government Green Paper titled, *The Next Ten Years: Public Expenditure and Taxation into the 1990s* (HM Government, 1984) argued that finance should determine expenditure, not expenditure determining finance. During the post-1945 period, emphasis had been laid on the volume of public sector outputs rather than on the cash outlay required to finance them. Outputs of public services such as education and health are difficult to measure. Hence, public expenditure planning focused on the levels of input required to provide services (e.g., teachers, nurses, police officers). While the desired volume of public sector services was inevitably influenced by what the economy was thought to be able to afford, the emphasis was on real (rather than cash) expenditures.

Public expenditure was effectively index-linked, with automatic adjustments being made to take account of inflation over the years (as many as five) between the initial plans and the actual delivery of services. This led to many different sets of financial figures on differing price bases for a given financial year. For example, during the 1970s, "survey prices" reflected price levels at the time of the Public Expenditure Survey, a quadrennial projection of estimated public expenditures on the basis of existing policies. Survey prices would then be revalued to derive "main estimates," which were presented to Parliament 1 year after the survey and still 1 year or more before expenditures would actually be incurred. "Supplementary estimates" would then be presented to the UK Parliament during the financial year to which the main estimates related so as to fund subsequent inflation. Actual final expenditures were referred to as "outturn expenditures."

These differing price bases for given financial years caused considerable confusion when comparing expenditure outcomes with plans, leading to the term "funny money" and obscuring financial transparency. Furthermore, the effective guarantee of additional funds did little to promote financial accountability. Moreover, although such repricing of expenditure plans was administratively convenient, it meant that changes in the relative prices and costs of public sector outputs were not explicitly considered by the budgeting process.

Cash limits were introduced by the UK Labour Party government in 1976 and tightened under UK Conservative Party governments during the 1980s and early 1990s. Cash limits covered 60% of total public expenditure, directly or indirectly. They excluded demand determined expenditures such as social security, where the volume of spending depends on the number of claimants eligible for benefit. Cash limits set an upper limit on the financial provision for inflation within both the main and supplementary estimates. The latter were effectively abandoned in the late 1970s, when main estimates were presented to the UK Parliament at price levels forecast for the forthcoming year, including the cash limit. If inflation turned out to be greater than forecasted and allowed for in the cash limit, then the volume of public services had to be reduced in order for spending departments to remain within their own cash limits. In effect, public expenditure plans continued to remain in volume terms, but it was no longer guaranteed that spending departments would receive full compensation for inflation.

In 1981, the UK government announced a major shift in the planning of public expenditure from volume to cash. Volume planning, in terms of physical inputs such as teachers and hospitals, had been consistent with what had then been the main role of macroeconomic policy, namely the management of aggregate demand through fiscal policy. However, the shift of emphasis toward the financial or monetary aspects of macroeconomic policy necessitated close control of cash amounts (Bailey, 2002).

Financial accountability was said to be improved by planning in cash, in that government ministers discuss the money that will actually be spent, rather than funny money figures that could be significantly different from actual outturn spending, and because expenditure figures can be more closely related to revenue projections. Hence, in principle, if not in practice, finance determines expenditure rather than the reverse. From a managerial perspective, program managers previously had little incentive to adapt their expenditures in response to changing relative costs. Cash planning supposedly gives them more incentive to consider alternative ways of sourcing resources and/or using resources in different ways to achieve program objectives. In other words, there is increased emphasis on the achievement of value for money. Nevertheless the major problem with cash planning is that realistic assumptions must be made about inflation, otherwise expenditures may either be constrained much more than was intended or cash plans be regarded as unrealistic.

The post-1997 UK Labour Party government oversaw sharp increases in planned public expenditure after fiscal year 1998/1999, especially for health, education, and physical infrastructure. This required restraint of expenditures on other services. To this end, the government introduced a new public expenditure budgeting and control regime in 1998. That regime distinguishes between current and capital expenditure, sets departmental expenditure limits (DELs) for 3 years at a time, and distinguishes annually managed expenditures (AMEs), which cannot reasonably be subject to multiyear limits, most notably social security benefits and debt interest. TME is the sum of DEL and AME. TME is defined as public sector current expenditure plus net investment and depreciation. Table 10-1 shows the current data at the time of writing.

Current expenditure includes spending on wages and salaries, supplies and services, rent and rates, social security transfers, payment of interest on government debt, among others. These are broadly considered to be consumable items, the benefits of which are consumed or exhausted within each financial year. Capital expenditure includes spending on fixed assets such as land, buildings, and plant and machinery, the benefits of which are more durable, lasting several years or decades.

Table 10-1 demonstrates the relatively small scale of capital expenditures. The capital budget is less than 13.5% of the DEL in all years. Moreover, depreciation accounts for almost 40% of the total capital budget in all years. Depreciation had been much greater than net investment in previous years because, historically, capital expenditures bore the brunt of public expenditure restraint as cash limits began to weigh heavily, with capital projects easily being shelved or postponed. The UK Labour Party government's intention has been to avoid worthwhile capital expenditures being squeezed out. This is also reflected in Table 10-1; capital budgets having steadily increased from 11.25% of the 2005/2006 DEL to 13.02% of the planned 2009/2010 DEL.

Table 10-1 also shows that local government self-financed expenditure accounted for less than 5% of the TME in all years. While total local government expenditure typically accounts for about 25% of public expenditure, less than 20% of local spending is financed by local authorities themselves. About 85% of their expenditure net of income

Table 10-1					
Summary of Public Expenditure, Fiscal Years 2005/2006 to 2009/2010					
	2005/2006	2006/2007	2007/2008	2008/2009	2009/2010
	Outturn	Outturn	Estimated outturn	Plans	Plans
Departmental expenditure limits (DELs)					
Current budget	277.6	291.2	313.1	324.3	338.7
Capital budget	35.2	38.9	43.9	48.1	50.7
DELs	312.8	330.1	357.0	372.4	389.4
Annually managed expenditures (AMEs)					
Main departmental programs	183.6	202.6	216.5	220.0	233.4
Locally financed expenditure	22.8	23.4	24.8	25.6	26.6
Other	0.6	(10.2)	(15.1)	(5.6)	(6.4)
AMEs	207.0	215.8	227.0	242.0	253.6
Capital					
AMEs	4.4	3.8	2.3	3.4	3.5
Total managed expenditure (TME)	524.2	549.7	586.3	617.8	646.5
Current expenditure	484.6	507.0	540.1	566.2	592.3
Net investment	23.6	25.8	28.5	32.9	34.7
Depreciation	16.0	16.9	17.7	18.7	19.5

Source: Public Expenditure Statistical Analyses 2008 Cmnd 7391–7407 (HM Treasury, 2008).

Notes: Amounts given in billions of pounds (£). Components may not sum to totals because of rounding. Figures in parentheses include various accounting adjustments.

from sales, fees, and charges is financed by grants from UK central and devolved territorial governments through intergovernmental grants. The main programs for the central government are social security, the NHS, and defense. Other central government programs, relatively minor in expenditure terms, include trade and industry, overseas development, transport and agriculture, fisheries, and food. The main local government programs are school education (accounting for about half of local spending), personal social services (such as care of the elderly), housing, and the police. Other local government programs include local environmental health, household waste collection and disposal, and leisure and recreation.

After holding real TME in check between fiscal years 1997/1998 and 1999/2000, the UK Labour Party government's Comprehensive Spending Review (CSR) announced plans for sharp increases in TME over the following 3 years, particularly for education and the NHS. Being exhaustive expenditures (i.e., spent on inputs and processes) control of education and health spending can, in principle, be achieved through genuine efficiency savings without reducing service levels (i.e., outputs) and quality (i.e., outcomes).

Such reforms are not feasible for social security expenditures as they are transfer payments (i.e., cash effectively given by taxpayers to benefit recipients). Reforms have been intended to make work financially worthwhile, crystallized in the Jobseeker's

Table 10-2

Forecast Government Spending by Function, Fiscal Year 2009/2010

Function	£ billion	Percent of total
Social protection	189	8.2
Health	119	17.7
Education	88	13.1
Defense	38	5.7
Public order and safety	35	5.2
Personal social services	31	4.6
Housing and environment	29	4.3
Debt interest	28	4.2
Transport	23	3.4
Industry, agriculture, employment, and training	20	3.0
Other	72	10.7
TME	671	100.0

Source: Budget 2009: Building Britain's Future (HM Treasury, 2009a).

Notes: Spending figures by function are calculated using methods specified in international standards. They are 2009/2010 near-cash projections and so are not directly comparable with Table 10-1. Other expenditure includes spending on general public services: recreation, culture, media and sport; international cooperation and development; public service pensions; plus spending yet to be allocated and some accounting adjustments. Social protection includes tax credit payments in excess of an individual's tax liability, which are now counted on AME, in line with Organisation for Economic Co-operation and Development (OECD) guidelines. Figures may not sum to totals because of rounding.

Allowance (JSA). However, in the late 1990s and 2000s, almost 50% of social security benefit expenditures was accounted for by elderly people, just more than 25%, by sick and disabled people, 20%, by families, and only 7%, by the unemployed.

The UK central government's response to the global credit crunch that began in 2007 is forecast to lead to a sharply increasing share of public expenditure within GDP both as recession-related expenditures rise and as GDP falls. A breakdown of TME by function as forecast in the April 2009 budget is provided in Table 10-2. Some 60% of spending budgeted for fiscal year 2009/2010 is accounted for by social protection, health, and education.

The April 2009 budget forecast expenditures in Table 10-2 were revised in the December 2009 Pre-Budget Report (PBR). Overall, forecast figures for government expenditures in 2009/2010 are little changed compared to those in the April 2009 budget. Largely due to the impact on the public expenditures of the recession following publication of the 2009 budget in April, there is a slight (0.7%) increase in the total from £671 billion to £676 billion. There are slight increases in forecast spending for social protection (i.e., social security, including unemployment-related benefits, and tax credits), public order and safety (i.e., policing, etc.), housing (e.g., municipal) and environment, debt interest, personal social services (mainly care of elderly people) and industry, agriculture, employment, and training. Spending on health (i.e., the NHS), education, defense, transport, and other is unchanged. No expenditure categories are forecast to fall.

Table 10-3		
Government Receipts, Fiscal Year 2009/2010		
Source	**£ billion**	**Percent of Total**
Income tax	141	28.4
National insurance	98	19.8
Value-added tax (VAT)	64	12.9
Excise duties	44	8.9
Corporation tax	35	7.1
Council tax	25	5.0
Business rates	24	4.8
Other	67	13.5
Total receipts	496	100.0

Source: Budget 2009: Building Britain's Future (HM Treasury, 2009a).

Notes: Receipts are 2009/2010 projections. Other receipts include capital taxes, stamp duties, vehicle excise duties, and some other tax and nontax receipts (i.e., interest and dividends). Figures may not sum to totals because of rounding.

Table 10-3 shows the different sources from which government revenue is raised. Public sector current receipts are expected to be around £496 billion in fiscal year 2009/2010. This is substantially less than the £671 billion forecast figure for spending in Table 10-2.

Figures for budgeted expenditures and receipts are published in spring each year, at the start of the financial year. The UK chancellor of the exchequer presents the UK government's budget statement to Parliament and the nation. It includes a detailed assessment of the state of the economy and the nation's finances. In that statement, the chancellor usually announces changes to taxes and new spending measures.

Since 1997, the chancellor has also presented a prebudget statement along with a PBR in the autumn. The PBR is an integral part of the annual budget process, providing a progress report on what the government has achieved since the budget earlier in the year and an updated assessment of the state of the economy and public finances. It sets out the direction of government policy in the run up to the following year's spring budget.

The PBR stimulates debate on key economic issues and on taxes and spending in advance of the spring budget. It seeks the views of people and business across the country and in all sectors of the economy so as to inform the government's subsequent budget decisions. The PBR for 2009 was delayed until December, the chancellor having postponed it from autumn in order to get a clearer picture of the impact of the 2009 recession on both the economy and the public finances.

In its 2009 PBR, the government emphasized that the report took place during the first contraction in the global economy in 60 years (HM Treasury, 2009b). The government responded with measures to support households, businesses, and the broader economy through the recession until the recovery is secured. Thereafter, it commits itself to reduce public borrowing by 50% over the following 4 years, while continuing to invest in public services, especially the NHS and school education.

The December 2009 PBR forecasts for government receipts in 2009/2010 are little changed compared to those in the April 2009 budget. Total receipts are forecast to rise from £496 billion to £498 billion. This 0.4% rise in receipts is based on the (perhaps optimistic) assumption that the recession concluded by the end of 2009 and that economic growth takes place. Nevertheless, due to the deeper and greater than expected recession following publication of the 2009 budget in March/April, there are falls in the forecasts for (personal) income tax, national insurance (a tax on employees paid by both employers and employees), and corporation tax (on companies' profits). However, there are forecast increases for value-added tax (VAT) and other receipts (see note to Table 10-3). Forecasts remain unchanged for excise duties (e.g., on alcohol and tobacco), council tax (a local property tax on the capital values of houses and flats), and business rates (a national property tax on the rental values of business properties).

The forecasted £5 billion rise in spending compared with the £2 billion rise in receipts results in an increased difference between total receipts and total expenditure, rising from £175 billion to £178 billion in fiscal year 2009/2010. This forecast increase in borrowing has occurred because the UK government decided not to change 2009/2010 DELS and to let AMEs rise further than expected in spring 2009 as a result of the deeper than expected recession during the remainder of 2009.

The UK Labour Party government is gambling on a return to moderate levels of economic growth to reduce the rise in public sector debt following the biggest fall in GDP (forecast by the government to be −4.75% in 2009) since 1931, the worst year of the Great Depression.

The UK's Territorial Budgets: The Barnett Formula

The UK central government allocates block grants to the three territorial governments of Northern Ireland, Scotland, and Wales based on both historic levels of spending and on a formula taking into account the share of the total UK population in each territory. That formula (called the Barnett Formula after the civil servant who devised it) is used to allocate among all four UK territories (including England) a substantial part of the annual changes in the aggregate level of UK public expenditure. In 2007/2008, the Barnett Formula accounted for around £49 billion of UK public spending (House of Lords, 2009), with TME being around £590 billion (Table 10-1).

The formula does not apply to nondevolved spending programs and to only part of devolved programs. In theory, the formula should lead to convergence of the remaining devolved expenditures per capita in Northern Ireland, Scotland, and Wales with *comparable* per capita expenditures in England (Fingland & Bailey, 2004).

The Barnett Formula does not determine *total public expenditures* in the three territories or changes in those expenditures. The formula is only applied to *devolved* expenditures that are *comparable* with England, for example, education, health and personal social services, housing, other environmental services, and law and order. Nondevolved services, such as social security payments and defense expenditures, are not subject to the formula.

The Barnett Formula has been used since 1978 to recognize higher per capita comparable expenditure needs in Scotland, Wales, and Northern Ireland when compared with England. Per capita comparable spending needs were thought to be higher in these three territories in the late 1970s. This was generally due to their greater sparsity of population (e.g., leading to smaller schools and class sizes, and so higher education spending per pupil), relative ill health, relatively adverse industrial structures (i.e., declining industries such as coal and iron and steel), and lower incomes per head compared with England.

In terms of the current public expenditure planning mechanism, the formula does not affect AMEs, which are mainly social security and also the EU's Common Agricultural Policy (CAP) and other spending. The formula only affects comparable DELs, such as health. It is only in respect of comparable expenditures that any convergence brought about by strict application of the Barnett Formula occurs. For example, in Scotland's case, the formula currently applies to less than half of public expenditure in its territory.

The formula works simply by giving to the three territories a fixed proportion of changes in the plans (DEL) for comparable English expenditure programs. That proportion is added to the UK central government block grant for each territory as the planned increases in comparable English public spending take effect.

Thus, the effect of the Barnett Formula is to prolong relatively high per capita comparable public spending in the three territories that existed long before the Barnett Formula was introduced. Over an extended period of time, the successive annual increments in each territory's comparable public expenditure account for an increasing proportion of public finance for comparable services. Hence, the effect of the base year level of finance (i.e., 1978, when the Barnett Formula was introduced) is progressively eroded. Complete convergence on per capita public expenditures in England could take many years, depending on just how fast UK comparable expenditures increase.

It has to be recognized, however, that territorial expenditure needs have changed since 1978. In particular, the three other territories are no longer characterized by an economic base comprised of an adverse industrial structure compared with England, the former preponderance of old declining heavy industries having long gone. Not surprisingly, therefore, the UK Treasury has been reviewing the Barnett Formula with a view to introducing a sustainable and justifiable methodology.

Critics of the formula argue that it results in overly generous annual payments of grant from the UK Treasury to the Scottish government. Public spending per head of population in Scotland has been about 20% more than that in England over many years. These generous annual budgets have allowed the Scottish government to provide some services free to their users, whereas people in England have to pay charges. The most notable examples are free university tuition, free personal care of elderly people, road and bridge crossings free of tolls, free NHS eyesight and dental checks, free parking at hospitals, and free prescription medicines (although charges are being progressively phased out in Scotland by 2011). The assemblies of Wales and Northern Ireland have also been able to abolish many of these charges, they too being generously funded by the Barnett Formula in comparison with England.

By 2011, England will be the only part of the UK where (most) patients will still have to pay charges for medicines prescribed by their NHS doctors (the exception being that in 2008, UK Prime Minister Gordon Brown announced the abolition of prescription charges for cancer patients).

As was the case for free personal care and university tuition, it could be expected that demand for prescription medicines will rise sharply once they are free, creating possibly severe pressures on Scotland's budgets and perhaps leading to the rationing of services by means other than charges. For example, Scottish local governments argue that their annual budgetary allocations from the Scottish government do not fully compensate for the extra demand created by abolishing charges for personal care, and so, elderly people eligible for care have to endure longer waiting times before care can be provided.

Critics of this overly generous funding of the three territories argue that block grants should be determined according to social and economic needs, rather than being determined by the relative populations of the four UK territories. Such formulas are already used by the UK territorial governments themselves for the distribution of intergovernmental grants between local governments within their respective territories (Bailey, 1999).

The reason why these fairly sophisticated grant distribution methodologies are not used to distribute the central government's block grants between territories seems to be the fear that the UK Labour Party government would alienate voters in the three territories and so reduce its chances of returning to power at the 2010 UK general election.

The Scottish government has been controlled by the Scottish National Party (SNP) since 2007. The SNP seeks independence for Scotland and a return to nationhood. It could capitalize on such voter discontent by invoking (for the first time since devolution in 1999) the Scottish Parliament's powers to raise the standard rate of UK personal income tax by up to 3% (i.e., 3 pence in the £) within Scotland. Arguing that this tax hike has been made necessary by the cuts in Scottish funding imposed by the UK central government, the SNP would hope to strengthen its case for independence.

Ultimately, it is not possible to develop a truly objective system of expenditure needs assessment and so any new grant distribution formula would probably be even more heavily politicized than the population shares-based Barnett Formula. To say the least, the share of any increase in comparable public expenditure enjoyed by the three territories would certainly not be as certain under a comprehensive objective annual expenditure needs assessment as it is now under the Barnett Formula.

Implications of the EU's Stability and Growth Pact for UK Budgets

Membership into the EU and adoption of the Euro currency requires national governments to observe the EU's SGP. The key objective of the SGP is the maintenance of a budgetary position close to balance, or in surplus, in each of the member states. Close to balance means maintaining a budget deficit of no more than 3% of GDP, so that fluctuations resulting from recessions or recoveries would be accommodated as long as balance was achieved over the economic cycle as a whole. Ultimately, all Eurozone countries, and those intending to adopt the euro, must comply with the PGP if economic and financial stability, as well as the pact's credibility and sustainability, is to be maintained.

The operation of the SGP has two aspects, the first of which is the monitoring of budgetary positions based on stability programs submitted by Eurozone members, and convergence plans submitted by those who are not Eurozone member states (including the UK). Failure to meet budgetary guidelines results in the implementation of the second aspect, the excessive deficit procedure. In theory, members have 4 months to take corrective action when a deficit exceeds 3%, with a view to reducing the deficit within a year, notwithstanding circumstances deemed exceptional by Regulation 1467/97, Article 2(1) of the Council of the European Union. Failure to act within these 4 months should result in the member being served notice to take deficit-reduction measures, with continued inaction resulting in the imposition of sanctions. These take the form of noninterest bearing deposits of 0.2% of GDP plus, 10% of the amount by which the deficit exceeds 3%. However, in practice, the excessive deficit procedure, as it is called, has not been evenly applied due to the uneven distribution of power within the EU, and difficulties resulting from statistics used to determine excessive deficits (Fingland & Bailey, 2008).

The one-size-fits-all approach resulted from the need for a system that was easy to monitor; however, the failures of the SGP has led to widespread calls for reform and changes proposed by the European Commission recognized the need for greater flexibility while retaining an emphasis on sound public finances. Calls for greater flexibility led to some reform of the SGP and a shift away from its initial focus on short-term targets. There has been an acknowledgment that monitoring the budgetary position over the period of the economic cycle may be more appropriate. Thus, recent reforms allow for country-specific medium-term budgetary objectives. As a quid pro quo, those who transgress the 3% target will be given a grace period of 2 years in which to correct the excessive deficit, with allowances made for special circumstances. Further, no excessive deficit procedures will be launched if a country has experienced negative growth or can cite relevant factors, which could include potential economic growth or structural reforms.

Whether the SGP was sustainable had already been questioned prior to the 2007 credit crunch because it remained to be seen whether the economic and monetary union and fiscal rules for joining the euro would remove and/or avoid structural gaps between (higher) public sector expenditures and (lower) revenues in the long term. These gaps between income and expenditure in public finances lead to persistent budget deficits and rising debt irrespective of the economic cycle. They can be hypothesized to arise as pressure groups (distributional coalitions) capture the bulk of benefits from incremental expenditures while the costs of financing them are shared across all current and future local taxpayers. Consistent with this hypothesis, the gap between tax revenues and current expenditures increased over the last four decades of the 20th century in the UK and other countries (Bailey, 2004). This is inevitable unless the economy grows faster than borrowing or unless rapid inflation and negative real interest rates reduce the real value of the stock of debt.

In effect, the SGP requires avoidance of structural gaps in public finances and discretionary fiscal policy measures to be taken by governments to counteract the negative effects on the public finances of falls in GDP. However, the recessionary impact of the global credit crunch on EU member states is so great that they have done precisely the opposite by greatly increasing their budget deficits (Bailey, Asenova, & Beck, 2009).

The 2007–2009 Global Credit Crunch and the UK's Prudential Borrowing Framework

The credit crunch refers to the collapse in bank lending as the cost of credit became prohibitively expensive or simply unavailable during the years 2007–2009. Simply put, it was the result of governments' deregulation of bank lending without introduction of sufficiently rigorous self-regulation, without appropriate governance arrangements, and without sufficient scrutiny of the financial risk models employed. These deficiencies severely compromised fiscal transparency and accountability.

In sharp contrast, the UK's PBF requires rigorous local self-regulation and governance. Since 2004, governance and accountability arrangements for UK local government borrowing under the new PBF have been based on the "professional discipline and control model" of budgetary governance (Bailey, Asenova, & Hood, 2009; Bailey, Asenova, Hood, & Manochin, in press). It replaced the earlier "centralized discipline and control model," whereby municipal borrowing had to be approved by the central government, thus providing an alternative to private finance initiatives and public–private partnerships for capital procurement. It grants UK local authorities a significant degree of freedom and flexibility to determine their own capital expenditures, provided that they meet requirements for prudent management of their financial affairs, while ensuring fiscal transparency and accountability. This follows decades of very strong central government control of local government borrowing (Bailey, 1999).

The associated Prudential Code requires local governments to ensure that they have the financial capacity to repay debt because their borrowing is unsecured by assets (i.e., they are not allowed to use their land, buildings, or other assets as collateral). However, they have no control over the amount of grants they receive from the UK central government and are constrained (to varying degrees) in their ability to increase the rates of their own taxes on residential and business properties. This explains the use of prudential borrowing to finance capital projects, which are expected to generate sufficient cost savings to repay the associated debt. These spend-to-save infrastructural investments are meant to protect local governments' future financial sustainability.

This approach to municipal fiscal prudence contrasts sharply not only with the approach adopted by banks and other financial institutions over the last several decades, but also with that now being adopted by national governments. The highly speculative, short-term financial model adopted by the senior executives of many banks to win them large annual bonuses has been criticized for long-term gambling with other people's money (i.e., their depositors and shareholders). Now national governments could similarly be criticized for being reckless with future taxpayers' money as they borrow increasingly large proportions of GDP in order to bail out those heavily indebted banks and other private sector organizations.

The International Monetary Fund (IMF) calculated the ratios of fiscal stimulus relative to GDP. The UK's ratio was 19.8% as of February 2009, by far the highest ratio in the G20 countries (as compared to "only" 6.8% in the United States). These ratios increased as further debt-financed measures were announced, and as GDP fell. The accelerating costs to the public purse of these measures raised questions about budgetary prudence, especially in the UK.

Between 1997 and 2007, UK central government budgets had been based on its much vaunted fiscal rectitude principle of "prudence for a purpose." Response to the credit crunch now seems to be "imprudence for a purpose." If the hoped for levels of economic growth are not forthcoming, a deepening and prolonged recession/ depression will make what had already been a long-term structural gap between government expenditures and revenues much greater. This will exacerbate any losses the government (and, ultimately, the taxpayer) incurs on its ongoing purchases of increasingly large proportions of bank shares, swaps of government bonds for toxic mortgage-backed bonds, guarantees of bank loans on both wholesale and retail money markets, among others.

Justifying the current high-risk fiscal largesse by arguing that doing nothing would be even more costly for the future health of the economy is an act of faith in the success of the ever-increasing bank bailouts and fails to address how the huge increases in government debt will be repaid. Repayment will be even more difficult if interest rates rise from their very low-to-zero levels of early 2009 and by any downgrading of sovereign debt (used to refinance loans) by credit ratings agencies.

The UK central government has abandoned its own fiscal rules, namely the golden investment rule (borrow only for capital, not current expenditure) and the sustainable investment rule (net public debt no greater than 40% of GDP). Its own figures show that net public debt exceeded 50% of GDP in January 2009 and forecast it to peak at almost 60% by fiscal year 2012/2013. Nevertheless, this still seems low compared with those Eurozone countries rapidly approaching breaches of the SGP.

Clearly, the UK's PBF and its associated Prudential Code is arguably a much stronger regulatory regime than what has existed for banks, other financial institutions, and even national governments themselves under the market discipline and control model (whereby borrowing is sanctioned by financial markets in accordance with the bond ratings they attribute to individual local governments).

The obvious deficiency of both the centralized discipline and control model and the market discipline and control model is the lack of an explicit professional discipline and control component. The professional discipline and control model requires local chief finance officers (CFOs) to assess the prudence and sustainability of borrowing in terms of local revenue and capital budgets. Municipalities must observe fiscal supervision rules, of which there are two categories. First, *flow-based accounting indices* control the levels of borrowing relative to (expected future) revenues. This is meant to ensure that there are sufficient revenues from local taxes, charges rents, leases, and other sources with which to repay debt instruments upon maturity after having financed ongoing current expenditures. Second, *stock-based accounting indices* control the level of debt relative to the net value of stock-based balance sheets that reflect fiscal conditions in each local government. This is meant to ensure a sustainable balance between assets and liabilities. Together, the flow-based and stock-based accounting indices are meant to ensure sustainability and prudence in UK local governments' accounts.

Local government CFOs assess the sustainability of borrowing and set limits in line with the Prudential Code. The code contains both the flow-based and stock-based accounting indices (see Table 10-4). The professional discipline and control model establishes a financial rubric devised by *national* associations of finance officers, which have to be observed by all municipalities.

Table 10-4

Prudential Indicators for the Prudential Borrowing Framework

Prudential indicators for affordability[a]

Estimates of the ratio of financing costs to net revenue stream (%)

Actual ratio of financing costs to net revenue stream (%)

Estimates of the incremental impact of capital investment decisions on council tax

Estimates of the incremental impact of capital investment decisions on housing rents

Prudential indicators for prudence[a]

Net borrowing and the capital financing requirement

Prudential indicators for capital expenditure[b]

Estimate of total capital expenditure (3 years)

Actual capital expenditure for previous year

Estimates of capital financing requirement (3 years)

Actual capital financing requirement for previous year

Prudential indicators for external debt[b]

Authorized limit for external debt (3 years)

Operational boundary for external debt (3 years)

Actual external debts as at March 31st of the previous year

Prudential indicators for treasury management

Adoption of CIPFA Code of Practice for Treasury Management in the Public Services

Upper limit on fixed interest rate exposures (3 years)

Upper limit on variable interest rate exposures (3 years)

Upper and lower limits for the maturity structure of borrowing

Prudential limits for principal sums invested for longer than 364 days

Source: The Prudential Code for Capital Finance in Local Authorities (CIPFA, 2003).

[a] Flow-based controls.

[b] Stock-based controls.

The PBF marks a significant shift from prescriptive statute-based control and from the centrally determined strategic priority areas such as education. The only significant limitations that remain in place are the prohibition on the mortgaging of local authority property as well as on the "securitization" of future revenue streams (e.g., rents) in return for immediate one-off payments.

It was recognized that the PBF had to be operationalized by a Prudential Code of financial practice that required borrowing decisions to be both prudent and sustainable. Prudence is judged in terms of the financial consequences of borrowing decisions for current and future generations of local taxpayers and tenants of municipal housing. Decisions have to take account of the financial burdens placed on them in the future as accumulated net debt comes to be repaid with interest. Future generations have no capacity to vote in the present and so both intergenerational inequity and a democratic deficit could result from unrestrained borrowing.

Furthermore, imprudently high levels of borrowing and debt would preempt current revenues (from intergovernmental grants, local taxes, and service charges) as they are increasingly used to service debt. Such preemption could reduce the revenues available for running services and so jeopardize the achievement of service objectives. Additionally, high levels of borrowing and debt could ultimately compromise the balanced-budget rule. Breaching that rule would be contrary to the fiduciary duty of local governments. This is in stark contrast with the budgetary position adopted by the UK central government in its response to the credit crunch.

The professional code of practice developed for the PBF is encapsulated in the Prudential Code developed by CIPFA. Thus, the previous centralized and highly detailed administrative control system has been replaced by one based on local autonomy tempered by professional financial advice offered within the code's rubric. This is intended to ensure adherence to certain purely financial rules (i.e., that all external borrowing is within prudent and sustainable limits, that capital expenditure plans are affordable, and that treasury management decisions correspond with professional good practice).

The code requires each authority's CFO to establish procedures for reporting to the capital finance decision-making body of the local authority. Mirroring the framework's rationale for performance monitoring every 3 years, the code sets down short- and medium-term prudential indicators of affordability and prudence (see Table 10-4). These indicators are intended to clarify the consequences of proposed investment policies, demonstrating transparency and accountability to community stakeholders.

CFOs are held accountable for observance of both the code and the indicators. They are required to estimate the indicators, recommend the limits and operational boundaries for their local authorities, recommend upper limits of fixed and variable interest rate exposures, and recommend limits for the maturity structure of borrowing and investments. In this way, CFOs are meant to guide decision making by their respective local authorities. Although those decisions are ultimately the responsibility of local politicians, CFOs are required to make abundantly clear the resulting financial burdens and strains on municipal budgets in the current and subsequent financial years of possible decisions to borrow. The estimates are then compared with the limits and operational boundaries for debt previously agreed to by councils, and so it is thought unlikely that they would wantonly breach them.

Local authorities are held financially accountable in terms of observance of the Prudential Code and its indicators. However, neither the professional body that developed the code and indicators (CIPFA), nor the UK territorial governments set the values for the various flow and stock indices or the associated treasury management indicators. This is because, given the move toward increased devolution and decentralization of decision making and responsibility in general, it was thought inappropriate for any person or organization other than local authorities themselves to set those ratios and limits.

Notwithstanding criticisms that the Prudential Code is too narrowly focused on quantitatively measurable financial ratios, compared with the lack of observance of such ratios by banks, other financial institutions and even national governments themselves, the code is to be lauded for its systematization of fiscal rectitude within local government. Although the code could no doubt be improved, adoption of such a code by financial institutions would almost certainly have avoided the imprudent borrowing (and lending) that led to the 2007–2009 credit crunch, and which arguably, underpins the national government's responses to it.

Resource Accounting and Budgeting

The development of RAB introduced accruals accounting in UK public sector budgets. As already noted, they were previously prepared on a cash basis even though accrual accounting was universal in the commercial world. The UK central government expenditure is now controlled and accounted for on the basis of expenditures incurred, with costs being recorded when they are incurred (i.e., when goods and services have been received or performed) rather than when they are paid. Items held in store are only charged to expenditure when they are issued, and capital projects and equipment are charged to expenditure over their lifetime (via depreciation accounting). There is also a charge to expenditure for the economic cost of capital assets. Local authorities, the NHS, nationalized industries, nondepartmental public bodies (NDPBs), and public corporations already had accrual accounting in place prior to its adoption by the central government departments (from fiscal year 1999/2000).

A timetable had previously been set for all government departments to establish systems capable of producing resource accounts within the financial statements produced by the government departments. These are the:

- Operating Cost Statement: showing the cost of resources consumed during the year;
- Balance Sheet: showing the assets and liabilities at the year-end, represented by taxpayers' equity;
- Cash Flow Statement: analyzing the net cash outflow by current/capital and the sources of finance;
- Main Objectives Analysis: comparing budgeted with actual results by main objective headings; and
- Output and Performance Analysis: comparing target with actual cost/output data for specific activities.

The framework of accounting principles and conventions is based on the UK Generally Accepted Accounting Practice (GAAP), in particular, the accounting and disclosure requirements of the Companies Act (1995) and accounting standards supplemented, where appropriate, to accommodate the particular requirements of the central government. This feature was called into question by Jones (1998) who argued that there are clear differences between the *Resource Accounting Manual (RAM)* produced by the UK Treasury (HM Treasury, 1997) and the requirement that resource accounting be based on company accounting.

Each department prepares one consolidated set of resource accounts and this has to include the assets and liabilities of its executive agencies, including trading funds. Resource accounting therefore provides the opportunity for departments to link the full costs of resources they consume to their objectives and outputs. It gives departments clear incentives to use assets to their full advantage or to dispose of them so as to reduce the annual costs of holding on to them. The annual costs are depreciation and a cost of capital charge reflecting the opportunity cost of holding assets (i.e., their value in the next best alternative use). The information so produced helps government departments and their agencies to better develop their long-term plans and manage their resources and also provides better information about the full cost of activities irrespective of whether or not there is a cash cost.

Besides allowing for better internal departmental planning and better external control of departmental plans, resource budgeting should also improve the decision-making process for the allocation of resources between departments as well as within them. In particular, a resource-based Public Expenditure Survey and control regime provides the opportunity to develop a more rational basis for the treatment of capital spending. Parliament and the general public are also able to scrutinize those plans and activities more effectively, transparency and accountability thereby being made clearer.

Resource budgeting also opens up the possibility of changing the basis of parliamentary as well as administrative control of public expenditure. In changing the public expenditure control total to an accruals basis, resource budgeting is consistent with maintaining control of public expenditure expressed as a proportion of GDP, which is also measured in accruals terms. However, there still has to be firm control over cash as the government is still responsible for managing its own cash flow.

It is important to note that the introduction of RAB into the UK central government departments in 1999/2000 was a systematic planned process, which included a large amount of consultation from all interested parties. The UK government formally initiated the process for the introduction of resource accounting in the 1995 Green Paper *Better Accounting for the Taxpayer's Money: The government proposals: Resource Accounting and Budgeting in Government* (HM Treasury, 1995). This consultation paper set out the government's main proposals for the introduction of RAB into central government departments, agencies, and trading funds. The UK National Audit Office also prepared various reports on the proposals and on the audit of resource accounts. Furthermore, the *RAM* (HM Treasury, 1997) is updated annually so as to ensure it remains fit for purpose and for use by all central government departments.

Whole of Government Accounts

Although it initiated the introduction of RAB in the late 1990s, the then UK Conservative Party government decided not to pursue the introduction of WGA, as introduced in New Zealand and Australia. The incoming 1997 UK Labour Party government announced that it would consider producing WGA to enhance both RAB and economic policy making, subject to the results of a feasibility study (HM Treasury, 1998a). The study (Chow, Humphrey, & Moll, 2008) concluded that the benefits from producing WGA would outweigh its costs. It was recommended that the government should first develop a whole of central government accounts (CGA), which would consolidate the resource accounts of the central government departments. Once the CGA was completed, it was recommended that it be extended to WGA. This would be a consolidation of CGA, local government accounts, and public corporations.

WGA are commercial-style accounts covering the whole of the public sector and including some 1300 separate bodies. In the UK, this includes government departments, agencies, trading funds, NHS bodies, local authorities, and other stated bodies. The introduction of WGA stems from the UK government's fiscal rules established in July 1997 and the Treasury's *The Code for Fiscal Stability* (HM Treasury, 1998b). The code was given statutory force by the Finance Act 1998, setting out the key principles of transparency, stability, responsibility, fairness, and efficiency to be applied in the formulation and implementation of fiscal policy.

WGA will be the first (fully audited) true and fair view of the UK government's financial performance and will enhance transparency and accountability to Parliament. It will also provide better quality financial information to underpin funding and investment decisions at the local and national levels. However, there are still issues to be resolved, which will affect the practical implementation of WGA.

The *Government Resources and Accounts Act* 2000 (HM Government, 2000) provides the framework for the UK Treasury to coordinate the preparation of WGA. The act places a duty on the Treasury to prepare a set of financial accounts for a group of bodies that exercise functions of a public nature or are entirely or substantially funded from public money. The Treasury will determine the form and content of the accounts, but it must ensure that they conform to the UK GAAP (subject to such adaptations as are necessary) and present a true and fair view. The Comptroller and Auditor General (C&AG) will audit the consolidated WGA against the true and fair criterion (there will be no opinion on regularity, which will continue to be covered in the underlying accounts). The December 2003 PBR (HM Treasury, 2003a) required local authorities be included in the development of WGA and set out a timetable for implementation. In Scotland, and to some extent in Northern Ireland, there will be some practical differences in the arrangements for WGA, but the broad principles for preparation and audit will be similar.

The Treasury has designated the bodies to be included in the accounts for any financial year, subject to consultation with the National Assembly for Wales, the Scottish government, and the Northern Ireland executive, where appropriate (HM Treasury, 2003b). The Treasury has written to the accounting officer (or equivalent) for each body to confirm its inclusion and explain the reporting requirements. *The Whole of Government Accounts (Designation of Bodies) Order* 2003 sets out those central and nondepartmental government bodies, trading funds, and public corporations currently included for England, Wales, and Northern Ireland.

Provisional lists of English and Welsh local authorities to be included are published on the local authority page of the Treasury's WGA Web site. These include unitary, shire district, metropolitan district councils, the Greater London Authority and London boroughs, police and fire authorities, waste disposal authorities, transport authorities, and the national parks authorities. NHS trusts and foundation hospital trusts are dealt with in a separate list.

The UK Treasury designation orders cannot apply in Scotland. Instead, the Scottish government will arrange for the required information to be prepared for Scottish bodies, which are expected to include all councils, police boards, and fire boards. In Northern Ireland, the Department of Finance and Personnel has designated the bodies to be included. They include city, district and borough councils, and health and social services trusts.

The stated objectives of the UK Treasury are that WGA will provide better quality data to underpin the operation of the golden rule and will allow the public sector balance sheet to be used more directly in fiscal management. Government planners and managers will have better and more transparent data for the conduct of fiscal policy, encouraging a medium- to long-term focus for policy making and the more efficient and effective distribution of resources. There will be increased consistency between fiscal policy data and that used for planning and controlling public spending. The overview of public finances provided by WGA will improve government accountability to Parliament and taxpayers.

The use of similar accounting policies throughout the public sector should be seen as beneficial to the users of the accounts. First, a reduced need for reconciliation of figures produced on different bases and correspondingly less scope for disputes over matters of interpretation. Second, communication will be more effective because everyone will be speaking the same language. Third, convergence of the different accounting rules for public sector bodies will enhance comparability of performance data and increase the opportunities for benchmarking. Fourth, it will also enable targets to be set and measured on a consistent basis, allowing relative trends in performance to be evaluated more accurately. Fifth, funding bids can be presented and assessed more efficiently. As part of their year-end accounts closure procedures, designated bodies will prepare WGA data returns containing summaries of their financial statements in the form of a standard chart of accounts, including analysis of transactions and balances with other bodies within the WGA umbrella.

For local government bodies, the information requirements will be agreed through a joint committee drawn from the central government, the Local Government Association and other interested parties. The requirements are likely to include a specific local government data return based on the annual statements of accounts that local authorities already prepared, rather than the standard chart of accounts. Income and expenditure will be analyzed under the subjective headings recommended in the Best Value Accounting Code of Practice.

Designated bodies will arrange for their returns to be reported upon by their existing auditors and submit them to the responsible government department. In England, these are the Department of Health for NHS bodies or independent regulator for foundation hospital trusts, the Home Office for police authorities, and the Office of the Deputy Prime Minister for local authorities including fire authorities. Elsewhere, responsibility lies with the National Assembly for Wales, the Scottish government, and the Northern Ireland executive.

Government departments will perform a subconsolidation for all the bodies within their responsibilities, aggregating the consolidation information and eliminating transactions and balances between these bodies. In England and Wales, departments will arrange for the subconsolidation to be audited by the C&AG and then submit the results to the UK Treasury. The Treasury will then consolidate the subconsolidations, eliminating transactions and balances between departmental groups, and prepare WGA for audit and for putting before Parliament. The C&AG will then examine the consolidated accounts and report whether they present a true and fair view.

As was the case for RAB, the UK Treasury decided that the WGA project would have a staged development process. The first stage of the process was two dry runs for the CGA for the fiscal years 2001/2002 and 2002/2003. This was followed by the preparation of a set of audited and published CGA to be prepared for the 2003/2004 fiscal year. Some useful lessons were learned from this process, for example, the importance of integrating WGA requirements into the annual accounting cycle and of strict adherence to deadlines, and the need to involve suitably qualified and experienced staff.

The second stage is preparation of WGA, also preceded by 2 years of dry runs. However, the initial timetable for WGA was put back many times to allow more time to solve issues relating to the alignment of local and central government accounting policies and to allow WGA to be published in accordance with introduction in 2009 of the International Financial Reporting Standards (IFRS). The first published set of WGA is intended to be for fiscal year 2009/2010.

However, the accounting policies used by local government have not been wholly consistent with those of WGA. Such alignment issues between local and central government have caused a number of problems, particularly the different valuation of their assets. For example, the local government road network is valued at historical cost whereas the motorway and the trunk road network (financed by central government) are valued at current cost on the CGA. As the Local Authority Statement of Recommended Practice (SORP; CIPFA, 2008) develops over time, these, already few areas of difference, are likely to reduce further.

A considerable amount of work has gone into minimizing the differences between the HM Treasury RAM, the accounting framework for central government bodies, and the NHS and local government. With regard to the NHS, the differences have been resolved with amendments to the Department of Health's Manual for Accounts. The situation with local authorities (including police and fire authorities) has been more complex as the issues affecting local authorities have been substantial, most notably with respect to the capital accounting treatment of fixed assets. The CIPFA/Local Authority (Scotland) Accounts Advisory Committee (LASAAC) joint committee has been heavily involved in resolving the differences between the local authority current accounting requirements, the RAM, and the UK GAAP. Local authorities will now provide additional information with the financial returns to take account of the differences in accounting policies between central and local government.

The National Audit Office will work with the auditors of the other WGA bodies (the Audit Commission for England and Wales, Audit Scotland, the Welsh Audit Office, the Northern Ireland Audit Office, and private sector firms) to establish group audit instructions for the WGA. Strategies have been prepared and are available for the different types of bodies that make up the WGA.

It is clear that there are many issues surrounding the implementation of the WGA, both on a positive and negative basis. The government had initially planned to publish the first set of WGA by fiscal year 2006/2007. However, as noted previously, this was pushed back to 2009/2010. This suggests that problems came to light that had not been anticipated. This will no doubt raise the cost of introducing a system for the production of WGA. As no actual WGA had yet been produced at the time of writing, only time will tell if the WGA system will achieve the expected results.

Conclusions

The historic development and evolution of budgeting in the UK has increasingly focused on its contribution to the achievement of key social policy priorities, to microeconomic as well as macroeconomic considerations, to achieving greater value for money in terms of outputs and outcomes as well as inputs and processes, to devolution and decentralization, to fiscal transparency and accountability, to sustainability and prudence, to governance, and to professional discipline and control.

This ongoing evolution has been based on the development of budgetary planning and control in cash (in place of real) terms, then on an accruals basis, replacement of historic costs by economic costing, the adoption of RAB, and now preparation of whole of government accounts. There has also been a move toward adoption of EU budgeting standards, such as the IFRS being adopted for public sector budgets in fiscal year 2009/2010. The IFRS also applies to the setting and measurement of performance targets, budgeting and forecasting, and financial reporting.

The benefits of these improvements to the principles and practice of budgeting may, however, be overwhelmed by the UK central government's response to the 2007 credit crunch. The sustainability and prudence of its own financing has been severely threatened by its budgetary response to the credit crunch, the borrowing and debt implications of which are enormous in absolute cash terms, in resource terms and relative to GDP. It has effectively abandoned both its own budgeting and borrowing rules and those of the EU. The relaxation of budgetary control mechanisms to deal with the credit crunch seems unprecedented and the sustainability of the resulting budgetary outcomes is crucially dependent upon whether deep and prolonged economic depression is avoided.

Prior to that response, there had been an increasing emphasis on what was affordable and this drove the shift from real resource to cash budgeting with cash limits.

This led to microeconomic distortions as capital expenditures were cut heavily to keep total spending within budgets. Subsequent movement toward inclusion of economic cost and resource accounting in UK budgeting and adoption of EU-wide accounting rules (i.e., IFRS) had been intended to make UK budgets more sustainable. This occurred at the same time as increasing decentralization of budgetary responsibility to UK territorial governments and local governments to improve fiscal transparency and accountability. Ironically, it is the national government's budgets that appear to be increasingly imprudent and unsustainable, with devolved budgets being much more conservatively managed.

The lesson from the UK experience is that while the practice of public sector budgeting can be continuously and significantly improved by the ongoing adoption of various technical measures and protocols, those improved budgetary procedures are easily overridden by political responses to exogenous economic crises.

Discussion Questions

1. Assess the rationale for the UK central government's adoption of 3-year budgeting and for the distinction between AMEs and DELs.
2. Critically appraise the arguments in support of planning public expenditures in cash rather than in real terms and the associated budgets on an accruals basis.
3. Review the determination of budgets for the devolved territorial governments in the UK and consider the need for a sustainable and justifiable methodology.
4. Consider the extent to which the 2007 credit crunch has compromised the UK's new budgeting framework and the EU's SGP.
5. Assess the rationale for, and limitations of, the professional discipline and control model applied to local government borrowing in the UK.
6. Explain the rationales for RAB and WGA and consider the problems of consolidation and implementation.

References

Audit Scotland. (2009). *Scotland's public finances: Preparing for the future.* Edinburgh: Audit Scotland. Available at: http://www.audit-scotland.gov.uk/docs/central/2009/nr_091105_scottish_public_finances.pdf. Accessed April 8, 2010.

Bailey, S. J. (1999). *Local government economics: Principles and practice.* Basingstoke, UK: Palgrave Macmillan.

Bailey, S. J. (2002). *Public sector economics: Theory, policy and practice* (2nd ed.). Basingstoke, UK: Palgrave Macmillan.

Bailey, S. J. (2004). *Strategic public finance.* Basingstoke, UK: Palgrave Macmillan.

Bailey, S. J., Asenova, D., & Beck, M. (2009). UK public private partnerships and the credit crunch: A case of risk contagion? *Journal of Risk and Governance,* 1(3).

Bailey, S. J., Asenova, D., & Hood, J. (2009). Making more widespread use of municipal bonds in Scotland? *Public Money and Management,* 29(1), 11–18.

Bailey, S. J., Asenova, D., Hood, J., & Manochin, M. (in press). An exploratory study of the utilisation of the UK's prudential borrowing framework. *Public Policy and Administration.*

The Chartered Institute of Public Finance and Accountancy. (2003). *The Prudential Code for capital finance in local authorities.* London: Author.

The Chartered Institute of Public Finance and Accountancy. (2006). *Guide to central government finance and financial management* (fully revised, 2nd ed.). London: Author.

The Chartered Institute of Public Finance and Accountancy. (2008). *Code of practice on local authority accounting ("the SORP"): Consultation on future governance framework.* Available at: http://www.hm-treasury .gov.uk/d/frab90_annexa_code_practice.pdf. Accessed April 8, 2010.

Chow, D., Humphrey, C., & Moll, J. (2008). *Whole of government accounting in the UK.* London: The Association of Chartered Accountants. Available at: http://www.accaglobal.com/general/activities/research/ reports/accountability/rr_101. Accessed April 8, 2010.

Fingland, L., & Bailey, S. J. (2004). Convergence of public expenditures in UK territories. *Regional Studies, 38* (7), 845–858.

Fingland, L., & Bailey, S. J. (2008). The stability and growth pact: Its credibility and sustainability. *Public Money and Management, 28*(4), 223–230.

Her Majesty's Government. (1984). *The next ten years: Public expenditure and taxation into the 1990s* (Cmnd 9189). London: Her Majesty's Stationery Office.

Her Majesty's Government. (2000). *Government resources and accounts act 2000.* London. Her Majesty's Stationery Office. Available at: http://www.opsi.gov.uk/acts/acts2000/ukpga_20000020_en_1. Accessed April 8, 2010.

Her Majesty's Treasury. (1995). *Better accounting for the taxpayer's money: The government proposals: Resource accounting and budgeting in government* (Cmnd 2929). London: Her Majesty's Stationery Office.

Her Majesty's Treasury. (1997). *Resource accounting manual.* London: Her Majesty's Stationery Office.

Her Majesty's Treasury. (1998a). *Whole of government accounts.* Available at: http://www.hm-treasury.gov.uk/ media/d/wga_scopingstudy.pdf. Accessed April 8, 2010.

Her Majesty's Treasury. (1998b). *The code for fiscal stability.* Available at http://www.hm-treasury.gov.uk/d/ fiscal_stability.pdf. Accessed April 8, 2010.

Her Majesty's Treasury. (2003a). *Pre-budget report 2003: The strength to take the long-term decisions for Britain: Seizing the opportunities of global recovery* (chap. 2, sec. 2.17). Available at: http://www.hm-treasury.gov.uk/d/ PBR03completerep[1].pdf. Accessed April 8, 2010.

Her Majesty's Treasury. (2003b). *The whole of government accounts (Designation of Bodies) order 2003* (statutory instruments 2003 No. 489). London: Her Majesty's Stationery Office. Available at: http://www.opsi.gov .uk/si/si2003/20030489.htm. Accessed April 8, 2010.

Her Majesty's Treasury. (2008). *Public expenditure statistical analyses 2008* (Cmnd 7391–7407). London: Her Majesty's Stationery Office. Available at: http://www.hm-treasury.gov.uk/d/pesa0809_complete.pdf. Accessed April 8, 2010.

Her Majesty's Treasury. (2009a, April). *Budget 2009: Building Britain's future. Economic and fiscal strategy report and financial statement and budget report.* London: Her Majesty's Stationery Office. Available at: www.hm-treasury .gov.uk/bud_bud09_index.htm. Accessed April 8, 2010.

Her Majesty's Treasury. (2009b, December). *Pre-budget report 2009: Securing the recovery: growth and opportunity.* London: Her Majesty's Stationery Office. Available at: http://www.hm-treasury.gov.uk/prebud_ pbr09_index.htm. Accessed April 8, 2010.

House of Lords. (2009, July). *Select committee on the Barnett formula.* London: Author.

Jones, R. (1998). The conceptual framework of resource accounting. *Public Money and Management, 18* (2), 11–16.

Middle East

Budgeting Under Resource Abundance and Hesitant Steps to Decentralized Investment Planning and Budgeting in Iraq[1]

Ronald W. Johnson and Ricardo Silva-Morales

Learning Objectives

- Understand the formal structure for budgetary decision making in contemporary Iraq, and the main political and economic influences on budgetary decisions.
- Understand the degree of decentralization of responsibilities from central government to provincial governments, in contrast to the totally centralized and autocratic regime that ruled prior to 2003.
- Understand the possibilities for provincial governments to influence public policy and service delivery within provinces in light of the relatively limited authorities provided for in the 2005 Constitution of the Republic of Iraq and the Law on Governorates Not Incorporated into the Region (Law 21 of 2008).
- Review budgeting in Iraq as a relatively wealthy, mineral-rich state in contrast to states with considerable resource constraints.
- Understand development planning and capital investment budgeting as sources of leverage for provincial governments in a system characterized as substantially centralized.

Introduction

This chapter describes Iraq's overall budgetary decision-making structure and process since the adoption of the 2005 Constitution and focuses on capital investment planning and budgeting. Iraq's budgetary structure and process is influenced by traditions from the previous regime and conflicts that became manifest after the Saddam Hussein regime was overthrown by the United States. Sectarian tensions since 2003 have intruded into the policy process, including budgetary decision making. Tensions between the desire by many to limit the power and authority of the central government, and concerns by others that a weak central government could not successfully address internal security conditions also have had an impact. The first part of this chapter focuses on the framework for budgetary decision making. The second part of this chapter focuses on investment planning and budgeting to address severe public service delivery deficits caused by a neglected and crumbling public infrastructure base.

Iraq's 2005 Constitution created a mixed federal/unitary system that gave constitutionally protected authority to regions and governorates (provinces), but ensured central legislative authority over important provincial structures and authorities. Central government ministries are responsible for providing basic public services throughout those provinces not organized into a regional government. However, public investment planning within regions and provinces is a decentralized authority. The central government makes modest central budget allocations to regional and provincial authorities for investment projects. The majority of capital investments is contained within central ministry budgets and is implemented by central ministries. Provincial operating budgets for elected provincial councils and governors (selected by councils) are appropriated in the annual central government Budget Law and, like the investment funds, are considered transfers or allocations of the central budget, not intergovernmental grants or revenue sharing.

Investment budgeting takes place in a context of tensions between those that prefer greater decentralization of authority, partly in response to excessive centralization of the previous regime, and those that prefer a more modest decentralization, partly out of fear of a tyranny of the majority and also from a strong tradition of central control that is comforting during periods of conflict. Budgeting, and other public sector decision making, is further complicated by ethnic and religious schisms and by weak central executive authority over functional and operating ministries.

Iraq is a country rich in natural resources. The politics of relative abundance, more so than the politics of relative scarcity, influence the budget process. Government in Iraq has historically dominated and currently dominates the economy. The government budget is between 55 and 65% of gross domestic product (GDP), and oil revenues constitute 90% or more of public sector revenues (Central Intelligence Agency [CIA], 2009). During the previous regime, public sector resources, mainly from oil and, to a lesser degree, agriculture, were redistributed to favored regions of the country and were controlled by favored party officials.

Budgeting in Iraq, like other natural resource-rich countries in which the state controls the distribution of wealth from natural resources, focuses more on the allocation of revenues from the exploitation of oil than on expenditure priorities. From 2006 through 2008, the planned budget had little correspondence with the executed budget. Budgeting activities in Iraq have focused more on mobilizing funds (from oil revenues) during the budget year than on developing and executing an expenditure plan.

Taxation, beneficiary charges, and other forms of generating public sector revenue have never played a significant role in budgetary decisions. The price of oil on the world market is the primary determinant of public sector revenue availability. Expenditures are subsequently adjusted to fit the expected revenue. Since the new government was elected after the 2005 Constitution, oil prices have fluctuated wildly, causing the government budget to range from approximately US$30 billion to US$70 billion in the budget years 2006 through 2008, with a planned 2009 revenue budget of approximately US$42.7 billion (US Embassy, 2009). The 2009 Budget Law estimated expenditures of US$58.6 billion (US Embassy, 2009). The deficit would be covered by reserves created by extraordinarily high oil prices in 2008, causing a carryover of unspent 2008 funds. The carryover was mainly caused by slower-than-planned implementation of capital investment projects from 2006 through 2008.[2]

Structure and Process

BUDGET FRAMEWORK AND BUDGET PREPARATION

Budgeting in a multiparty framework is new to Iraq, dating from the development of a parliamentary democracy following the overthrow of Saddam Hussein's regime in 2003 by the United States. The budgetary process reflects a constitutional structure created in 2005 and implemented with national elections in 2006, with a modest degree of decentralization of authority and responsibility to subnational units of government. The politics of the budgetary process is shaped by the process of reconciling historic regional conflicts within Iraq, as well as sectarian conflicts awakened by the destruction of the previous authoritarian regime. Continuing security costs have dominated budget allocation among sectors, with about half of the budget going to various security functions.

The budgetary process in Iraq is evolving from a history of centralized regimes that were dominated by executive power emulating Soviet-style central planning to a system with a greater degree of separation of powers at the center and modest decentralization of authority to subnational governments. Under the most recent regime prior to its overthrow by the United States in 2003, centralization had reached an extreme with a formal structure favoring executive power and no delegation of authority to regions or provinces. In addition, the president wielded both formal and informal control over all societal resources through his leadership of a single party, the Ba'athist Party. Leadership succession in the Ba'athist Party was often marked by coups and violent overthrow.

The constitution grants specific authority to the national government, including the authority to exploit the oil resources, to control water sources that originate outside the borders—mainly the Tigris and Euphrates Rivers—and to formulate foreign and national security policies. Other authorities are shared between national government and regional or provincial-level government, including regulating electrical energy, environmental policies, development planning, public health and education policy, and internal water resources. All other powers "not stipulated in the exclusive powers of the federal government belong to the authorities of the regions and governorates that are not organized in a region" (Article 115 of the constitution; Constitution of Iraq, 2007). There are considerable differences between the powers reserved to a region and to provinces. The constitution permits provinces to form regional governments, with the Kurdistan Regional Government (KRG) having been recognized simultaneously with the adoption of the constitution. Regions may write their own constitutions, as long as they do not contradict any part of the national constitution. A regional government enjoys considerable autonomy over governmental structure and authority within the region, as well as public finance.

Provinces, on the other hand, yield to considerable central legislative authority over the provincial-level exercise of constitutional powers. Detailed specifications of the structure of provincial government, revenue authority, and other functions are subject to national legislation. Article 122 of the constitution stipulates that "A law shall regulate the election of the Governorate Council, the governor, and their powers." Article 123 of the constitution states that "Powers exercised by the federal government can be delegated to the governorates or vice versa, with the consent of both governments, and this shall be regulated by law."

The draft general budget and the development plan for the state is the responsibility of the Council of Ministers under the direction of the prime minister (PM; Article 80 of the Constitution). Iraq's first elected government under the 2005 Constitution was initially characterized by a weak and complex coalition of political parties. Ministry leadership posts were negotiated with key parties and factions in the coalition. Hence, the Council of Ministers included numerous ministers more loyal to their party or faction than to the government. The provincial elections of 2009 resulted in a somewhat surprising show of strength for the PM party at the provincial level, potentially strengthening his hand for later national elections and with the Council of Ministers. However, as is typical of parliamentary systems, some ministers have greater control over ministry budgets than the PM, given the necessity of negotiating a coalition in order to form a government (Sutherland, 2009).

The draft general budget is to be submitted to the elected Council of Representatives (COR) prior to the next budget year (January 1 through December 31). Typically, the draft general budget and the Budget Law are not completed before the beginning of the budget year, and ministries spend in accord with a continuing resolution. Once the COR passes the Budget Law, the Presidency Council has the authority to review and comment and, on occasion, recommend changes in the legislation. Once negotiations between the Presidency Council and the COR are complete, or the COR overrides the Presidency Council with a 60% majority, the annual General Federal Budget Law is decreed. The decree is followed by implementation instructions from the Ministry of Finance (MOF). Budget authorizations are limited

Table 11-1

Total Government of Iraq Budget, Fiscal Years 2006–2009

	2006	2007	2008 Initial	2008 Supplemental	2008 Total	2009
Total government budget	**33,975**	**41,118**	**49,885**	**22,352**	**72,237**	**58,615**
Current (operating) expenditures	25,794	31,055	36,826	14,298	51,124	45,888
Investment (capital) expenditures	8,181	10,063	13,059	8,054	21,113	12,727
Central-government-only investment	5,681	6,432	7,511	3,771	11,282	10,293
Allocation to KRG for investment	500	1,560	2,528	1,173	3,701	292
Allocation to provinces for investment	2,000	2,071	3,333	3,110	6,443	2,142
Total subnational allocations for investment	2,500	3,631	5,861	4,283	10,144	2,434
Percent of expenditures and investments as percents of total budget						
Current expenditures	76%	76%	74%	64%	71%	78%
Budgeted investment	24%	24%	26%	36%	29%	22%
Central-investment-only investment	17%	16%	15%	17%	16%	18%
Regional (KRG) + provinces investment	7%	9%	12%	19%	14%	4%
KRG investment[a]	1%	4%	5%	5%	5%	0%
Provinces investment	6%	5%	7%	14%	9%	4%
Regional (KRG) + Provinces Investment as Percent of Investment Expenditures	31%	36%	45%	53%	48%	19%

Source: The data for 2006, 2007, and 2008 are from MOF (2008). The figures for 2009 are from *Government of Iraq: The Federal Budget Law of 2009* (US Embassy unofficial translation), US Embassy in Iraq. (2009, March 5).

Notes: Amounts given in millions of US dollars. Small discrepancies among Tables 11-1, 11-2, and 11-3 are caused by different treatments of nonfinancial assets and how allocation to the KRG is treated by the MOF in different MOF source documents.

[a] After the 2007 budget, allocations to KRG, specifically from the Accelerated Reconstruction and Development Program, were no longer fully distinguished from other allocations to KRG. The figures for 2006 through 2009 make clear the effects of the 2008 oil price spike. A supplemental appropriation—a 40% addition to the original 2008 budget—was approved in mid-2008, bringing the original US$50 billion budget to just more than US$72 billion for the year. Subsequent oil price drops brought the anticipated revenue for 2009 back down to 2007 levels.

to the budget year, and do not carry over to the following year, although exceptions can be granted (RTI International, 2008).

Table 11-1 illustrates the budgeted amounts for the main budget categories for 2006 through 2009. The table also illustrates the budget split between capital or investment budget and current operating budget—typically 24 to 29% of the total budget has been appropriated for capital investment projects since 2006. Of the total investment budget, 30 to just more than 50% has been allocated to investment or capital projects/acquisitions under the authority of the provincial or regional governments. The 2009 Budget Law that was passed in March 2009 reflected the drop in oil prices below US$50 per barrel. The biggest loser in the budget cuts for 2009 was the category of allocations to provincial and regional governments and capital investments in general. Budgeted investment as a percentage of total budget was down in 2009 to 22%, but provincial and regional government absorbed most of the cuts with their share of the investment budget falling below 20%.

BUDGET IMPLEMENTATION

Table 11-1 illustrates budget appropriations. Implementation of budget appropriations has consistently lagged since the first budget after the 2005 Constitution. Central ministries, and to a somewhat lesser degree provinces, have consistently been unable to implement the full budget. Between 2006 and 2008, only 65 to 75% of the budget actually was expended during the budget year (US Government Accountability Office [US GAO], 2008a). A US General Accounting Office (GAO) analysis notes that the Iraqi government spent 80% of the current operating budget, but only 25% of the funds allocated to capital investments.

Table 11-2 displays the MOF's official record of budgeted versus actual expenditures, in broad terms.

According to the MOF's figures, between 67 and 69% of the 2006 through 2008 budgets were executed, on a cash basis, during the budget year (by the end of December 31st). Just more than 30% of the budgeted funds were not expensed in those budget years. Table 11-2 also illustrates the differences between operating and investment budget execution. For example, in 2008, 80% of the operating budget was executed in the budget year, but only 40% of the investment budget. Of the investment budget, the performance of the KRG and the 15 provinces in capital investment execution was better than the performance of central ministries, as will be discussed more fully in the next section on development planning and budgeting.

There are practical and technical explanations for the large discrepancies between budgeted and expended amounts. High levels of violence from mid-2006 to early 2008 contributed to a much slower execution of construction projects. Additionally, skilled personnel in key ministry positions were lost in the years 2003 to 2004 to the de-Ba'athification process and migration outside Iraq by many technical professionals

Table 11-2

Budgeted Versus Executed Expenditures, Fiscal Years 2006–2008

	Budgeted			Executed		
	Total operating budget	Projects and reconstruction budget	Total budget	Total operating expenditure	Total projects and reconstruction expenditures	Total expenditure through December 31st of the budget year
2006	25,794	8,181	33,975	20,298	2,491	22,789
2007	31,055	10,063	41,118	21,977	4,623	26,600
2008[a]	51,124	21,113	72,237	41,032	8,471	49,503

Source: Ministry of Finance (2008).

Notes: Amounts given in millions of US dollars. Expenditures from 2008 are provisional, and include the supplemental budget for that year. All expenditure figures are cash based as of the end of budget year (December 31st). Authors reclassified budgeted central allocations to KRG and provinces as capital; MOF includes operational expenditures as transfers. Budget amounts are only those appropriated in that year and exclude carry over from previous year's unspent funds.

in government employ. Further, there are significant differences in accounting for expended funds. As the US GAO noted in an analysis of data weaknesses in assessing Iraq budget performance, the government of Iraq operates on a cash basis (US GAO, 2008b). Funds are considered expenditures only after receipts are presented and funds are paid out. Based on these accounting methods, capital investment expenditures lag considerably behind current operating expenses and substantially behind expenditures for government employee salaries.

Overall, budget implementation in Iraq reflects the budgetary politics of relative resource abundance. Budgeting is about anticipating revenues from oil, and expenditure plans generally are not up to revenue levels. In the future, starting with 2009, it would not be surprising to see actual expenditures come much closer to the budget figures in years in which oil prices are lower on the world market. That would be consistent with budgeting in other countries that are wealthy in resources.

Capital Investment Planning and Budgeting

The legacy of the Iran–Iraq war, Iraq's invasion of Kuwait and the subsequent first Gulf War, a decade of international sanctions following that war, and mismanagement of the country's public resources was a crumbling infrastructure base. Both the US reconstruction program and the government of Iraq's budget process have struggled to remedy this situation (Special Inspector General for Iraq Reconstruction, 2009).

Budget reform to address the public infrastructure deficit since 2003 has had both political and technical dimensions. The political dimension has been the attempt to balance the tensions between control of investment budget decisions by the central government and by regions and provinces. Technical budget reform, both during the US Coalition Provisional Authority administration of Iraq and since the adoption of the 2005 Constitution, has focused on improving the capital investment planning and budgeting process more so than current operations budgeting. Donor participation in budget reform has focused on the development planning process and, through the International Compact with Iraq (ICI) in 2006, attempts to assist Iraq in developing a Medium-Term Expenditure Framework (MTEF) approach. The following sections analyze the development planning framework and process, and capital investment budgeting and execution.

Multiyear Development Planning: Central Versus Local

Capital investment planning in Iraq is a subset of the larger national development planning process. Public administration in the modern era (since the 1950s) reflects a tradition of multiyear national development planning dominated by the central planning agency—today the Ministry of Planning and Development Cooperation (MOPDC). Historically, central planning in Iraq was influenced by assistance to the Ba'ath Party government from the Socialist Republic of Poland. This model of central planning corresponded closely to the Soviet Union's approach to managing public finances. In the former Soviet central planning approach, the central planning committee (Gosplan), controlled decisions on all available resources including public funds, particularly capital investment funds. Emulating the Soviet style, Iraq's MOF was more an implementation agent for central planning and the responsible party, along with the Central Bank for the treasury function of controlling financial flows. Multiyear (5-year) development plans under the Ministry of Planning's control encompassed both the allocation of national economic resources to the public sector and the allocation of the investment portion of the budget among public sector functions. With as much as 80% of the economy in the public sector, the control of the development planning process was the top political prize.

Since 2003, Iraq's centralized national planning model has been challenged on several fronts. The first serious challenge to central government control of development planning was the US reconstruction program. The sheer size of the US reconstruction program was, from 2003 to 2004, the dominant source of "public sector" investment capital. This US$17 billion reconstruction program, whatever its successes and failures in effectively rebuilding the infrastructure base, introduced a planning and decision-making process largely outside the influence of Iraqi authority, even after the end of the formal occupation (Special Inspector General for Iraq Reconstruction, 2009). Throughout the interim and transitional Iraqi governments (mid-2004 through 2005) and the first years of the constitutional government (2006–2007), external donor funding, mainly from the United States, created a donor-driven capital investment budget decision-making process parallel to that of the government of Iraq. Donor-funded investment choices were based largely on donor perceptions of investment needs and not integrated with the government's investment decision-making processes. From 2003 to 2004, virtually the only investment spending was the externally funded reconstruction program. From 2005 to 2006, externally funded investment spending in total was still a major proportion of total investment spending. This donor-driven process weakened the function of central planning, although initially it did not contribute to the development of an alternative. However, as the government of Iraq's own allocation to capital investment starting in 2006 grew from approximately US$2.5 billion to approximately US$8.5 billion in 2008 (see investment expenditures in Table 11-2), the quantitative impact of external investment funding on Iraq's own investment planning and budgeting waned.

The second challenge to the historic dominance of central planning in Iraq was the shift in US strategy for building the capacity of Iraqi institutions. The initial US focus on strengthening the central government shifted to an equal or greater focus on strengthening the role and capacity of provincial and regional governments in order to reinforce the modest decentralization features in the Iraqi Constitution (Article 112). The introduction of Provincial Reconstruction Teams (PRTs) in late 2005 to 2006 by the United States focused much of the development effort on strengthening provincial and regional government. The PRTs promoted a more decentralized decision-making process that emphasized, at least somewhat, provincial priorities in capital investments. Further, the overall international donor community's engagement with Iraq, formalized initially in the ICI in 2006, represented a key role for subnational government in development planning and budgeting. The compact emphasized devolution in the planning process, noting that Iraq was undergoing a "major transition from a highly centralized model of managing the economy to one based on devolution." Further, the compact expressed the government of Iraq's pledge that the

> transition to regional, governorate and area-based development is a central theme in Iraq's National Development Strategy and will be supported in the Compact implementation. Transition should be a gradual process, given the high degree of centralization in the Iraqi economy at present, legislative and regulatory gaps and low and variable planning and execution capacities at both national and sub-national levels. (ICI, 2007)

The international donor focus exemplified in the ICI also stressed Iraq's adoption of the MTEF approach as the vehicle for integrating macroeconomic forecasts and policies with investment planning and budgeting. The MTEF approach seeks to integrate multiyear development planning, macroeconomic forecasting (especially public sector revenue forecasts), and multiyear capital or investment budgeting.[3] The donor community sees the MTEF as a particularly important tool for Iraq because of the dominance of oil in the country's economy and the public sector budget, and the volatility of oil prices. The MTEF's objective in Iraq is to develop a rational public sector investment planning and budgeting process that can operate within a safe margin of oil price fluctuations, while planning for an effective use of surpluses that arise from unanticipated price increases. For Iraq, the complications have been largely on the side of integrating development planning; translating development planning into specific, multiyear capital budgets; and implementing budgeted capital projects. At least in Iraq, the MTEF approach has tended to strengthen the hand of the MOPDC.

The third challenge to a completely centralized investment planning process is Iraq's own national legislation that further specifies the powers and authority of provincial-level governments, the *Law of Governorates Not Incorporated into a Region* (Iraq LGP, 2008). Article 7, paragraph 4, specifies that the governorate (provincial) council shall: "Outline, in the development of the plans for the governorate, the general policies in coordination with the competent ministries" (Iraq LGP, 2008). In conjunction with the general provisions of the constitution that assign all powers not specifically designated to the central government or shared with central government to regions and provinces and the National Development Strategy, this paragraph generally is interpreted to give subnational government the authority to prepare multiyear development plans that either contain or implicitly lead to multiyear investment plans.

Developments in the Practice of Provincial Development Planning

Within the context of the formal policies and the mainly external circumstances that have led away from total central control over development planning to a shared responsibility with regional and provincial government, the 18 provinces began a process in 2007 of preparing a *provincial development strategy* (PDS) as a local initiative. No formal instructions or guidelines from MOPDC preceded this bottom-up process of provincial development planning (RTI International, 2007).[4] External donor assistance by the US Agency for International Development [USAID] provided logistics and financial support, technical support for facilitating the process in each province, and various other external resources, including the technical and logistic capabilities of PRTs.

Each province created a PDS planning or coordinating committee, usually at the invitation of the governor or the provincial council. In some provinces, the PDS chairperson and other key leadership positions were filled by elected provincial officials; in other provinces, provincial government supported and participated in the process, but business, professional, and traditional leaders (tribal and religious) and other private citizens provided the primary leadership. Workshops facilitated by private Iraqi citizens trained in participatory planning processes established committees to carry out functional tasks, reviewed and discussed committee reports, formulated broad statements of economic and social vision, and ultimately developed, to varying degrees of specificity, a statement of longer term strategy. Longer term meant different things in different provinces. Basrah Province, for example, prepared a 2-year strategy, whereas Babil, Baghdad, and other provinces prepared 4- to 5-year strategies.

The general form for each PDS was similar across the provinces. An assessment phase of the planning process identified key economic, social, and public services weaknesses. Some assessments were impressionistic views resulting from open public meetings. Other provincial assessments were more quantitative, relying on data from various central government ministries on service delivery, economic base (mainly state-owned enterprises), and social issues, such as numbers of displaced persons. The assessment phase was followed by general discussions in the PDS committees, including several large, open public forums in some provinces to identify the highest priority issues. Anbar Province's PDS committee was composed of approximately 100 individuals from provincial-, district-, and subdistrict-level governments; some traditional leaders; and leaders of private business (transportation, construction, and engineering). This committee met mostly outside the province because of the high-intensity conflict occurring at that time. Kirkuk Province's PDS committee involved hundreds of citizens through numerous public meetings.

From the priority setting process, a broad statement of ambition or vision was developed in most of the provinces. Some provinces started with a broad vision statement prior to assessing conditions in the province. Several provinces had extensive involvement from central ministries responsible for service provision at the provincial and cross-provincial levels, while others had limited input and coordination with central ministries. Baghdad Province, for example, had representatives from more than 30 central ministries in almost every general session and many of the working group sessions. Muthanna Province had little involvement from central ministry personnel in the province, likely because it is remote from Baghdad and central ministry management and central ministry leaders issued no instructions or guidelines for province-based personnel to participate in the PDS process.

The culmination of the PDS process was the formal delivery of bound copies of their PDS by each of the provinces in an official ceremony in May 2008, which was presided over by the PM and the Minister of Planning and Development Cooperation. All 18 provinces participated in the ceremony, and the central government leadership committed to incorporating the basic provincial strategies in the overall national development strategy in ensuing years. To observers, MOPDC was caught somewhat by surprise that the process would have produced strategies that represented a fairly broad swath of Iraqi society in every single province.[5] One of the subsequent responses was for the MOPDC to increase its staff in the provinces, creating offices to coordinate provincial planning among the ministries. This action was interpreted by some as an attempt by the MOPDC to regain the initiative from the bottom-up provincial process.[6]

Linking PDS to Investment Planning

The importance of the decentralized PDS process for capital investment planning and budgeting is the extent to which strategies lead to investment priorities that, in turn, result in the development of detailed investment plans and budgets. In that respect, the variation across Iraq's provinces was pronounced. The Baghdad PDS, for example, contains approximately 50 pages of text describing conditions in the province and laying out a broad strategic vision. This is followed by 70 pages that briefly list several hundred capital investment projects organized by sector, problems addressed, parties responsible (a specified central ministry budget or planned by the province to be funded through the MOF investment budget allocations to Baghdad Province), implementation schedule between the years 2008 and 2012, and estimated costs by year (Baghdad Provincial Council, 2007). Other provinces include no specifically identified capital projects at all, deferring the process to the subsequent preparation of a provincial development plan; and still other provinces' PDSs contain only those projects the respective province anticipated funding in the year the strategy was prepared from funds allocated by the MOF.

With the provincial elections of January 2009 and the subsequent formation of new provincial governments, experience has not been sufficient to predict whether the PDS process will continue with periodic review and revision of basic strategies and with the development of more thorough multiyear capital investment plans and budgets. Some provinces used the process to generate broad population support to address provincial priorities (e.g., Kirkuk). Other provinces used the PDS process to generate comprehensive economic development programs. For example, from the PDS process and other activities by the governor and provincial council, Najaf launched a major program of capital investment financed by revenues produced by religious pilgrimages to holy sites in Najaf and nearby provinces. The PDSs of the three provinces of the KRG had their strategies subsumed by and into the more comprehensive regional economic development strategy.

The draft 2009 Budget Law contained a reference to substantial decentralization of central ministry functions to provincial governments, but the reference did not appear in the budget bill that passed. Two pieces of legislation were introduced in 2009 to respectively decentralize the municipalities' functions (basic urban services such as water, sewerage, streets, solid waste collection, and disposal) from the

Ministry of Municipalities and Public Works to provincial governments and modest social welfare functions from the Ministry of Labor and Social Affairs (social protection and juvenile reform) to provincial governments. Passage of either or both of those bills was uncertain as of early 2010. The draft 2010 Budget Law decreased funding for capital allocations to provincial governments in favor of increased capital funding in central ministries. These apparently contradictory proposed laws and draft budget were caught up in the political maneuvering leading up to the March 2010 parliamentary election.

Iraq's Performance in Capital Budgeting and Budget Execution

Although some PDSs contain capital investment projects that are planned to be executed over several years (5 years in Baghdad's PDS) and include capital projects to be implemented by central ministries and by provincial authority, capital budgeting and implementation has not had a stellar track record since 2006. Table 11-2 shows that since the formation of the constitutional government in 2006, in no year did capital budget execution reach 50% of budgeted funds, whereas operating expenditures each year have reached between 70 and 80% of budgeted funds.

Provincial-level capital budget execution, however, has been more successful in two respects: in the proportion of budgeted funds actually being implemented and in the project selection process. Table 11-3 differentiates capital budget execution by central government ministries versus provincial capital budget execution.

During the years 2006 to 2008, the central ministry capital budget execution ranged from as high as 46% to as low as 23% of budgeted amounts. By contrast, provincial capital budget implemented (expensed) as a percentage of the budgeted total was 57% in 2007 and 60% in 2008. The provincial capital budget expensed was low in 2006, at 31%, because the capital allocation to provinces was made 4 months into the budget year, and this was the first time the provincial-level governments had the authority to

Table 11-3									
Budgeted Versus Actual Capital Projects for Central and Provincial Governments									
	Central ministries' budgeted funds	Central ministries' expended funds	KRG and provinces' budgeted funds	KRG and provinces' expended funds	Total budgeted funds	Total expended funds	Expended as percent budgeted		
2006	3,681	1,704	2,500	787	6,181	2,491	46%	31%	40%
2007	6,224	2,415	3,846	2,208	10,070	4,623	39%	57%	46%
2008	11,282	2,617	9,831	5,854	21,113	8,471	23%	60%	40%

Source: Ministry of Finance (MOF) (2008).

Notes: Amounts given in millions of US dollars. Marsh lands rehabilitation program were included as federal expenses. Provincial capital allocations were originally classified under MOF operational expenses for 2006. Figures for 2008 include the supplemental budget. Planned amounts exclude amounts carried over from the previous year's unspent budget allocations.

make capital budget decisions and implement capital projects. It is also noteworthy that the central ministry performance, as low as it is, is still somewhat exaggerated. In 2007 and 2008, letters of credit issued in advance of expenditures were counted as executed budget for the central government. This deviates from the otherwise cash or expense accounting basis for budget execution. The letter of credit mechanism enables ministries to purchase equipment from abroad or to enter into other contracts. However, a letter of credit does not represent an actual transaction; only when a vendor is paid on the letter of credit has an expenditure taken place. For example, during 2007, of the around US$8 billion in letters of credit requested by central ministries, only 50% actually turned into expenditures. The average processing time was 10 months (MOF, 2008). If calculations had been made only on a cash basis, central ministry execution would have been less than reported in Table 11-3.

There are three related explanations for the difference in performance between central ministries and the provinces. First, the letter of credit process, as noted in the previous paragraph, delays capital budget execution because central ministry projects involve more imported capital goods. Capital goods imports, in turn, depend upon issuance of letters of credit. Hence, the slow process of obtaining letters of credit delays imports, and in turn delays capital project execution. Second, central ministry projects generally are larger and more technically complex than the capital projects implemented by provincial governments and require more time to implement. Third, provincial governments have more political stake in demonstrating public service improvements. The implementing authorities are the elected provincial councils and the governors, and their execution of the budget is likely to influence voter behavior. The provincial elections of January 2009 seem to support this assertion. About 80% of the provincial council members elected were first-time council members, reflecting general public dissatisfaction with the pace of improvement in basic conditions in Iraq.[7] On the other hand, central ministry budget execution is much less visible to voters, and the incentives to perform are more related to bureaucratic incentives. It is important to note that a substantial proportion of the low level of capital budget implementation is concentrated in only a few ministries, mainly the oil ministry. Nonetheless, the decentralized portion of the capital budget has been characterized by better performance than the central ministry portion.

A second aspect of provincial performance in capital budget planning and execution has been in project selection. Under the centralized planning model and a regime that was not subjected to any form of accountability to the public, central ministries made decisions without any means of public input. In the 3 years that provincial authorities have had capital funds at their discretion (2006 to 2008), they have been subject to election and, by virtue of the local nature of projects budgeted and executed, their performance has been more visible. It may even be the case that provincial officials elected in 2006 suffered in the 2009 elections for the overall weak performance of central and provincial government in revitalizing Iraq's public infrastructure base.

To the provinces' credit, there are partial data that indicate attempts on the part of provincial officials to fund investments that conform to the population's expectations. Table 11-4 illustrates preliminary data for 2006 investment project implementation by 10 provincial governments.[8]

Table 11-4

Sectoral Distribution of Capital Projects in 10 Provinces, Fiscal Year 2006

Sector	Amount	Percent
Drinking water and water resources	83,431	15.9%
Health care	81,513	15.5%
Municipalities	79,807	15.2%
Elementary education	66,062	12.6%
Sewage and sanitation	54,714	10.4%
Roads and bridges	45,179	8.6%
Provincial capital city	44,690	8.5%
Power generation and distribution	38,127	7.2%
Higher education	11,721	2.2%
Others	6,018	1.1%
Communications	3,298	0.6%
Sports and youth	2,885	0.5%
Agriculture	1,586	0.3%
Intermediate and vocational education	1,470	0.3%
Local management	1,246	0.2%
Trade	1,093	0.2%
Garbage collection and disposal	960	0.2%
Security	891	0.2%
Environment	619	0.1%
Urban planning and development	540	0.1%
Parks and recreation facilities	226	0.0%
Islamic Foundations for Social, Religious, and Welfare Affairs (Awqaf)	138	0.0%
Court buildings	99	0.0%
Total	**526,313**	**100.0%**

Sources: Provincial Reconstruction Teams and USAID Local Governance Program Staff.

Notes: Amounts given in thousands of US dollars. The 10 provinces included are Babil, Baghdad, Basrah, Diyala, Karbala, Maysan, Najaf, Ninawa, Salah ad Din, and Wasit.

The table shows the US dollar amount and percentage of project value implemented in those 10 provinces by sector. Priority areas were the improvement of water, health care, and municipalities' services. Municipalities' services include solid waste collection and disposal, street maintenance, street lighting, drainage, and similar basic municipal functions. A second cluster is also apparent—education and sewage. Almost 94% of the investments were concentrated in the eight sectors that have consistently been shown to be the highest priority in various public opinion polls.[9]

Since 2007, as described in the discussion of the PDS process, provincial capital investment planning has been increasingly characterized by participatory processes that involve district and subdistrict levels of government, as well as citizens, opinion leaders, and, in some provinces, hundreds of individuals. At a minimum, the selection of capital improvements sectors in which to invest at the provincial level generally has a basis in public opinion and in participatory processes.

There has been push back from those that continue to favor a more centralized state, including the central planning ministry. Since 2008, the MOPDC has been successful in inserting a chapter in the annual budget describing the approved projects by name, which makes the reorganization of capital investment initiatives inflexible during the year. This list includes both projects identified by the provinces and projects planned by central ministries. While there is no evidence from 2008 that MOPDC used this device to reorder provincial priorities, this reassertion of the prerogatives of the central planning ministry reflects the ongoing tensions between decentralization and recentralization of power and authority.

Conclusions

Iraq's budgetary framework, and the experience to date from 3 years of a new constitutional government, reflects a departure from a highly centralized tradition. The extent to which regional and provincial governments will play a major role in public sector budgeting remains unclear because there are forces in favor of centralized authority as well as decentralized authority. Evidence on budget execution tends to support the proposition that regional and provincial governments are performing better than central ministries in addressing Iraq's serious infrastructure deficits that are the legacy of decades of war, neglect, and misuse of public funds. The 2009 provincial elections also showed some support for the proposition that voters paid attention to performance, which may strengthen the position of regional and provincial government in delivering basic public services. However, future national elections, and the continuing tension between proponents of strong central authority who believe it is necessary to address ongoing security issues and proponents of decentralized authority, are likely to mean a budgetary process will be in flux for some years to come.

Discussion Questions

1. What are some of the differences in the politics and economics of the budgetary process in a wealthy state like Iraq in comparison with countries with limited natural and other resources?
2. What have been the main challenges since 2003 to the previously totally centralized regime with respect to the role of central government versus provincial governments?
3. Research provisions of international donor compacts with nation states with respect to economic and social development planning and the role of the central versus subnational units of government and compare with Iraq.

4. What are the ways in which elected provincial officials in Iraq, with relatively limited authorities and responsibilities, can enhance the effective and efficient delivery of public services within their respective provinces?

References

Baghdad Provincial Council. (2007, October 10). *Baghdad Provincial Council Strategic Plan, 2008–2012* (Unofficial English translation). Available at: http://www.lgp-iraq.org/publications/index.cfm?fuseaction= throwpub&ID=130. Accessed April 8, 2010.

Central Intelligence Agency. (2009). *The world factbook: Iraq.* Washington, DC: Author. Available at: https:// www.cia.gov/library/publications/the-world-factbook/print/iz.html.

Constitution of Iraq: 2005. (2007). Reprinted in RTI International (Ed.), *Republic of Iraq District Government Field Manual* (Vol. I). Research Triangle Park (RTP), NC: Author. Available at: http://www.lgp-iraq .org/search/index.cfm?fuseaction=throwpub&id=173. Accessed April 8, 2010.

International Compact with Iraq. (2007). Available at: www.mop-iraq.org/mopdc/resources/ images/Planning%20&20Dev/INTERNATIONAL_COMPACT_WITH_IRAQ_FINAL__English_ final.pdf. Accessed April 8, 2010.

Iraq Local Governance Program. (2008, June). *Law of governorates not incorporated into a region: An annotated text.* Washington, DC: USAID. Available at: http://www.lgp-iraq.org/publications/index.cfm?fuseaction= throwpub&ID=274. Accessed April 8, 2010.

Ministry of Finance. (2008). Interview with Iraqui budget officials in 2006, 2007, and 2008.

RTI International. (2007, November). *Writing the future: Provincial development strategies in Iraq* (Vol. 1). Washington, DC: USAID. Available at: http://www.lgp-iraq.org/publications/index.cfm?fuseaction=throwpub& ID=187. Accessed April 8, 2010.

RTI International. (2008). *Government of Iraq federal budget process: Investment budget.* Washington DC: USAID. Available at: http://www.lgp-iraq.org/publications/index.cfm?CatId=70&domainStartNode=70&showStart Node=1 Accessed April 18, 2009.

Special Inspector General for Iraq Reconstruction. (2009). *Hard lessons learned: The Iraq reconstruction experience.* Washington, DC: US Government Printing Office.

Sutherland, J. J. (2009, February 5). Iraqi Prime Minister's party tops election results. *National Public Radio.* Available at: http://www.npr.org/templates/story/story.php?storyId=100297561. Accessed April 19, 2009.

US Government Accountability Office. (2008a). *Stabilizing and rebuilding Iraq: Iraq revenues, expenditures and surplus.* Washington, DC: US Government Printing Office.

US Government Accountability Office. (2008b). *Iraq reconstruction: Better data needed to assess Iraq's budget execution.* Washington, DC: U.S. Government Printing Office.

US Embassy in Iraq. (2009, March 5). *The federal budget law of 2009* (unofficial translation of the US Embassy in Iraq).

ENDNOTES

1. This chapter was made possible through support provided by the USAID Mission in Baghdad, the US Agency for International Development, under the terms of Contract No. DFD-I-03-05-00128_00 LGPIII. The opinions expressed herein are those of the authors and do not necessarily reflect the views of the US Agency for International Development, or the author's employer, RTI International.

2. Authors' observations and various unofficial statements of Ministry of Finance officials.

3.   A list of documents with country case studies, descriptive material, and critical commentary on the practicality of implementing MTEF is available at: http://web.worldbank.org/WBSITE/EXTERNAL/TOPICS/EXTPUBLICSECTORANDGOVERNANCE/EXTPUBLICFINANCE/0,,contentMDK:20235448~pagePK:148956~piPK:216618~theSitePK:1339564,00.html.

4.   Discussion of the PDS process is based on this document and the authors' participation in phases of the process.

5.   Based on the authors' observations of the formal presentation ceremony and comments made by the PM and other ministry staff at the workshops to discuss next steps, held on the same day as the formal presentation.

6.   Based on the authors' interviews with the coordinator who was appointed by the Minister of Planning during the workshop.

7.   Figures are unofficial counts by RTI staff implementing the USAID-funded Local Governance Program (LGP). Opinion expressed is solely that of the authors.

8.   Caution is necessary in interpreting Table 11-4 because the records only cover 10 of the 18 provinces, and are, in some cases, incomplete in the 10 provinces. The results reported in the table should be considered indicative, rather than definitive.

9.   Various polls conducted for and reported by ABC/BBC news services, usually at least four times a year since 2005 are readily available. For example: *Iraq and Afghanistan Polls: Where Things Stand*. Available at: http://abcnews.go.com/PollingUnit/story?id=6627152&page=1. Accessed April 8, 2010.

Chapter 12

Budget Discipline and Undisciplined Politics: The Case of Jordan

Jamil E. Jreisat

Learning Objectives

- Understand the political and economic foundations of Jordan.
- Recognize links between performance budgeting and the overall professional development of public management, the institutional context, and the tradition and culture of Jordan.
- Realize that success of budget implementation requires clear commitment and adjustment of the political system.
- Develop an awareness that implementation of a performance budget system underlines the importance of competence and commitment of the central financial institutions that provide guidelines to agencies, audit results, and train employees in the necessary skills.
- Identify various elements of performance budgeting that require skillful development such as operational goals, indicators, continuous data collection, and expert interpretation of data.
- Understand that inducing compliance and motivating staff through incentives are key factors for success.

Introduction

Traditionally, public managers defined success in terms of budget growth, increase in the number of employees, and expansion of organizational assets and facilities. Such a view tends to overshadow accomplishments and obscure performance data. A shift of focus in the past 2 decades is gradually changing evaluation criteria in budgetary decisions and allocations from input-driven to output- or outcome-driven measurement. Actually, many countries, such as the United States, Canada, Australia, The Netherlands, and many countries of the Organisation for Economic Co-operation and Development (OECD), have already changed their public budgeting processes to emphasize results and performance (Bouckaert & Halligan, 2008; Kettl, 1997).

In 1999, the government of Jordan also decided to change its budget system from the traditional input-oriented, line-item format, to a performance-based budget system. Jordan's Ministry of Finance, including the Department of Budgeting within it, requested help from the German Technical Cooperation (GTZ) in making this change. The stated reasoning by Jordanian officials for seeking to change their budget system includes what they perceived as expected benefits from the new system. Namely, Jordanian officials were hoping that the adoption of performance budgeting would give them better information on results, improve accountability, and allow greater control over cost. The response of the GTZ program was to invite an "international team of experts" to develop a plan for introducing performance budgeting to Jordan. The international team met in Amman, Jordan, several times for this purpose.[1]

This chapter describes the process of introducing performance budgeting to Jordan, defines objectives, specifies necessary steps in the execution of the proposed master plan, assesses conditions conducive or inimical to the process of change, and articulates the roles of key agencies involved. Lessons learned from this case are relevant to many countries embarking on or contemplating such changes in their own budget systems.

Background Information

Jordan is a constitutional monarchy of about six million people. The country suffers from great economic and social challenges. The country has a legislative branch, elected through universal suffrage. During the past few years, the annual economic growth ranged between 5 and 6% (fixed prices). Inflation rate reached 20% during 2008, but has been declining according to the most recent estimates (Fanek, 2009b). Although the official unemployment level has often been estimated between 10 and 15%, this number is less reliable for various reasons. This includes part-time employment and poor recordkeeping. Independent, nongovernmental calculations put the number of unemployed at much higher rates.

Income distribution is grossly uneven and all efforts to fight poverty seem to produce only modest results. A study for the Center for Strategic Studies at the University of Jordan, points out that 30% of the population earns 60% of the income. The disparities in standards of living are also growing as the government has reduced subsidies and canceled welfare programs despite the fact that unemployment is increasing and the

Table 12-1	
Estimated Public Revenues, Fiscal Year 2009	
Domestic revenues	**4783**
Taxes on income and capital gains	664
Taxes on property	120
Taxes on goods and services	2100
Taxes on international trade	307
Other taxes	65
Total tax revenues	**3257**
Nontax revenues	**1526**
Property income and other revenues	674
Revenues from selling goods and services	760
Fines, penalties, and forfeits	63
Foreign grants	**684**
TOTAL REVENUES	**5467**

Source: *General Budget Law for the Fiscal year 2009*, p.8, by Jordan's General Budget Department, Ministry of Finance, 2009.

Notes: Amounts are given in millions of Jordanian dinars (JD). JD1 equals US$1.4.

total population is continually rising. Moreover, the tax structure is primarily regressive. The main sources of internal revenue are a flat-rate income tax, customs duties, excise tax, various fees, and a recent and fast-growing sales tax that amounts to 24% of local public revenues (Abbadi, 2008). All internal (local) revenue sources add up to about 85% of government annual expenditures of more than US$8.5 billion (see Table 12-1). The chronic deficit or revenue shortfall has been funded from foreign assistance and through public debt.

Over the past several years, Jordan adopted various social, legal, and cultural changes, such as increasing women's participation in governance and amending election law to empower women to elect and to be elected, guaranteeing a minimum number of women in Parliament and city councils. In education, health, and local authorities, important changes have been initiated and legislated to decentralize the authority system and to improve services. Education is universal and the literacy rate is more than 80%. Overall, the citizens enjoy a measured level of political and religious freedom.

Planning a Performance Budget System

The government of Jordan has been advocating economic reform to reduce macro imbalances, improve delivery of public services, and decrease poverty. To meet these objectives, the government initiated many public policies that culminated with a strategic shift to performance budgeting. Discussions by members of the team of consultants and with senior Jordanian budget officials established these expected advantages:

- Performance budgeting provides information about the effectiveness and efficiency of government activities and services;
- Public managers are able to view their operations methodically to identify problems and to deal with them promptly;
- Policy makers (prime minister [PM], cabinet, and Parliament) are able to improve the quality of strategic and operational decisions;
- Departments and agencies will be able to identify, implement, and document improvements;
- Resource allocation would improve and be more responsive to societal needs;
- Citizens' satisfaction becomes known and problems are easier to address;
- Performance measurement provides managers the necessary data for better decision making, improved unit cost estimates, and enhanced accountability; and
- Measurement improves fairness of the incentive system that should reward excellence, correct deficiencies, and encourage creativity and innovation.

With agreement on anticipated benefits, the focus of the team of consultants shifted to the domain of action and challenges. Successful implementation of performance budgeting requires, at an early phase, that germane activities be grouped (bundled) into programs of well-defined services and outputs. This requires a functional review of the various public sector services, and, in some cases, a reconsideration of the organizational configuration. The development of a mission statement for each public agency is a reminder of the overall strategic commitments that guide operational goals and underscore accountability.

The implementation, however, is intricate, involving far more elements than the preparation of the annual budget document. Effective performance budgeting has political, economic, and managerial dimensions as well as medium- and long-range horizons (Rubin, 2010). Transforming sound principles and plans to application remains a work in progress, typically extending from 3 to 5 years. The presence of the following elements of financial management was deemed vital for the process of implementing performance budgeting in Jordan:

1. Central strategic policy direction at the initial phase of the annual budget process is essential to signify national policies and priorities that need to be reflected in budget allocations. Primarily, this is a responsibility of the political leadership such as the PM, the cabinet, and the Parliament, as well as the senior public managers. Strategic capacity at the political and organizational levels offers a flexible deliberate outlook, not necessarily tied to a formalized strategic plan. An effective strategy or approach "integrates resources, tactics, and goals" (Meyers, 1996, p. 1). A set of guidelines and a multiyear framework for improving reallocation of resources based on shifting priorities will go a long way in the direction of developing a strategic capacity.

2. Guidelines and operational instructions are to be issued promptly by the central budget office (the Budget Department) in order to introduce the proposed change and ensure compliance with relevant laws and regulations. Essentially, the Budget Department guides public agencies in the preparation of the budget, and takes the initiative in translation, interpretation, and transmittal of strategic policies and priorities of the political leadership, including setting ceilings that limit spending by departments.

3. Setting operational goals for determining outputs and outcomes, and measuring them begins with identifying legitimate primary objectives (overall policies) of each public organization, particularly those specified in the enabling law. Goal setting is a relatively complex job. Goals have to be derived from a legitimate public policy, few enough to be manageable, represent consensus or general agreement, and must be measurable (Jreisat, 1997, p. 213).

4. Development of performance indicators facilitates gathering data to gauge progress in reaching organizational goals. Work indicators are the instruments for the measurement of results and for providing information on effectiveness, efficiency, quantity, and quality of services.

5. Investing in an appropriate management information system that provides for the collection, recording, storing, classifying, summarizing, and retrieving of data about the indicators. Such an information system is essential for improved decision making as well as facilitating performance audit and evaluation.

6. Periodic, reliable reports are indispensable for the proper functioning of a financial system. Quarterly and annual reports aggregate and communicate financial data.

7. Devolution of responsibilities is a concern in a highly centralized system of governance, as in Jordan. Performance budgeting is premised on the idea of empowering managers to manage, guided by overall policies and the operational requirements of their goals. In contrast, the traditional line-item budgeting permits only a minimum administrative discretion while maximizing control over employees' abilities to consider, let alone adopt, alternative actions.

In addition to these vital elements, revising and reorienting the financial control process was recognized as an initial and necessary step. It is worth noting that the president of the Bureau of Accounting and Audit faced considerable resistance from members of the cabinet who were unwilling to commit to a strong independent audit function when he attempted to update the enabling law of accounting and audit. The proposed change would strengthen the bureau's independence, allow vigorous prosecution of violations, extend performance audit to all activities of the government, and allow the bureau to audit before or after spending, as needed (personal communication with the president of the Bureau of Accounting and Audits, July 15, 1999 and June 24, 2001). To be sure, some changes were enacted recently but their impact cannot be evaluated yet. Certainly, restricting the functions of central accounting and audit produces a chilling effect on the operational systems of performance, accountability, and audit. Finally, it is important to point out that the head of the Bureau of Accounting and Audit is appointed and dismissed at the will of the PM and the cabinet, significantly limiting the autonomy and the independence of the auditing function.

Responsibilities and Implementation

Primarily, the responsibility for performance measurement is with departments and agencies (Bouckaert & Halligan, 2008, p. 237). The legitimacy and sustainability of a shift from a line-item to a performance budget format, however, would be far more authentic and reliable when the planned change is grounded in a legislative mandate that institutes the new framework. Political buy-in at the highest executive and legislative levels of authority is the best way to cement the political commitment to the new performance measurement system. Political support and operational capacity of departments and agencies are among the most crucial requirements of a successful implementation strategy.

The designated responsibility for leading the process of budget reform in Jordan is in the Budget Department, which operates as a semiautonomous unit within the Ministry of Finance.[2] The Budget Department plays a central role in the design of budget procedures that determine the form, the calendar, and the guidelines for the submission of estimates by line agencies. A significant aspect of procedures is determining flow of information to and from line agencies. Procedures and regulations shape coordination of requests for funds and set restrictions on a variety of decisions in areas such as personnel, procurement, and capital spending.

The role of the Budget Department also includes responsibility for examining, coordinating, and approving requests for funds before submission for the appropriate authorization by the cabinet and, subsequently, the Parliament. The director of the Budget Department reviews annual funding requests, interacts with executive agencies, and regularly consults with the minister of finance and with the Bureau of Accounting and Audit. The monitoring authority gives the department a special role in introducing change, particularly while gauging management efficiency and quality of service in each unit requesting or receiving public funds. Usually, operational information is reported according to a specified format to ensure comparability. The Budget Department is authorized to verify and check the quality and the integrity of submitted information.

The minister of finance has an influential position in the cabinet and among line agencies. Not unlike the chancellor of the exchequer in the British system, the minister has a special fiduciary responsibility for revenues. The minister's special status in the cabinet is not only because of a commanding role in decisions involving money, but also because of coordination with the PM and the power to initiate limits and to arbitrate disputes over funding among agencies or between agencies and the Budget Department. The minister of finance also acts as a buffer zone by being the authority that turns down requests from line agencies for new funds. His standard response is: "We do not have the money." Such requests are not only for new funds, but also for the release of already appropriated funds that the minister of finance is impounding for whatever reason. Unquestionably, the institutional framework for financial management in Jordan is set by the Ministry of Finance, which has major responsibilities for the overall economic and financial policies, and is in charge of a number of other functions ranging from forecasting revenue to administering public debt and cash management.[3]

Line agencies are the main source of cost estimates for government operations. Although a high ratio of these costs is fixed as salaries, the rest of their expenditures are not based on real or exact measurements. Historic data and political factors often sway the outcome of the negotiations between line agencies, the Budget Department, and the Finance Ministry. Generally, the top leadership of each line agency determines the critical question of how much money to ask for. Although the finance or budget officers in each administrative unit may participate in the calculations of estimates, generally these finance managers are limited to specific duties such as monitoring compliance with accepted accounting principles, developing financial reports, and facilitating annual audit and inspections. Still, line agencies are the operational centers where the information on performance and financial transactions originates.

Formalism and Legislative Authority

A permanent finance committee in the Parliament reviews the budget request as a whole before sending it with recommendations for a vote by the total membership. A similar process is followed in the Senate. Typically, the conclusions of these debates do not result in increasing spending and rarely affect, meaningfully, the final outcome (Fanek, 2009a). The vote usually is on the total budget bill, up or down. The cabinet, if convinced during the debate in the Parliament, may promise on its own to increase or decrease spending decisions in the future according to appropriate procedures. As expected, exhortations from the Parliament's podium, criticisms, questions, and requests for reduction or for additional funds are voiced. Some legislators actually vote against the government financial package because it does not include projects or policies they deem necessary. Typically, the government's response, after a polite acknowledgement, is a promise to take their opinions and views into serious consideration.

Disapproval of the PM's budget by Parliament is a vote of no confidence in the government. However, no one recalls such an event ever occurring in recent history. After executive and legislative approval, line agencies start the execution phase following elaborate procedures for payments, monitored from within each unit, and from without by the Budget Department and the Bureau of Accounting and Audit. The bureau provides a basic control on spending by monitoring compliance and by verifying conformance to the technical spending rules throughout the executive branch. The bureau submits its annual audit report to the Parliament, the PM, and minister of finance simultaneously. In cooperation with the Budget Department and the Ministry of Finance, the bureau takes the lead in standardizing and enforcing generally accepted accounting principles (GAAP) in line agencies. In theory, the Bureau of Accounting and Audit reviews public management performance to align it with organizational mission and to satisfy improved work processes. In actual practice, these concepts remain targets to be achieved rather than a reality because of limitations in staffing, legal mandates, and technical resources. The role of the bureau is still unfolding in relation to effective redefinition of its mission and expansion of its mandate to include performance reviews.

Analysis and Assessment

Budgeting is essentially making choices among alternatives. It involves institutions, individuals, relationships, goals, norms, and values, all of which produce outputs in patterns not immediately evident from studying only the budget documents (Lee, Johnson, & Joyce, 2008, pp. 7–18). In a centralized system of authority, as in Jordan, the PM and the cabinet seek to constrain behavior through rules and regulations that define and limit the ways in which budgets are prepared, approved, and implemented. In many aspects, the process of budgeting in Jordan is a lesson in crisis management and uncertainty. A combination of factors complicates the process, thus requiring a particular focus and evaluation methodology. Examples include the following.

BUDGET DISCIPLINE AND POLITICS

Financial discipline involves certain formal budget constraints and restraints, notwithstanding frequent noncompliance and exceptions. Prior constraints include laws, social norms, constitutional clauses, and the like that restrict the decision powers of policy makers and predetermine certain budgetary outcomes by placing bounds and ceilings on spending or on deficit. Post restraints include restraints on changing levels of spending and how uncertainties are resolved and contingencies foreseen after the beginning of the fiscal year. These "constraints" and "restraints" are applied in tandem with preparation, approval, and execution of the budget cycle, a distinction that helps to separate information and improve its organization and analysis. The accent on phases of the budget cycle helps to focus on a wide range of information that clarifies the broad outlook and delineate aggregate characteristics of the budget while defining most effective mechanisms that restrict overspending. Compliance with the prior constraints and post restraints of the budget is an indicator of the discipline in the execution phase. In Jordan, individual positions of power within the institutions, particularly the king and the PM have extraordinary powers of decision making that can reach any aspect of the system, as well as make exceptions as they see necessary.

Line agencies habitually and creatively attempt to circumvent the substance of rules and regulations through exceptions sanctioned by the PM. A range of political influences and personal considerations determine the success of an agency in receiving such exceptions. A decisive post restraint on spending is applied by the PM during the execution of the budget when a revenue shortfall is eminent, or when expected loans or grants do not materialize. The PM, at the recommendation of the minister of finance and the Budget Department, is often able to stop, reduce, slow down, or postpone spending on a variety of items in the budget without prior legislative authorization. As a result, the actual budget is often significantly different from the appropriated one. One immediate reason is the frequent change of the PM and the cabinet. The new government regularly finds itself not obligated to honor financial allocations made by the previous regime. Another factor for the tentativeness of the budget is the habit of exceeding appropriated expenditures based on the expectation of issuing a budget supplement in the future, either by another government, or after a long time when the decision is a far gone conclusion. Thus, legislative approval of public spending is made ineffective or reduced to a mere formality.

An interesting conception of authority by the top executive leadership is that legislative approval of the budget is an approval of the ceiling on the authority to spend. Consequently, as long as the numbers are kept below the ceiling, as approved by the legislators, a de facto approval remains operative. When spending exceeds legislative authorization, it is not regarded as a violation because a retroactive request for a supplement would be submitted to Parliament for approval, even after many months had passed. As an example, the deficit of the 2007 budget was doubled as a result of supplements and adjustments that were not included in the original budget approved by Parliament, but were added subsequently (Fanek, 2009a).

AGGREGATE FISCAL DISCIPLINE

Jordan's budget lacks comprehensiveness because significant components are handled outside of the budget instead of within the budget process, diluting fiscal discipline. Military expenditure is one example of those autonomous components, subjected only to the minimal scrutiny and evaluation by the central budget office. The military's budget is consistently determined by the top political level. Military and security forces consume more than 33% of the budget, yet the central budget agencies have little control over the growth or the management of this large portion of the budget. More importantly, the institutional arrangements behind these components create incentives for increased expenditures, which can potentially drive the fiscal situation out of control. In addition to the military, security forces, intelligence operations (*Muckabarat*), the judiciary, the royal court, and pension benefits are legally and politically assured of their fiscally autonomous status (nondiscretionary). Moreover, although public enterprises were granted administrative autonomy, the government remained obligated to their solvency and a guarantor of their debts. The significance of this obligation, however, decreased after many enterprises were privatized. In brief, by conceding its fiscal responsibility, and allowing such off-budget budgets, the government has weakened fiscal discipline and budget comprehensiveness.

Another important factor weakening fiscal discipline of the budget is heavy reliance on loans and foreign assistance. Jordan's budget suffers from a chronic dependence on foreign aid and loans, even for funding operational expenses. More than 14% of the annual expenditures have usually been funded by loans and foreign aid. This condition is restrictive and creates formidable uncertainties. In effect, it undermines the independence of public decision making and discourages serious strategic mid-term and long-term planning. Jordan's economy has been burdened by the heavy weight of public debt and a persistent budget deficit. Although external (foreign) debt has been reduced from US$7.4 billion in 2007 (44.8% of GDP) to US$5 billion in 2008 (25% of GDP), total external and internal debt continue to grow (a 3.1% increase in 2008 from the previous year). Internal public debt increased to about US$11.8 billion, equal to 61% of GDP (Ministry of Finance, 2009). The increase in domestic borrowing is mainly to pay operating budgetary obligations.

ALLOCATIVE EFFICIENCY

Efficiency of allocation involves issues such as the use of objective criteria for prioritization, use of a macroeconomic framework, systematic cost–benefit analysis, performance measurement, and the time horizon of public expenditure plans. In Jordan, however, the following conditions continue to sidetrack the process:

First, legislative approval of the budget has been reduced to an ineffective formalistic ritual that is ill-defined, poorly understood by its own members, and ineptly carried out. Overall, the legislature has neither been effective in utilizing its powers of appropriation nor educated in monitoring government within a clear set of rules. Budget procedures already allow far too much reshuffling of accounts after legislative approval, which often undermines the purpose of the initial budget. While these changes may allow greater attention to momentous exigencies, they often weaken strategic interests and objectives. Timidly and reluctantly, legislators regularly defer to executive discretion for lack of confidence in their own information and knowledge.

Second, undisciplined politics and chronic deficit spending increase reliance on grants, loans, and deferrals. The dilemma is manifested in economic distortions caused by current account of the balance of payments, which could not be covered except by borrowing or by invading the reserves. In addition, disaggregating domestic revenues often reveals significant funds "rotated" from the previous year. The government of Jordan refers to these funds as "savings in the current budget." In reality, just as the presidential impoundment of funds may occur in the US budget, the government in Jordan (PM, minister of finance, and the director of the Budget Department) is also able to halt spending on a project for a variety of reasons. The most common claim, however, is a lack of funds. Frequently, the "saving" is accomplished through delays or postponement of payments rather than outright denial.

Third, invariably, the government is in a crisis management mode (a fire department approach) with little or no strategic focus. The budget has not served the purpose of defining and updating national policies and priorities in an intermediate or long-range vision. The political and organizational settings, short on strategic capacity and shackled by financial scarcity, have not been able to effectively respond to compelling changes in the domestic, regional, and global environments. In this context, public administration has been relatively disconnected from the political leadership. Reform initiatives have produced only unfulfilled promises, mutual blaming, and a remarkable lack of accountability where public institutions are answerable for their performance of duties and responsibilities. According to a report sponsored by United Nations Development Program and the Swedish Fund (United Nations Office for Project Service & the Swedish Fund for Consultancy Services, 1998), Jordan's financial system leads to a situation in which it is difficult, or even impossible, to find out what various programs and projects really cost. Budget estimates are not based on the long-term, full costs of activities, and rarely apply cost–benefit analysis or other objective criteria for project selection.

Fourth, a high ratio of nondevelopmental expenditures such as salaries of military and civilian personnel, retirement benefits, and other fixed costs consume more than half of the total public expenditures. After adding debt service and other restricted expenditures, nondevelopmental budget allocations exceed 80% of total public spending

(83% in the 2010 budget). Thus, only a small part of the budget could be targeted to economic growth and job creation. Even spending classified as capital is mostly spent on acquiring automobiles for senior officials, office furniture, and projects of the type known in US financial practices as "turkeys," that mainly reward influential public figures and their followers.

The allocative efficiency of budgetary institutions may be evaluated in terms of producing the desired outcomes of fiscal policy such as low unemployment, low inflation, economic growth, balanced budget, and a reduction in the trade gap. Another type of evaluation is in terms of efficient and effective delivery of public services to citizens such as education, health, and social services. Failures of budgetary institutions to allocate financial resources efficiently compounded Jordan's economic entanglement under an excessive load of debt and chronic budget deficit. The macro picture of fiscal performance in Jordan underlines the complexity of the economic situation. Fiscal discipline is more than balancing the financial books: It is making decisions about what is important enough for the country and the citizens to justify the taxes collected.

TECHNICAL EFFICIENCY

Technical efficiency determines the extent of reliance on merit-based recruitment and promotion as well as the level of overall professional development of public service. This includes educational attainment and various measures that highlight competence and quality of the pool from which public employees are recruited.

The early financial management system of Jordan was an incremental process using line-item format, cash-based accounting, and a traditional financial audit. Such a method of operation makes it difficult to differentiate the cost of various programs or determine what types of services are supplied and to what consequences. In other words, political decision makers do not reliably know what they are getting for the money they spend. The information is simply not available. Poor resource allocation, inefficiency of operations, and poor customer focus remain entrenched habits. Accountability has many dimensions: (1) It is expressed in terms of results, performance measurement, performance-based incentives, and employing cost–benefit analysis in making allocative decisions; (2) it means utilizing sound accounting principles, conducting effective and timely audits, and consistently and fairly applying clear rules and regulations; and (3) accountability involves freedom of the public and the press to investigate public decisions, to receive information, and to expect transparency of public actions (Kelly & Rivenbark, 2003, p. 3).

Generally, it is assumed that centralization of the budget by limiting the number of actors in the budget-making process leads to smaller deficits and reduces fragmentation (Poterba & von Jurgen, 1999). But key dimensions of such centralization are transparency and entrepreneurship, and neither of them is a distinction of past performance for the government of Jordan. Actually, centralization has reduced the autonomy of executive agencies in the sense that they lost flexibility in making decisions and in managing their resources according to facts on the ground. Managers of line agencies fear central decisions that may further shrink their functions or abruptly reduce their operations.

Table 12-2

Functional Classification of Estimated Public Expenditures, Fiscal Year 2009

Functional division	Current expenditures	Capital expenditures	Total
General public services	847,507	120,083	967,590
Defense	959,500	21,000	980,500
Public order and safety	592,229	93,500	685,729
Economic affairs	81,548	544,179	625,727
Environmental protection	1,218	5,000	6,218
Housing and community amenities	20,352	165,575	185,927
Health	447,282	188,650	635,932
Recreation, culture, and religion	73,849	49,702	123,551
Education	507,108	93,181	600,289
Social protection	1,259,882	84,126	1,344,008
TOTALS	**4,790,475**	**1,364,996**	**6,155,471**

Source: General Budget Law for the Fiscal Year 2009, p. 19, by Jordan's General Budget Department, Ministry of Finance, 2009.

Notes: Amounts given in JD.

LIMITED PARTICIPATION

In the end, few individuals in the executive branch of government ultimately determine the main allocations among public functions. Certainly, the Jordanian public is neither a participant in setting budgetary priorities, nor a participant in debating its policies. Only recently, the financial system began to practice a modest measure of transparency. Line agencies prepare the estimates and execute the budget law, but within carefully confined administrative discretion. Jordan's public agencies and departments, including key institutions as the Budget Department and Bureau of Accounting and Audit, operate with narrow perceptions of their duties because of inadequate organizational capabilities and uncertain political support. These units have not succeeded in refining or expanding their functions in alignment with their organizational missions and goals. Under current conditions of heavy workload, understaffing, and overall low technical skills of the staff, these two key budget organizations are seriously restrained or held down in enforcing performance budget rules and objectives.

Conclusions

After 3 years from submission of the master plan for performance budgeting in Jordan in 1999, a follow-up consultant's report concludes: "The current format of the Budget law does not support a result-oriented debate" (Allied Business Advisors, 2002). Subsequent visits in 2008 and 2009 by this author and conversations with senior officials in the Budget Department indicate that "very little has been done" toward operational implementation of a performance budgeting process in Jordan. The most compelling question, then, is why no significant progress has been made in executing the plan of reform where fiscal imbalance is a constant threat to the country's economic vitality?

The uncertainty caused by chronic structural deficits and the subsequent reliance on foreign sources (see Table 12-2) to shore up these deficits have effectively prevented shifting the emphasis back to microbudget negotiations. The political leadership has been using "lack of revenue" as a financial shield to deny or to postpone urgent and popular requests for funding. Instead of promoting microbudget reforms, the budget problems have been used as a rationale for ambiguity, centralization of power, inaction, and often for arbitrary decisions. Thus, on transferability of this budget reform to Jordan, Irene Rubin (personal communication, November 14, 2005) suggested that the reform may have been a "mismatch" because of the many problems encountered that the reform was not what was intended. Consequently, during implementation, the real challenges emerged and eventually unsettled the process, particularly these two key factors:

First, the technical and managerial competence necessary were not present at the senior levels of political and administrative leadership. Lack of relevant experience and knowledge of management by results and performance measurement within the Jordanian public administration system in general were insurmountable impediments in a short time frame. Old habits of appointments to senior positions do not change fast enough to produce a group of qualified public managers. It was not easy to build professional managerial competence of leadership when a system of recruitment to senior positions was dominated by nepotism and favoritism, instead of professional qualifications and potential. Merit-based recruitment and promotion to senior management positions means restricting political appointments, and applying objective performance criteria to recruit, reward, and promote personnel. These shortcomings were clearly noticeable in the central budget office, a relatively weak institution, neither exercising enough leadership, nor deploying a sufficient level of resources to effectively guide the reform process. Arrangements for the use of macroeconomic programming and institutional limits on borrowing and spending exist, but they have not been enforced.

Second, it is commonly acknowledged that public budgeting is largely a political process (Rubin, 2010; Wildavsky & Caiden, 2001). In Jordan, however, in an economy of severe scarcity and with a highly centralized political authority, the top political leaders were not sufficiently committed to the new approach. The evidence suggests that the political leadership never intended to loosen its grip on decision making, particularly where money was involved. While political leaders offered verbal support to the plan, their actions regularly undermined budget discipline. Poor discipline and weak comprehensiveness were consequences of political rather than objective considerations. A number of laws and procedures governing the conduct of public management in general had to undergo substantive changes to reorient the administrative system and to shift attention to the outcome of policies and to outputs of administrative units. The PM and the cabinet were not ready for such change of responsibility and accountability.

The experience of Jordan in searching for a more effective budgeting process illustrates how the political, economic, and managerial dimensions are intertwined. Focusing on results and providing reliable information on outputs was subordinated to the economic reality of controlling aggregate spending and reliance on foreign sources of funding. Thus, linking broad organizational goals, society's needs, and the overall strategies of the political leadership always seemed contingent on the availability of funds. Also, weak discipline and comprehensiveness of the budget process contributed to further centralization and less transparency as well as compounded the complexity of implementing an effective performance measurement system.

Evidently, the government of Jordan had limited choices in its search to correct a serious financial imbalance, either by controlling aggregate spending, by focusing on improving technical efficiency, or by introducing mechanisms to facilitate strategic prioritization and enhancing allocative efficiency. In either case, reliable information about results, defining goals, developing indicators, and collecting data were essential to achieve higher efficiencies and better spending disciplines. Moreover, performance budgeting had little chance of success without appropriate understanding and support of the political leadership that appeared to have rushed into reform without realizing that they would have to change their own behaviors and play by their new rules. In the end, they were trapped into a mechanistic view of the process, void of strategic input, realistic indicators, or any meaningful output measurement.

A contextual element that had a serious impact on budget reform is the inadequacy of the existing traditional audit system. With poor budget information, limited freedom of the press, and weak democratic institutions, appropriate and effective audits became particularly difficult. Actually, the main mechanism that helped maintain fiscal discipline in Jordan was prior agreements that bind spending and deficit reduction before the budget proposal was drafted. Even this was routinely modified by the PM in light of uncontrollable deficit spending.

Eventually, better governance is the only factor of reform for which the government is fully responsible, and, the only factor that is also fully under its control. In Jordan as elsewhere, fiscal institutions are important determinants of fiscal outcomes. Although the processes of interaction among the numerous participants of public budgeting vary with each phase of the budget cycle, links and interactions between fiscal rules and fiscal outcomes have been largely shaped by the growing budget deficit. The deficit problem affected not only the budget aggregate but also the effectiveness of fiscal institutions and their abilities to plan, coordinate, and monitor expenditures.

While the primary responsibility for implementation of performance budgeting is with agencies and departments, the Ministry of Finance and the Budget Department had to formulate appropriate guidelines and directions as well as provide training and development programs to facilitate the change. All this had to be within a system of accountability that makes institutions answerable for their performance of delegated duties and responsibilities. In Jordan, the recommended change was neither accompanied by change in the nature of public policy and management in government, nor included explicit political commitment for reform and for leadership capable of coordinating all the pieces of reform into a coherent plan of action.

Discussion Questions

1. What overt or covert factors motivate a developing country to transform its budget system to a performance budget format?
2. What contextual factors, besides issues of money, are important for the initial phase of implementing a performance budget?
3. Could there be a budget reform separate from a comprehensive administrative reform in a developing country, such as Jordan?
4. Is it necessary to enact a budget reform into law even when the executive leadership is entrusted with the task of public management? Under what conditions is legislative mandate essential?
5. Technical and behavioral qualifications of public employees are important factors for the success of budget change. What actions can be taken to ensure employees have the required qualifications?
6. What is performance audit and how it is different from financial audit?

References

Abbadi, H. (2008, July 14). Investigative study. *Alrai*.

Allied Business Advisors. (2002). *The budgeting process in Jordan* (An unpublished consultant report submitted to the Jordanian Budget Department).

Bouckaert, G., & Halligan, J. (2008). *Managing performance: International comparisons*. London, UK: Routledge.

Fanek, F. (2009a, February 9). On the margin of the public budget [Op ed]. *Alrai*.

Fanek, F. (2009b, February 25). Regarding the budget [Op ed]. *Alrai*.

Jreisat, J. E. (1997). *Public organization management*. Westport, CT: Greenwood.

Kelly, J. M., & Rivenbark, W. C. (2003). *Performance budgeting for state and local government*. New York: M. E. Sharpe.

Kettl, D. (1997). The global revolution in public management: Driving themes, missing links. *Journal of Policy Analysis and Management*, 16(3), 446–462.

Lee, R. D., Jr., Johnson, R. W., & Joyce, P. G. (2008). *Public budgeting systems* (8th ed.). Boston: Jones and Bartlett Publishers.

Meyers, R. T. (1996). *Strategic budgeting*. Ann Arbor: University of Michigan Press.

Ministry of Finance. (2009, February 21). Updates on the public debt. *Alrai*.

Poterba, J. M., & von Hagen, J. (1999). Introduction. In J. M. Poterba & J. von Hagen (Eds.), *Fiscal institutions and fiscal performance*. Chicago: University of Chicago Press.

Rubin, I. S. (2010). *The politics of public budgeting* (6th ed.). Washington DC: CQ Press.

United Nations Office for Project Service & the Swedish Fund for Consultancy Services. (1998, July 15). *Jordan: Program and performance budgeting*. Stockholm, Sweden: Alfred Bretschneider. Unpublished manuscript.

Wildavsky, A., & Caiden, N. (2001). *The new politics of the budgetary process*. New York: Longman.

ENDNOTES

1. The author served as chair of an international team of experts, with membership representing The World Bank, United Nations Development Program, the General Budgeting Department of Jordan, and individuals from France, Germany, and New Zealand. The author wrote the master plan for implementing performance budgeting in Jordan. Some elements of the plan are integrated in this chapter.

2. The Budget Department has more than 75 career employees of various grades. It is organized into four budget directorates, in addition to special Directorates of Evaluation and Development.

3. The Ministry of Finance encompasses the Income Tax Department, the Customs Department, the General Budget Department, and other entities. The ministry has more than 1000 employees, grouped into 15 administrative units.

Chapter 13

Budget Making and Intergovernmental Fiscal Relations in Pakistan

Roy Bahl, Musharraf R. Cyan, and Sally Wallace

Learning Objectives

- ▦ Understand the institutional makeup of budget making in Pakistan.
- ▦ Understand how institutions and policy often together define budget-making practices.
- ▦ Know and understand subnational governments and their roles in central government expenditure allocation and fulfilling national priorities.
- ▦ Know and understand provincial governments and capital budgeting.
- ▦ Know and understand transparency and intergovernmental transfers.

Introduction

Federal countries are characterized by multilevel budgeting and by the devolution of fiscal powers to lower level governments. The link between these two is the system of intergovernmental fiscal relations. An important and often missed point is that the success of this structure in achieving the objectives of fiscal decentralization depends on the incentives embodied in the intergovernmental fiscal system. This chapter is about the experience in Pakistan.[1] We begin with a description of the multilevel budgeting system, and then turn to an analysis of why provincial governments have mobilized so few fiscal resources, rendering their budgeting dependent on central decisions and revenue performance. We conclude with some discussion of reform options and their implications for budget making.

The analysis here is best understood in the context of the wide regional disparities in economic development and socioeconomic makeup. Pakistan is a multitiered federation with four provinces, three federally administered areas, and the autonomous region of Kashmir. It has a total estimated population of about 160 million. Most of the population lives in the four provinces but there are great disparities. According to the last census held in 1998,[2] Punjab has a population of 73 million and the highest per capita income in the nation, Sindh has a population of 30 million and includes Pakistan's largest city, Karachi. The largest concentration of poverty is in North-West Frontier Province (NWFP) where the total population is 18 million. Baluchistan Province has a population of 7 million but a very large land area. About 5 million people live in the federally administered territories in the north, Federally Administered Tribal Areas and Islamabad Capital Territory, while Pakistani-administered Kashmir contains another 3 million.

Pakistan has a federal structure of government. At the top two levels are the federal government and provinces. The federal government and provinces derive their functions and powers from a constitution. At the lower level, the three-tier local government is created by provincial laws and is treated as a provincial subject. For budgetary purposes, the main players are the Federal Ministry of Finance and the Planning Commission at the federal level. In the provinces, their counterparts are the finance department and planning department of the province. The National Finance Commission (NFC) is an intergovernmental body created by the president under a constitutional provision. It lays down the size of the intergovernmental transfer pool and the formula for deciding provincial shares. The budgets are prepared by the finance ministry or department and presented to the respective legislature for debate and approval. The accounts are maintained centrally. Disregarding the constitutional provisions in 2001, the federal government promulgated an ordinance to reorganize a hierarchic accounting bureaucracy with provincial accountants general directly responsible to the central controller general of accounts. The accountant general works through district level accounts offices where the control is shared between the provinces and the federal accounts bureaucracy. The accounts are audited by the auditor general of Pakistan for all levels of government except lower level local governments. The audited accounts are presented to the legislatures at each level of government.

The Structure of Budget Making

Budget making in Pakistan is a well-defined process organized through a hierarchy of laws and institutional processes and linkages. Fiscal decision-making powers are allocated to the federal government and the provincial governments, with the provinces in turn decentralizing some authority to local governments. The provinces have a recognized status in the constitution, but the local governments have a much weaker position. Their expenditure responsibility and revenue authority has changed over time. Incremental budgeting is the norm at all levels, with some recent experimentation with performance-based budgeting.

LEGAL FOUNDATIONS

The 1973 constitution was written in the aftermath of the separation of Bangladesh from the earlier Pakistani federation. This history continues to be relevant to inter-governmental relations and to the political economy of budget making in Pakistan. In 1955, the four western provinces of Punjab, Baluchistan, Sindh, and NWFP were amalgamated into "one unit." The separation of Bangladesh led to the recognition of provincial rights in the constitution (drafted in 1970) and to the creation of the four provinces. Important powers were decentralized to the provinces (Baxter, 1974). The provinces can make their own budgets without approval by the federal government, formulate financial management rules, and incur expenditures according to their own priorities. Provincial revenue-raising powers are assigned in the constitution.

To respond to the provincial demands for fiscal decentralization, two "legislative lists" were created in the constitution.[3] These legislative lists were devised as a mechanism for expenditure and revenue assignment, and were the result of negotiation between various political parties. The legislatures, national and provincial, derive law-making powers from the legislative or expenditure lists. When subjects were assigned to the provinces through the legislative lists, the provinces automatically gained the expenditure making responsibilities for those areas. A number of subjects appear in the "federal-only" list indicating a consensus (reached in 1973) on the responsibilities of the federal government. The other legislative list is the "concurrent list," which allows both federal and provincial governments to carry out those expenditures. Any residual functions stay with the provinces. The makers of the constitution saw the concurrent list as an interim arrangement to be abolished in due course of time, although there was no constitutional provision for this. As time has passed, the concurrent list has remained in place, and federal presence in provincial domain continues to be as strong as ever.

The clear expenditure assignments in the constitution reflected a compromise in favor of a strong role for the provinces, envisaging it as a safeguard against federal encroachment on provincial budgetary authorities. The provinces have continued to build up their role in expenditure making. They have developed elaborate manuals and processes for spending and service delivery. But similar capacity has not emerged on the revenue side (Bahl, Wallace, & Cyan, 2008). While provinces were given a less dominant role on the revenue side, they still were assigned some sources with significant revenue potential. This potential has not been realized. The lesson here is that legal clarity may be a necessary condition for optimal subnational government revenue effort, but it is not a sufficient condition.[4] The underlying problem, as we will argue, is a system of intergovernmental fiscal relations that carries perverse incentives for revenue mobilization.

MULTITIERED BUDGETS

The constitutional scheme in Pakistan makes provision for federal and provincial level budget making. This is an important requirement for successful fiscal decentralization. For each level, legal accounting entities are defined. The most important of these are the consolidated funds, created by Articles 78 and 118 of the constitution. These funds include all revenues that accrue to a government.

The consolidated funds provide for a clear mechanism to lay down the foundation of budgetary transparency. Parallel accounts are not allowed. Once the consolidated funds are recognized as accounting entities, the budget-making processes and authorities, powers and processes to keep accounts, powers to carry out audit, and mechanisms for legislative oversight are organized around them. The annual budget statement (ABS) is prepared for all the monies in the consolidated fund. Preparation of ABS as a report on the consolidated fund is a constitutional obligation of the relevant ministry or department of finance. The ABS also allows the executive branch to lay out its expenditure program for the fiscal year and seek approval from the legislature.

The ABS defines expenditures from the consolidated fund and lays down parameters for budget execution from this account. The financial rules are also formulated under the constitutional provisions. The accountants general, at different levels of government, federal and provincial, are mandated to prepare a statement of accounts for all budgetary transactions, leaving a clear trail of expenditures (Government of Pakistan, 2001b). The auditor general, as the supreme audit institution, lays down the principles, forms, and methods of accounting and also carries out audit at all levels of government (Government of Pakistan, 2001a). The only departure from this rule is at the two lower tiers of government where special arrangements have been made. Together, the constitutional provisions relating to finance and the subordinate legislation carried out under them, define a codified system of budget making, expenditure tracking, and preparation of accounts and audit.

At the federal level, all revenues collected by the federal agencies go into the Federal Consolidated Fund, with two important exceptions. The first exception is the public account where monies are held in trust. For example, court deposits are placed in the public account.

The second exception to the consolidated fund principle laid down in the constitution is given in Article 160, subarticle 4, which pertains to the NFC. The NFC sits after an interval of no more than 5 years. It makes recommendations on the vertical and horizontal sharing of tax revenue between the federal government and provinces and among the provinces. The decisions of the NFC are given effect by a statutory order promulgated by the president. The latter has no authority to amend the commission's recommendations. The effect of Article 160 is that it automatically removes the provincial shares of central taxes from the Federal Consolidated Fund and takes them directly to the Provincial Consolidated Funds. In this manner, Parliament does not have any authority over determination of the provincial shares. This has important implications for the Pakistani budget making. By definition, it means that the federal government and its Ministry of Finance get no powers to attach any conditions to the provincial revenue shares. No wonder that some provinces, in their budget documents, describe the share of revenues received under the NFC formula as their own source revenues.[5]

Another important feature of the NFC award is that the provinces take these revenues as an entitlement, and would not countenance any conditions attached to these grants. They would expect the transfers to flow to them without hindrance and without any conditions. The provincial shares have indeed been transferred to the provinces without fail, in time and with no conditions attached (Ahmad & Wasti, 2003).

Due to provincial dependence on the federal budgetary decisions, the budget calendars are organized so that the provincial budgets follow the federal budget in June, the last month of the fiscal year. Several important committees meet in the preceding months to indicate resources available to the provinces, allowing them a planning figure for their budgets. Three of these important committees are: (1) the Annual Plan Coordination Committee (APCC), which is chaired by the Planning Commission, has provincial membership, and recommends capital investments and decides on the capital grants to provinces; (2) the Appropriations Committee, chaired by the federal finance division finalizes the recommendations of the APCC and indicates the size of transfers during the following fiscal year to the provinces; and (3) National Economic Council (NEC), which is chaired by the prime minister (PM) and its members include the provincial chief ministers along with important federal ministers. It derives its mandate from the constitution. This body coordinates budget making at the highest level and meets at the beginning of June every year. The NEC forum also takes up any further intergovernmental coordination that may be required.

SUBNATIONAL GOVERNMENT BUDGET AUTONOMY

The constitution was written against the backdrop of dissolving the one unit government system. The dissolution of one unit and the recreation of four provinces was hailed as a fulfillment for the demand for decentralization. The makers of the constitution wanted to give clear revenue assignments to the provinces to make them less dependent on federal transfers. This resulted in the insertion of two types of provisions in the constitution. First, certain taxing powers were delegated to the provincial governments. For instance, the tax on professions was recorded as a provincial tax.[6] Second, the legislative lists mechanism and enumerates the tax bases that are either awarded to the federal governments or shared between the federal government and the provinces. The constitutional assignment of taxes is described in Table 13-1. The award to the federal government is exclusive and provinces do not have the right to tax those bases. Similarly, if a tax base is not mentioned in either of the lists, it falls to the provincial domain. The federal government in these cases has no right to tax the base.

The mismatch between the relatively heavy assignment of expenditures to provinces and their weaker revenue assignment is resolved by the NFC awards. In this case, federal taxes are shared, but defining the base and setting rates and administration of these taxes is exclusively a federal authority. These taxes include personal income tax (except agriculture income), corporate income tax, customs, sales tax on goods, excise duty (except on alcohol and narcotics), and capital value tax. Most of the national

Table 13-1	

Constitutional Assignment of Revenues

Revenue assignment/tax	Legal provision
Federal revenues	
1. Personal income tax (except agricultural income)	Federal List (subject 47)
2. Corporate income tax	Federal List (subject 48)
3. Customs	Federal List (subject 43)
4. Sales tax on goods	Federal List (subject 48)
5. Excise duty (except on alcohol, narcotics)	Federal List (subject 44)
6. Capital value tax	Federal List (subject 50)
7. Estate duty	Federal List (subjects 45, 46)
8. Mineral oil, minerals, natural gas	Federal List (subject 51)
9. Tax on production capacity	Federal List (subject 52)
10. Terminal taxes on goods and passenger transportation	Federal List (subject 53)
11. User charges on federal subjects	Federal List (subject 54)
Provincial revenues	
12. Excise duty on alcohol, liquor, narcotics	Assigned to province by bar on the federation in the Federal List (subject 44)
13. Sales tax on services	Residuary assignment
14. Tax on professions	Article 163 of the constitution
15. Motor vehicle tax	Residuary assignment
16. Property tax	Residuary, but there is bar in the Federal List (subject 51)
17. Capital gains	Assigned through bar on the federation in the Federal List (subject 50)
18. Agriculture income tax	Through bar on the federation in the Federal List (subject 47)
19. Stamp duty	Residuary assignment
20. Registration fee	Residuary assignment
21. Mutation fee	Residuary assignment
22. Natural gas excise duty	Article 161 of the constitution
23. Net hydro profits	Article 161 of the constitution
24. Electricity duty	Article 157(2)(b) of the constitution
25. User charges	Residuary assignment

Note: Taxes at number 1 to 6 in the table are shared revenues under the NFC clauses of the constitution. The base and rate are set by the federation.

revenue is collected from these taxes. Table 13-2 shows a detail of revenue structure. Provinces, even when claiming these as "shared taxes," abdicate all responsibility for taxation to the federal government. Due to the provincial claim on the revenue from these taxes, they do not have further right to impose another tax on the same base. Provincial governments simply budget their entitlements from federal taxes.

Table 13-2

Revenue Structure of Federal Government, Fiscal Year 2008/2009

Revenue items	Amount	Percent of total
Total tax	**1,180,462**	**66.2**
Direct taxes	**461,000**	**25.8**
Income tax	443,341	24.9
Worker participation tax	11,618	0.7
Capital value tax	6,041	0.3
Indirect taxes	**719,462**	**40.3**
Customs	145,000	8.1
Sales tax	457,000	25.6
Federal excise	116,000	6.5
Other taxes	1,402	0.1
Airport tax	60	0.0
Nontax revenue	**603,140**	**33.8**
Income from property and enterprises	107,807	6.0
Receipts from civil administration	236,915	13.3
Miscellaneous receipts	258,418	14.5
Total revenue	**1,783,602**	**100.0**

Source: Budget in Brief, 2009–2010, Tables 9 and 10, Ministry of Finance, Government of Pakistan.

Note: Amounts given in millions of rupees (Rs) and based on revised estimates of collection for fiscal year ending June 30, 2009.

From one perspective, it can be argued that separation of bases, as in Pakistan, allows for clear revenue assignment and prevents any tax competition. This system would appear to give subnational governments considerable autonomy in determining the size of the budget envelope. In practice, however, it has resulted in unintended consequences. Most of the revenue productive bases are assigned to the federal level, and NFC awards to the provinces have been generous. As a result, there has been very little tax effort at the subnational government level. As the NFC awards have grown and grants have flowed in, there has been further dampening of provincial revenue efforts.

INTERGOVERNMENTAL INFLUENCES

In the hierarchic system, grants link budget making at all levels. Grants are an expenditure in the federal budget and a revenue in the provincial budget, and define the amount of direct expenditures that can be budgeted at either level. There are five types of federal grants offered to the provinces in Pakistan. The federal government cannot make a direct grant to a three-tier local government unless it is for a specific purpose.[7]

The five types of federal transfers are: (1) shared tax revenues; (2) mandated pass-through grants for local government; (3) subventions; (4) natural resource royalties; and (5) discretionary federal grants. The first three grants are created by the NFC, which lays down their size and distribution formulas. The third is also decided by the NFC and lump sum amounts are announced each year. The system of transfers to provinces in Pakistan is quite transparent by comparison with many developing countries. The structure of this system raises no problems with respect to certainly in budgeting.

The NFC award, comprising the first three transfers, is by far the largest of the grants in the system. The NFC is charged with making a decision every 5th year on the size of the sharing pool and on the distribution of this amount among the four provinces.[8] It has a major influence on budget making at all levels. The NFC itself is composed of two representatives each from the federal and from the four provincial governments. The finance minister and one other technical representative from each of the five governments meet for several months or longer to reach a consensus on the sharing formula. The recommendations of the NFC are governed by a powerful constitutional provision: The president is obliged to promulgate the recommendations as a statutory order without making any changes to them. Once promulgated, the NFC formula regulates the vertical and horizontal sharing of important taxes between the federal government and the provinces (the vertical share) and among the provinces (the horizontal share) until the next NFC makes its recommendations.

The provincial share of the NFC award was set as 41.5% of the shared federal taxes in 2006 and is scheduled to increase by 1% per year, up to 46.5% by 2011 (Government of Pakistan, 2006). According to the structure of the NFC grant program, the only revenue growth for a province during an award period comes from increases in federal government tax revenues. So, there is stability in the distribution system that helps long-term fiscal planning at both levels of government.

Federal grants are the main sources of revenue in the provincial budgets, accounting for more than 80% of provincial revenue. The local governments, in turn, depend on the provinces for their revenue. On average, district and lower level governments derive between 70 and 97% of their revenue from the provinces (Asian Development Bank, Department for International Development, & The World Bank, 2004). An important federal grant was created in 2002 as a compensation for an abolished local government sales tax.[9] This pass-through grant transfers one sixth of the value-added tax revenue collected by the federal government to the provinces for further allotment to local governments. Some local governments are heavily dependent on this grant to a major extent.

CAPITAL FACILITY BUDGETS

Pakistan appears to be transitioning away from central planning. The Ninth Plan, 1998–2003 initiated a switch toward "indicative planning" (Pasha et. al., 1996). The Planning Commission prepares planning documents with the participation of different government and nongovernmental entities. For the period between 1996 and 2001, the provincial governments were dependent on federal funds for capital investments. Most of the dependence arose out of the unrealistic revenue projections, which formed the basis of the 1996 NFC. The provinces did not have the revenue to carry out planned capital investment after meeting their recurrent expenditures. The federal government gave them loans for capital investment purposes, albeit at very high interest rates (17 to 18%). After 2002, the fiscal situation improved and the provinces did not need further loans. The result was that provinces began deciding investment priorities on their own.

The Planning Commission tracks provincial capital investments. Project appraisal and approval powers were given to various authorities by the federal government on the advice of the Planning Commission. When some federal funding is involved, all projects with a total cost above a specified threshold level must be approved by the Planning Commission. The project approval requires that provincial projects be prepared in a format provided by the federal government, and that they meet the appraisal criteria set by the commission.

The provinces are allowed to borrow for capital investment and commodity operations. For the former, borrowing is only allowed from the federal government, an overdraft facility with the State Bank, or from multilateral agencies. In the last case, the operations are supervised by the federal government. Foreign loans to the provinces are processed by the federal government. The Federal Ministry of Finance oversees such loans and their project implementation by the provinces.

MULTILEVEL BUDGETS AND DECENTRALIZATION

In principle, there is no inconsistency between multilevel budgets and fiscal decentralization. Each level of government has revenue and expenditure assignments, their expenditure level is set by a combination of own source revenue mobilization and intergovernmental transfers, and each has substantial budget autonomy. So long as there is a hard budget constraint for the subnational governments, there is no compelling reason to have a consolidated budget for all levels of government. This is true for both industrialized and developing countries.

A problem arises in coupling multilevel budgets with fiscal decentralization. The goal of decentralization is to provide some degree of fiscal autonomy at the subnational government level, so that voter preferences can be matched by expenditure and revenue outcomes. On the revenue side, voters need to be able to have a say not only about the amount of revenues that will be raised locally, but about how this revenue will be raised. Revenue mobilization at the provincial level is a key to making provincial officials accountable for the quality of services delivered. In Pakistan, as in many developing countries, the incentives embodied in the intergovernmental fiscal system are perverse with respect to stimulating tax reform that will match fiscal decentralization goals. Multilevel budgeting works in that a hard budget constraint is imposed at the subnational government level, and there is provincial discretion about how to obey this constraint, but the revenue mobilization dimension of fiscal decentralization has failed.

BUDGET MAKING IN RECENT YEARS

Budget preparation follows incremental approach. Each year, finance departments issue a budget call letter at the end of September, which coincides with the end of the first quarter of the fiscal year. The call letter lays out various stages of submission of expenditure estimates. Generally, it allows an incremental increase in the sector's share based on the revenue projections and policy targets of the government. Pay raises and other recurrent expenditures are deemed to be protected unless specifically indicated. Departments are allowed to carry out intrasector changes. Designated budget execution authorities are well specified within each department with clear powers under the rules. They are called the drawing and disbursing officers (DDOs). Each DDO prepares a budget on the given format following the general instructions and protecting the previous expenditures and adding incremental changes, like salary raises. For the latter, the DDOs follow the centrally laid down schedule of salary raises. Any new positions or expenditures for replacement of equipment are submitted separately using the forms for the Schedule of New Expenditures (SNEs). Both the recurrent expenditure estimates and SNEs are processed in the department and then submitted to the finance department by the end of the third quarter of the fiscal year. At that stage, the finance department holds a series of meetings with line departments to go over the submitted proposals for expenditures. Once agreed, the proposals are included in the budget estimates and presented to the assembly as the ABS.

In recent years, despite the overall integration of planning and budgeting or the capital and recurrent budgets, the process of budget making both at the federal and provincial levels takes place as two separate streams (Gable & LaPorte, 1983). Planning or capital budgeting begins with the Planning Commission–led periodic development plans setting priorities for sectors and projects. At the provincial level, the same mandate is exercised by the planning departments. Ministries and departments initiate projects rather than sectoral capital investment plans. The latter, if they are developed for a sector, have remained as guiding principles rather than operational plans. For example, the multiyear expenditure frameworks developed by the federal government and Punjab do not specify strict sectoral planning figures but only indicative figures. The budget-making cycle culminates each year with approval of a number of new and ongoing projects. Mostly new projects, unless already appraised and given technical approval by planning agencies, receive indicative financing only. Ongoing projects are allocated funds according to their stage of completion to be achieved in the following fiscal year. Ordinarily, ongoing projects are not dropped from the projects. Over the past two decades, change of government has been followed by review of ongoing projects, sometimes resulting in closure of ongoing projects that did not find favor with the incoming political government.

The projects are the main agency for accessing capital investment in a sector. Individual projects are reviewed by planning departments and approved by committees chaired by them. Only in case of small projects, the line departments are allowed to approve projects on their own. For the federal agencies, the upper limit has been specified at Rs 40 million (US$0.5 million). Projects costing more than this are submitted for appraisal and approval to the planning commission (Government of Pakistan, 2008). The provincial planning departments can approve projects costing Rs 5 billion (US$62.5 million) or less. Projects with a higher cost are submitted for appraisal and approval to the planning commission at the federal level.

Appraised and approved projects are combined to formulate each sector's capital budget. This methodology has certain strengths and weaknesses. On the positive side, it has allowed the line departments to carry out project identification and selection at their level, using their better information bases and understanding of the sector. It has, in practice, become a fairly decentralized system catering to departmental initiatives even in the presence of central planning agencies at the two levels of government. Within a loose sectoral planning figure, departments are able to generate capital investment proposals and implement them after approval. On the other side, the system suffers from important weaknesses. Responding to demands for development, departments keep on adding projects to the portfolio within the existing sector share of the capital budget. Each year, new projects are added at the time of budget preparation. The inclusions carry token allocations to keep the overall sector share within the allocation made by the planning agency. As a result of this mechanism of budgeting, the portfolio of projects has often swelled to several times the capital budget of the government, requiring periodic pruning, which sunk costs of ongoing projects. The individual projects and sector objectives are often not reconciled correctly. Project appraisal looks at matches between project objectives and sector objectives. But where sector objectives are not clearly defined, most projects pass the muster if they are aiming to contribute in any way to development goals of the sector. This mechanism does not cater to selection of the highest value projects.

Despite the centralized project appraisal and approval, projection identification, preparation, and implementation is with the concerned line ministries. There is one exception to this rule. The capital funds are controlled by the planning departments. For most of the projects, planning departments authorize funds on a quarterly basis often after ascertaining amounts that had been authorized earlier. This mechanism allows a central capital budget programming. This is important at the provincial level because provinces depend on federal transfers and can only operate within overdraft limits specified by the State Bank of Pakistan. Planning departments at the provincial level authorize funds to individual projects of the line departments, keeping in view the financial situation intimated by the finance department.

Subnational Government Revenue Mobilization

Provincial governments do have access to some revenue sources that are potentially revenue productive (see Table 13-1). To demonstrate the success with revenue raising in Pakistan, we use data from two of the four provinces: Punjab (the largest) and the NWFP (the poorest).[10] Together, these provinces account for about 60% of the national population.

Table 13-3

Revenue Mobilization in Punjab and NWFP, Fiscal Years 2002–2006				
	Punjab		**NWFP**	
Revenue source	**2001–2002**	**2005–2006**	**2001–2002**	**2005–2006**
Urban property tax	0.001	0.026	0.039	0.041
Excise duty	0.021	0.019	0.005	0.004
Land taxes	0.086	0.077	0.049	0.045
Motor vehicle taxes	0.064	0.094	0.110	0.093
Professions tax	0.007	0.005	0.010	0.010
Other taxes	0.000	0.001	0.014	0.005
Fees and charges	0.196	0.135	0.255	0.209
Total	0.375	0.358	0.482	0.424

Source: Provincial Revenue Time Series Data, 2001–2006, The World Bank, Islamabad.

Note: The revenues are listed as a percentage of gross domestic product (GDP).

The time frame of revenue mobilization for the two provinces, by major revenue source, is described in Table 13-3. The results for both provinces show little change in the rate of revenue mobilization (relative to gross domestic product [GDP]). over the 2002–2006 period. In fact, the overall level has declined between 2002 and 2006 in both provinces (bottom row of Table 13-3). Various analysts have offered several reasons to explain this weak revenue—GDP elasticity (buoyancy).[11]

First, provincial taxable capacity is low and the tax base is hard to reach. NWFP is the poorest province in Pakistan and has a high concentration of poverty, leading provincial officials to argue that it is tough to expect to get much more out of the system. A similar argument is made in Punjab. Per capita GDP is higher, but there also is a high concentration of poverty and large informal sector. Even so, many would argue that the economic base is strong enough to give up more in provincial government tax revenues than the 0.36% and 0.42% of GDP that were collected in Punjab and NWFP, respectively, in fiscal year 2005/2006. Moreover, both provinces have shown significant growth in GDP in recent years. The "low taxable capacity" argument for low revenue buoyancy is not persuasive.

Second, the tax administration machinery has not been effective in either province.[12] Both provinces are plagued by incomplete and out of date records, suggesting that there is not a good sense of the true tax base. Moreover, most tax subjects (e.g., professions tax, land taxes) have not been recently surveyed, hence tax bases are understated. Most of the recordkeeping in both provinces is manual.

Particularly in NWFP, there are serious constraints on assessment and collection. Revenue collections, except for some excises, take place only in urban areas. For example, there are 24 districts in NWFP but 70% of all property tax collections are from Peshawar (the capital city). More than 50% of excises come from seven districts.

In fact, some districts in NWFP are all but excluded from the tax system. About one third of the NWFP is made up of Provincially Administered Tribal Areas (PATA). Only a few taxes are collected in these districts (e.g., tax on the transfer of property, stamp duty, and the local rate). Urban immovable property tax (UIPT) is collected in only 16 of 24 districts. While there is no question about NWFP facing a challenging environment for tax collection, the situation is by no means hopeless. A thorough review and analysis of the tax administration system in NWFP points out numerous approaches to overcoming some of these obstacles (Khan, 2004).

In Punjab, the tax administration does not appear to be effectively mining the significant taxable capacity in urban areas. Property values have grown but property tax collections have not, the number of motor vehicles has grown but motor vehicle tax (MVT) revenues have not kept pace, and so on. Part of the problem is that the province has given away much of its tax base in the form of preferential treatment, but another part of the problem is that underassessment is considerable and collection rates are low. With respect to rural areas in Punjab, the story of underassessment and low collection rates is much the same.

The two provinces have a common administrative problem of not being able to effectively reach the agricultural sector. Neither of the provinces do a particularly good job with collection of agricultural income tax or with property transfer taxes. Certainly part of the problem is with the structure of these taxes, but there are also major administrative failings. These include poor recordkeeping and surveillance, exclusion of part of the tax base, and a failure to update valuation information.

Third, the structure of taxes is such that significant increases in revenue relative to GDP should not be expected. One reason for this is that the tax structure is partly based on specific rates. Another is that land is being acquired by government and nonprofits, thereby taking it off the tax rolls. It is also the case that provincial governments are not taking discretionary action to increase the effective rate of tax collection, such as revaluation of property or increases in nominal rates. Finally, the growth in tax revenues might have been slowed because some faster growing components of the tax base are not taxed, are given exemption, or preferential treatment (e.g., owner-occupied property, industrial property and vacant land, and the consumption of services).

All of these factors no doubt contribute to the weak revenue mobilization by provincial governments. But perhaps the dominant explanation is the perverse incentives that are embedded in the system of intergovernmental fiscal relations. Increases in intergovernmental transfers from the center have been large enough to allow a slowing of the effort exerted to collect provincial taxes. The increase in central government assistance has been significant in both provinces while the growth in own source revenues has been nearly flat. This pattern should come as no surprise. There is no incentive built into the transfer formula that would reward provinces for increasing their tax effort, or penalize them for not doing so.

It is also the case that the central government has encroached enough on provincial tax bases that potential revenue growth has been dampened. The provincial government has been limited by the federal government in terms of the fiscal space it has been given. Some of these limits stem from the constitution, but there also are limits imposed by federal government policy. Four examples, regularly mentioned by provincial officials, include the following:

- The only tax, which provinces alone are specifically empowered to levy, is the tax on professions, trades, and callings. The fact that more revenue-productive taxes are not assigned exclusively to the subnational governments is a limiting factor on revenue growth.
- The UIPT is a provincial government tax, but most of the revenue collected is assigned to local governments.[13]
- Motor vehicle registration and licensing taxes (MVT) belong to the provincial governments. The collection rate is only about 70%. Some argue that the collection rate is this low because there is mandatory collection of the (federal) presumptive income tax at the time of vehicle registration. This additional tax payment stiffens resistance to payment of MVTs and reinforces opposition to any proposed increase in the provincial levy on MVTs. It is in this sense that the federal government is seen as encroaching on the provincial tax base.
- The federal government imposes a 2% capital value tax on property transfers, raising the total rate on each transfer and arguably reducing the rate of compliance with provincial stamp duty and registration taxes.

The result plays to the motives of elected local officials who are hesitant to increase tax effort for fear of losing political support. There have been no increases in tax rates or expansions in tax bases for 8 years in NWFP and 5 years in Punjab. The provincial government in Punjab postponed the introduction of the new property tax valuation roll, due in 2007, in part because of upcoming elections. Enforcement is lax in both provinces. Politics has been perhaps the major reason why provincial tax structures have not developed. Clearly, politicians have felt pressure from strong interest groups (agriculture, property owners) to hold off on increasing taxes, and in a sense they have been "protected" by increased intergovernmental transfers under the NFC. In NWFP, political leadership has not insisted on an aggressive administration in regions of civil unrest.

Intergovernmental Transfers

The system of (three) NFC transfers to provinces in Pakistan is quite transparent. In practice, the NFC awards have not been so simple to execute. In the last iteration, the NFC was not able to reach agreement on the sharing formula. The NFC distribution formula decided in 1996, initially valid for 5 years, was continued through 2005. The 7th NFC Award was finalized only in January 2006 after the NFC could not reach a consensus on the sharing arrangement despite 11 meetings after July 2000.[14]

The fundamental issue with the NFC award is that the constitution mandates that the four provinces must agree on the proposed formula. Given the great differences in wealth, needs, and demographic conditions in the four provinces, agreement is quite unlikely. This consensus requirement has held up the final decision of the NFC. In January 2006, the president announced a formula for sharing of resources, which is technically not an NFC award.[15]

At present, the provincial pool for the NFC award is 41.5% of the federal divisible pool and is scheduled to increase by 1% per year up to 46.25% by 2011. The distribution of this pool among provinces is by population shares: NWFP receives 13.82% and Punjab receives 52%. The pattern of distribution of intergovernmental transfers to the two provinces is described in Table 13-4. From the data presented here, we can see that the shares of Punjab and NWFP have remained approximately constant since 1999. According to the structure of the NFC grant program, the only revenue growth for a province during an award period comes from increases in the rupee amount of the vertical share. This in turn depends on the growth in federal government tax revenues. So, there is stability in the distribution system that helps long-term fiscal planning.

The largest increases in the real per capita amounts received came at the time of the formation of the new award, in fiscal year 2004/2005, because of the increased vertical share for provincial governments. We might look back at the 2000–2006 period

Table 13-4

The Growth in Federal Transfers

Fiscal year	Transfers received as percent of provincial GDP		Transfers received as percent of total expenditure		Transfers received as percent of total federal transfers	
	Punjab	NWFP	Punjab	NWFP	Punjab	NWFP
2000–2001	3	5	–	–	52	12
2001–2002	3	5	–	–	51	12
2002–2003	3	5	68	–	52	12
2003–2004	3	5	58	–	51	13
2004–2005	3	5	50	58	53	13
2005–2006	3	5	46	40	52	13

Fiscal year	Total federal transfers as percent of GDP	Total federal expenditures as percent of GDP	Federal transfers as percent of federal expenditures
2000–2001	3.64	–	–
2001–2002	3.60	–	–
2002–2003	3.74	–	–
2003–2004	3.28	10.33	31.77
2004–2005	3.62	10.46	34.63
2005–2006	3.53	10.26	34.38

Sources: For federal expenditures, we used Table 5.10 in *Economic Survey: 2006–2007* (Government of Pakistan, 2007); for transfers we have relied on the provincial time series data provided by The World Bank, Islamabad, 2001—2006.

Notes: Transfers include only shared taxes.

and ask whether the growth in revenues from the NFC awards has been buoyant. The answer we get is that for every 1% increase in provincial GDP over this period, NFC revenues increased by 1.01% in Punjab and 1.18% in NWFP. Certainly for NWFP, the balance between transfers received and own source revenues has changed in favor of transfers during the past 7 years. This pattern holds for all provinces taken together.

We examine the stability in the composition of the flow of NFC transfers to Punjab and NWFP and report this in Table 13-4. The considerable stability that we find suggests that provinces can rightly view this flow as an annual entitlement.

In the top panel of Table 13-4, we can see the following:

- Transfers received as a percentage of provincial GDP have remained constant for both provinces. Note that the transfer share of provincial GDP in NWFP remains higher than that in Punjab. The equal per capita distribution of the NFC awards makes the system implicitly equalizing because per capita GDP is lower in NWFP and Balochistan.
- The dependence on the NFC award as a source of financing total expenditures has fallen in both Punjab and NWFP because of the significant increase in loan-financed projects, debt retirement, and structural adjustment credits. Since loans to provinces are allocations that are either made or approved by the central government, they also might be viewed as transfers. If we had used this metric, the importance of transfers in financing provincial expenditures would have shown an increase over this period.

We might ask whether the federal government's emphasis on intergovernmental transfers has changed in the past few years. We can study the determinants of changes in the federal government's emphasis on transfers to provincial governments with the data presented in the bottom panel of Table 13-4. The determinants of federal transfers to provinces (FT) as a percentage of GDP (FT/GDP) are the product of: (1) the federal expenditure share of GDP (FE/GDP) and (2) the federal transfer share of federal expenditures, (FT/FE), or:

$$FT/GDP = (FE/GDP) (FT/FE)$$

As may be seen in Table 13-4, the federal government has held the level of transfers to provinces between 3.3 and 3.7% of GDP (i.e., the GDP elasticity of transfers is about 1.0). Neither have the components of this growth changed very much. NFC awards have remained within a narrow band between 32 and 35% of federal expenditures, and federal expenditures have remained at a level equivalent to about 10% of GDP.

Conclusions

There are good opportunities for reforming the system of provincial level taxation and fiscal decentralization in Pakistan. There are certainly available opportunities for both structural reforms and administrative improvements to increase own source revenues.

A properly designed reform must at once allow the federal government to satisfy its objective of increasing provincial level taxes in a framework of good tax policy, while the provincial government is able to satisfy its objective of enhancing both public service levels and fiscal autonomy. The design of the reform will center on determining appropriate targets for provincial tax revenues and on putting appropriate incentives in place to encourage provinces to implement tax reforms that will generate increased revenues. The budget authority at the provincial level will face new challenges as increased reliance on own source revenues will require more effort in the areas of revenue forecasting.

How much tax revenue should be raised by provincial governments? The most conservative of politicians will favor low-risk options, usually only tinkering with the present system. But tinkering will not raise much money. Revenue enhancement calls for a more far-reaching set of reforms, and much higher revenue targets. This is perhaps the key matter for policy makers to sort out. How much would the federal government like to see raised and how much would local government officials be willing to raise?

Estimating a tax revenue target for Pakistan's provinces is at best a subjective exercise. For example, the federal government has called for an increase in provincial taxes to reach a level equivalent to 1% of GDP.[16] Achieving this target would require a doubling of the present level of revenues in both provinces.

There are systematic approaches to fixing on provincial revenue targets. Probably the best approach is to start with expenditure targets that reflect minimum acceptable service levels (ME). From the equation:

$$ME - Tr = OSR$$

where
$$Tr = \textbf{transfers}$$
$$OSR = \textbf{own source revenues,}$$
$$= \textbf{an affordability parameter}$$

one can develop a revenue target for provincial governments. After accounting for financing from intergovernmental transfers, the remainder of the cost of providing minimum service levels would be covered by own source revenues. This normative service level approach to determining the minimum needed level of tax effort is what each provincial government would be required to do (i.e., revenue needs would be based on an expenditure plan).[17] Setting target expenditure levels would be good budget practice for provincial governments, but by itself would not lead to increased revenue mobilization. Incentives to stimulate increased revenue mobilization are needed.

The problem that is more central to this analysis is that provincial government revenue mobilization is not increasing, arguably because the NFC award is carrying so much of the revenue load. In theory, the federal government could address this issue by building a greater equalization component into the formula, thereby reducing the assignment of NFC awards to the provinces where revenue mobilization potential is greatest. This would force the higher income provincial governments (Punjab and Sindh) to either increase taxes or cut services. A second alternative is to build an incentive for increased tax effort directly into the allocation formula.

Discussion Questions

1. What are the advantages of a hierarchic budget-making system in a federation?
2. How has centralized planning for the capital budget given way to decentralized initiatives in Pakistan? Explain strengths and weaknesses of the approach.
3. How has weak revenue mobilization at the provincial level impacted the growth of subnational expenditures in Pakistan? Is the outcome intuitively the same as would be expected with weak subnational revenue mobilization?
4. What is the importance of the NFC to budget making in Pakistan?
5. Identify three important reforms that would suit the budget-making processes in Pakistan.

References

Asian Development Bank, Department for International Development, & The World Bank. (2004). *Devolution in Pakistan.* Islamabad: Authors.

Ahmad, I., Mustafa, U., & Khalid, M. (2007). *National Finance Commission awards in Pakistan: A historical perspective* (PIDE Working Papers). Pakistan: Institute of Development Economics.

Ahmad, N., & Wasti, S. A. (2003). Pakistan. In Y. H. Kim & P. Smoke (Eds.), *Intergovernmental fiscal transfers in Asia: Current practice and challenges for the future.* Manila: Asian Development Bank.

Bahl, R., Wallace, S., & Cyan, M. (2008). *Pakistan provincial government taxation* (ISP Working Paper 08-07). Atlanta: Andrew Young School of Policy Studies, Georgia State University.

Baxter, C. (1974). Constitution making: The development of federalism in Pakistan. *Asian Survey, 14*(12), 1074–1085.

Gable, R. W., & LaPorte, R., Jr. (1983). Planning and budgeting in Pakistan. *Public Administration and Development, 3*, 135–149.

Government of Pakistan. (1973). *The Constitution of the Islamic Republic of Pakistan.* Cabinet Division, Government of Pakistan.

Government of Pakistan. (2001a). *The auditor general of Pakistan ordinance 2001.* Finance Division, Ministry of Finance, Government of Pakistan.

Government of Pakistan. (2001b). *The controller general of Pakistan ordinance 2001.* Finance Division, Ministry of Finance, Government of Pakistan.

Government of Pakistan. (2006). *NFC award, January 2006.* Finance Division, Government of Pakistan.

Government of Pakistan. (2007). *Economic survey: 2006–2007.* Ministry of Finance, Government of Pakistan.

Government of Pakistan. (2008). *Guidelines for project management.* Planning Commission, Government of Pakistan.

Government of Punjab. (2001). *Punjab local government of ordinance 2001.* Lahore: Local Government and Rural Development Department, Government of Punjab.

Government of Sindh. (2008). *The annual budget statement 2008–2009.* Karachi: Department of Finance, Government of Sindh.

Khan, A. (2004). *Reform of tax administration in NWFP* (Report of the Study Sponsored by DFID, Mimeograph).

Pasha, H. A., Ghaus-Pasha, A., Ismail, Z. H., Husaini Jagirdar, S. A., Bengali, K., Zaidi, S. A., . . . Rasheed, A. (1996). *The ninth five year plan: Issues paper.* Karachi: Social Policy and Development Center.

ENDNOTES

1. We draw heavily on Bahl, Wallace, and Cyan (2008).
2. The total population at the time of the census was 132 million.
3. The lists are given in the Fourth Schedule, Government of Pakistan (1973).
4. Revenue assignment to provinces is through the provincial lists or through articles of the constitution. Despite this clear assignment, as for example in the cases of the tax on professions and natural resource royalties, implementation of the legal provisions has not been free of problems.
5. For instance, see Government of Sindh (2008).
6. See Article 163, Government of Pakistan (1973).
7. See Chapter XII in Government of Punjab (2001). It provides for grants to flow through the provincial government only. Local government laws in the other three provinces have similar provisions.
8. This is under the constitutional provision, Article 160, Government of Pakistan (1973).
9. These taxes were levied at the local jurisdictional boundaries and were abolished in 1998 by the federal government.
10. Most of the information reported here was gathered in interviews with provincial and federal officials and from a variety of budgets and financial reports (Bahl et al., 2008).
11. Technically, the revenue GDP elasticity is the percentage change in revenue divided by the percentage change in GDP, assuming that all revenue increases due to discretionary changes have been removed from the numerator. If the revenue impacts of discretionary changes have not been removed, the term "revenue buoyancy" is used. In Punjab and NWFP, discretionary changes have been so infrequent that the buoyancy and elasticity coefficients are about the same.
12. The collection *cost* for all taxes in Punjab is reported (by provincial officials) to be equivalent to 4% of collections. The collection *rate*, which would take into account the difference between the base assessed and the true tax base, is much smaller.
13. This assignment was made under the Local Government Ordinances 2001, which some of the provinces perceive to be a result of a federally driven reform.
14. The finalization came as a presidential decision (Ahmad, Mustafa, & Khalid, 2007).
15. In the 1990s, NFCs always finalized the awards during "caretaker" setups when provinces were not represented by elected governments. Therefore, arriving at a consensus was easier. Since 2002, elected governments have been in place in the provinces. The 2001 award was held up largely because the provinces did not agree on a distribution formula. The current formula was promulgated in January 2006 by the president (and per se is not an NFC award). Technically, an NFC award is an outcome of the NFC deliberations.
16. This target was presented in the *Economic Survey* (Government of Pakistan, 2007, p. 65).
17. The revenue target for MVTs, for example, was set in reference to roadway expenditures. This is an example of expenditure needs driving a revenue target.

Chapter 14

Budgetary Systems in Saudi Arabia: Reform Needed

Bassam ALBassam

Learning Objectives

- Understand the political and economic foundations in Saudi Arabia.
- Understand the public budget cycle in Saudi Arabia.
- Analyze political and administrative reforms taking place in Saudi Arabia.
- Analyze the relationship between the political system, administrative system, and budgetary system in Saudi Arabia.

Introduction

Similar to other countries around the globe, Saudi Arabia has not been immune to changes in its budgeting and financial management systems. In this chapter, I will focus on exploring and discussing Saudi Arabia's budget system, as well as its structure and procedures. In addition, I will also discuss the budget cycle and its different phases. Last, the chapter introduces the main players in Saudi Arabia's financial system and concludes by exploring studies that have analyzed the country's financial system.

Background Information

Saudi Arabia has an oil-based economy, with strong government controls over major economic activities. It owns more than 20% of the world's proven petroleum reserves, ranks as the largest exporter of petroleum, and plays a leading role in the Organization of the Petroleum Exporting Countries (OPEC, 2007; see Table 14-1). The petroleum sector accounted for roughly 75% of budget revenues in 2008, 45% of GDP, and 90% of export earnings. About 40% of the GDP comes from the private sector. Roughly, 5.5 million foreign workers play an important role in the Saudi economy, particularly in the oil and service sectors (Central Intelligence Agency, 2007; Ministry of Finance [MOF], 2008).

High oil prices have boosted growth, government revenues, and Saudi ownership of foreign assets, while enabling the Saudi government to pay down domestic debt. At the end of fiscal year 2008, estimates suggested that public debt had dropped to around US$63.2 billion, which represented 13% of gross domestic product (GDP) for 2008 compared to 18.7% in 2007. The stock of debt is totally domestic (MOF, 2008). In general, all of the government's plans have centered on revenues from the oil industry despite the tenuous nature of oil prices. Hence, the creation of a long-term plan is difficult or nearly impossible.

Despite the focus on oil, the government is encouraging private sector growth—especially in power generation, telecommunications, natural gas exploration, and petrochemicals—to reduce the kingdom's dependence on oil exports and to increase employment opportunities for the rapidly increasing Saudi population, of which nearly 40% are youths younger than 15 years of age (Ministry of Economy and Planning, 2008). Unemployment is high, at nearly 9.8%, and the large youth population generally lacks the education and technical skills the private sector requires (Ministry of Labour, 2009). Therefore, the Saudi Arabian government has substantially boosted spending on job training and education, infrastructure development, and government salaries.

Table 14-1					
		Actual Oil and Non-Oil Revenues			
	Oil Revenues		Non-Oil Revenues		
Year	Amount	% Share	Amount	% Share	Total Revenues
2003	61,600	78.84	16,533	21.16	78,133
2004	88,000	84.12	16,611	15.88	104,611
2005	134,544	89.40	15,945	10.60	150,489
2006	161,192	89.73	18,457	10.27	179,649
2007	159,916	88.15	21,497	11.85	181,413
2008	98,666	82.22	21,333	17.78	119,999

Source: Ministry of Finance, 2009b. *Statistical Tables.*

Notes: Amounts given in millions of US$.

As a part of the government's efforts to attract foreign investment and diversify the economy, Saudi Arabia acceded to the World Trade Organization (WTO) in December 2005 after many years of negotiations. After that, the government announced plans to establish six "economic cities" in different regions of the country to promote development and diversification.

According to the Saudi Arabian General Investment Authority (SAGIA), the six economic cities will cost more than US$60 billion to establish. The kingdom has planned and begun construction of four metropolitan marvels; a project that promises to significantly alter the economic landscape of Saudi Arabia, while providing a wealth of green field opportunities to investors. The new economic cities will contribute US$150 billion to the country's GDP by the year 2020. Ideally, these efforts will generate job opportunities for 1.3 million people (Saudi Arabian General Investment Authority, 2008).

Although the private sector contributes 28.4% to GDP, the government fully owns or has shares in more than 70% of the corporations and financial institutions listed on the Saudi Stock Exchange (Tadawul, 2007). Government ownership comes through two kinds of institutions and government agencies: direct ownership from the government through agencies such as the Public Investment Fund, and indirect ownership with complete authority and supervision from the government over the agency, such as the General Organization for Social Insurance and the Public Pension Agency. Like any other government agency, these agencies have their own budgets (revenues and expenditures), with all expenditures coming from and all revenues going into the government budget.

It is clear that the government budget concentrates on expenditures (control and spending) rather than revenues, since the majority of these revenues come from one resource, oil. This explains why the Saudi government has utilized the traditional line-item budget since 1954, because it perceives this system provides more control over expenditures.

Government Structure

The government structure in Saudi Arabia is based on a monarch, where the king has absolute power, and is not constrained by a written constitution, a legislative assembly, or elections. The king appoints the Council of Ministers, led by the king or his deputy, which acts as the legislative and executive branch.

The Council of Ministers has the power to issue regulations, control the government and government agencies, and authorize and control the government's budget. The *Majlis Ash Shura*, or Consultative Council, has 150 members, all appointed by the king. The Consultative Council does not have actual legislative power, but rather serves as an advisory body that can make recommendations to the king (Metz, 1992).

Budget System and Structure

Saudi Arabia uses a traditional line-item budget. The fiscal year starts on January 1st and ends on December 31st. The MOF is responsible for preparing the kingdom's general budget, discussing it with other government agencies, and monitoring the implementation thereof. In addition, the MOF is responsible for controlling spending from budget allocation in all government agencies, overseeing the kingdom's revenue gathering procedures, ensuring the conformity of these procedures with an established set of regulations and bylaws, and overseeing the finalization of the government's annual closing accounts record of expenditures (Al-Shaibani, 1998; MOF, 2008).

A line-item budget is designed to "Focus on controlling budget revenue and public expenditure, carry out spending in accordance with the laws, rules, and regulations, and reduce or prevent financial misappropriations or irregularities" (Asfour, 1994, p. 23; Menifield, 2009, p. 3). The traditional line-item budget was adopted as the budget system to prepare the state budget in the Kingdom of Saudi Arabia starting in fiscal year 1938, and the rules are still applicable.

The budgetary system of Saudi Arabia has a specific classification, which depends on expenditure usage. Ten sectors in the Budget Department at the MOF discuss and follow up on the implementation of the state's general budget; these sectors are defense, security, public administration, municipalities, economic resources, infrastructure, transportation and communications, labor force, social development, and administrative regions (Al-Sultan & Abu Makarim, 1998; MOF, 2008).

BUDGET FORMAT (CHAPTERS)

The government budget consists of four chapters, which are referred to as sections in this manuscript, that relate to its preparation and spending stage. These sections are: (1) salaries, allowances, and wages; (2) operational costs, consumption, and expenditure on subsidies; (3) operating, maintenance, and hygiene; and (4) projects (investment).

Salaries, Allowances, and Wages

This section of the budget contains the basic, essential parts of the budget, such as salaries of civilians, allowances of civilian employees, salaries of military employees, allowances of military employees, temporary allowances, and wages of workers. The budget regulations do not allow any modification or funds transfer from one section to another. In addition, this section covers a large percentage of the government's budget. In some cases, more than 80% of the agency or ministry's budget depends on the nature of the work of organizations that receive government funds. Figures that show the percentage that each section represents in the government's budget were not available.

Operational Costs, Consumption, and Expenditure on Subsidies

This section of the budget includes all sections related to operations and basic daily demands such as travel expenses, personal transportation, electricity consumption, miscellaneous expenses, furniture and office supplies, fuel, maintenance, transportation, and equipment.

Operating, Maintenance, and Hygiene

Section three of the budget covers operating services in Saudi Arabia's budget system. It includes items such as software for computers, and the maintenance and upkeep of the ministries and government departments. Government agencies have two ways of undertaking these tasks. Some agencies and ministries hire people directly to do the job, while some agencies and ministries outsource these jobs to private companies.

Operating, maintenance, and hygiene services are managed primarily through contracts between government agencies and private companies. Each organization estimates the amounts it requires to carry out operating, maintaining, and cleaning services in the next fiscal year and adds them to their budget. In the move toward greater privatization, and the government's stated aim of supporting the private sector and ensuring greater job quality, it has strongly recommended and advised all government agencies and ministries to let private companies handle the operating, maintenance, and hygiene process by outsourcing contracts to the private sector.

Projects (Investment)

This section of the budget is exclusively for projects and infrastructures. The budget is split into two main categories: new projects and projects under implementation. In the 2008 budget, new projects accounted for more than 40% of the government's budget.

New projects are those projects that have requested accreditation for the first time in the state budget. The Ministry's Engineering Department plays a major role in conducting visible studies and reviewing estimated expenditures for new projects. Cost estimation depends on a new project's components. After the MOF has approved a project, the department can add the cost of the project for the first fiscal year. If the project plan covers more than one fiscal year, the remaining funds are held in the government's account, and 1 fiscal year the government will add the cost of that fiscal year to the department's budget until the project is completed.

Projects under implementation are approved projects that have been implemented either in the present year or in previous fiscal years. The funds necessary for the project in a fiscal year are held in the government's account from the beginning of the project. If there is any change to the cost, departments prepare a draft budget, which includes the change of the cost, and send it to the MOF for analysis. The MOF then determines the cost that should be added to the budget. Each department and agency is responsible for providing information on projects under implementation. The monitoring of appropriations for the project under implementation for the next fiscal year is determined according to the information provided by the agency that owns the project. Note that allocations for each project are from year to year until the full implementation of the project.

Budget Legal Declaration

The Royal Decree No. 38 in 1957 organized authorization of the government budget by the executive cabinet, the Council of Ministers. This organized the budget process from preparation to execution (Asfour, 1994; MOF, 2005). The key components of the royal decree related to the budget process are as follows:

- Article 28: All financial affairs of the state have to be approved by the Council of Ministers.

■ Article 37: The Council of Ministers' authorization of the annual state budget includes a forecast of imports and expenses for that year. The budget is then given to the king for approval. If something happens that leads to delays in getting the budget approved, the budget must follow the previous fiscal year's budget on a monthly basis until the new budget is approved.

■ Article 38: Any increase in the budget has to be under royal order or a decision from the Council of Ministers.

Budget Cycle

There are four stages, or phases, in the Saudi Arabia budgeting process:

1. Preparation of the government budget,
2. Approval of the government budget,
3. The implementation phase, and
4. Controlling and monitoring the implementation.

PHASE I: PREPARING THE GENERAL BUDGET

The executive branch in Saudi Arabia, represented by the MOF (Budget Department), government ministries, departments, and agencies, have the task of preparing the government budget. The MOF plays a major role in all budget preparation steps, from gathering information and issuing regulations, to approving the budget. After the Council of Ministers approves the budget, the MOF supervises the implementation process.

The preparatory steps start 1 to 5 years in advance. These steps include: a study of the state's economic and financial situation conducted by the MOF and the Ministry of Economy and Planning, based on previous budget performances; and a review of the national economy based on a 5-year strategic plan, which is issued as a guideline for the government (Ministry of Economy and Planning, 2008; MOF, 2008).

On January 1st of each year, the MOF issues guidelines for all government agencies to prepare the budget, which forms they should use, and the timeline to submit the first and final drafts of their budgets and projects. Agencies and ministries then set internal guidelines and timetables, based on the MOF statement, so they can meet the requirements for preparing their budget.

The MOF has the power and ability to intervene in all stages of the preparation process and monitors the process on a daily basis, either in the preparation stage or during the execution period. The role of the MOF is to prepare the ministry budget, prepare the estimation of government income (the general revenues of the state), and to collect the budget drafts of the ministries and government agencies in order to analyze and discuss the drafts with these agencies and ministries. The draft budget has to be ready for discussion with the MOF no later than July of each fiscal year, and if the agency has a new project in their budget, they have to send it to the MOF between April and June of that year (MOF, 2008). The draft budget usually contains revenues estimates and expenditures for every agency and ministry, as well as tables of income and expenditure, which is the largest penalty of the budget document.

The final and official draft of the budget usually comes as a royal decree and contains the formal authorization for agencies and ministries to apply the budget. This statement authorizes the collection of income and opening credits (leave spending). It also includes provisions for the implementation of the budget. The statement of the MOF include the state's economic and financial situation, the budget deficit or surplus, economic or financial prospects for the next fiscal year, the distribution method for allocated funds for the next fiscal year, and the revenue shares for each sector. In the preparation phase each year, government agencies fill out specific forms, and the MOF sends these forms to all government agencies annually (MOF, 2005).

Problems often arise during the preparation process because of the bureaucracy and central supervision by the MOF. Problems in preparing the government's budget fall into two categories. First, there are preparation problems from the perspective of the MOF. Examples include:

- Excessive and sometimes unjustified appropriations for some items;
- Increases in amendments without proof of substantiating the increase;
- The lack of economic feasibility studies of projects submitted; and
- Frequent requests for transfers between items in the budget during implementation, which are not justified at times.

In contrast, there are preparation problems from the perspective of government agencies and ministries, such as:

- Lack of confidence in the MOF regarding estimates submitted by the agencies and ministries;
- A tendency by the MOF to reduce permanent appropriations items during the discussion prior to approval;
- The MOFs dependence on previous budgets for the adoption of any item, even in the presence of a justification to explain an increase that might occur in any budget item; and
- Insufficient time to adjust the budget items requested by the MOF after the budget discussion.

PHASE II: APPROVAL OF THE BUDGET

Authorization steps and the timeline of the government's budget in the Kingdom of Saudi Arabia are usually the same every fiscal year, and are based on a statement issued by the MOF at the beginning of the fiscal year (all dates are approximate).

1. The MOF studies and analyzes the draft of the government's budget that comes from agencies and ministries, and then sends it to the Council of Ministers for consideration and acknowledgment (April–November).
2. The draft budget is forwarded to the finance committee in the Council of Ministers to prepare a report on the budget (November).
3. The draft budget is discussed at a meeting of the Council of Ministers (November).

4. The royal decree announces the government's budget in a special meeting for the Council of Ministers (last week of December).

5. The official budget, through the MOF, is distributed to all government agencies and ministries in order to implement it as issued (last week of December).

PHASE III: IMPLEMENTATION OF THE GOVERNMENT BUDGET

Revenue collection and disbursement of expenditures is conducted by two government agencies: the Saudi Arabian Monetary Agency (SAMA), which is the central bank in the Saudi Arabian financial system, and the MOF. The implementation of the government budget in Saudi Arabia comprises five main operations: revenues collection, expenditures distributions, treasury transactions, budget corrections (transfers), and the government closing account.

Revenue Collection

The collection of revenues is the function of the MOF and other ministries and departments. All revenues are deposited into the government's account at SAMA. These revenues are categorized in two parts: revenues from the production and sale of oil, and direct and indirect taxes or fees. For direct taxes, such as the tax applicable to a foreign company operating in Saudi Arabia, a specific formula shows how to calculate the amount of relevant taxes. Local corporations have a similar formula called a *Zakat*, which is based on the corporation's total income, type of corporation, and operations performed. There is a specific formula to assess *Zakat*, and it is a part of the Islamic law.

The Department of Zakat and Income Tax (DZIT) is responsible for collecting Zakat and the income tax in Saudi Arabia's financial system.

> The mission of DZIT is briefly to administer and collect Zakat on commercial goods from Saudi individuals and to administer and collect tax from non-Saudi individuals doing business in the Kingdom, resident Saudi companies on shares of non-Saudi partners, and non-resident companies doing business in the Kingdom through a permanent establishment or deriving income from a source in the Kingdom. (Department of Zakat and Income Tax, 2008, para. 1)

The second type of taxes are indirect taxes, which are fees produced by processes such as getting a driver's license. Compared to other countries, the indirect tax in Saudi Arabia is low, so it makes only a small contribution to the government's budget. Note that there are no other types of individual taxes such as income or property taxes. As a result, non-oil revenues, including Zakat and customs, contributed around 12.5% to the 2008 budget (Saudi Arabian Monetary Agency, 2008).

Expenditure Distribution

Expenditure distribution is the step whereby the MOF distributes and spends the agency and ministry's share of the budget. All spending must follow the instructions that come from the MOF after the Council of Ministers approves the government's budget and the monarch issues the royal decree. The government performs and operates under the centralization system, in which the MOF must approve any financial issues or spending

Table 14-2					
Actual Current and Capital Expenditure					
	Current expenditure		**Capital expenditure**		
Year	Amount	% Share	Amount	% Share	Total expenditures
2003	59,608	86.98	8,925	13.02	68,533
2004	66,040	86.83	10,014	13.17	76,054
2005	75,779	82.02	16,614	17.98	92,393
2006	85,976	81.97	18,910	18.03	104,886
2007	92,586	74.46	31,764	25.54	124,350
2008	120,000	52.33	109,333	47.67	229,333

Source: Ministry of Finance, 2009b. *Statistical Tables.*

Note: Amounts given in millions of US$.

before it occurs. Hence, none of the agencies has a free hand over their own budget. In addition, since 87.5% of government revenues come from oil, the primary and most important task of the government is the distribution of expenditures, which explains why the Saudi government is still using the traditional line-item budget system because it allows for more control features than other budget systems. Table 14-2 shows the current and capital expenditures for the 2003–2007 fiscal years.

Treasury Transactions

Treasury transactions are the link between the collection of revenues and the disbursement of expenditures. The SAMA manages treasury transactions in consultation with the MOF. In the treasury transaction operation, SAMA performs the following tasks: collects revenues and disburses expenditures on behalf of the state; manages the collection of operation revenues and disbursements of expenditures; and provides the funds to pay for expenditures when needed. The treasury, in fact, is a legal personality or moral treasury (accounts) and does not relate to material money (bank notes; SAMA, 2008).

Budget Corrections (Transfers)

Transferring funds between chapters, sections, and items of the government budget occurs when needed from the items where there is a surplus over those experiencing deficits. Regulations are in place for budget correction when this happens. In general, the Council of Ministers has to approve any transfer from chapter to chapter or any transfer that exceeds US$37.75 million. The MOF approves transfers less than US$37.75 million. It is the MOF's responsibility to manage and direct any transfer, in consultation with the agency or ministry asking for the budget correction.

The transfer process gives some kind of flexibility to the government budget, as the budget figures are projections for the next fiscal year, which contains an estimate of expenditures, not actual numbers. There are no exact numbers that delineate the number and extent of budget corrections during the fiscal year, but it has been a problem for the MOF and other government agencies. Poor planning and estimation of government expenditures during the budget preparation, and a lack of confidence between the MOF and other government agencies are responsible for the misuse of the budget's corrections tool.

Government Closing Account

The closing account includes all actual amounts of revenues and expenditures for the closing fiscal year and the cash surplus or deficit. It is one of the most important financial statements prepared by the government. The closing accounts reflect the execution of the government budget in accordance with the rules, regulations, and financial instructions. It shows the state's rights and obligations, and, if the difference between government revenues and expenditures is positive, the state has achieved a savings (an increase in assets); on the contrary, if the difference between revenues and expenses is negative, the state has achieved a deficit (shortfall of assets).

The Department of General Accounts at the MOF is responsible for preparing the government closing accounts, and it must be ready no later than April of the new fiscal year. The accrual basis (cash base) is the account base that the government of Saudi Arabia has adopted for the preparation of the government's closing account. The state's closing account starts with an explanatory memorandum indicating the amount of revenues, which includes the extent of the expenses and the actual amounts spent. This process is reconciled (in terms of deficits and surpluses) based on the budget of the closing account. The closing account concludes with a detailed breakdown of the budget items (revenues and expenditures).

In order to verify the closing account balance for each ministry and agency, the Department of General Accounts in the MOF prepares a comprehensive account balance to be compared to the final accounting from each ministry and agency. After completion of the summaries of the closing accounts of all ministries and agencies, all reports are gathered into one full report. The MOF sends the final report to the Council of Ministers and the General Auditing Bureau (GAB) no later than April of the following fiscal year.

PHASE IV: CONTROLLING THE IMPLEMENTATION OF THE GOVERNMENT BUDGET

After the adoption of the budget by the executive branch (Council of Ministers) and issuance of the royal decree, the MOF informs the ministries and government agencies to begin work on their newly allocated budgets. Control over the implementation of the budget is to ensure the commitment of the government units included in the budget appropriations and the extent of compliance with instructions and the administrative and financial regulations.

The control process is a set of actions that are identical to ensure the effective implementation of the budget and to examine the reasons for any deviation in implementation. Control over the implementation of the budget is one of the most important stages in the budget session; it ensures safety and accuracy in estimating public expenditure and revenues in the budget. The control process also helps the government ensure revenue collection and disbursement of expenditures (budget assessments and forecasting) to be in the range of the specified estimates in the budget.

There are three types of controls over the implementation of the government budget in Saudi Arabia: time of control (before and after implementation), administrative control, and nature of control. In general, the control processes exist simultaneously and complement each other.

Time of Control

The control time frames are divided into two types: previous control (expenditures only) and subsequent control. Previous control aims to scrutinize transactions before they are implemented in order to prevent any financial irregularities. The government agencies and the MOF implement this kind of control internally. This control aims at reducing opportunities to commit financial irregularities and thus protect public funds. It also aims at maintaining precision in the application of rules, regulations, and financial instructions. At the same time, one of the downsides of previous control is the work delays that occur because of the time required to accomplish the control prior to authorizing spending.

Subsequent control (comparing spending to revenues) takes place after the budget is implemented and after the disbursement of expenditures and collection of revenues. The main object of this control is to discover financial irregularities. In the Saudi Arabia financial system, two agencies perform subsequent control: the MOF and the General Auditing Bureau.

This kind of control does not impede the implementation of actions or cause delays in financial transactions. In addition, it encourages agencies to be more accurate because they know in advance that there will be a control at the end of the fiscal year. On the other hand, it does not prevent financial mistakes and irregularities because it takes place after financial errors had been committed.

Administrative Control

Administrative control is the control process that takes place inside the agency by the executive branch of that organization. It provides both financial and administrative control. Another face of administrative control is policy control—the control exercised by the organizations responsible for legislation and regulations, such as the Council of Ministers. In this process, these agencies control and monitor the implementation of the budget legislation and regulations, so it is more of a regulatory formality process than one dealing with basic daily monitoring. Administrative control focuses more on the budget plans and objectives rather than on issues that crop up on a daily basis, and deals with the state's long-term plans regarding financial and nonfinancial issues.

Natural Control

There are two types of natural control in Saudi Arabia's financial system: accounts control and evaluative control. The first, accounts control, is designed to ensure the accuracy of revenues collection and disbursement of expenditures, and focuses on the accuracy of accounting procedures. Agencies and ministries perform this kind of control either internally, by having a financial director at the agency, or externally, by the MOF and the GAB.

Secondly, there is evaluative control (economic control), which not only is a bookkeeping process, but also includes follow-up actions and the implementation of projects and programs, and ensures the efficiency of existing implementation. In addition, evaluation control ensures that budget implementation proceeds according to the government's long-term plans. This control ensures that programs are on schedule and achieve targeted results. Natural control also includes studying and analyzing the impact of the implementation on the national economy in general. The Ministry of Economy and Planning and the MOF attend to this control.

Financial Regulator Authorities in Saudi Arabia

Several government agencies in Saudi Arabia control and monitor the financial activities in all ministries and departments. Each of these agencies plays a specific role in monitoring the regulatory process for the integration of efforts to ensure proper control of financial activities. The Council of Ministers is the legislative authority charged with the responsibility of issuing regulations and financial legislation, and regulates the performance of government agencies. The MOF follows up and monitors the implementation of those regulations. The MOF and the GAB assess the performance of government agencies and discuss the financial reports with officials (Alhoiml & AlHussein, 2006).

Many agencies and bureaus in the structure of the Saudi financial system are responsible for monitoring and controlling the government budget. Most of them have a consultative role, not an executive role. The main players who have an executive or consultative role in preparing, authorizing, mentoring, and controlling the government budget are discussed here.

COUNCIL OF MINISTERS

The Council of Ministers and the prime minister (PM), usually the king himself, act as the supreme executive power behind the consolidation of all activities and functions. The Council of Ministers establishes domestic and foreign policy, as well as financial, economic, educational, defense and all the state's public affairs and supervises their implementation.

The Council of Ministers monitors the process of implementation of the government budget and discusses any additional appropriations when any government unit requests it. After the implementation of the budget, the Council of Ministers examines the closing (final) account for approval. The biggest part of the budget cycle, in all aspects, goes through the Council of Ministers where the council discusses, analyzes, and authorizes the collection of revenues and disbursement of expenditures, and monitors and controls the government budget. They also monitor the implementation of laws and regulations, make decisions, and follow up on the implementation of the overall plan for development. Last, they create committees to investigate the functioning of the ministries and other governmental agencies (Al-Sultan & Abu Makarim, 1998; Asfour, 1994).

MINISTRY OF FINANCE

The MOF plans the management of public resources, in addition to imposing control over the collection of revenue and disbursement of expenditures by the ministries and governmental departments. Therefore, the MOF is the main player in all financial matters and assumes sole responsibility for all the financial affairs in the kingdom. The aims and functions of the MOF are as follows:

- Oversee the kingdom's financial and monetary policies and monitor implementation by competent agencies.
- Prepare the kingdom's general budget, discuss it with other government agencies, and monitor the implementation.
- Maintain the records of all current accounts between the MOF and other government agencies.
- Exercise subsequent control over budget allocations in all government agencies.
- Oversee the kingdom's revenue gathering procedures and ensure conformity with these procedures by applying established regulations and bylaws.
- Prepare the closing account for the government's budget.

SAUDI ARABIAN MONETARY AGENCY

The SAMA, established in 1952, is the central bank for the Kingdom of Saudi Arabia. The SAMA oversees and implements monetary policy in Saudi Arabia, including the deposits of all state revenues and payment of all expenses. The aims and functions of the SAMA (2008) are as follows:

- Acts as a banker to the government.
- Supervises commercial banks.
- Manages the kingdom's foreign exchange reserves.
- Conducts monetary policy for promoting price and exchange rate stability.
- Promotes growth and ensures the soundness of the financial system.

GENERAL AUDITING BUREAU

The GAB is an independent government agency that reports directly to the PM. GAB control focuses on subsequent spending (after spending) control, which takes place after the implementation of the government's budget. The main objectives are accounting and administrative controls over the government's agencies to ensure commitment to government rules and regulations in the administrative and financial implementation of the state budget.

The GAB is also required to watch over the state's fixed and current resources and to oversee proper deployment and maintenance of these resources (General Auditing Bureau, 2001). The role of the GAB is an advisory role and not an executive role because the GAB's role ends when it sends the final report to the PM. The aims and functions of the GAB (2008) include:

- Providing assurances that the state's revenues and due amounts in cash or services have been appropriately collected and entered into accounting books, according to the prevailing regulations, and ensuring that expenditures have been consumed in accordance with the provisions contained in the annual budget statement and in accordance with prevailing regulations.
- Monitoring the implementation of projects and ensuring that they are within the estimated costs and are completed on time, as well as evaluating the results and achievement of its objectives (performance audit).
- Issuing an annual report for each fiscal year, including the results of the final audit and assessment of the financial management of the state in general and the financial management assessment of each of the entities subject to supervision.
- Issuing a statement on the closing account for that year and making appropriate recommendations aimed at improving the performance and development of financial management at state level.

New Reforms

A number of structural reforms were implemented from 1999 to 2007 to organize the privatization process, raise the contribution percentage of the private sector on the GDP, and to reduce dependence on oil revenues on the government budget. In 1999, steps were taken to corporatize and restructure the telecommunications and electricity sectors; the stock market was opened to foreign investors through open-ended mutual funds; and reform of the tax and customs administration continued. In 2000, the new Investment Law was implemented, allowing foreign investors full ownership of business in almost all activities, including the oil and energy distribution sectors. In addition, the Saudi Arabian General Investment Authority was established to encourage foreign direct investment. In addition, steps were taken by the Ministry of Education and the Technical and Vocational Training Corporation (TVTC) to train the Saudi labor force and to prepare them for employment in the private sector.

Conclusions

Several studies, papers, and articles researching various aspects of the Saudi economy and financial system have been published in the last 10 years (Alfozan, 2008; Belayachi & Haidar, 2008; International Monetary Fund, 2001, 2008; United Nations Development Program, 2006; World Bank, 2007; Wurm, 2008). Despite the various subjects discussed, all of them value the political and economic reforms that have taken place within the past decade. This includes the new Investment Law in 2000, the Judiciary System Law in 2007, and the Governance Law in 2007.

To ensure that the new economic and political reforms are successful, the Saudi government should combine economic reforms with improving the performance of public finance in general and the government budget in particular, because the government's contribution to GDP is large enough to influence the performance of the economy in general.

On the other hand, these studies recommend a review of the government budget in all aspects and in all stages of planning, preparation, and implementation to more efficiently manage public finance, because the government budget is the capstone of the economy. The structure of the budget and the budget system that has been in affect since 1954 have had only minor updates and reforms. In addition, these studies recommend financial and administrative enhancement of public sector performance through transparency and clearer procedures of control.

Availability of data is one of the issues that have arisen in many studies. As studies such as the IMF (2008) have found, fiscal data are not available, which contributes to increased acts of corruption and misuse of power. In addition, the absence of fiscal data reduces the effectiveness of the government to control its own performance. Transparency International (TI) had the same concern about the availability of data and information, and its consequences. According to the Corruption Perceptions Index (CPI), issued by the Transparency International in 2008, Saudi Arabia scored a 3.5 out of 5, which indicates a serious corruption problem (Transparency International, 2008). "Unsurprisingly, Saudi Arabia is also among approximately half of the world's countries that cannot be treated on Transparency International's corruption perceptions index because reliable data is not available" (Eigen, 1998, p. 179).

Control and reduced spending in the government's budget, especially spending on wages, is one of the main recommendations of most studies. An IMF (2008) study, for instance, reports "directors urged the authorities to further tighten current spending, in particular for wages, and to target more narrowly large implicit water and energy subsidies" (para. 9).

The government needs budget performance criteria and needs to establish goals by having long-term plans and by sticking to the government's budget, because in many cases, the rulers add projects and spending, that are not included in the original government's budget. This excessive spending on projects affects the economy in general and the ability of the government to have clear goals for the economy. In addition, the absence of fixed criteria makes the evaluation process almost impossible. "The absence of fixed criteria for success and failure, which apply regardless of time and place, is a serious problem" (Bovens & t'Hart, 1996).

The development of a long-term strategy to take advantage of the rise in oil prices is one of the most important recommendations made in order for the state to take advantage of budget surpluses and to ensure the stability of economic growth in the kingdom. Lack of long-term plans in the past, in 1982 for example, led to a failure to take advantage of the increase in income and therefore resulted in a large deficit in the government's budget for many years thereafter. In 2003, there was a deficit of US$160 billion. "Preliminary estimates indicate that public debt will drop to around SR237 (US $63.2) billion at the end of fiscal year 2008, which represents 13.5% of projected GDP for 2008, as compared with 18.7% in 2007. The stock of debt is totally domestic" (MOF, 2009a, p. 1). Therefore, it is highly recommended that clear and long-time strategic plans need to be in place to avoid having the same situation in the future. "Directors encouraged the authorities to develop a long-term strategy of accumulating foreign assets beyond stabilization purposes, so that the benefits of the current oil wealth can be shared with future generations" (IMF, 2008, para. 9).

Finally, all agencies responsible for controlling and monitoring administrative and financial activities for the government's agencies, such as the GAB and the Consultative Council have a consultative role without any authority. These agencies file reports to the king in an advisory capacity. Giving controlling agencies an executive and independent role in monitoring the government budget will enhance the ability of these agencies to be more powerful in controlling corruption and in supervising the execution of the government's budget, as well as bringing about economic and financial reforms. These suggestions and recommendations stress the optimum use of public funds, and the importance of ensuring continued growth for generations to come.

Discussion Questions

1. The political system in Saudi Arabia is a monarchy-based system, where the final word of all state's affairs extends back to the king. So, how can other political institution influence the budgetary system in Saudi Arabia?
2. It is clear that the MOF exerts much power over the budget cycle in Saudi Arabia. Do you think this situation has negative or positive influences in transparency and quality of the government's budget? Explain.
3. From the discussion in this chapter, it is clear that the financial system faces many challenges and one of these challenges focuses on the implementation of the budget. How can Saudi officials bridge the gap between policy creation and policy implementation?
4. If you had the opportunity to make substantive changes in any of the four stages of the Saudi budget, in which stage would you make the changes and how would this affect the remaining stages?
5. Controlling agencies have an advisory role in the budgetary system in Saudi Arabia. How does this affect transparency and the quality of the public budget in Saudi Arabia?

References

Alfozan, A. (2008). Are there any other incomes not included in the budget? *Alwatan News Paper*. Available at: http://www.alwatan.com.sa. Accessed April 9, 2010.

Alhoiml, S., & AlHussein, A. (2006). *Accountability in government agencies in Saudi Arabia*. Riyadh, Saudi Arabia: Institute of Public Administration.

Al-Shaibani, M. (1998). *The general budget and its applications in the kingdom*. Riyadh, Saudi Arabia: Institute of Public Administration.

Al-Sultan, S., & Abu Makarim, W. (1998). *Accounting in government units and other social organizations*. Riyadh, Saudi Arabia: Mars Publishing House.

Asfour, M. (1994). *The assets of the general budget*. Riyadh, Saudi Arabia: Institute of Public Administration.

Belayachi, K., & Haidar, J. (2008). *Competitiveness from innovation, not inheritance: Case study–Saudi Arabia*. Washington, DC: World Bank.

Bovens, M., & t'Hart, P. (1996). Quoted in Howlett, M., & Ramesh, M. (2003). *Studying public policy: Policy cycles and policy subsystems* (2nd ed., pp. 207–208). New York: Oxford University Press.

Central Intelligence Agency. (2007). *Factbook: Saudi Arabia*. Available at: https://www.cia.gov/library/publications/the-world-factbook/geos/sa.html. Accessed April 9, 2010.

Department of Zakat and Income Tax. (2008). *The department of Zakat and income tax (DZIT)*. Available at: http://www.dzit.gov.sa/en/GeneralInfo/generalinfo1.shtml. Accessed April 9, 2010.

Eigen, P. (1998). Quoted in Champion, D. (2005). *The paradoxical kingdom: Saudi Arabia and the momentum of reform*. New York: Columbia University Press.

General Auditing Bureau. (2001). *The royal decree establishing GAB*. Available at: http://www.gab.gov.sa/article_e.php?id=32. Accessed April 9, 2010.

International Monetary Fund. (2001). *IMF concludes 2001 Article IV consultation with Saudi Arabia (01/119)*. Washington, DC: Author.

International Monetary Fund. (2008). *IMF concludes 2008 Article IV consultation with Saudi Arabia (08/102)*. Washington, DC: Author. Available at: http://www.imf.org/external/np/sec/pn/2008/pn08102.htm. Accessed April 9, 2010.

Menifield, C. (2009). *The basics of public budgeting and financial management: A handbook for academics and practitioners*. Lanham, MD: University Press of America.

Metz, H. (Ed.). (1992). *Saudi Arabia: A country study*. Washington, DC: GPO for the Library of Congress. Available at: http://countrystudies.us/saudi-arabia/. Accessed April 9, 2010.

Ministry of Economy and Planning. (2008). *The eighth development plan*. Available at: http://www.planning.gov.sa/. Accessed April 9, 2010.

Ministry of Finance. (2005). *Instructions and budget models*. Riyadh, Saudi Arabia: Government Printing Office.

Ministry of Finance. (2008). *Instructions of accounts closing and preparing the final account*. Available at: http://www.mof.gov.sa/en/docs/rules. Accessed April 9, 2010.

Ministry of Finance. (2009a). *Press release*. Available at: http://www.mof.gov.sa/en/docs/news/budget1430.pdf. Accessed April 9, 2010.

Ministry of Finance. (2009b). *Statistical tables*. Available at: http://www.mof.gov.sa/en/docs/stats/index.htm. Accessed April 9, 2010.

Ministry of Labour. (2009). *The low rate of unemployment and increase the number of Saudi workers*. Available at: http://www.mol.gov.sa/ar/accomplishments/pages/enjaz1.aspx. Accessed April 9, 2010.

Organization of the Petroleum Exporting Countries. (2007). *Annual statistical bulletin*. Austria: Ueberreuter Print und Digimedia.

Saudi Arabian General Investment Authority. (2008). *The Saudi Arabian general investment authority (SAGIA)*. Available at: http://sagia.gov.sa/. Accessed April 9, 2010.

Saudi Arabian Monetary Agency. (2008). *45th annual report*. Riyadh, Saudi Arabia: Government Printing Office.

Tadawul. (2007). *Annual statistical report*. Available at: http://www.tadawul.com.sa/static/pages/en/Publication/PDF/. Accessed April 9, 2010.

Transparency International. (2008). *Middle East and North Africa (MENA)*. Available at: http://www.transparency.org/regional_pages/africa_middle_east. Accessed April 9, 2010.

United Nations Development Program. (2006). *Executive board of the United Nations development programme and of the United Nations population fund*. New York: Author.

World Bank. (2007). *Annual report: Middle East and North Africa*. Available at: http://go.worldbank.org/D738A4O6B0. Accessed April 9, 2010.

Wurm, I. (2008). *Operation: Reforming the kingdom; External and internal triggers of the reform process in Saudi Arabia*. Paper prepared for presentation at the 49th ISA Annual Convention, San Francisco, CA.

Chapter 15

Finance Reform and Performance-Based Budgeting in the United Arab Emirates

Deniz Zeynep Leuenberger

Learning Objectives

- Understand the impacts and relevance of United Arab Emirates' (UAE) federal level budget reforms.
- Know and understand the unique characteristics of the UAE's financial and political infrastructure.
- Explore the importance of transparency and accountability in budgeting decision making, especially in securing international confidence.
- Explore the economic influence and relevance of the UAE in a global context.

Introduction

Following September 11, 2001, the UAE's banking and financing practices came under increased international scrutiny. Some of the financing for the bombing of the World Trade Center had been run through its banks. Global governments and investors pressured for increased transparency in financial management across the Middle East. With hopes of becoming a global financial center, the UAE undertook steps to reform its public budgeting and finance infrastructures, as well to increase its oversight of private investments. Accountability, efficiency, oversight, transparency, security, and citizen participation processes began to be integrated into government agency planning and decision making through budget and finance reforms. These reforms have changed the relationship between governments and nongovernmental organizations (NGOs) operating in the area, with governments increasing budget review, oversight, and auditing over NGOs. Related changes to participation and transparency processes are altering civil society and social capital in the region and transforming the role of key federal regulatory agencies in the UAE.

A question of finance reforms in the UAE have recently again come under question in 2008, after financial tremors from the global economic crisis sent markets and real estate values crashing in the UAE, especially in the Emirate of Dubai. Unlike Abu Dhabi, the larger and oil-rich emirate, Dubai's economy is anchored in tourism, banking, business, and has a service-based focus. Dubai World, which is Dubai's primary development, holding, and investment enterprise and which investors had believed, until the crisis, would be fully government backed, is nearly $60 billion in debt and has asked for an extension on its November 2009 payments. In addition, the government of Dubai is approximately $19 billion in debt and in the middle of construction on a number of state-funded infrastructure projects, all funded without taxes. The estimated debt of Dubai is between $80 and $90 billion. Abu Dhabi has stepped in with $10 billion to assist, but it is becoming clear that there are political costs for Dubai. Abu Dhabi, which is more conservative, larger, and more financially stable, is increasingly overshadowing Dubai. Dubai's attempt to brand itself as a center of business and finance is likely to end as it hands that role over to Abu Dhabi. On January 4, 2010, the tallest building in the world, called Burj Dubai, was unveiled under its new name, Burj Khalifa, after the president of the UAE and head of the Abu Dhabi government. As development projects sit unfinished and the value of housing in Dubai has fallen as much as 50% from 2007 to 2010, the financial woes of the emirate are not likely to be resolved quickly.

The close connection between private development and government budget in the UAE also requires attention. Further, the lack of transparency is not an oversight, but is largely a planned component of government decision making. The lack of transparency and accountability, however, is likely to continue to impact the role of the UAE as a global financial center, especially in an increasingly economically risk averse world. Added to the international demand for security, the restructuring of decision-making process is critical. In 2006 for instance, Dubai World's Dubai Port Authority was pressured to sell off US port assets after purchasing P&O Ports because of political mistrust of US citizens. The economic and political climate is likely to lead to additional pressures for reform or for reluctance by the international community to collaborate with the UAE in development and in markets.

In order to better understand the infrastructures that underlie the public and private financial system of the UAE and the impacts of these infrastructures globally, this chapter describes processes and stakeholders of the federal level budget. This chapter outlines the budget system and its relationship to the political process in the UAE. It provides foundational information on budget actors, budget cycles, auditing and accounting systems, and a discussion of revenue and expenditure allocations. It introduces the catalyzing role of performance-based budgeting (PBB) and describes the relationship between the federal governments, regional governments, and NGOs operating in the region. Finally, the chapter discusses the impacts of recent finance reforms in the region.

Background and Political Structures

The UAE is a federation of seven independently led states, each with its own government, ruler, and ruling family. Located in the Arabian Gulf, the federation is increasingly becoming an international hub with growing economic influence. Of the emirates, Abu Dhabi is the largest, covering more than 26,000 square miles of the 30,000 square mile nation (Cordes & Scholz, 1980). It also holds the largest portion of oil reserves in the UAE. As the most politically and financially powerful state, it subsidizes up to 85% of the cost of public services such as free education and free health care in the remainder of the federation (Cordes & Scholz). Dubai, the second largest emirate with 1500 square miles, is the center of trade and tourism in the region (Cordes & Scholz). The remaining states are Sharjah, Ras al-Khaimah, Ajman, Fujairah, and Umm al-Qawain. All of the emirates retain autonomy and maintain control their own economic development, resembling a city-state model of government at the regional level.

After traditional tribal and regional rivalries were largely set aside during the 1971–2004 presidential rule of Sheikh Zayed bin Sultan Al Nahyan, the federation quickly invested in development efforts and moved from an economy focused on pearling, agriculture, fishing, and boat building to an economy founded on oil and natural gas exports (US Department of State, 2007). There continues to be some rivalry between the emirates, especially between Abu Dhabi and Dubai, over a leadership role in developing the nations identity in the global context. Officially, Abu Dhabi has the federation's leadership in hand and has increased its power after backing Dubai following the 2008 financial crisis. Abu Dhabi has the largest amount of oil resources and its leader is also the president of the UAE. Dubai, however, had attempted to diversify its development as its oil resources diminished and has marketed itself as a luxury vacation site and a center for business. The debt problems of Dubai in 2008 through 2010 are likely to hand the role of global business and financial power over to Abu Dhabi. The UAE, as a whole, has increased its development in international business, banking, trade, and tourism as a long-term solution to an expected decline in oil and natural gas reserves. Even in light of the economic problems of 2008 and 2009, extensive international investments make the UAE a key player in the world marketplace and it is likely to continue to remain a key player in the long run.

BALANCING TRADITION AND DEVELOPMENT

It is important to state the influence of religion in the financial and legal structures of the UAE. *Shariah* law, based on Islamic principles, informs the legal system in the UAE. The majority of nationals are practitioners of Sunni Islam and religious values impact laws, business practices, and social behavior. As the nation balances traditional values and influences from external forces, it has become a center for exchange, trade, and communication between the Middle East and Western nations. After a rapid influx of labor as a result of development, 85% of the population consists of nonnationals working and living in the country, with the remaining 15% of residents holding citizenship (Cordes & Scholz, 1980). Free trade and communication zones and large construction projects attract foreign business and labor. While the nation follows conservative laws and government rules and policies, it is relatively accepting of other cultural and religious practices. There are often separate expectations and practices for national and nonnational led organizations. All businesses outside of the free trade zones, for instance, must have at least 51% ownership and investment by nationals. Taxes on business outside of the free trade zones and revenues from fossil fuel reserves fund government agencies, services, and projects. The UAE collects no income tax from its national and nonnational workforce and collects most of its business-related taxes from the oil and banking industries.

The UAE, as a developing nation, is also balancing issues of equity in its labor force. The workforce is increasingly seeing the addition of female employees, although the total population of the nation reflects a higher number of males to females due to the high number of male laborers residing in the country. Among nationals, a larger portion of women than men enter and graduate from the free public higher education system. The "emiratization" policy of the nation has required that nationals be shown preference by public and private agencies and a large number of nationals work in government positions. There was little oversight of public employee work practices in the past and there were also difficulties for nationals seeking employment in private organizations due to a perception of poor performance. Under recent reforms, government employees are more closely monitored regarding performance and attendance and a growing number of nationals are working in private organizations and in businesses of their own. As there are no laws providing protections to nonnationals on wage or hiring equity, there tend to be disparities in pay and benefits between nationals and nonnationals. As the UAE has stopped some of its larger construction projects as real estate prices plummeted and debts rose, laborers from poorer nations, especially India, have experienced the largest layoffs and hardships.

Finally, the UAE balances Islamic law and Western banking models. The world's self-reputed oldest Islamic bank, the Dubai Islamic Bank, is an example of the type of change emerging in the region. This institution represents one translation of economic and banking practices into forms with a unique Islamic identity. The development of the UAE as an international center for finance is itself an example of the same phenomenon. The economic development of non-oil exporting countries in the region is increasingly impacted by the increased use of Islamic religious law in financial practices. For instance, Islamic banking, in its ideal form, would be a full-reserve system and would also charge no interest to borrowers.

In practice, banks enter into contracts with parties wherein they may purchase an item on that individual's behalf and sell it to that individual at a profit and on a payment plan. They may also enter into profit–loss sharing arrangements or arrangements similar to "layaway" and "rent-to-own" financing. They may also provide benevolent loans, wherein persons with need pay no interest on a loan. Another example of the religion influenced financial structure is the move by Dubai, in October of 2009 to issue both a $4 billion bond and a $2.5 billion sukuk, a type of Islamic bond, for government projects.

As citizens in these regions demand financial practices aligned with Islamic religious law in private ventures, there is increased demand for translating infrastructural systems in governments and NGOs as well. Facilitation of efficient, outcome-based financial and budget systems that respect local sensibilities is a key component of budget and finance reform. Additionally, the UAE must adopt increasingly transparent and accountable systems if it is to continue to attract international investment following the crisis of September 11, 2001 and the 2008 economic crisis.

POLITICAL STRUCTURE

The political structure of the UAE is a key influence on the transparency and accountability of budget decision making and financial reporting. While each emirate is controlled by its own ruling family and leaders, the UAE's overall government decision making is led by the Supreme Council of Rulers (US Department of State, 2007). The Supreme Council consists of the seven individual state monarchs. The ruler of Abu Dhabi acts as the president of the Council and of the UAE and the ruler of Dubai acts as the vice president and prime minister. A UAE Cabinet manages the administrative responsibilities of the nation, proposes laws and policies, and has the right of approval over the federal general budget (US Department of State, 2007).

In addition, there is a forty member Federal National Council, half of which is appointed by members of the Supreme Council of Rulers and the other half of which is elected by a vote of the nationals of the country as established in 2006 (US Department of State, 2007). There is no other federal level voting mechanism and there is no allowance for political parties (US Department of State, 2007). The concept of citizen participation in political and financial decisions is largely unfamiliar to the citizens of the UAE. Although informal reporting demonstrates satisfaction with government leaders, the limited transparency and self-censorship in the media provides little reliable information on citizen views. The fact that up to 85% of the residents of the country are nonnationals also makes full participation unlikely. Transparency and accountability, a demand on democratic government, is not a component of most federal economic and political decision making in the UAE.

Budgeting and Finance Structures

The economy of the UAE has grown rapidly in the 21st century. The growth gross domestic product (GDP) is an indicator of economic change and is described in Table 15-1. The GDP is composed of three major sectors with industry at 61.8%, services at 36.6%, and agriculture at 1.6% (Central Intelligence Agency [CIA], 2009). The UAE had an external debt of 73.71 billion in 2008, balanced with reserves of gold and foreign exchange of 67.24 billion US dollars (CIA, 2009). In light of the 2008 financial crisis, the growth of the UAE, especially of Dubai, has been challenged as too rapid and international demands for improved infrastructure are increasing.

The federal budget of the UAE documents revenues of $83.15 billion in 2008 and expenditures of $48.3 billion (CIA, 2009). Taxes on oil companies and banks bring

Table 15-1					
United Arab Emirates GDP Growth 2000, 2005–2008					
	2000	2005	2006	2007	2008
GDP in billions	$70.59	$133.00	$163.00	$191.46	$270.00
GDP growth rate	–	–	9.4	7.6	7.7
GDP per capita	–	–	$37,300	$38,600	$40,000

Sources: CIA, 2009; The World Bank, 2009; UNData, 2009.

in the largest amount of revenues in the UAE (Federal Research Division of the Library of Congress, 1993). Defense, education, and social services are provided by the federal government. Education services are fully subsidized for citizens from primary to higher education and social and health services are free of charge. The federal budget is funded through contributions from Abu Dhabi, which provides nearly 80% of revenues, and Dubai, which provides nearly 10% of revenues (Federal Research Division of the Library of Congress, 1993). Individual emirates draw up their own budgets for additional municipal and industrial projects, but these budgets are rarely published and seldom publicly available.

The Central Bank of the UAE issues currency, maintains gold and foreign currency reserves, regulates and controls credit, and advises government leaders on monetary policy (US Library of Congress, 1989). Since the 1980s, the Central Bank has also expanded its auditing and inspections responsibilities and has a strong influence on banking regulation and policy. It also has a role in ensuring stability of currency. The practice of the UAE has been to peg the UAE dirham to the US dollar; however, all revenues and expenditures for government budgets must be recorded in the UAE dirham.

In addition, the Ministry of Finance and Industry (MoFI) prepares all policies and laws regarding the national budget and also has responsibilities for the expenditure framework for government agencies. The MoFI also provides a financial circular that defines budget preparation guidelines in the fourth month of the fiscal year and requires government agencies to prepare preliminary estimates for expenditures and revenues (UAE Federal Law 23, 2005). The fiscal year for the general federal budget is January 1 to December 3 and all government agencies must use a 3-year program agreement for planning purposes (UAE Federal Law 23, 2005). Projects may be continued into subsequent years, but all changes in appropriation must be approved by the UAE Cabinet and all unused revenues must be returned by agencies (UAE Federal Law 23, 2005). The current year's estimate must be compared to the previous year's spending. If mandated agencies do not submit estimates to MoFI, it prepares the estimates on their behalf (UAE Federal Law 23, 2005). If expenditure estimates exceed revenue estimates, MoFI has the authority to define the ceiling for expenditures.

The MoFI prepares a general budget using the estimates provided by individual agencies (UAE Federal Law 23, 2005). The general budget is submitted to the UAE Cabinet for changes and approval. The budget is then submitted to the Federal National

Council, which must approve the budget at least 2 months before the beginning of the financial year. The MoFI informs other agencies of allocation decisions. Each government agency must complete its own final account and an aggregated final account must also be completed by MoFI.

Additionally, the UAE has established independent government agencies that also provide resources for public services and projects. These autonomous entities do not fall under the jurisdiction of regulating bodies. The budgets in these autonomous structures are controlled directly by rulers, and the budget documents are not publicly available. The allocation of resources from these structures requires no oversight by MoFI or the Central Bank, nor does it require consultation with the UAE Cabinet.

The UAE has been under pressure to revise its budgeting and regulatory practices, especially after accusations that some terrorist funding had been traced through UAE bank accounts following the tragic events of September 11, 2001 and the debt crisis, which escalated in 2008 and 2009. These suggested reforms have been critical to a nation with interest in remaining a leader in international banking. Internal and external economic and political pressures have led to a demand for added transparency and outcomes measurement for federal agency budgets, especially because of the blurring of boundaries between private and public investment in the UAE.

Federal Agency Budget Reforms

The events of September 11, 2001 and the crisis of 2008 and 2009 revealed weaknesses in the political systems and domestic policies of the Gulf states. The 1980s and 1990s introduced changes such as increased political prospects, growth of the population, urbanization, anticipation of reduced revenues from oil sources, and greater freedoms for NGOs (al-Sayegh, 2004). These events catalyzed the introduction of educational, economic, and political reforms in the UAE (al-Sayegh). As a state with high hopes of becoming a leader in international finance and tourism, the UAE has developed a strong relationship with Western nations. In the early 1990s, the UAE joined the United States in the Gulf War in an attempt to remove Iraq from Kuwait, resulting in the United States becoming a strategic security force in the area (al-Sayegh). At the writing of this work, the UAE hailed as the only Middle Eastern nation without an act of terrorism on its soils. Nonetheless, ties of 9/11 hijackers to UAE held bank accounts led to increased scrutiny of its financial systems. In 2005, these ties were listed as a primary reason by opponents of the Dubai Port Authority management of US ports. The UAE eventually backed away from the business proposal, although the transaction had the support of then US President George W. Bush.

The UAE has, since 2003, undertaken efforts to reform its public budgeting infrastructures. Specifically, the adoption of PBB has impacted accountability, efficiency, oversight, transparency, security, and citizen participation processes. The goal was to "improve decision-making by providing better information on how well Government services meet the community's needs and by adopting economy (cost of inputs), efficiency, and effectiveness as tenets of good government" (UAE MoFI, 2005, p. 3).

A series of training workshops, guidelines, and curriculum documents were created to assist federal agencies with implementation (UAE MoFI, 2005).

In 2005, UAE Federal Law 23 reiterated the commitment to PBB requiring all ministries and agencies to include performance measures and efficiency indicators in preparation of the general budget (UAE Federal Law 23, 2005). The budget reforms, for the first time, mandate that all nonautonomous federal agencies and departments use outcomes measurements for agency planning. The decision process now also requires additional transparency of the budget and added oversight and regulation by MoFI and the UAE Cabinet.

Impact of Reform

Budget reform in the UAE increases the regulatory power of the MoFI and requires the integration of performance measurements in decision making. In addition, regulation of banking and finance by the Central Bank has been increased. These reforms have had a number of consequences for government agencies. The reforms have also impacted nongovernmental organizations operating in the region and have the potential to impact citizen participation in government decision making. The question continues to be whether these reforms are enough to regain the trust of an increasingly risk averse international community.

Impact on Government Organizations

UAE government agencies have long faced allegations of inefficiency. Government agencies have been accused of not monitoring employee performance, not setting achievable goals, and not using outcomes measures in agency planning. Reforms have increased expectations for organizational performance, with the budget process as a key component of planning and decision making improvements. PBB has established consistent formal outcomes measurement and planning across public agencies. It has, in some agencies, integrated meaningful performance measures in government decision making for the first time. PBB has become an important tool because it has established a standard for agency budgeting and has allowed increased communication in the oversight process.

As PBB has been a government practice for a limited period of time, it is difficult to assess what all of its impacts on public agencies will be. It has, already, increased transparency of the budget process for select agencies. Whether this transparency will lead to increased public participation or whether the decision-making process will improve program outcomes is yet unclear. These reforms are important because the introduction of performance measurement into the budget process is itself novel in the Arabic gulf region, where the majority of governments are autocratic, limiting transparency, program assessment, and citizen participation. The reforms also model compliance with international standards of public administration practice, especially relevant as the UAE seeks to be a central player in international finance. This compliance addresses some of the past and potential criticism that a lack of regulation of agencies, both internal and external to the government, increases the risk of funds being funneled into terrorist action. The government has used the budget process to voice its commitment to stopping terrorism, a commitment that protects the stability of the current political leadership as well as addresses the demands of international stakeholders. The reforms have allowed the UAE Cabinet, the Federal National Council, and the Supreme Council of Rulers to increase their oversight and control of government agency decision making.

Impact on Nongovernmental Organizations and Civil Society

The reforms have also changed the relationship between government and NGOs operating in the area, with the UAE government increasing budget review, oversight, and auditing over NGOs as well. The events of 9/11 dramatically altered the manner in which NGOs interacted and acted in the international community, as well as the regulatory policies in oversight of NGOs (Levitt, 2002). Across the world, nations began to question the "capacity of Muslim and especially Arab countries to establish modern, democratic, secular, and gender egalitarian systems" (Moghadam, 2004). The largest changes include increased regulation of NGO activities, increased emphasis on balancing government funding for human welfare and domestic development versus funding for military action, and increased difficulty in raising funds for NGO activities in the region from private donors.

The recent reforms led by the UAE government are aligned with internal review process models supported by international nongovernmental organizations (INGOs) such as the World Bank. Increased transparency of budgets and outcome measurements have become a part of the financial decision-making process for both public organizations and NGOs. The impact of budgeting reform on governments has just begun to emerge as a valuable tool for civil society development. As accountability, efficiency, and effectiveness have come to be a part of budget curriculum training for federal employees, civil society partners have been invited as both budget trainers and trainees as governments adopt outcome-based decision making. The long-term impacts of reforms will become increasingly apparent in the coming decade, as nations move from training and implementation to maintenance of reforms and as they move from program-focused reforms to nationwide implementation.

A number of policy changes were also initiated in the UAE to regulate financial transfers and NGO actions following the attacks of 9/11. The transfer of funds from immigrants to other nations through the *hawalah* system was restricted, eliminating the unregulated exchange of finances on the international market (al-Sayegh, 2004). Also, regulation of prayer service was implemented and no political discussions were allowed to be combined with religious teachings (al-Sayegh). This also had an impact on charitable organizations in the UAE as religious and charitable actions are closely tied in Islamic practice in the region. Further, educational reforms included formation of local committees to review textbooks and curriculum, limiting any politically volatile material from entering the classroom (al-Sayegh). Finally, NGO behaviors are also held in check as a number of charitable organizations are headed by members of Emirati royal families.

Conclusions

Budget and finance reforms, powered by the UAE's desire to become leaders in the global market place, provide both opportunities and challenges for the UAE government and for civil society members within its borders. Opportunities include increased efficiency, effectiveness, and transparency in the budget decision making and allocation. These concepts may also be used to improve other types of the planning structures within the UAE, perhaps adding outcome-based decision making through the use of tools such as strategic planning. The reforms may also lead to an increased role in international finance, especially if political risks can be regulated and managed. Further, there is the possibility that increased transparency in the budget process may lead to increased citizen participation in budgeting decisions and in the larger political process. Finally, the reforms may provide models for other Gulf nations, who are under similar pressures to improve finance and budgeting practices.

The UAE also faces challenges as it implements reforms. One concern is that while PBB is used "on paper," it may not have true transformative powers over the budget itself. The autocratic nature of the political process may limit true transparency or citizen participation. Regulation and oversight, in themselves, can be tools for political leadership to control decision making and to eliminate internal opposition. While NGOs and INGOs may serve as partners in the development process, dissent by civil society members may be controlled through this oversight process. The PBB process and reforms, because of variations in implementation, have the potential to both increase or to decrease democratic voice in decision making. New discussions in 2009 of implementing zero-based budgeting may also significantly impact reforms if zero-based budgeting is eventually adopted by the federal government.

It is still early to determine if PBB and other reforms will have a long impact on decision making in the UAE. It will be important to watch the process of change as a model of reform for other nations in the Gulf region. The UAE, to date, appears to have addressed some of the concerns raised by the international community tied to management of security and terrorism in the economic system. The fact that the highest levels of leadership in the government are not held to the same levels of transparency as government departments or NGOs operating in the region, may be an influence on the lack of trust in the UAE 2008 debt crisis. Perhaps greater federal level budget transparency is the key to assuring the international community that their investments are secure in the long run. Lessons learned as the UAE works to create its own unique brand of performance-focused planning may have relevance to other developing countries in the region and will hopefully benefit them in their reform efforts.

Discussion Questions

1. The UAE limits citizen participation in the budget decision-making process. What are the potential intended and unintended impacts of budget reforms on citizen participation in the budget decision-making process?

2. What are the potential political, social, and economic impacts of increased transparency in the budgeting process? What are some specific mechanisms and tools that may improve budgeting transparency?
3. The influence of religion is a prominent factor in approaches to economic development in the UAE. What are the anticipated benefits and barriers of religious influence on the UAE's growth as a global economic leader?
4. What are the appropriate roles of NGOs and INGOs in reforming the budget processes of developing and developed nations?
5. How should budgeting reforms of nations with a high level of economic resources versus those with low assets be planned, designed, and implemented? Do economic health and level economic development impact the structure of reforms?

References

al-Sayegh, F. (2004). Post 9/11 changes in the Gulf: The case of the UAE. *Middle East Policy*, 11(2), 107–124.

Central Intelligence Agency. (2009). *The world factbook: United Arab Emirates*. Available at: https://www.cia.gov/library/publications/the-world-factbook/geos/ae.html. Accessed April 19, 2010.

Cordes, R., & Scholz, F. (1980). *Bedouins, wealth, and change: A study of rural development in the United Arab Emirates and the sultanate of Oman*. Tokyo: United Nations University.

Federal Research Division of the Library of Congress. (1993, January). *United Arab Emirates: Budget*. Available at: www.country-data.com/cgi-bin/query/r-14228.html. Accessed April 19, 2010.

Levitt, M. A. (2002). The political economy of Middle East terrorism. *Middle East Review of International Affairs*, 6(4). Available at: http://meria.id.ac.il/journal/2002/issue4/jv6n4a3.html. Accessed April 19, 2010.

Moghadam, V. M. (2004). *Towards gender equality in the Arab/Middle East region: Islam, culture, and feminist activism*. New York: United Nations Development Program.

UAE Federal Law 23. (2005). *Federal law no (23) year 2005 regarding the general budget and the final accounts preparation rules*. Available at: http://www1.worldbank.org/publicsector/pe/countrybudgetlaws.cfm. Accessed April 19, 2010.

UAE Ministry of Finance and Industry. (2005, March). *2006 guidelines for developing and implementing performance-based budgeting in the United Arab Emirates*. Available at: http://www.uae.gov.ae/mofi/English/e_mofi_budget_PDF/2006–2008%20Performance-Budgeting-Guidelines%20-%20EN.pdf. Accessed April 19, 2010.

UNData. (2009). *United Arab Emirates*. Available at: http://data.un.org/CountryProfile.aspx?crName=United%20Arab%20Emirates. Accessed April 19, 2010.

US Department of State. (2007, June). *Background note: United Arab Emirates*. Available at: http://www.state.gov/r/pa/ei/bgn/5444.htm. Accessed April 19, 2010.

US Library of Congress. (1989). *United Arab Emirates: Banking and finance*. Available at: http://countrystudies.us/persian-gulf-states/89.htm. Accessed April 19, 2010.

The World Bank. (2009). *Data & statistics: United Arab Emirates*. Available at: http://go.worldbank.org/1SF48T40L0. Accessed April 19. 2010.

Part **5**

North America

Chapter 16

Review and Reallocation in the Canadian Federal Government's Budgetary System

Mike Joyce

Learning Objectives

- Understand Canada's system of government.
- Comprehend the nature of Canada's budget process and the organizations and individuals that play key roles within it.
- Understand the fiscal framework and how it underpins budget decision making in Canada.
- Understand the mechanisms by which spending is controlled and the government is held accountable for the results it achieves with the spending the legislature has authorized.
- Understand the Canadian experience with review and reallocation initiatives and factors that influence the degree to which such exercises have succeeded.

Introduction

Review and reallocation have become persistent themes in Canadian federal budgets although the results achieved have not always met the expectations set. The first half of this chapter provides an overview of Canada's form of government and the budgetary process that plays out within that framework. The latter part of the chapter considers a number of review and reallocation initiatives and draws tentative conclusions on factors that affect the degree of success achieved.

Canada's System of Government

Canada's system of responsible government sets the framework within which the federal government develops its budgets and manages spending. Canada is a federal state and a constitutional monarchy with its system of government based on the British Westminster parliamentary model (Forsey, 2005). Canada's constitution is both written and unwritten. The written part is set out in the Constitution Act (Constitution Act, 1982). The unwritten part consists of a series of precedents that have been established over time (Jaconelli, 1999).

The federal legislature consists of the two Houses of Parliament: the House of Commons and the Senate. Members of the House of Commons are elected and colloquially referred to as MPs (Member of Parliament). There are presently 308 seats in the House of Commons each of which corresponds to a geographical electoral district (or riding). Each district elects an MP in a single-member plurality (or first-past-the-post) voting system. Electoral districts are established on the combined basis of population, community of interest and of identity, and "a manageable geographic size for districts in sparsely populated, rural or northern regions" and are reviewed every 10 years by independent commissions (Department of Justice, 1985). The Senate, described by Canada's first prime minister (PM) as a place of "sober second thought" has 105 seats that the constitution distributed in equal numbers to Canada's principal geographic regions and to which senators are appointed by the government of the day and serve until the age of 75.[1]

Two of the principal tenets of responsible government are the confidence convention and ministerial responsibility.[2] The former requires that the government, consisting of the PM and the cabinet, must be able to retain the confidence of the House of Commons and must resign or face a general election if it cannot. Ministerial responsibility has two aspects: Ministers are collectively responsible for carrying out the government's decisions, and ministers are individually responsible for the powers that they have been assigned as well as for those of the portfolio of departments and agencies assigned to them by the PM. This convention ensures that a designated minister can be held responsible for the exercise of powers granted by Parliament whether those powers are exercised by the ministers themselves or by departmental officials in their name. Ministers are accountable under this convention because they have the power to take corrective action (i.e., they are answerable rather than accountable for mistakes that have been made by their departmental officials, but they are accountable for taking action to make sure the mistake is corrected and does not happen again). Parliament has no power to terminate a minister—only the PM can appoint or remove a minister from office. Parliament's role in holding the government to account rests largely on the pressure it can bring to bear in shaming and blaming individual ministers or, ultimately, in voting no confidence in the government as a whole.

The confidence convention has a particular significance for the budgetary process because, by another aspect of constitutional convention, all money bills are considered to be matters of confidence. In practice, that means that the government will have lost the confidence of the House of Commons if it loses a vote on the government's motion to accept its budget, on budget implementation legislation or on legislation dealing with revenue or spending.

Canada has a professional, nonpartisan public service within which appointments and promotions are based on merit. The public service is organized into departments and agencies, each of which is led by a minister (i.e., a member of cabinet appointed by the PM) and a deputy minister. Although deputy ministers are appointed by the PM also, there is a strong tradition, verging on a constitutional convention, that these appointments are nonpartisan. In that sense, deputy ministers form part of the permanent public service and are usually appointed from the ranks of the permanent public service. In the few cases where deputy head appointments have been made from outside those ranks, these individuals have been appointed predominantly for the expertise or experience they bring, not for political considerations.

Participants in the Budget Process

Among the many institutions (organizations) and individuals that actually or potentially play into the budgetary process, the principal players are the legislature, the executive (i.e., the PM and cabinet), and central budget agencies. The House of Commons plays the primary role in the budget process because that is where the annual budget is tabled, where money bills must originate, and where confidence can be lost if the government loses a vote on any of these. Standing committees of both houses review detailed information on departmental[3] spending plans before legislation seeking spending authority is tabled. Three standing committees in the House of Commons play additional and more specific roles in the budgetary process roles: the Committee on Finance in budgetary policy and in prebudget consultation; the Public Accounts Committee in reviewing reports of the Auditor General and in focusing on the government's accountability for federal spending more generally; and the Committee on Government Operations and Estimates, a relatively new committee that has the potential to examine the form and content of the government's spending estimates and the parliamentary processes that these documents support.

Within the political executive, the PM and the minister of finance are solely responsible and accountable for final decisions on the government's annual budget (Office of the Auditor General Canada, 2006, p. 10; Treasury Board of Canada Secretariat (TBS), 1995, p. 11). With the possible exception of the Planning and Priorities Committee that existed in the late 1960s and early 1970s under PM Trudeau, Canada has not had a cabinet committee with specific responsibility for budget matters (French, 1980). Although the Treasury Board[4] has an expenditure management role, it has not played a significant allocation role in the budget process since the mid-1970s (Kelly & Lindquist, 2003). The PM is supported by two organizations. The PM's Office (PMO) provides political advice to the PM with staff that are appointed by the PM and do not form part of the public service. The Privy Council Office (PCO) is a department of government whose staff are public servants, led by the Clerk of the Privy Council who also functions as head of the public service. One of PCO's primary roles is to facilitate the smooth and effective operations of the cabinet and its committees.

While a number of specific cabinet committees are responsible for considering and making recommendations on policy, in recent times, they have not been given any funds to allocate and so carry out their policy development role without any fiscal constraint.[5] As Savoie (1999) notes, the cabinet has evolved from a decision-making body under Pearson "to a focus group under Trudeau in his later years in office and also under both Mulroney and Chrétien" (p. 3). He repeats the comment in a more recent publication (Savoie, 2008).

Three central agencies constitute the principal public service players in the budgetary process: the PCO; the Department of Finance (DoF); and the TBS. Together, with the PMO, these three institutions constitute a central budget office network in which they work together of a necessity born of the different information each possesses and the different roles each plays. But they do so in an environment that is contentious and competitive and each owes its primary allegiance to the deputy and political heads they support.

Key Steps in the Budget Process

This section provides an overview of the key steps in the budgetary process, starting with new policy development, moving through budget decision making and spending approval to reporting and accountability. Canada's fiscal year runs from April 1st to March 31st and the annual budget is typically tabled in late February/early March although there is neither a constitutional or legislative timing requirement nor indeed any requirement to table a budget annually.

DEVELOPING NEW POLICY

The government signals its policy priorities in its election platform, in the most recent Speech from the Throne, and in subsequent speeches and statements. More specific policy priorities are often contained in the mandate letter that each minister receives from the PM on appointment, although these are not made public. In most cases, a single minister and his or her department take the lead in developing a particular policy in a process that involves consultation with relevant experts and stakeholders. Within government, other departments that would be directly implicated in implementing a proposed policy are closely engaged in the development process. Broader internal consultation proceeds through a series of interdepartmental meetings in which the three central agencies participate and take a direct interest.

At the ministerial level, the formal instrument for seeking approval of a policy is a Memorandum to Cabinet (MC) that the lead minister signs and presents to the appropriate cabinet policy committee. That process is closely controlled by the unit within the PCO, which provides secretariat services to the committee in question.

The MOF and the president of the Treasury Board are ex officio members of all policy committees and a senior official from each of their departments attends policy committee meetings as an observer whether or not their ministers are in attendance. PCO provides a briefing note to the policy committee's chair in which it will identify issues with the policy being proposed along with recommendations to the chair on strategy for managing the meeting. Although PCO will have consulted with its sister central agencies in developing this note, this role gives it considerable influence in the policy development process, as does its role in managing committee agendas. Policy committees have no authority to approve a policy and their decisions take the form of a Committee Recommendation (CR). Those recommendations are then considered by the full cabinet, which issues a formal Record of Decision (RD).

From a budgeting perspective, two particular features of the policy development process at the ministerial level are worth noting. The first is that policy committees are not given any funds to allocate; neither is there any requirement for a source of funds to be obtained as a prerequisite to bringing an MC forward for consideration. Consequently, the process tends to produce a large number of policy recommendations that, in aggregate, significantly exceed funds that are eventually made available for allocation in the budget process. Another consequence is the lack of an incentive for a policy committee to reject any individual policy. Ministers are unlikely to risk offending a fellow committee member when they will want support for their own policy proposals. That is not to say that the policy discussion that occurs in committee is not useful in refining policies and in ensuring that they are adequately developed before being recommended. Neither does discussion take place in a fiscal vacuum as MCs are required to include implementation cost estimates. If there is any lack of discipline, it is in managing the aggregate number of policies that are brought forward and recommended rather than in the process of considering individual MCs.

The second feature is that effective approval of individual policy proposals occurs in the budget decision-making process, not in the full cabinet. That is entirely consistent with responsibility for budget decisions resting solely with the PM and the MOF, as noted earlier. Any cabinet approval that is given in advance of a budget allocation decisions being made will, in all probability, be conditional on funds being allocated. It is also possible that a policy that has been recommended by a committee may need to be reconsidered in light of the amount of funding eventually allocated. There have also been occasions when the budget has allocated a block of funds to a broad policy theme or priority, leaving specific allocation decisions to be made by the appropriate policy committee in a postbudget process.[6]

The Fiscal Framework and Budget Decision Making

A fiscal framework is the set of numbers that articulate government revenue and spending and thus the surplus or deficit for the period in question. For budget planning, the fiscal framework sets out these numbers on a policy status quo basis (i.e., the forecasts assume no change in tax rates or in cost recovery fees and that existing programs continue to operate as currently constituted). Since 1994, the Canadian government's

Table 16-1

Illustrative Fiscal Framework

| | Actual | Projection | | | | | |
	2006–2007	2007–2008	2008–2009	2009–2010	2010–2011	2011–2012	2012–2013
Budgetary revenues							
Personal income tax	110.5	113.5	121.3	127.8	135.6	143.4	152.2
Corporate income tax	37.7	41.5	37.9	38.0	39.0	39.3	38.3
Excise taxes/duties	45.3	44.5	41.8	43.2	44.4	45.9	47.5
Employment insurance premiums	16.8	16.5	16.5	17.0	17.5	18.0	18.8
Other revenues	25.6	27.9	28.3	29.3	30.1	31.2	32.3
Total budgetary revenues	236.0	243.9	245.8	255.4	266.7	277.8	288.9
Budgetary expenses							
Program expenses	188.3	198.4	207.6	217.0	225.1	233.7	242.9
Major transfers to persons							
Elderly benefits	30.3	32.0	33.6	35.1	36.7	38.5	40.5
Employment insurance benefits	4.1						

Source: Adapted from *Strong Leadership: A Better Canada (Economic Statement)*, by DoF Canada, 2007.

practice has been to provide these numbers in a fiscal update document released in the fall each year as the basis for parliamentary and public consultation.[7] Table 16-1 shows main components of the fiscal framework, taken from the October 2007 economic statement (Department of Finance Canada, 2007b).

There are three main elements to the fiscal forecasting process:

■ Finance is responsible for developing forecasts for tax revenue and major statutory program spending, all of which involve modeling based on forecasts of economic and demographic variables.

■ TBS is responsible for reviewing departmental estimates of direct program spending and establishing policy status quo levels for these programs.

■ Finance incorporates TBS's direct program spending estimates with its own forecasts and simple arithmetic yields the forecast surplus or deficit for each year addressed.

One of the more critical steps in the decision-making process is that of establishing an upper limit on the amount of incremental funds available for allocation. Fiscal flexibility, as it is termed, is the difference between the *forecast* budgetary balance and the *outcome* level that the government desires or sets as a target. For example, if the forecast budgetary balance is for a surplus of 10 billion Canadian dollars and the desired outcome is a surplus of $2 billion, then there will be $8 billion of fiscal flexibility to allocate. If the forecast was for a surplus of $1 billion and the desired outcome was a surplus of $5 billion, then the fiscal flexibility would be a negative $4 billion, there would be no flexibility to allocate, and the government would have to cut spending, increase taxes, or do both to achieve its desired budgetary balance. A deficit forecast does not necessarily mean that there will be no flexibility to allocate, as the government could set its desired outcome at a higher level of deficit than that forecast (e.g., if the forecast was for a deficit of $6 billion, the government could set its target outcome as a deficit of $8 billion, which would provide it with fiscal flexibility of $2 billion).

In order to manage the risk of missing its fiscal targets, governments since 1994 have applied a structured prudent budget planning framework, principle elements of which include using the average of a wide range of private sector forecasts of key economic variables as the basis for its fiscal forecasting and introducing prudence factors into the fiscal framework that have the effect of reducing flexibility available for allocation.[8]

Clearly, the process is neither as linear nor as simple as the previous steps suggest. There are many iterations of these steps up and down the chain of actors involved as forecasts are refined, trade-offs between new policy options are considered, and the potential to increase flexibility by cutting existing spending is examined. The principal players in this endgame are the PM, the PMO, the MOF, PCO, and the DoF. The final budgetary balance target established will be the residual result of a combination of political judgments on budget communication strategy, trade-offs between policy priorities and their affordability, sensitivity to the economic situation, the accuracy of the fiscal forecasts, and the degree of fiscal risk the government is willing to take.

Parliamentary Spending Approval

Being a winner with budgetary stakes does not mean that a department can start spending. As indicated earlier, a basic tenet of responsible government is that the government cannot spend without parliamentary approval. The House of Commons' debate on the government's budget is based on a motion "that this House approves in general the budgetary policy of the government." The vote on that motion is a matter of confidence but it does not deal with spending authority. Parliament approves spending through two types of legislation: annual supply bills, or in a specific spending provision included in other legislation. Supply legislation is the conventional means and the spending authority it confers is referred to as voted as the legislation is divided into individual votes that provide spending authority for a single fiscal year.[9] Spending authority conferred through other legislation is referred to as statutory and has generally been used to provide ongoing spending authority where the amount authorized is determined by a formula, typically based on economic or demographic variables. In effect, both Parliament and the government have relinquished any discretion to vary statutory spending without amending the legislation concerned. Unlike voted spending that is provided 1 year a time, most statutory authority continues as long as the legislation remains in force.

The annual or voted part of the parliamentary supply process proceeds on the basis of two sets of documents provided by the government. The estimates provide Parliament with information on the spending authority the government is seeking. The supply bill is the instrument through which Parliament provides that authority.

Control

The individual votes in appropriation legislation constitute the basic unit of parliamentary expenditure control. Departments must not spend more than the vote amount and it must be spent only on the purposes specified in the vote wording. In most cases, however, the vote wording is very general and departments have considerable flexibility managing spending. No parliamentary constraint flows from the considerable further spending detail provided in the estimates.

More generally, the Treasury Board's constituent legislation confers a wide range of powers that it can deploy in exercising expenditure management control. Relevant powers include those for general administrative policy; organization of the public service; financial management and accounts; the estimates; revenues from the disposition of property; and review of annual and longer term departmental expenditure plans and the determination of priorities (Department of Justice, 1985, sec. 7).

Accountability

While not perfect, there is no shortage of information that provides a basis for the public and Parliament to hold the government to account for the money it spends. The Reports on Plans and Priorities prepared by each department that form part of the estimates establish the basis for accountability, and their counterpart, Departmental Performance Reports, report on achievements. In addition, the Treasury Board publishes an annual report to Parliament on the government's overall performance (Treasury Board of Canada Secretariat, 2007a). The Auditor General releases audit reports throughout the year that provide considerable fodder for Parliament to hold the government to account.[10] Treasury Board policy also requires that departments publicly disclose their internal audit and evaluation reports (Treasury Board of Canada Secretariat, 2005).

Two parliamentary arenas provide opportunities to extract expenditure management accountability from the government: the daily question period and committee meetings. The former is highly partisan and can be viewed as a form of pre-audit. If the accusations leveled at the government stick, then there is likely to be follow-up action; if they do not, there will not be. As a number of parliamentarians have quipped "it's question period, not answer period." Although parliamentary committees provide the potential for effective accountability, a number of observers, including parliamentarians, have lamented the limited degree to which House of Commons committees realize that potential. Issues that have been identified as impediments to greater House of Commons committee effectiveness include: the lack of incentive for members to make committee work a priority (Chenier, Dewing, & Stillborn, 2005, p. 205); lack of research resources (Thomas, 1980); frequency of committee membership changes (House of Commons, 2003, min. 1845); excessive partisanship (Savoie, 2006); and the practice of limiting the time individual members have to question witnesses to 8 or 10 minutes in each rotation of speakers. While Senate committees are not perfect, their relatively lower degree of partisanship, the greater time that senators are willing and able to spend in committee, as well as the greater constancy of membership are among the factors that explain their relatively greater effectiveness.

Within government, the focus on expenditure management accountability lies predominantly with the Treasury Board and its Secretariat. In part, that plays out within the Management Accountability Framework that "sets out the Treasury Board's expectations of senior public service managers for good public service management" (Treasury Board of Canada Secretariat, 2007c).

A significantly greater focus on expenditure accountability flows from a more recent initiative that requires each department to develop a Program Activity Architecture (PAA), shown diagrammatically in Figure 16-1.

The underlying concept is simple: to link resources that have been allocated to the results they are intended to achieve. As Figure 16-1 shows, that is done at progressively

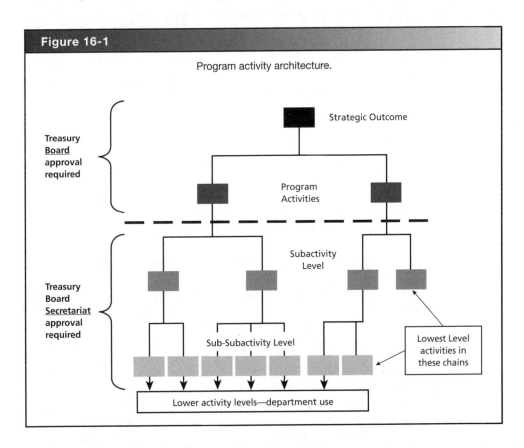

Figure 16-1

Program activity architecture.

Strategic Outcome

Treasury **Board** approval required

Program Activities

Treasury Board **Secretariat** approval required

Subactivity Level

Sub-Subactivity Level

Lowest Level activities in these chains

Lower activity levels—department use

lower levels of resource allocation, starting with the funds that have been allocated to each of a department's business lines. Within each business line, the lower levels reflect the way that departmental management has suballocated to individual managers. At the departmental level, the results articulated are expected to be well toward the outcome end of the spectrum while lower levels of the PAA will show progressively greater output characteristics. Although both TBS and departments are still gaining experience with PAAs, they have formed an essential part of the strategic reviews that the current government recently implemented and that are discussed in the next section. It is unclear, however, whether PAAs are being used to create a more specific accountability relationship between departments and the Treasury Board.

Results-Based Budgeting

In simple terms, results-based budgeting completes the budgeting cycle by feeding back information on the performance of existing programs into the budget decision-making process. There is considerable literature available on this topic,[11] and while significant progress has been made, achieving the full potential that feedback would yield has presented as much of a challenge for the Canadian government as it has for many other jurisdictions that are progressing down that road. Lee McCormack's (2008) recent publication provides a good and current account of both the progress that has been made in Canada as well as the challenges that remain. Further integration of performance information in the budget process is a specific objective of strategic reviews that are among the initiatives addressed in the next section.

Reallocation Since the Early 1990s

An Organisation for Economic Co-operation and Development (OECD) study defines reallocation as "the readjustment of expenditures in relation to the current budgetary or medium-term estimates" (Kraan & Kelly, 2005, p. 9). In budgetary terms, reallocation is usually and more pointedly understood to involve taking funds away from one element of the fiscal framework and giving it to another. For the purposes of this chapter, the focus is on reallocation that originates from central budget decision making and that can be characterized as follows.

Internal reallocation occurs where the program activities cut and those augmented by the resultant savings are all within the same department. At its simplest, decisions on this type of reallocation are made by departmental management and its results have no impact on the fiscal framework. As internal reallocation can be used to partially or completely offset the cost of new spending initiatives and so relieve pressure on the fiscal framework, it is possible for central budget decision makers to force internal allocation either by specific direction or by deliberately allocating significantly less funds than required to implement a particular budget measure. With internal reallocation, the task of managing the winners and losers falls primarily to departmental management.

Direct reallocation results from a central decision to cut the existing or planned level of funding for an identified program activity in one department in order to increase the funding levels in another department. That can be done to offset pressure to provide additional funding to an existing program activity or to offset the cost of a new spending measure. To state the obvious, in this type of reallocation the winners and losers are explicitly identified and linked, and this can create significant communication and management challenges for the government in implementing its budget, as well as for the "losing" department.

Disconnected reallocation, where the link between the activities being cut and the recipient of the resultant savings is weakened or broken, represents one technique for managing this winner/loser issue. For example, if the yield from cuts is incorporated into the fiscal framework in order to add to existing fiscal flexibility, the budgetary winners and losers are still identified but they are not individually matched. As will be seen in some of the examples that follow, it is also possible to disconnect the reallocation decisions in time, where cuts are either made in advance of new funding allocations or follow.

Taxpayer reallocation occurs when taxes are increased to provide or contribute to new spending allocations or, in the other direction, if the yield from program activity cuts is allocated to tax reductions.

Intertemporal reallocation occurs when funds are shifted between time periods. Conceptually, the reallocation winner can also be the fiscal framework generally. That can occur, for example, when the total amount of new spending allocations is less than any cuts that have been made and the fiscal framework is a reallocation winner. This represents reallocation between current and future time periods as the net increase in fiscal flexibility that results from the cut either reduces borrowing requirements or increases debt reduction, depending on the state of the fiscal framework at the time of the cuts. Either way, the result is increased flexibility in all future fiscal years because of the reduced debt interest charges relative to precut fiscal forecasts. In a sense, this type of reallocation could be considered intergenerational.

MOTIVATION FOR REALLOCATION

Why reallocate if it is so politically contentious? One answer is that it probably happens less frequently than it should for that very reason. And when it does happen, it is often with less success than its advocates hope for because political will weakens. Nonetheless, significant pressure to reallocate can originate from the following situations:[12]

- Fiscal stress – where spending needs to be cut or taxes increased in order to achieve a desired budgetary balance;
- Fiscal abundance – where fiscal performance produces budgetary balances in excess of those desired as a matter of fiscal policy;
- Excessive growth in spending – where limiting the rate of growth in government spending (or, in the extreme, reducing the size of government) becomes a political priority;
- Fiscal discipline – where fiscal flexibility is insufficient to fund new spending priorities and achieve the desired budgetary balance; and

■ Good management – where changes in program design or supporting infrastructure are needed to increase efficiency or effectiveness of delivery within
existing policies and priorities.

CANADIAN EXPERIENCE WITH REVIEW AND REALLOCATION

Pressure to reallocate has been a factor in Canadian budget making dating back to
the 1970s. The following summarizes some of the reallocation initiatives that were
launched in which review formed a specific part.

X-budgets is a term that came to be used to describe centrally driven, untargeted, and
equal percentage across-the-board cuts. One of the earlier examples in recent history
was when Prime Minister Trudeau returned from a meeting with Germany's Chancellor
Helmut Schmidt in 1978 with strengthened fiscal resolve and announced a $2 billion
cut from expenditures. The exercise was dubbed The Guns of August because so few
of Trudeau's ministers or advisors were forewarned, let alone consulted (Savoie, 1999,
p. 166). That exercise marked the start of a series of X-budgets. Motivated primarily by
fiscal stress, the general pattern was one where the central budget office officials provided advice on specific programs that could be reduced or cut but political will faded
when it came to singling out individual programs. The end result was generalized,
across-the-board cuts that were insufficient to halt increasing annual deficits. The review
component of these exercises was not particularly strong as it was focused primarily
within central budget offices with little systematic engagement of departments.[13]

Program Review, initiated in 1994 as a one-time exercise by the then newly elected
Chrétien government, is generally considered the most successful review and reallocation exercise in recent history. Primarily driven by concern over persistent and
increasing annual deficits, the exercise had the twin objectives of reducing expenditures to achieve specific deficit reduction targets and "getting government right" by
rationalizing existing programs. Implementation was coordinated from the PCO with
the DoF and TBS each playing roles. Expenditure reduction targets established by the
DoF constituted a key driver of the exercise with departments required to conduct
their own reviews, based on six program review tests.[14] A coordinating committee of
ministers, a "shadow" committee of deputy ministers, and the three central agencies
all played a challenge role. Fiscal discipline was maintained by strong support from
the PM and a clear message that any reduction to a target that had been established
for one department or agency would require concomitant increases to the cut targets
that had been set for others (Greenspon & Wilson-Smith, 1996, p. 164). A key factor
in Program Review's success was a strong political will to achieve the deficit and debt
reduction targets that were set. That political will was buttressed by widespread public
awareness of a need to eliminate persistent annual deficits that had reached a point of
criticality and so, a lack of any strong adverse reaction to the specific program cuts that
were needed. Any potential for that resolve to soften was removed when, on the heels
of the Mexican peso crisis, Moody's threatened to downgrade Canada's credit rating in
the early days of program review's implementation.[15]

Program Integrity was an initiative developed by the TBS in 1999. Its short-term objective was to address situations where inadequacies in approved funding levels created a

critical risk to the sustainability of existing programs with a focus on the health and safety of Canadians and on degradation of the government's capital infrastructure (or capital rust-out as it came to be known). The initiative's longer term objective was to restore both the capacity and credibility of TBS in its expenditure management role by gradually taking greater responsibility for the direct program spending envelope. The overall framework within which that central management and oversight function was to be developed was one of sustainable program structures and results within approved funding levels. It was to be made operational by developing a direct accountability relationship between departments and the Treasury Board. Departments would be required to identify the program results for which they were prepared to be accountable to the Treasury Board within their approved resource levels. The Treasury Board's acceptance (but not approval) of those result levels would effectively sanction what, in many cases, was expected to be a lowering of previous service delivery expectations. Within its authority, the Treasury Board would approve measures necessary to improve program delivery structures, including internal reallocations. To the extent that lower than previously expected program result levels or proposed reallocations were of a magnitude to raise policy issues, the Treasury Board would refer these issues to the appropriate policy committee who would consider the merits of additional funding as an alternative to reduced service levels.

In the first round, the TBS succeeded in extracting $1 billion in annual ongoing funding from the fiscal framework in Budget 2000 for allocation to critical program issues, somewhat to the DoF's chagrin who had not anticipated the degree to which PCO and PMO would support TBS's claim. TBS had clearly signaled in the first round that it had deferred consideration of a number of additional program integrity issues to a second round the following year. With the intervening election and the decreased political sensitivities to program integrity risks that the first year of a new mandate brought, the DoF effectively killed the Program Integrity Initiative in its second round by cutting off any further ongoing funding allocations (Kelly & Lindquist, 2003).

Departmental Assessments were introduced by PCO in 2001 as a graceful exit from program integrity with the objective of formalizing reallocation within departments. The concept was that departments with significant program integrity issues would examine less costly ways of delivering existing programs as well as opportunities for scaling back or eliminating low priority program activities and would seek the necessary approvals from the Treasury Board. Although the internal reallocation objective for Departmental Assessments was consistent with the longer term objectives that TBS had established for its Program Integrity Initiative, the initiative failed for a number of reasons:

- TBS had not had the time to develop either the capacity or the credibility that would have resulted from the longer transition planned for the Program Integrity Initiative;
- Preparation of a Departmental Assessment was voluntary and, in the absence of a sustainable program structure accountability framework, there was neither any need nor any incentive for departments to participate; and
- "Surprise" surpluses were continuing to emerge throughout the year and the prospect that held for additional funds despite the discontinuation of Program Integrity funding added to the lack of incentive for departments to take any initiative in proposing internal reallocation.

A $1 billion Exercise was launched by the government in Budget 2003 "[t]o demonstrate its commitment to reallocating spending and improving efficiency" along with a statement that it would "reallocate $1 billion from existing spending beginning in 2003–04 to fund higher government priorities" with details to be announced by the president of the Treasury Board in early May (DoF Canada, 2003, p. 177). The fiscal flexibility on which Budget 2003 allocations were based assumed that these cuts would be achieved and the Treasury Board had no option but to make these reallocations after the fact by cutting $1 billion from the direct program spending base. The exercise proved politically fraught for two primary reasons. One was the tension that was created by the DoF's seemingly unilateral action to stick the Treasury Board and its secretariat with the dirty work of finding cuts while it and its minister had managed the more rewarding task of allocating new funds. The other, in the face of continuing fiscal overperformance, was the lack of credibility that cuts were necessary to maintain fiscal framework integrity. Consequently, political will weakened and, when the results of this exercise were announced some 5 months later than promised in the budget, it was evident from the news release that much of the $1 billion that had been cut did not represent cuts to existing program activities, but constituted less politically painful reductions in unallocated funding that was part of the fiscal framework (Treasury Board of Canada Secretariat, 2003c).

Expenditure and Management Reviews were implemented in 2003 as a "broad review of expenditures and management in all departments and agencies over a 5-year cycle" with two explicit objectives:

- "[T]o make reallocation from lower to higher priorities an integral part of the way [the government] manages" (DoF Canada, 2003, p. 176); and
- "[M]ore efficient, effective and sustainable programs, increased satisfaction with levels of service, easier access to government services and reallocation from lower to higher priorities" (Treasury Board of Canada Secretariat, 2003b).

The process for this review was quite different from the Program Review in a number of respects. Although initially driven and announced by the DoF as part of the budget development process, implementation of the review was the sole responsibility of the Treasury Board and its secretariat. No fiscal targets were set and the reviews took place in an environment of continued fiscal overperformance. The reviews were conducted by Treasury Board Secretariat internal review teams in consultation with departments. These reviews made little significant progress towards the objectives that had been set and were essentially abandoned after the first cycle.

Expenditure Reviews were initiated in December 2003 through the establishment of an ad hoc Expenditure Review Committee (ERC) of cabinet chaired by the president of the Treasury Board. The news release stated that:

> The review will create a cycle of continuous management improvement and the pursuit of excellence in the public service. Resources will be reallocated from the old to the new, from the good to the better. The committee starts work tomorrow. (Treasury Board of Canada Secretariat, 2003a)

A new expenditure review secretariat was to be set up within TBS and all program spending was to be tested against a set of test questions that were essentially the same as those employed by the 1994 Program Review (Treasury Board of Canada Secretariat, 2003a).

Subsequently, Budget 2004 committed the committee to an explicit reduction target of "$3 billion in annual ongoing savings within four years" (DoF Canada, 2004, p. 54). At the same time, the ERC was made a subcommittee of the Treasury Board but the PM subsequently replaced the TB president as ERC's chair with another minister and a new unit was established within the Privy Council Office to provide secretariat support services to the committee. Despite the ERC's status as a subcommittee of the cabinet and statements by the TB president that it would report through the Treasury Board, the ERC effectively functioned as a committee in its own right. The review process proceeded by inviting ministers to propose how they might be able to achieve the nonbinding targets that the committee had established for each department.

Budget 2005 declared that the committee had identified "nearly $11 billion in savings that will be achieved over the next five years" (DoF Canada, 2005a). However, close to 90% of that total was from proposed efficiency measures rather than from eliminating or scaling back programs. Efficiency savings were to be achieved in three areas: property management (including revising accommodation standards and lower cost accommodation outside municipal cores and outsourcing); procurement (leveraging buying power by consolidating purchasing); and service delivery (one-stop points of service with savings being realized through technology-related investments and reducing overpayments in employment insurance and Canada Pension Plan programs) (DoF Canada, 2005b, p. 7).

In 2006, the newly elected conservative government reiterated the commitment to achieve those savings in its first budget (DoF Canada, 2006a, p. 171). But, in the fall of that year the government indicated that the procurement savings had been "significantly overestimated" (DoF Canada, 2006b, p. 36). By the time Budget 2007 was tabled, the government was indicating similar doubts that the full amount of savings that had been booked for Service Canada would be achieved (DoF Canada, 2007a, p. 285). Little or no communication prominence was given to whether any progress had been made on the initiative's managerial objectives. The new PM chose not to continue with an Expenditure Review Committee and the unit providing secretariat services within PCO was disbanded.

Strategic Reviews are a work in progress and represent the government's most recent review initiative that emerged from a commitment to renew the expenditure management system that the conservative government made in its first budget in 2006. Led by the president of the Treasury Board, the system was to be based on three principles: a focus on results and value for money; government programs consistent with federal responsibilities; and the elimination of programs that no longer served the purpose for which they were created (DoF Canada, 2006a, p. 54). In a speech later that year, the president of the Treasury Board, perhaps because the audience was public service executives, considerably softened that message by characterizing the overall thrust of expenditure management renewal as "focused on results—results in decision-making, results in managing and results in reporting" (Treasury Board of Canada Secretariat, 2007b). But that softening was also reflected in Budget 2007, which indicated that the new system to be announced by the president would "focus on good management and value for money" without reference to the earlier and harsher program elimination message (DoF Canada, 2007a, p. 158).

Strategic reviews have emerged as a major component of expenditure management system renewal and the Treasury Board secretariat's lead role in implementing a review of each department's spending was announced in the 2007 Budget:

> The first reviews will start this spring and the results will be reported in the 2008 budget. The Government's objective is to conduct these reviews on a four-year cycle. . .[t]he results of the reviews will be integrated into budget planning. (DoF Canada, 2007a, pp. 158–159)

Although not explicitly identified as an expenditure reduction exercise, departments in the first round of these reviews were each asked to identify 5% of their spending that they considered their lowest priority.[16] In announcing the results of the first round, Budget 2008 identified savings totalling $896 million over three years—an annual average of 2% of the spending base that was reviewed. Of the total savings, $81 million or 9% was reallocated to new spending in other departments and the remainder "reinvested" to higher priorities within the departments concerned (DoF Canada, 2008, p. 253). Budget 2009 provides a greater level of detail on the results of the second round of strategic reviews. Savings achieved through this round are stated to rise over 3 years to an annual ongoing amount of $586 million, which represents 2.3% of the total spending reviewed (DoF Canada, 2009, pp. 267–278).

While it may be premature to cast judgment on an initiative that is only midway through its cycle and in which the key players are still gaining experience, the Treasury Board secretariat in particular, a number of observations can be made. The fact that the initiative is alive and well after two rounds is positive, particularly in comparison to the shorter than intended life of some of its predecessors. It is also apparent from the second round that significant progress has been made toward the goal of integrating both the reviews and, more significantly, the Treasury Board secretariat itself, into the budget process. It would, however, be useful if the quantitative results of the reviews were presented in a manner that provided a basis for accountability on the extent to which they will have been achieved—if not in budget material, then in the estimates documents for which the Treasury Board has oversight.

Conclusions

Table 16-2 summarizes key characteristics of the initiatives previously discussed along with a somewhat subjective assessment of the degree to which each succeeded in meeting its objectives. Fiscal targets appear to be a factor in reallocation success even when an initiative is motivated by fiscal discipline rather than the relatively stronger fiscal stress. Success in achieving good management objectives is much weaker overall, but success would appear more probable when linked to a successful reallocation initiative, as was the case with Program Review.

With the DoF's singular focus on fiscal responsibilities and its influence over budget messaging, it is not surprising that review initiatives have been announced

Table 16-2

Assessment of Reallocation Initiatives

Initiative	Reallocation type	Motivation	Objectives	Fiscal target?	Degree of success
X-budgets	Disconnected	Fiscal discipline	To limit growth rate of debt	Yes	Medium
Program review (1994)	Disconnected	Fiscal stress	To reduce debt	Yes	High
		Good management	To rationalize existing programs	N/A	Medium
Program integrity (1999) short-term		Fiscal abundance; good management	To restore program integrity	N/A	High
Program integrity (1999) long-term	Internal	Fiscal discipline	TBS's responsibility for managing the direct spending envelope	N/A	Low
		Good management	To create sustainable programs within approved funding	N/A	Low
Departmental Assessments (2001)	Internal	Fiscal discipline	To manage internal reallocation	No	Low
$1 Billion Exercise (2003)	Disconnected	Fiscal discipline	To create cuts to existing program base	Yes	Medium
Expenditure & Management Reviews (2003)	Disconnected	Fiscal Discipline	To reallocate from higher to lower priorities	No	Low
		Good management	To create more efficient, effective, and sustainable programs	N/A	Low
Expenditure Reviews (2003)	Direct	Fiscal discipline	To create cuts to existing program base	Yes	Medium
Strategic Reviews	Disconnected Internal	Fiscal discipline; good management	To provide good management and value for money	No	Too early to assess.

with greater emphasis on fiscal objectives than on good management. Although the stridency of that fiscal rhetoric has a tendency to be softened over time, that initial emphasis can do little to help TBS in balancing its twin responsibilities for management and expenditure oversight. The sustained progress that TBS is making with strategic reviews coupled with the more realistic objectives they have been given hold significant promise both for meeting these objectives as well as regaining its past status in the central budget office network.

However, further research is needed to test out and further develop these tentative conclusions, based as they are on a relatively subjective assessment of the initiatives discussed. And, to do full justice to the issue, would require access to more information than is currently in the public domain.

Table 16-3					
Fiscal Framework—Policy Status Quo Basis					
	Year 1	Year 2	Year 3	Year 4	Year 5
Revenue	20.1	20.7	21.3	22.0	22.6
Spending	19.8	20.6	21.4	22.3	23.2
Surplus (deficit)	0.3	0.1	(0.1)	(0.3)	(0.5)

Note: Amounts given in millions of $.

Discussion Questions

1. Who are the key players in Canada's budget process? If you were an interest group outside the government lobbying for a budget allocation for the sector you represent, which three players would you target as your highest priority? Why?

2. Describe the main steps in the process by which a new policy moves from a priority idea in a new government's election platform to obtaining the funds needed to implement it.

3. The government, which is in the final stages of developing what is expected to be a preelection budget, has made a number of promises over the past year. It has also reiterated its commitment to "balanced or better" budgets, a commitment that it has been successful in achieving since it was elected 4 years ago. The finance department has provided the following fiscal framework in Table 16-3, forecast on a policy status quo basis (i.e., on the assumption that there is no change in existing policy or the way that programs are delivered). Implementation costs for its spending promises are estimated in Table 16-4. What are the government's options for keeping its promises?

Table 16-4					
New Spending Promises					
	Year 1	Year 2	Year 3	Year 4	Year 5
Promise 1	50.0	–	–	–	–
Promise 2	–	100.0	200.0	10.0	10.0
Promise 3	75.0	75.0	75.0	75.0	75.–
Promise 4	200.0	–	–	–	–
Promise 5	10.0	20.0	30.0	40.0	40.0
Totals	335.0	195.0	305.0	125.0	125.0

Notes: Amounts given in millions of $.

4. In a minority government situation (i.e., the opposition parties have elected more members to the House of Commons than the governing party has), what opportunities do the opposition parties have to use a budget issue to force an election?
5. The government has just won a general election with a majority in the House of Commons. A key election promise it made was to reduce the debt/GDP ratio from 35% to 25% over the next 5 years by reducing government spending. What review and reallocation approaches could be considered to do this and which one would you recommend? Would your recommendation change if the government was in a minority situation?

References

Aucoin, P., Smith, J., & Dinsdale, G. (2004). *Responsible government: Clarifying essentials, dispelling myths and exploring change.* Ottawa: Canadian Centre for Management Development.

Chenier, J. A., Dewing, M., & Stillborn, J. (2005). Does parliament care? Parliamentary committees and the estimates. In G. B. Doern (Ed.), *How Ottawa spends 2005–2006.* Montreal & Kingston: McGill-Queen's University Press.

Constitution Act. (1982). *Enacted Schedule B to the Canada Act 1982* (U.K.), 1982, c.11. Retrieved from http://laws.justice.gc.ca/en/const/10.html#anchorsc:8. Accessed April 20, 2010.

Curristine, T. (Ed.). (2007). *Performance budgeting in OECD countries.* Paris: OECD.

Department of Finance Canada. (1995). *Budget 1995 fact sheets 6: Getting government right.* Available at: http://www.fin.gc.ca/budget95/fact/FACT_6-eng.asp. Accessed April 20, 2010.

Department of Finance Canada. (2003). *The budget plan 2003.* Available at: www.fin.gc.ca/budget03/bp/bptoc-eng.asp. Accessed April 20, 2010.

Department of Finance Canada. (2004). *The budget plan 2004.* Available at: www.fin.gc.ca/budget04/bp/bptoc-eng.asp. Accessed April 20, 2010.

Department of Finance Canada. (2005a, February 23). *Budget 2005: Delivering on commitments.* Available at: http://www.fin.gc.ca/n05/2005-014-eng.asp. Accessed April 20, 2010.

Department of Finance Canada. (2005b). *Expenditure review for sound financial management.* Available at: http://www.fin.gc.ca/budget05/pdf/bkexpe.pdf. Accessed April 20, 2010.

Department of Finance Canada. (2006a). *The budget plan 2006.* Available at: http://www.fin.gc.ca/budget06/bp/bptoc-eng.asp. Accessed April 20, 2010.

Department of Finance Canada. (2006b). *The economic and fiscal update 2006.* Available at: http://www.fin.gc.ca/budtoc/2006/ec06-eng.asp. Accessed April 20, 2010.

Department of Finance Canada. (2007a). *The budget plan 2007.* Available at: http://www.budget.gc.ca/2007/plan/bptoc-eng.html. Accessed April 20, 2010.

Department of Finance Canada. (2007b, October 30). *Strong leadership: A better Canada* (economic statement). Available at: http://www.fin.gc.ca/budtoc/2007/ec07_-eng.asp. Accessed April 20, 2010.

Department of Finance Canada. (2008). *The budget plan 2008.* Available at: http://www.budget.gc.ca/2008/home-accueil-eng.html. Accessed April 20, 2010.

Department of Finance Canada. (2009). *The budget plan 2009.* Available at: http://www.fin.gc.ca/n08/09-011-eng.asp. Accessed April 20, 2010.

Department of Justice Canada. (1985). *Electoral Boundaries Readjustment Act* (R. S., 1985, c. E-3). Available at: http://laws.justice.gc.ca/en/E-3/text.html. Accessed April 20, 2010.

Doyle, S. (2007, September 10). Cabinet to review low-performing programs this fall for budget process. *The Hill Times.* Available at: www.thehilltimes.ca/page/view/.2007.september.10.civiccircles. Accessed April 20, 2010.

Department of Justice. (1985). Financial Administration Act. (R.S., 1985, c. F-10). Available at: http://laws.justice.gc.ca/en/ShowFullDoc/cs/F-11///en. Accessed April 20, 2010.

Forsey, E. A. (2005). *How Canadians govern themselves* (6th ed.). Ottawa: Library of Parliament.

French, R. D. (1980). *How Ottawa decides: Planning and industrial policy-making 1968–1980.* Toronto: J. Lorimer & Canadian Institute for Economic Policy.

Gow, D. (1973). *The progress of budgetary reform in the government of Canada.* Ottawa: Information Canada.

Greenspon, E., & Wilson-Smith, A. (1996). *Double bision: The inside story of the liberals in power.* Toronto: Doubleday Canada Ltd.

Hartle, D. G. (1978). *The expenditure budget process in the government of Canada.* Toronto: Canadian Tax Foundation.

Hartle, D. G. (1988). *The expenditure budget process of the government of Canada: A public choice-rent-seeking perspective.* Toronto: Canadian Tax Foundation.

House of Commons. (2003, May). *Informal committee meeting, evidence number 10, 7* Available at: http://parliamentarycentre.com/publications/pdf/number10.pdf. Accessed May, 2003

Jaconelli, J. (1999). The nature of constitutional convention. *Legal Studies, 19*(1), 24–46.

Joyce, M. (2009). Prudent budgeting and budgetary process effectiveness: The Canadian government's experience. *Institute for Research on Public Policy: Policy Matters Series Vol 15, no. 6.*

Joyce, P. G. (2008). Does more (or even better) information lead to better budgeting? A new perspective. *Journal of Policy Analysis and Management, 27*(4), 945–960.

Kelly, J., & Lindquist, E. A. (2003). Metamorphosis in Kafka's castle: The changing balance of power among the central budget agencies of Canada. In J. Wanna, L. Jensen, & J. de Vries (Eds.), *Controlling public expenditure: The changing roles of central budget agencies—Better guardians?* (pp. 85–105). Northhampton, MA: Edward Elgar Publishing, Inc.

Kraan, D.-J., & Kelly, J. (2005). *Reallocation: The role of budget institutions.* Paris: OECD.

Kroeger, A. (1998). The central agencies and program review. In P. Aucoin, & D. J. Savoie (Eds.), *Managing strategic change: Learning from program review.* Ottawa: Canadian Centre for Management Development.

McCormack, L. (2008). *Institutional foundations for performance budgeting: The case of the government of Canada.* Ottawa: Canadian Comprehensive Auditing Foundation.

Office of the Auditor General of Canada. (2006). *An overview of the federal government's expenditure management system.* Available at: http://www.oag-bvg.gc.ca/internet/docs/20061100ce.pdf. Accessed April 20, 2010.

Robinson, M., & Brumby, J. (2005). Does performance budgeting work? An analytical review of the empirical literature (Working paper no. 05/210). Washington, D.C.: IMF. Available at: http://www.imf.org/external/pubs/cat/longres.cfm?sk=18321.0. Accessed April 20, 2010.

Savoie, D. J. (1999). *Governing from the centre: The concentration of power in Canadian politics.* Toronto: University of Toronto Press.

Savoie, D. J. (2006). The Canadian public service has a personality. *Canadian Public Administration, 49*(3), 261–281.

Savoie, D. J. (2008). *Court government and the collapse of accountability in Canada and the United Kingdom.* Toronto: University of Toronto Press.

Thomas, P. G. (1980). Parliament and the purse strings. In H. D. Clarke (Ed.), *Parliament, policy and representation.* Toronto: Methuen.

Treasury Board of Canada Secretariat. (1995). *The expenditure management system of the government of Canada.* Available at: http://www.tbs-sct.gc.ca/pubs_pol/opepubs/TB_H/dwnld/exma-eng.rtf. Accessed April 20, 2010.

Treasury Board of Canada Secretariat. (2003a, December 16). *Government takes action to control spending.* Available at: http://www.tbs-sct.gc.ca/media/nr-cp/2003/1216-eng.asp. Accessed April 20, 2010.

Treasury Board of Canada Secretariat. (2003b, May 29). President of the Treasury Board announces expenditure and management reviews. Available at: www.tbs-sct.gc.ca/media/nr-cp/2003/0529-eng.asp. Accessed April 20, 2010.

Treasury Board of Canada Secretariat. (2003c, September 29). *President of the Treasury Board reports on reallocation.* Available at: http://www.tbs-sct.gc.ca/media/nr-cp/2003/0929-eng.asp. Accessed April 20, 2010.

Treasury Board of Canada Secretariat. (2005). *Policy on internal audit.* Available at: http://www.tbs-sct.gc.ca/pol/doc-eng.aspx?id=12340. Accessed April 20, 2010.

Treasury Board of Canada Secretariat. (2007a). *Canada's performance: The government of Canada's contribution 2006–07.* Available at: http://www.tbs-sct.gc.ca/reports-rapports/cp-rc/2006–2007/cp-rc-eng.pdf. Accessed April 20, 2010.

Treasury Board of Canada Secretariat. (2007b, May 9). *President of the Treasury Board of Canada to the APEX National Symposium.* Available at: http://www.tbs-sct.gc.ca/media/ps-dp/2007/0509-eng.asp. Accessed April 20, 2010.

Treasury Board of Canada Secretariat. (2007c). *TB management accountability framework.* Available at: http://www.tbs-sct.gc.ca/maf-crg/index-eng.asp. Accessed April 20, 2010.

Treasury Board of Canada Secretariat. (2009). *2008–09 parts I and II: Main estimates.* Available at: http://www.tbs-sct.gc.ca/est-pre/20082009/me-bd/pub/ME-001_e.pdf. Accessed April 20, 2010.

ENDNOTES

1. Allocated to each of the Maritimes, Ontario, Quebec, and Western Canada are 24 seats, with an additional six seats provided for Newfoundland and Labrador (the last province to enter confederation) and one each to the recently created territories (Northwest, Yukon, and Nunavut).

2. For an excellent exploration of Canada's parliamentary democracy, see the publication authored by Aucoin, Smith, and Dinsdale (2004), from which this summary treatment is drawn.

3. Unless otherwise qualified, the term *department* or departmental is used to refer to both departments and agencies. These are listed in schedules to the Financial Administration Act (Department of Justice, 1985).

4. The Treasury Board is the only cabinet committee established by statute (Department of Justice, 1985, sec. 5). That statute gives the Treasury Board a broad mandate to oversee expenditures and management. It is also the only committee that is empowered to make decisions without ratification by the full cabinet. It is also the only committee served by a secretariat that is not part of the Privy Council Office. All other cabinet committees are created and their membership and chair determined at the discretion of the PM.

5. For a current list of committees, see the PM's Web site (http://www.pm.gc.ca/eng/feature.asp?pageId=53, accessed April 30, 2009). At the time of writing, cabinet policy committees are those on: Social Affairs, Economic Growth and Long-term Prosperity; Foreign Affairs and Security; Environment and Energy Security; and Afghanistan.

6. Post-9/11 security and the Green Plan funding are examples.

7. The initial 1994 update was titled, A New Framework for Economic Policy. Subsequent releases were titled Economic and Fiscal Update, until 2007 and 2008 when the title was changed to Economic Statement and Economic and Fiscal Statement respectively. Copies of these and other budget documents are available electronically at http://www.fin.gc.ca/access/budinfo-eng.asp. Accessed April 20, 2010.

8. For an assessment of prudent budget planning, from the risks it has created to the effectiveness of the budgetary process and the impact of a recession-induced return to deficit budgeting, see Joyce (2008).

9. Votes for larger departments are split into an operating vote, a capital vote if capital spending is $5 million or more and a grants and contributions vote if spending on these items is $5 million or more. Smaller departments whose spending does not reach either of those $5 million thresholds have a single program expenditure vote (Treasury Board of Canada Secretariat, 2009, pp. 1–50).

10. For a list and access to these reports, see the Office of the Auditor General's Web site at http://www.oag-bvg.gc.ca/internet/English/rp_fs_e_44.html. Accessed April 20, 2010.

11. For a survey of progress in the United States, see the article by Joyce (2008). For information on progress in OECD countries see Curristine (2007). For a review of the literature, see Robinson and Brumby's IMF working paper (2005).

12. While not inconsistent with the motives identified by Kraan and Kelly (2005, pp. 9–25), the following typology relates more directly to Canadian experience and the examples described in this chapter.

13. For further information on expenditure management during this era by two authors that were directly engaged, see publications by Gow (1973) and Hartle (1978; 1988).

14. The six tests were: serving the public interest; necessity of government involvement; appropriate federal role; scope for public sector/private sector partnerships; scope for increased efficiency; and affordability (Department of Finance Canada, 1995).

15. For further information on and an assessment of program review, see Kroeger (1998).

16. Treasury Board spokesperson Pierre-Alain Bujold, as quoted in Doyle (2007).

Chapter 17

Decentralization, Budgets, and the Challenge of Intergovernmental Coordination: Lessons from Mexico[1]

Salvador Espinosa P.

Learning Objectives

- Know and understand how performance budgets improve efficiency and effectiveness in Mexico.
- Know and understand the subnational governments and their roles in promoting national priorities in Mexico.
- Know and understand how assessing performance using a System of Performance Evaluation works in Mexico.
- Know and understand the accountability and performance measures used in Mexico.

Introduction

Transforming the political and economic institutions of a country is a difficult endeavor that is usually characterized by tension and uncertainty. Mexico is experiencing these difficulties as it tries to move along the path of decentralization. The transition has not been smooth and its effects on the budget process must be carefully pondered.

The Mexican state of Oaxaca serves as an example of the struggles associated with decentralization. In 2004, Oaxaca denied the Federal Auditor's Office (*Auditoría Superior de la Federación*) access to the records documenting the use of earmarked transfers designated for social infrastructure.[2–3] These resources are part of a branch of the federal budget that has grown significantly. In principle, conditional transfers should be used to attain policy goals that the federal government considers a priority. However, due to the fact that these transfers have become one of the most important sources of subnational revenue, states and municipalities have been trying to increase their control over these funds. Their actions are partly a result of an ongoing transformation in the political system, which has impacted procedures to decide public spending allocations.

For more than 7 decades, the president made the most important decisions in terms of government expenditures and service provision in Mexico. Congress was more an extension of the executive branch of government rather than a sovereign entity. States and municipalities were administrators of federal programs rather than independent levels of government with the capacity to design and implement their own public policies. But now that those times are over and subnational governments are regaining decision-making power, problems of intergovernmental coordination are more visible.

This chapter explains the events that impacted these coordination problems and how the difficulties may affect budget reform. A budget, as we know, is what allows governments to articulate policy choices and set spending priorities. The process to decide this is rather complex, especially since it is difficult to balance economic efficiency and political feasibility. Additionally, even in the context of a favorable economic scenario, the available revenues will always be insufficient to fulfill all the needs for government services. Fiscal scarcity tends to be the norm rather than the exception.

Now, consider what happens when the number of entities participating in the negotiation of the annual budget increases. It is likely that most of them will have contrasting visions about the use that governments should give to public revenues. This means that the basic problem in the world of budgeting is not only about deciding how to allocate scarce resources among competing activities. The puzzle is to try to allocate those resources efficiently while accommodating the demands of those who have the capacity to influence the final outcomes. It is reasonable to believe that as the number of participants in the budget process increases, so does the difficulty of attaining the intended policy goals. Mexico, however, is confronting these issues.

Although the constitution establishes that Mexico is a federation comprised of 31 sovereign states and a federal district, the political system that emerged from the 1917 revolution led to a highly centralized form of government where the president dominated every stage of the decision-making process. This system was in place for almost 7 decades. In 1997, the president's party lost its majority in congress for the first time since 1929. The same party lost its first presidential election in 2000. The demise of a system that relied on the figure of the president and the emergence of other political actors made clear that many of the existing procedures were no longer operational. The need for a comprehensive reform to Mexico's public administration was unavoidable. One of the most pressing needs was a reform of the process by which annual budgets get planned, approved, and audited.

There are contrasting views on the ways to carry out the needed changes. State governors have acquired significant power and are using it to push for policies that bestow decision-making power to subnational governments. This is one of the driving forces of decentralization reform. Nonetheless, states are not the only actors seeking a more active role in decision making. The federal government has made clear that while subnational governments should have an active role in the design and implementation of public policy, they must also be part of the efforts to augment transparency and accountability. Such efforts include a plan to introduce the notion of performance to the federal budget. A performance-oriented budget allocates government revenues based on government results (outputs and outcomes) rather than the money needed to operate (inputs).

The Mexican experience raises an important question that should not be bypassed. On the one hand, we have subnational governments' quest for decision-making power. But as the case of Oaxaca illustrates, this desire may not be accompanied by efforts to promote transparency in the use of public monies. On the other hand, the federal government plans to improve spending efficiency and government accountability. Are these policy objectives conflicting? Can decentralization become an obstacle for the introduction of budget reforms aimed at making better use of scarce public revenues?

This chapter addresses these timely issues in four sections. The first section, Political Transition and Budget Reform, provides the reader with the background to understand the motivations for budget reform. It explains the evolution from a single-party to a multiparty system and the implications that this may have on the recent efforts to introduce performance-oriented budgets. The second section, Budget Reforms and Processes: Overview, reviews Mexico's budgetary legal framework, as well as the reforms that the federal government has promoted as part of its efforts to reform the existing budget institutions. The reader will observe that although subnational governments are sovereign entities with their own budgetary procedures, they receive a substantial amount of fiscal resources in the form of federal transfers. And as the 2006 Federal Budget and Fiscal Responsibility Act (*Ley Federal de Presupuesto y Responsabilidad Hacendaria*) establishes, all entities receiving federal funds are required to report details about the use of public funds through periodic performance assessments. The likely implications of these requirements are discussed in the third section of the chapter, Decentralization, Budgets, and the Challenge of Intergovernmental Coordination. The closing arguments and the issues that must be further debated are presented in the last section.

Political Transition and Budget Reform

To understand the opportunities and limitations of Mexico's budget reforms, one must situate the discussion in the context of its political transition. The postrevolutionary history of the country can be explained by a long period of hegemonic control by a single party and a more recent period of multiparty government.

The first stage, which Mexican scholars usually refer to as *Presidencialismo*, can be traced back to the beginning of the National Revolutionary Party. The leaders of the party (that would later be known as the Institutional Revolutionary Party or PRI) governed for more than 70 years with a system in which a newly elected president would automatically become head of the executive branch, head of state, and head of the political party which had power over all the states, municipalities, and the federal congress. This concentration of power led down an inevitable path of centralism that affected almost every aspect of the government's decision-making process. Centralism allowed the president to shape policy around his preferences, as long as those decisions did not affect the interests of the groups on which the PRI relied (Lehoucq, Negretto, Aparicio, Nacif, & Benton, 2008). The one-party regime was built around numerous unwritten rules that contributed to an environment of relative political stability, which had the effect of minimizing conflicts over the allocation of federal tax resources. The approval of the annual budget became more of a formality than a forum for a discussion of how to allocate scarce public funds.

Even though the constitution establishes the principle of separation of powers and congress is an autonomous entity, the PRI was able to maintain continuous control over the Chamber of Deputies and the senate. The PRI's power and the lack of visible opposition permitted the president to act as a dominant player in the setting of the budget agenda. The annual spending plan was designed by the federal secretariats, whose top officials were appointed directly the president. In most cases, the heads of such agencies negotiated and reached agreements pertaining to the budget even before the document was sent to congress for discussion or approval.

The one-party system described here had an important benefit: political stability. However, the trade-offs were significant. One of them was that decision making became very inflexible, heavily centralized, and biased towards the groups or individuals who had close ties to the party or the president. As Lehoucq and colleagues (2008) point out, "[t]he clientelistic organization of hegemonic one-party government meant that social spending benefited the urban-based, corporatist pillars of the regime" (p. 28).

Another shortcoming of the system was its inability to adapt to a changing political landscape. As local governments demands started growing and opposition parties gained voices, the foundations of the one-party system began to erode. Mexico entered into a period of democratic transformation that concluded with the loss of the PRI's dominance. In 1989, the party suffered its first defeat in a state election (in the northern state of Baja California); the loss of its majority in congress in 1997; and, finally, defeat in the 2000 presidential election.

These events forced a reallocation of power and the emergence of a multiparty system paved the way for a political transformation that introduced new participants to the decision-making arena. The rising power of state governors and the new composition of congress are perhaps two of the most important events affecting current budget negotiations.

Under the old one-party rule, governors were seen as local political administrators acting on behalf of the president. A system of incentives rewarded their loyalty with the promise of a political career at the federal level; punishment for instability in their jurisdictions might be removal from office. The changes that were part of the transformation to a multiparty system have changed the role of the governor. While maintaining control over local affairs, their lobbying capacity with respect to the federal government has increased. Governors have become central players in the allocation of tax resources and have played key roles in the creation of new funds to channel federal money to their jurisdictions.

A second institutional player is congress. Since the legislative election of 1997, a political party has been unable to approve the annual budget without the support of at least another party, because, since 1997, no party has obtained a simple majority in congress.[4] This situation forces the president to negotiate his spending priorities. The power balance that resulted from the 1997 election changed the budget-setting scenario significantly, as the deputies elected for the LVII legislature[5] promoted important reductions and reallocations to the president's proposed budget. This legislature was also characterized by a significant increase in conditional transfers to states and municipalities (Sour, Ortega, & Sebastián, 2003).

Conditional transfers are financial resources that one level of government delivers to another, accompanied by a series of predetermined requirements that the recipient must fulfill. The federal budget groups most of these transfers in a fund that is commonly known as *Ramo* 33. As of 2006, about 25% of federal tax collections were allocated to this fund (Secretary of Finance and Public Credit, 2007), making it one of the pillars of the intergovernmental fiscal system.

It is worthwhile mentioning that Mexican states depend almost completely on federal transfers to provide government services and cover administrative costs. Approximately 90 cents out of every peso[6] of state revenue are from conditional transfers (*Ramo* 33) and revenue sharing (*Ramo* 28; Espinosa, 2008). These two types of federal transfers differ on an important basis: Because there are no conditions imposed on revenue sharing transfers, states have no obligation to report to the federal government how the resources are used. This is not the case with conditional transfers, as recipients are required to demonstrate that they complied with the spending guidelines set forth by congress.

The way in which states use conditional transfers lies at the core of Mexico's devolution debate. As the auditor general correctly points out, they are one of the most obscure areas in terms of transparency and accountability (González de Aragón, 2009). A timely question that budget analysts must address involves what sorts of reforms will enhance accountability among recipients of federal funds. The task is certainly not an easy one. There is an ongoing international discussion about policy measures to improve public spending efficiency,[7] yet there are significant political constraints that a devolution process like the one occurring in Mexico may impose. The emergence of new actors and the shift of power away from the president add to the complexity of the budget approval process. Though conditional transfers are growing in importance, the existing institutional setting may not be sufficient to achieve and maintain accountability among state governments. Intergovernmental coordination is crucial for both the preparation of the annual budget and the setting of multiyear goals.

What is the Mexican government doing about this? As stated previously, in 2006, congress enacted the Federal Budget and Fiscal Responsibility Act, a piece of legislation that includes the general guidelines that must be followed to maintain fiscal discipline and avoid wasteful spending. The act provides guidance for many of the issues that previously contributed to the lack of transparency in public finances, including the way in which local governments spend federal funds. The 85th article specifies that, "all resources that are allocated among federal entities, municipalities or the Federal

District are to be assessed by independent entities instances using strategic indicators of performance."[8] This clearly reflects an intention to make the budgetary system more dependent on results and less on the factors that guide the more traditional line-item budgets.[9]

This requirement poses numerous challenges in terms of implementation as it calls for the development of measures to determine whether or not a recipient of federal aid is fulfilling the conditions attached to its delivery. Despite the fact that Mexican states are autonomous entities with their own laws and governing institutions, making them part of a program to improve the quality of public spending is a timely policy issue. In countries where multiple participants with the capacity to shape policy outcomes interact, there is a clear need for effective intergovernmental coordination. But since the devil is in the details, devising effective mechanisms to increase accountability among local governments is a task that must be approached with care. Having a federal law requiring states to subject their accounts to external scrutiny is one thing. Creating an institutional framework that promotes cooperation and transparency is something else.

The transition to a multiparty system of government has added a multiplicity of actors to the budget process. Since it is unlikely that their goals and incentives will always be compatible with those of the federal government, there is always the possibility that they will behave strategically and will try to use federal transfers for the attainment of their own policy objectives. How can transparency and accountability in an intergovernmental system be achieved if participants have differing goals? How can the government ensure that the delivery of federal transfers will not undermine efforts to improve the quality of public spending in subnational governments? The close link that exists between transfers, grants, and subnational fiscal performance constitutes one of the main dilemmas of fiscal decentralization (Rodden, 2002). In order to find answers to the important questions that have been raised, it is necessary to gain a basic understanding of the workings of Mexico's budgetary process.

Budget Reforms and Processes: Overview

The course of action that the federal government follows in the preparation of its annual budget does not vary significantly with respect to countries with similar forms of government. One of the central players in the preparation and negotiation of the federal budget is the Secretariat of Finance and Public Credit, which coordinates the integration of the president's budget and provides detailed reports about likely macroeconomic scenarios that should be expected in the upcoming fiscal year. These guidelines (called *Criterios Generales de Política Económica*) are sent to the different congressional committees before the proposed budget to provide legislators with sufficient information about the economic environment and the way in which it could affect public finances.

The budget calendar establishes that the president's budget be sent to congress for discussion in September of the fiscal year. The package must contain the proposed revenue plan (known as *Ley de Ingresos*) and the budget (known as *Presupuesto de Egresos*), both of which must be approved by mid-November. It is interesting to mention that these deadlines were introduced as part of a constitutional reform enacted in 2004.

Prior to such reform, the constitutional deadline was December 31st. This situation created serious problems when the PRI lost its majority in congress because there were no provisions to establish the course of action in cases where parties could not reach an agreement before the start of the new fiscal year.

The end of presidential control over budget affairs unveiled a number of inadequacies in the budget framework and the existence of power imbalances that made budget agreements difficult to attain. The Mexican constitution vests congress with substantial powers over budget affairs. While many countries restrict the capacity of their legislatures to modify the proposal from the executive branch, the possibilities that the Mexican congress has are, in principle, unlimited (Casar Pérez, 2001). Interestingly, only the Chamber of Representatives has the capacity to make changes to the president's budget. The constitution does not give the senate this power; the senate is only able to vote on the president's revenue plan. This is one of the cases that illustrates the need to redefine the roles and responsibilities that each of the participants in the budgetary process should have.[10] As of today, this remains as one of the pending issues in the reform of the Mexican state.

In terms of budget reforms, one can affirm that the most recent reform efforts are in line with an international trend characterized by a shift from the more traditional, input-oriented budgets, to spending plans focusing on performance and results. This type of budget format includes rules and norms aimed at inducing public representatives and managers to concentrate on outcomes and outputs rather than inputs and procedures (Andrews, 2005). But while it is true that Mexico's political transition triggered many of the reform efforts that took place in recent years, redesigning the governments' administrative procedures has been ongoing since the mid-1970s.

From 1930 to 1976, the core of Mexico's budget system relied on input-oriented formats. The advantages and disadvantages of this method to classify expenditures are well documented in the literature. Although this method may enhance effectiveness in policy management and planning, governments around the world have long considered it an important element to maintain control over spending and accountability (Mikesell, 2007). In 1976, the government introduced a program-based budget format designed to enhance the efficiency of public spending. This method organizes budgets according to programs, objectives, and goals that are defined annually but that should be aligned with a long-term spending strategy that is part of the National Development Plan (Guerrero-Amparán & Valdéz-Palacio, 2000).

In a subsequent round of reforms, the Mexican government launched a program in 1995 to further the modernization of its administrative systems. The program, known as PROMAP (*Programa de Modernización Administrativa*), tried to improve public service delivery by developing a culture of results and performance. Its broad goals were not limited to the budget process, but it contained elements that influenced all the stages of the budgetary process. One of the salient elements of PROMAP was that it set the foundation for many of the reforms that the government has been implementing ever since. The Mexican government believed these changes would enhance methods to measure and assess public-sector performance (Guerrero-Amparán & López-Ortega, 2001). As the authors also explain, the programming structure that emerged from these changes included new guidelines to classify government activities, so as to better link organizational objectives, actions, and results (Guerrero-Amparán & López-Ortega, 2001). As explained later in this chapter, some of the recent efforts to redesign the intergovernmental budget system are anchored in these broad policy goals.

LEGAL FRAMEWORK

A pertinent question at this point concerns the norms that frame the preparation of the annual budget in Mexico. The cornerstone of the budgetary system is the constitution and the norms and regulations derived from it (usually referred to as *leyes secundarias*, or secondary laws). Figure 17-1 shows the legal framework for Mexico's budgetary system. The rules that regulate the budgetary process are contained in five federal acts (labeled with Roman numerals) and seven pieces of legislation that detail specific norms that ought to be followed (labeled with letters A–G). Details about the roles and responsibilities of each of the formal participants are contained in the Federal Public Administration Act (*Ley Orgánica de la Administración Pública Federal*).

The process to determine the allocation of federal funds starts with the Planning Act (*Ley de Planeación*). This document establishes that the government's goals should be

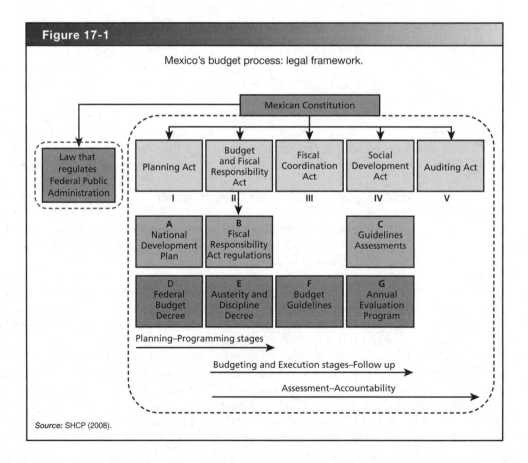

Figure 17-1

Mexico's budget process: legal framework.

Source: SHCP (2008).

set in the context of a long-term program known as National Development Plan (*Plan Nacional de Desarrollo*). This plan, which is usually outlined at the beginning of a new presidential term, articulates the actions of all government agencies and sets strategic priorities in terms of public spending.[11]

There are two pieces of legislation that have a significant role in the setting of spending goals and in the delineation of rights and responsibilities for subnational governments in terms of budget preparation and reporting. The first is the Fiscal Coordination Act (*Ley de Coordinación Fiscal*), which is the law that regulates the fiscal interactions among states, municipalities, and the federal government. This is one of the pillars of Mexico's fiscal system, as it defines the type of collaboration that different government levels may have in terms of the collection and administration of the tax bases. But one of the act's most salient features is that it determines the taxes that will be controlled by the federation, as well as the criteria to distribute the revenue to be obtained from these levies.

The second is the Federal Budget and Fiscal Responsibility Act, which provides the legal foundation to guide the planning and programming of the federal budget. This act discusses multiple issues that affect the finances of the public sector. As mentioned in a preceding section of this chapter, its relevance in terms of the intergovernmental system stems from the requirement to monitor the use that governments give to federal transfers more closely, and to develop mechanisms to assess their results.

Figure 17-1 also mentions a Social Development Act (*Ley General de Desarrollo Social*) and an Auditing Act (*Ley de Fiscalización Superior*). The former supplements the National Development Plan by setting social development objectives that the government must attain; it provides the government with guidelines to set priorities in terms of public spending. The latter delineates the responsibilities and scope of the entities in charge of the auditing stage of the budget cycle.

As is usually the case with legislation, the majority of articles contained in the laws approved by congress are broad mandates and not specific policy guidelines. The details about the procedures to be followed are contained in a series of programs, presidential decrees, rulings, and guidelines. In the case of Mexico, there are decrees with policy prescriptions in terms of public spending, austerity, and fiscal discipline, as well as multiple operating rules and guidelines in terms of budgeting and evaluation.

PERFORMANCE-ORIENTED BUDGETS AND INTERGOVERNMENTAL RELATIONS

Over the past decade, the Mexican government has taken steps to introduce a budget method that focuses more on program outcomes and policy impact. The new institutional framework is the result of a series of reforms that include changes to the way in which governments do their accounting,[12] as well as the mechanisms to evaluate the efficiency of public expenditures. These actions are aimed at increasing the quantity and quality of government services, reducing operating expenses, and maximizing the effect of government policies on the welfare of the population.

An important element of this reform process has been the introduction of a system to evaluate government performance and improve the link between public spending and program results. As explained by the Secretariat of Finances, the purpose of the System of Performance Evaluation (hereafter, I will refer to it by its Spanish acronym, SED) is to create a mechanism that facilitates the periodic evaluation of all the programs, institutions, and policies that are funded by the federal government (SHCP, 2008).

Scholars and practitioners have paid closer attention to these types of programs in recent years. In counties like Mexico, the change has been triggered by the need to get the highest benefit from a limited pool of tax resources. However, reform such as this should also be part of an international discussion about strategies to enhance government accountability.

The Mexican government has crafted a performance-based system that is comprehensive and tightly integrated (Schick, 2008). At first, one gets the impression that nothing has been left for speculation and that all the pieces of the budget puzzle fit together neatly. However, the challenges that the new multiparty system and the ongoing decentralization process entail are formidable. One of these challenges relates to the indicators that the federal government plans on using to evaluating program results and government performance.

According to the Secretariat of Finance, one of the goals of the SED is to introduce a series of objective measures to monitor performance at every stage of the budget cycle (i.e., planning, preparation, execution, evaluation, and auditing) (see Figure 17-2).

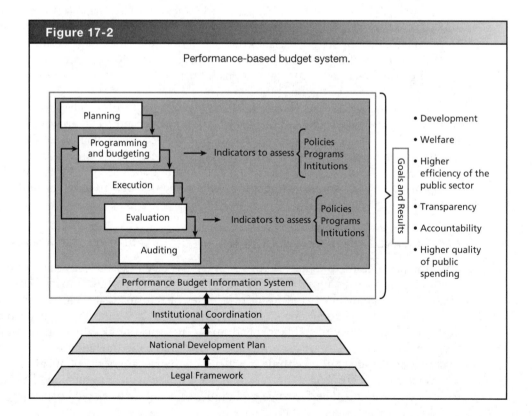

Figure 17-2

Performance-based budget system.

- Development
- Welfare
- Higher efficiency of the public sector
- Transparency
- Accountability
- Higher quality of public spending

As Figure 17-2 shows, the first set of indicators is introduced during the preparation stage of the budget. The goal is to create a benchmark that will be used to assess the accomplishments of an agency during the evaluation stage. The expectation is to have a constant flow of information about government performance that will enable managers to improve the quality of the indicators, but also to make sure that program outcomes are compatible with the National Development Plan. The expectation is that these actions will contribute to the attainment of specific results that will promote development, welfare, public management efficiency, accountability, transparency, and the quality of public spending. Each of these objectives is laudable. Due to the complexities of a multiparty, decentralizing system, it is important to identify any factors that may affect the goals of the new performance-based budget. One of the factors that emerge when an intergovernmental scenario is analyzed relates to the criteria used to select the indicators of performance that will be part of the SED. A related question is whether or not the benchmarks will be accurate measures in assessing the effectiveness of public spending among states.

It has been mentioned that conditional transfers are an important source of revenue for state governments, and that the Fiscal Responsibility Act requires any recipient of federal funds to participate in the evaluation of program results. The SED guidelines establish that the federal government formulates the initial list of indicators to carry out this task. These indicators are then presented to local governments so that they can review them, make observations, and agree upon the ones that will be used in the evaluation process. Once the final list is available, they will be reported to congress and become part of an information system that categorizes all the strategic management indicators to be used in the assessment.

This situation introduces an interesting issue for discussion. Subnational governments may agree to participate in the process to select the indicators. But what makes one think that they will actually use them as a tool to improve the efficiency of expenditure allocations? Even if the federal legislation determines that participation in the system is mandatory, some of the biggest challenges may occur during the implementation stage. In order to make results-oriented budgets a success, subnational governments must find the whole process beneficial. Reaching that point requires reforms that may need to go beyond changing the ways in which budgets are prepared. The challenges that this may entail, as well as the policies that a decentralizing country such as Mexico should consider, are the subject of the following section of the chapter.

Decentralization, Budgets, and the Challenge of Intergovernmental Coordination

Even though traditional, input-oriented budgets are widely used in many countries, there is a growing interest in the advantages of results-oriented budgets. It should be pointed out that the trend has not been to substitute one budget format with another but to add performance budgets to the procedures that were already in operation.

It is important to be careful about the complications that this coexistence may entail, particularly in the context of a decentralization process such as the one that is occurring in Mexico.

Introducing a new system to evaluate public spending in subnational governments can not only render important benefits in terms of allocation efficiency but also pose challenges that may reduce the probability of success. One of the problems that must be considered is related to the informational overload or the data shortages that may follow from the introduction of a new budget format, as it can increase the cost of generating and processing budget information (Schick, 2008). This can be particularly troublesome for countries that are going through a process of fiscal decentralization. The devolution of tax and expenditure responsibilities to subnational governments is a process that requires careful sequencing (Bahl & Martínez-Vázquez, 2006). If this is not properly done, and recipients lack an adequate institutional infrastructure, the demands that a performance-based budget could impose on local budget managers could be too cumbersome.

Mexico is already experiencing a situation like this. As already explained, the importance of conditional transfers in state finances is such that subnational governments have no choice but to participate in the performance evaluation system that the federal government has enacted. As in other countries, the new guidelines and informational demands of the new system are added to ones that are already in place.

For the Federal Secretariat of Finance, the effort is worthwhile because the system will generate new information to support decision making and to improve the connection between strategic priorities and program results. But when the issue is analyzed from the perspective of the states, there are two elements that raise concerns. The first is a financial issue. The second is a matter of willingness on the parts of local officials and budget managers to participate in the new program and accept the results of performance evaluation.

Generating indicators of performance carries administrative costs that someone must finance. These costs emerge from the need to train budget managers and from the time involved in learning a new system. It is not clear if subnational governments in Mexico can handle these costs. The introduction of a results-based system imposes informational needs that may end up creating additional burdens for local managers. If a financial sacrifice is also involved, introducing a system of performance indicators can force local governments to divert scarce tax resources from other strategic areas. However, if the generation of performance indicators is not a priority, local administrators may choose to spend the minimum amount of time fulfilling federal guidelines. State and local governments, which may benefit greatly from the new budget system, would only see it as another layer of bureaucracy to be circumnavigated in order to access much needed federal transfers. In this scenario, performance evaluation would certainly not be used to its full potential.

The willingness of local government officials and budget managers is another key element that will determine the success of the new budget system. There is much to be done in this regard, given the problems that Mexican states face in the formulation and execution stages of their budget processes (Amieva-Huerta, 2004). Successful budget reforms at the subnational level are only possible if state governors support changes to their budgetary frameworks. What is not that clear is whether they will consider these changes advantageous and make budget reform a priority.

In the process of judging the usefulness of adding a performance evaluation system to existing budgetary frameworks, the quality of the chosen indicators is an important factor. Users of this information must be convinced that the indicators are accurate measures of the various dimensions of performance. Certain elements of Mexico's SED raise questions about the quality and usefulness of the proposed indicators. An interesting feature of the SED is that the selection of performance indicators is negotiated by entities that will later be assessed. According to the SED guidelines, the Federal Ministry of Finance will craft a list of performance indicators that will be sent to participating entities for comments and approval. If consensus is achieved, the chosen indicators will become part of an information system (known by its Spanish acronym, SISED) that categorizes all the measures to be used in the assessments.

What criteria will subnational governments use when participating in the selection of performance indicators? This is an issue of great relevance that will determine the success of performance-based evaluations, especially if one takes into account the possible trade-off between the effectiveness of the indicators of performance and political negotiation. There could be a difference between the best possible measure of a phenomenon and the measure that the entity to be assessed would like to see. It is too soon to make an assertion such as this because the selection of the measures to be included in the SISED has just been completed.[13] However, in the opinion of some local government officials, one of the obvious shortcomings is that most of the indices to be included in the system will not be sufficient to evaluate the true impact of a program.[14]

There is a final challenge involved for countries immersed in a political transition. It is the issue of political liability and accountability. Mexican governors have been acquiring significant power since the demise of the one-party system. Consequently, their capacity to make spending allocation decisions has increased as well. The SED provides detailed information about the objectives and advantages of performance-based budgets. It also makes clear that all entities receiving federal funds must participate in the evaluations. However, several questions remain: What will happen when the recipient of those funds does not perform as expected? Who is held liable if the goals of a program are not met or if the indicators show deficient performance?

Performance indicators not only facilitate the monitoring of spending outcomes, but they also draw attention to low-performing entities and increase public scrutiny. Establishing adequate avenues of political accountability is highly desirable but difficult to attain. Interestingly, the SED does not specify what measures would be taken if transfer recipients do not meet performance expectations. For this reason, agreements between the federal government and subnational governments, as well as clearly defined penalties, are necessary conditions for the success of a performance-based budget system. Political commitments play a large role in determining the effectiveness of fiscal institutions (Schick, 2004). The challenge is to find ways to move in that direction.

Cooperation does not occur automatically. It is the result of a comprehensive process of institutional reform that goes beyond the mere introduction of additional budget procedures. The need for this type of reform can be better understood if the problem is analyzed using a principal-agent framework. This analytic tool is used when public spending involves delegation from one participant in the decision-making process to another (von Hagen, 2005). Although a large number of studies focus on the link between voters and elected officials, the principal-agent framework can also be helpful to explain interactions between subnational governments and the federal government.

Consider the federal government as the principal and each of the 31 states as the agents. The principal entrusts the agents with tax resources (i.e., the funds from *Ramo* 33) to carry out a series of predetermined policy goals (i.e., the objectives that are contained in the National Development Plan). In its simplest form, the framework suggests that if proper constraints are not in place, the agents will be tempted to use part of the money they receive to attain their own policy objectives. The challenge consists in designing effective institutional mechanisms to limit such behavior. As von Hagen (2007) explains, there are various strategies that can be used to limit the principal-agent problem. These strategies may include policy reforms such as the introduction of ex ante controls, constitutional limitations, or even changes to the electoral rules (von Hagen, 2007).

The status of Mexico's political transition, the current composition of congress and the difficulties among political parties as they try to reach agreements make changing the constitution or the electoral rules unlikely (at least in the short term). The idea of establishing ex ante controls appears to be a logical step in the introduction of an effective performance-based budget. The objective would be to introduce explicit rules and norms to limit potentially harmful actions of the agents in charge of the provision of government services. Governments have experimented with various forms of controls.[15] However, the benefit of adopting some of these measures should undergo careful and detailed analysis.

Conclusions

This chapter illustrates some of the challenges faced when budget reform is introduced in a decentralizing country like Mexico. This is a nation that is currently engaged in a transition from a one-party system where the president dominated budget affairs to a system where there are multiple participants, which increases the complexity of the budgetary process significantly.

The Mexican experience with the introduction of performance-oriented budgets is a good example of the difficulties that budget reform in an intergovernmental context entail. The federal government has come up with a comprehensive and well-crafted method to assess spending performance. Since subnational governments are sovereign and autonomous, one may think that it should not be mandatory for them to participate in such evaluations. However, the Fiscal Responsibility Act establishes that all entities that receive federal funds be subject to periodic performance assessments.

Performance evaluations have numerous advantages, but they also pose significant challenges. The emergence of new participants with the power to influence budget allocations raises questions about the extent to which they can make the system a failure or a success. The case of Mexico offers a good example of the problems that may arise when a government promotes budgetary reform in the context of a decentralization process.

This chapter introduced the reader to the transition that is taking place in Mexico and the reforms that have resulted from it. Even though the reform process encompasses many areas of public administration, the locus of attention is on the budget realm. By means of a new System of Performance Evaluation (SED), the federal government has engaged subnational governments (as well as its own agencies) in a process to improve the efficiency and effectiveness of public spending. Following an international trend, Mexico has introduced a series of reforms to its budget formats. Now, in addition to the traditional input-oriented budgets, agencies will incorporate performance-based standards. Federal legislation establishes that any entity that receives federal funds must comply with this requirement. It should be clear, nonetheless, that the introduction of a federal mandate is not sufficient to assure the success of the new reform. To accomplish this, it is necessary to develop incentives to make performance assessment advantageous for subnational governments. The current order of things does not seem to facilitate this. The decentralization process that is still taking place in Mexico has increased the number of participants that have the capacity to influence budget decisions, and yet, a clear definition of their rights and responsibilities remains unclear. Who should be accountable if performance objectives are not met? Will subnational governments have the financial and technical capacity to deal with the demands that the generation of performance indicators entail?

There is also another factor that may affect the outcomes of a performance budget reform negatively: an institutional infrastructure that promotes inefficient spending on the part of subnational governments. The problem arises because there is an agent (i.e., a subnational government) that receives substantial amounts from the principal (i.e., the federal government). Despite the fact that a growing percentage of federal transfers to subnational governments are of a conditional nature, the recipients of these funds will try to use them in their own benefit. The incentives to do so can only be reduced with adequate institutional constraints. Without these constraints, the delivery of federal transfers can introduce significant biases in public spending. Cases like this serve to highlight some of the dangers of decentralization.

Performance-based budgets are, in principle, a good idea. It is important to know what governments do with taxpayers' money. It is equally important to know that scarce public resources are being spent in the best possible way. Achieving this level of transparency, however, requires that reforms go beyond the introduction of new budgetary formats. The introduction of a SED in Mexico is a laudable effort. Unfortunately, the idea will not go far if the users of that information do not have the political willingness to promote transparency and accountability. In their discourses, they will likely claim that they do. But as much as one would like to believe this is true, we cannot forget that budgets are essentially political documents. Without a well-established institutional infrastructure, the spending efficiency that results-oriented budgets seek to promote will collide with the political interests of those who participate in the evaluation of those results. Addressing this remains a pending issue in Mexico's budget reform efforts.

Discussion Questions

1. As the chapter explains, the federal government in Mexico considers that performance budgets will enhance efficiency. The introduction of this budget method is occurring when the country is in a process of decentralization that incorporates new actors to the decision-making process. Do you consider decentralization to be an obstacle for the introduction of budget reforms aimed at making better use of scarce public monies? Is centralization a necessary condition to attain efficient budget allocations?

2. What are the main differences between traditional, line-item budgets and budgets that focus on performance? Do you consider that performance budgeting is a better method to allocate public monies?

3. Review the discussion about Mexico's SED. What procedures will be followed to assess performance? What are the advantages and limitations of this system?

4. For Schick (2008), Mexico has introduced a performance-based system that is comprehensive and tightly integrated. But if one takes into account the increased competition in local elections, it is not clear if subnational governments have incentives to introduce reforms that would increase their political liability and accountability. How can policymakers address this issue?

5. Using performance indicators in the budget process would facilitate the monitoring of spending outcomes and draw attention to low-performing entities. Who should be liable if the goals of a program are not met? What measures should be taken if a program is not performing as expected? At what cost?

References

Amieva-Huerta, J. (2004). *Finanzas públicas en México* [Public finances in Mexico]. Mexico City: Porrúa/INAP.

Andrews, M. (2005). Performance-based budget reform: Progress, problems, and pointers. In A. Shah, (Ed.) *Fiscal management* (pp. 31–70). Washington, DC: The World Bank.

Bahl, R., & Martínez-Vázquez, J. (2006). *Sequencing fiscal decentralization* (Policy research working paper, WPS 3914). Washington, DC: The World Bank.

Casar Pérez, M. A. (2001). *El Proceso de negociación presupuestal en el primer gobierno sin mayoría: Un estudio de caso* [Budget negotiation process in the first government without majority: A case study] (Working paper 137). Mexico, DF: CIDE.

Chamber of Deputies. (n.d.). *Leyes federales vigentes* [Current federal acts]. Available at: http://www.diputados .gob.mx/LeyesBiblio/index.htm. Accessed April 21, 2010.

Espinosa, S. (2008). *On devolution, revenue sharing and government behavior: Assessing the determinants of subnational fiscal behavior and their impact on the creation of a decentralized tax system for Mexico* (Doctoral dissertation). Bloomington, IN: Indiana University.

González de Aragón, A. (2009, February 26). *Áreas sensibles de la gestión pública* [Sensitive areas in public management]. Keynote given at the National Institute of Public Administration, Mexico D.F.

Guerrero-Amparán, J. P., & López-Ortega, M. (2001). *Manual sobre el marco jurídico del presupuesto público federal* [Handbook on the legal framework of the federal public budget]. Mexico, DF: CIDE.

Guerrero-Amparán, J. P., & Valdéz-Palacio, Y. (2000). *La clasificación económica del gasto público en México* [The economic classification of public spending in Mexico] (Manual). Mexico, DF: CIDE.

Lehoucq, F., Negretto, G., Aparicio, F., Nacif, B., & Benton, A. (2008). Policymaking in Mexico under one-party hegemony and divided Government. In E. Stein & M. Tommasi (Eds.), *Policymaking in Latin America: How politics shapes policies*. Washington, DC: Inter-American Development Bank.

Mikesell, J. (2007). *Fiscal administration: Analysis and applications for the public sector*. Fort Worth, TX: Thomson Wadsworth.

Rodden, J. (2002). The dilemma of fiscal federalism: Grants and fiscal performance around the world. *American Journal of Political Science, 46*(3), 670–687.

Schick, A. (2004). Fiscal institutions versus political will. In G. Kopits (Ed.), *Rules-based fiscal policy in emerging markets*. New York: International Monetary Fund.

Schick, A. (2008, June). *Getting performance budgeting to perform*. Paper presented at the Conference on Results-Oriented Budgets (*Presupuesto Basado en Resultados*). Mexico City, Mexico.

Secretary of Finance and Public Credit (SHCP). (2007). *Diagnóstico integral de la situación actual de las haciendas estatales y municipales* [Comprehensive diagnosis of the current situation of state and municipal finances]. Mexico, DF: SHCP.

Secretary of Finance and Public Credit (SHCP). (2008). *Sistema de evaluación del desempeño* [Performance asessment system]. Mexico, DF SHCP.

Secretary of Finance and Public Credit (SHCP). (2009). *Indicadores de desempeño de los fondos de aportaciones federales del Ramo 33* [Performance indicators for federal grant funds of Ramo 33]. Mexico, DF: Author; Secretary of Expenditures, Unit of Policy and Budgetary Control.

Shah, A. (Ed.) (2007a). *Budgeting and budgetary institutions*. Washington, DC: The World Bank.

Shah, A. (Ed.) (2007b). *Participatory budgeting*. Washington, DC: The World Bank.

Sour, L., Ortega, I., & Sebastián, S. S. (2003). *Política prespuestaria durante la transición a la democracia en México: 1997–2003* [Budget policy during the transition to democracy in Mexico: 1997–2003] (Working paper). Mexico, DF: CIDE.

Supreme Court of the Nation. (2006, December 1). *Controversia constitucional 42/2004. Sentencia Ejecutoria de Pleno* [Constitutional controversy 42/2004. House final judgement]. Mexico, DF.

von Hagen, J. (2005). Budgeting institutions and public spending. In A. Shah, (Ed.), *Fiscal management*. Washington, DC: The World Bank.

von Hagen, J. (2007). Budgeting institutions for better fiscal performance. In A. Shah, (Ed.), *Budgeting and budgetary institutions*. Washington, DC: The World Bank.

ENDNOTES

1. My gratitude to Laura Sour, Mounah Abdel-Samad, Javier Luna, and Stefani Espinosa for their comments and advice.

2. Earmarked transfers are fiscal resources that one level of government delivers to another on the condition that they will be used on specific programs or policies (also known as conditional transfers). In Mexico, the majority of conditional transfers are grouped in the federal budget Branch 33 (*Ramo 33*). Another core component of the intergovernmental transfer system are unconditional transfers called *participaciones federales*. These funds, which are grouped in Branch 28 of the federal budget, are formula-based allocations that do not impose any type of conditions on states and municipalities.

3. Details about the constitutional controversy and the resolution of the Mexico Supreme Court can be found on Suprema Corte de Justicia de la Nación (2006, December 1).

4. Although there are various political parties represented in congress, there are three parties that control the majority of seats in the Chamber of Deputies and the senate: the Institutional Revolutionary Party (PRI), the National Action Party (PAN), and the Democratic Revolutionary Party (PRD).

5. Mexico has a bicameral legislative system. The members of the Chamber of Representatives are elected for periods of 3 years without the possibility to be reelected for a consecutive period. The members of the Chamber of Senators are elected for 6-year terms, also without the possibility of reelection for a consecutive term.

6. The Mexican peso is the currency for the country. As of May 2009, the exchange rate with respect to the US dollar was Mx$13.5 = US$1.

7. Interested readers can review the books that comprise the Public Sector Governance and Accountability Series published by The World Bank. The volumes that discuss budget reforms are *Participatory Budgeting* (Shah, 2007b) and *Budgeting and Budgetary Institutions* (Shah, 2007a).

8. The acts and regulations mentioned in this chapter are available in Spanish on the Chamber of Deputies website (http://www.diputados.gob.mx/LeyesBiblio/index.htm). Accessed May 2009.

9. As Mikesell explains, in this type of budget the focus is on the resources (e.g., labor, equipment, or supplies) that governments must purchase to be able to respond to the demand for services (Mikesell, 2007, p. 42)

10. Although the discussion of those reforms is beyond the scope of this chapter, it is important to mention issues such as the assignment of a veto power to the executive branch and the lack of multiannual budget.

11. The reader should take into account that the Mexican president is elected for a period of 6 years without the possibility to be reelected. This situation implies that scope of the National Development Plan will usually be 6 years.

12. Congress approved a General Accounting Act (*Ley General de Contabilidad*) in December 2008 in an attempt to have homogeneous accounting standards in all government agencies and levels of government.

13. The final list of performance indicators was completed on December 2008. States are expected to incorporate them to their own budget processes over the course of fiscal year 2009. See SHCP (2009).

14. The names of the interviewees are not disclosed as they were not authorized to give an opinion.

15. Interested readers may want to review experiences such as the one of the European Union with deficit targets or that of the United States with balanced-budget rules.

Chapter 18

Federal Budgeting in the United States

Marvin Phaup and Charlotte Kirschner[1]

Learning Objectives

- Understand the complexities of US federal budgeting including the distinctive environment and institutions in which the system functions.
- Understand recent aggregate financial outcomes of the US budget process, including the long-term outlook.
- Understand several notable conceptual features of the US budget.

Introduction

Understanding public budgeting as practiced in a particular country requires a vision of the essential features of its budget process and some knowledge of the operating details of the system. Accordingly, this chapter introduces US federal budgeting from two perspectives. The first is a broad discussion of the interplay among environmental factors, budgetary institutions, and budgetary outcomes. The second examines more closely a few notable conceptual features of the US budget, including use of a modified cash basis of accounting, absence of a capital budget, limited coverage of the federal budget, use and effects of trust fund accounts, and efforts to move toward performance budgeting.

US Federal Budgeting: Environment, Institutions, and Aggregate Outcomes

Public budget processes, documents, and decisions are shaped by the social and political setting in which the activity takes place. For the United States, environmental factors include the multiple uses and users of budget information, the constitutional separation of powers between the executive and legislative branches, and the federalist structure of government. Those influences help explain some of the budget's most evident characteristics: the detailed contents and volume of US budget documents, the complexity of the budget formulation process (including multiple versions of the budget), and the relatively small size of the federal budget compared with some other countries.

BUDGETING IN THE US POLITICAL ENVIRONMENT

In the United States, as in most democracies, there are many users of budget information: policy makers, administrators, and the public. Each has somewhat different information needs. Policy makers making future plans need to know the amount of usable resources expected to be available along with projected uses under current and alternative policies. Administrators charged with executing budget decisions look to the budget documents for detailed guidance. The media, if not individual members of the public, need to be able to monitor the decisions of elected officials, so constituents may hold them accountable. Multiple users and user needs increase the volume of information that is required in the budget. US budget documents may lead the world in total weight, number of pages, and detail.

The significant role of the Congress in budget formulation greatly increases the complexity of the US budget process because it doubles the number of institutional framers and requires coordination between different branches of government. For example, there are multiple proposed budgets: the president's initial and modified proposals (the latter is the midsession review); and the congressional budget resolution, with or without adjustment for effects of economic changes, supplemental appropriations, and other budget year legislation. The president's initial budget proposal may have the strongest claim to the title of the budget because of its detail and inclusion of budget actuals for the most recently completed fiscal year.

Finally, the federalist structure of government in the United States is one factor that affects the size of the national government's budget as a share of the national economy, especially in comparison to unitary governments. That is, many functions of government financed at the national level in other countries, including primary and secondary education, criminal justice, and transportation, are assigned primarily to state and local governments. In the United States, most resources supporting those activities appear in the budgets of subnational jurisdictions rather than in the federal budget, except to the extent that the federal government provides financial assistance to those entities. Nor are the budgets of state and local governments easily consolidated into a single national budget because the federal and state accounting rules are not uniform, and fiscal years differ across jurisdictions. Only two states and about 6% of local governments have fiscal years that align with the federal government's fiscal year (US Census Bureau, 2006, p. 3.17).

THE US BUDGET: INSTITUTIONS AND RULES

The US budget process has an annual cycle. The fiscal year runs from October 1st to September 30th, chosen to permit a new Congress, whose term begins in January, to complete its work before the fiscal year begins. Fiscal years are numbered according to the calendar year of the January included in the fiscal year. That is, fiscal year 2011 runs from October 1, 2010 through September 30, 2011. Throughout the budget cycle, the primary emphasis of decision makers is on the single budget year under consideration, even though congressional and presidential budget documents project annual aggregate budget numbers 5 or 10 years out. Those projections are based on the budget agency's forecast of economic developments and specified assumptions about enactment of proposed policies and the continuation of expiring legislation.

As shown in Table 18-1, the formal budget process begins when the president transmits the administration's budget proposal to Congress. During the term of a sitting president, the Office of Management and Budget (OMB) begins developing the budget in the late summer. The president normally transmits the budget to Congress in early February. However, the first budget of a president taking office in January may be delayed several months to enable the new administration to develop a budget based on its own priorities. For example, President Obama submitted a budget blueprint on February 26, 2009, but delayed release of a detailed budget until May. In any case, the dates shown in Table 18-1 are set in law but there is no penalty for noncompliance, and they are frequently missed.

The president's budget is an expression of the administration's fiscal plan for the budget year and beyond. But because of its extraordinary detail, it is also a reference document. To that end, the US Government Printing Office provides both paper and electronic copies of the five volumes and the five supporting documents for public use. The *Appendix* includes measures of the projected use of authority to enter into obligations

Table 18-1	
US Budget Calendar	
Between the 1st Monday in January and the 1st Monday in February	The president transmits the budget.
6 weeks later	Congressional committees report budget plans and estimates to Budget Committees.
April 15th	Action to be completed on congressional budget resolution.
June 15th	Action on reconciliation (changes in authorizing legislation required to conform actual spending with the fiscal limits set in the budget resolution) completed.
June 30th	Action on appropriations completed by Congress.
July 15th	The president transmits midsession review of the budget submitted earlier in the year, with revised estimates of revenues, outlays, and deficits for the current and proposed budget years.
October 1st	The fiscal year begins.

Source: Office of Management and Budget. (2010). *Analytical Perspectives: Budget of the United States Government, Fiscal Year 2011*. Washington, D.C.: Author, p. 116.

(budget authority) and gross and net outlays by *individual budget account* for the most recent completed budget year (actuals), the current year (estimates), and budget year (proposed). Another volume, *Analytical Perspectives*, includes extensive discussions and tabulations of data for such topics as federal credit activity and insurance by program, tax expenditures, capital spending, budget concepts, and analyses of policy areas that cut across program lines.

At about the same time that OMB is preparing the president's budget, the Congressional Budget Office (CBO) is developing its forecast for the economy and baseline projection for the budget on the assumption that current policy is maintained for the projection period. This baseline—the administration prepares a similar one—is central to the development of a budget proposal because it provides policy makers with a path for future budgets if policy is left unchanged. It thus enables policy makers to focus on a limited number of policy changes to address unanticipated developments and changed priorities. The current policy baseline also supports the objective of maintaining a stable set of policies that enable constituents to develop and realize their own budget and financial plans.

In support of the Congressional budget resolution, the CBO uses its baseline and economic forecast to reestimate the budgetary and economic effects of the president's proposals. During this same period, Congressional Budget Committees solicit the budget plans of the authorizing and tax committees.[2] Based on the CBO forecast and the estimated effects of planned policy changes, the budget resolution that emerges in each house consists of ceilings on budget authority and outlays for various budget functions (e.g., agriculture, defense, and commerce and housing credit). Differences in the budget resolutions passed by the two houses must be resolved in Conference, a meeting of senior members of both House and Senate budget committees. The joint resolution adopted by the Conference is then submitted for adoption by both houses. However, in 4 of the past 9 fiscal years, Congress failed to adopt budget resolutions (Joyce, 2009). In those years, each house operated as though its own budget resolution had been adopted. This was usually accomplished through the passage of a "deeming resolution" or other provision in legislation that provides for the enforcement of maximum budgeted amounts for the budget cycle.[3]

The Congressional budget resolution is not enacted into law, which would require the signature of the president, but rather is embedded in the rules of procedure for the two houses of Congress. The congressional budget plan omits much of the program level detail found in the president's budget and instead aims to set aggregate limits for subsequently enacted legislation.

Once a resolution has been agreed to by both the House and the Senate (or a deeming resolution has been enacted), the ceilings on outlays and the floors on revenues are enforced through rules of procedure. Specifically, a point of order, a formal assertion that a rule of procedure is being violated, may be raised against consideration of legislation that would violate the budget resolution. However, Congress retains the flexibility inherent in controlling its own rules. In the House, a motion to suspend the rules and take up the offending legislation requires only a majority vote. In the Senate, three-fifths of the members must agree.

The Congress may use the process of reconciliation to adjust projected mandatory spending or revenues to those levels specified in the budget resolution (Schick). The House and Senate budget resolutions each include separate reconciliation instructions for authorizing or financing committees to report legislation that changes current law. The instructions do not specify how the budgetary changes are to be realized as that would threaten the division of responsibility between the budget committees and the other committees. When more than one committee is required to propose amendments to legislation by reconciliation, the budget committees consolidate the changes into an omnibus reconciliation bill. As a result, reconciliation usually produces large, complex bills. Reconciliation bills amend existing statutes and hence must be signed into law by the president, or a veto must be overridden.

Eventually, the presidential and congressional budgets are forged into an enacted budget, along with features found in neither. The enacted budget is adopted piece-meal through discrete pieces of authorizing and appropriations legislation. Over the last 3 decades, the Congress has been able to adopt all the required appropriations bills before the beginning of the fiscal year in only a few years (Lee, Johnson, & Joyce, 2008). To avoid a shutdown of the government, they have usually agreed to pass continuing resolutions that provide minimal stopgap funding for a portion of the fiscal year. In any case, legislation must be passed by the Congress and signed by the president unless, as rarely happens, both houses of the Congress can consistently override the president's opposition with a vote of two-thirds of the members present in both houses. This shared authority, combined with unexpected events during the legislative process, means that the enacted budget almost always differs from both the president's initial budget proposal and the congressional resolution.

The enacted budget for the US government is not the subject of any single report in part because it is enacted through many separate pieces of legislation including supplemental appropriations and other legislative action throughout the fiscal year. In addition, the fiscal outcome of budget decisions depends to a high degree on the performance of the economy and the public's demand for federal services. The "final" budget for any fiscal year consists of the body of law, including appropriations, effective during the period. The fiscal outcome of that final budget is reported in the "actual" budget numbers included in the president's proposed budgets for the next fiscal year.

AGGREGATE RESULTS

The effectiveness of the US budget process is difficult to assess because the process is intended to be neutral with respect to budget outcomes. Nonetheless, expressions of dissatisfaction with the federal budget process are widespread. Some of the most common criticisms are that the process is too complicated and therefore too hard to understand (Rubin, 2007), the budget is rarely completed on time (Meyers, 1997), spending and taxes are too high, the allocation of resources is inconsistent with maximizing public welfare, deficits are too big (Joyce, 2008), and current policy cannot be sustained indefinitely because of a long-term imbalance between projected revenues and spending (Congressional Budget Office, 2009). Space and time limits rule out any possibility of evaluating all those criticisms. Instead, we simply report some results of current budget processes and practices and leave assessment to readers and others.

Outlays, Revenues, and the Deficit

As shown in Figure 18-1, outlays remained within a fairly narrow range of 18–21% of GDP over the period 1998–2008. Stability in outlays in periods when the economy is performing well is consistent with the proposition that budget decisions are mostly made at the margins of current policy. This results in a high degree of program and budget continuity and stability. Revenues as a share of GDP declined in part because of the income tax reductions enacted during this period. That decline combined with a small increase in outlays turned the surpluses at the beginning of the period into deficits that averaged about 2% of GDP over the last 5 years.

The 2008–2009 global recession triggered declines in revenues and countercyclical increases in outlays for most countries. For the United States, the 2009 federal deficit reached a record US$1.4 trillion—close to 10% of GDP, with little improvement expected for 2010 (see Table 18-2). Most of the increase in the deficit was due to efforts to stimulate the economy through increased federal spending, including federal purchases of financial assets that are likely to produce future cash inflows. However, deficits are expected to remain above 4% of GDP for the next 3 years and under current policy would begin to rise again through the remainder of the 10-year projection period.

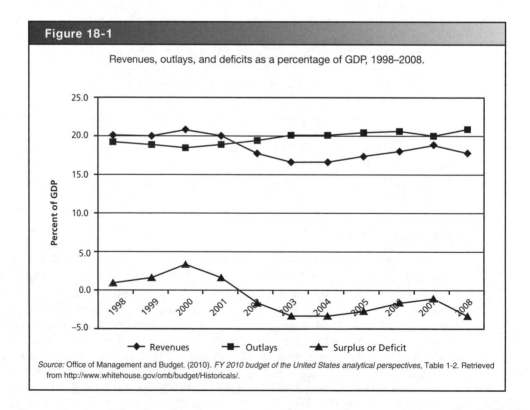

Figure 18-1

Revenues, outlays, and deficits as a percentage of GDP, 1998–2008.

Source: Office of Management and Budget. (2010). *FY 2010 budget of the United States analytical perspectives*, Table 1-2. Retrieved from http://www.whitehouse.gov/omb/budget/Historicals/.

Table 18-2

Congressional Budget Office Projections of Revenues, Outlays, and the Deficit, March 2010			
	Revenues	**Outlays**	**Deficit**
	Billions of U.S. Dollars	Billions of U.S. Dollars	Percentage of GDP
2009 (actuals)	2,105	3,518	9.9%
2010	2,176	3,545	9.4%
2011	2,673	3,668	6.6%
2012	2,967	3,609	4.1%
2013	3,221	3,746	3.1%
2014	3,469	3,931	2.6%
2015	3,629	4,101	2.6%
2016	3,818	4,331	2.7%
2017	4,000	4,521	2.6%
2018	4,174	4,708	2.6%
2019	4,355	4,996	3.0%
2020	4,567	5,251	3.0%
Total 2011–2015	15,598	19,055	3.2%
Total 2011–2020	36,872	42,862	3.2%

Source: Congressional Budget Office. (2010). *Comparison of projected revenues, outlays, and deficits in CBO's March 2010 baseline and CBO's estimate of the president's budget* Available at: http://www.cbo.gov/budget/budproj.shtml. Accessed May 5, 2010.

Deficits may distort taxpayers' views about the current cost of government because they shift those costs to future taxpayers. In times of economic crisis, however, the costs of fiscal inaction from lost output and income may be so severe that lawmakers are willing to risk a substantial increase in future tax burdens. The case for big deficits is that future taxpayers will be better off than current ones, in part because of today's spending, and hence they will be better able to bear those costs. An alternative view is that the predominance of deficits over surpluses, or a structural deficit, in recent decades is the result of the inability of the current budget process to discipline federal spending. That inability, it is argued, is imposing excessive and unfair tax burdens on future taxpayers.

Composition of Outlays and Receipts

The last year before the recession began to have a major effect on the budget was fiscal year 2007. Taking that year as representative of the basic structure of the US budget, Figure 18-2 indicates that nearly 60% of federal noninterest outlays are consumed by three activities: national defense, Social Security (old age pensions, support for the disabled, and minor survivors of deceased parents), and Medicare (health insurance for those of retirement age). The 2010 health care legislation, enacted too late to be included in this analysis, did not reduce the dominant importance of the Big Three.

The largest share of federal spending is accounted for by mandatory programs that provide benefits to all who qualify on the basis of age—primarily Social Security and

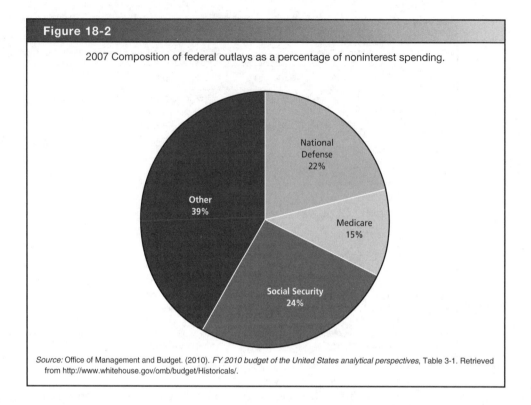

Figure 18-2

2007 Composition of federal outlays as a percentage of noninterest spending.

National Defense 22%

Other 39%

Medicare 15%

Social Security 24%

Source: Office of Management and Budget. (2010). *FY 2010 budget of the United States analytical perspectives*, Table 3-1. Retrieved from http://www.whitehouse.gov/omb/budget/Historicals/.

Medicare. Projected growth in these programs poses a threat to the long-term viability of current policies. Specifically, retirement of the baby boomers (the large cohort born just after World War II), and the rapid increase in the cost of medical care are projected to increase the cost of those two programs to the point that they consume all federal revenues by about 2075 (see Figure 18-3). Maintaining the current level of services in the face of such growth would result in either massive structural deficits or tax rates that are regarded as politically infeasible.

Mandatory spending can be limited through changes in authorizing legislation that specifies eligibility and benefits. The difficulty is that doing so requires a long-term planning perspective. People have been encouraged to incorporate the benefits of those social insurance programs into their lifetime saving and retirement plans and decisions. Having promoted reliance on promised benefits, it would be difficult for elected officials to terminate or significantly reduce benefits, especially for those who are retired or approaching retirement and have few means of reversing the effects of their past decisions.

On the revenue side, the general fund of the Treasury is financed primarily through the personal income tax (see Figure 18-4). Payroll taxes are the second largest source of income but those collections are earmarked for social insurance programs, most notably Social Security and Medicare. The share of revenues accounted for by payroll

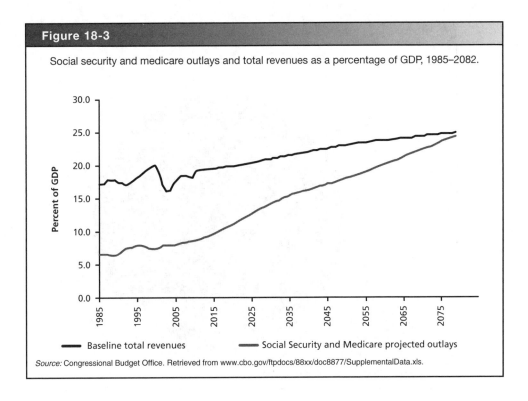

Figure 18-3

Social security and medicare outlays and total revenues as a percentage of GDP, 1985–2082.

Source: Congressional Budget Office. Retrieved from www.cbo.gov/ftpdocs/88xx/doc8877/SupplementalData.xls.

taxes has been increasing in the past several decades. This trend is widely regarded as undesirable because payroll taxes are regressive; they are levied at flat rates per dollar of wages and Social Security taxes are subject to a wage cap. Payroll taxes are also disincentives to employment and work. However, the prospects for shifting more of the burden to broader-based taxes are not favorable because of long-standing opposition to general fund financing for those programs, which are often described as earned, or at least prepaid through payroll taxes.

Some Notable Conceptual Features of the US Budget

The US budget has a number of features that may distinguish it from the budgets of other countries. Here we focus on a few elements that have been the subject of some controversy in recent years: cash-basis of accounting, with some (accrual) exceptions; the absence of a capital budget; the scope of activities included in the budget; the use and misuse of so-called trust funds; and the US experience with performance budgeting. Other interesting features of US budgeting not included here for lack of space but treated elsewhere (see "Where to Find More Information about the US Federal Budget and Finances" at the end of this chapter) include: the effects of the congressional committee structure on the budget process; the historic evolution of budget

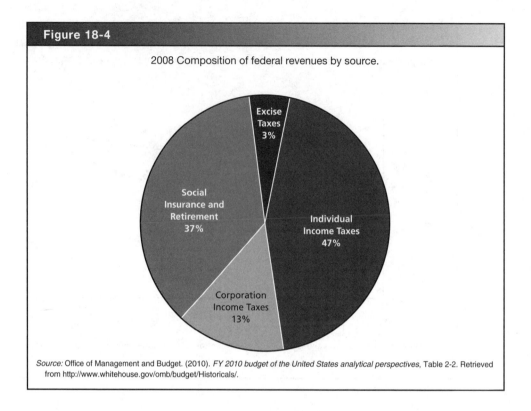

Figure 18-4

2008 Composition of federal revenues by source.

Excise Taxes 3%

Social Insurance and Retirement 37%

Individual Income Taxes 47%

Corporation Income Taxes 13%

Source: Office of Management and Budget. (2010). *FY 2010 budget of the United States analytical perspectives,* Table 2-2. Retrieved from http://www.whitehouse.gov/omb/budget/Historicals/.

institutions; and, the American experience with various budget rules such as pay as you go (PAYGO) and the use of sequestration to enforce deficit targets.

CASH-BASIS OF ACCOUNTING

The budget of the US government *largely* uses a cash basis of accounting to measure revenues and outlays. For most transactions and activities, resource inflows are recognized when cash is received by the government from outside entities while uses of resources or costs are recognized when cash flows to nonfederal recipients. Thus, revenues are dollar amounts expected or actually collected (depending on whether the budget is for future planned or past recorded events) in the fiscal year.

Not all cash that is received or paid out is recorded as revenues or outlays, however. Following universal practices, cash that is borrowed to cover fiscal shortfalls and net repayments of existing debt from budget surpluses are not counted as revenues or outlays. Otherwise, the budget would always be balanced because measured deficits could be eliminated by borrowing, and surpluses disposed of by repaying debt. Cash flows associated with issues and repayment of federal debt and other means of financing deficits or disposing of surpluses are included in the budget, but "below the (deficit) line" in the means of financing the deficit (see Table 18-3). The measured budget deficit is thereby insulated from those transactions, which finance rather than effect a deficit or surplus.

Table 18-3		
Components of the Budget Deficit and Its Financing, Fiscal Year 2008		
		In billions of US dollars
Revenues		2524
Gross Outlays	−3316	
Offsetting Collections	333	
Net Outlays		−2983
Deficit (−)/Surplus (+)		−459
Means of Financing the Deficit:		
Increase in Treasury Operating Balance (largely in support of Central Bank operations)		−296
Net Disbursements of Credit Financing Accounts		−33
Other Factors which Provided Net Cash		20
Total Requirement to Borrow From the Public		768

Note: Signs are operators rather than indicating positive or negative numbers.

Source: Office of Management and Budget, *Budget of the United States Government: Fiscal Year 2010*, 2009.

In addition, cash flows that arise from the sale of goods and services by government entities are recorded as offsetting collections and netted against gross outlays. Thus, if a government account incurs outlays to acquire resources which it transforms and resells; its outlays are reported net of offsetting collections from sales in the budget period. The accounting is cash basis, but the amounts are reported net rather than gross. This treatment is also followed by other countries and is consistent with the use of the budget as a measure of the size of government defined in terms of its exercise of the sovereign power to tax. Commercial production and sales do not directly involve the power to compel payment. Hence, they are shown as the net loss from the activity in the period, or the amount that imposes a burden on taxpayers (see Table 18-3).

Budget Authority (BA) Accounting

The US federal budget also includes a subaccounting system for expenditures that meet the commonly understood definition of accrual: It recognizes the use of resources when the government enters into obligations that are likely to lead to an outflow of resources. This subsystem tracks the granting of budget authority through appropriations and the use of this authority by executive branch agencies and other federal entities. Prior to the 1960s, when discretionary programs accounted for the lion's share of federal spending, budgeting was largely about the provision of annual discretionary budget authority under the jurisdiction of the Appropriations Committees (Schick, 2007). As mandatory or direct spending—payments to all those who are eligible to receive benefit—has grown as a share of total outlays, discretionary appropriations have become less effective in controlling aggregate spending. Although direct spending legislation provides permanent BA for those programs and benefit terms can be changed, discrete control of entitlement spending is weaker than for discretionary programs.

The cash-basis and BA accounting systems are linked in the budget through the concept of "spend-out rates." Budget authority is converted to outlays through an estimate of the rate at which new obligations are liquidated. For many programs, BA provided in one year will not lead to outlays until the next or subsequent years. For example, the homeland security grants obligated to state and local governments in one year require current year BA, but spend out over several years. Thus, outlays in any single budget year may result from current year or prior year budget authority.

Estimated spend-out rates are essential to developing outlay estimates for discretionary programs. Higher spend-out rates lead to larger near-term budget outlay costs per dollar of budget authority. For that reason, program advocates who prefer smaller up-front cost estimates also prefer slower spend-out rates. Advocates, therefore, sometimes challenge the spend-out rates used in budget formulation by arguing that current estimated rates are too high.

The Deferred Payments Exception

A major exception to the US budget's cash basis of accounting applies to transactions that result in foreseeable future cash flows between the federal government and nonfederal entities. Examples include interest accrued but not yet paid on federal debt held by the public, payments to be made by the government under lease-purchase agreements, and federal direct loans and loan guarantees. In those cases, the government recognizes the expected net value of future payments in budget outlays in the year the payment accrues (interest on the public debt) or in the year that the agreement is made (lease-purchase), or when the direct or guaranteed loan is disbursed to the borrower (federal credit). Those treatments are consistent with a core principle of federal budgeting in the United States: the full cost of a transaction should be recognized up front, when the decision is made to incur it.

The simplest of these cases involves interest on the outstanding debt. At the end of the fiscal year, the budget recognizes the amount of interest accrued on the debt which has not yet been paid. Recognition is accomplished by the transfer of the accrued sum from the general fund of the Treasury to an account in the means of financing section of the budget. This latter component is included in "Other" means of financing the deficit shown in Table 18-3. Payments from above-the-deficit-line accounts to below-the-line accounts are included in aggregate outlays and the deficit. Consequently, all interest costs incurred in a fiscal year are recognized in that year even if they are not paid. Because the transfer is intragovernmental, it does not increase the federal borrowing requirement, even though it increases the budget deficit. Thus, an increase in the balance of the interest payable account is a means of financing the deficit other than borrowing from the public. When the government subsequently pays the interest to the holder of the debt, the outlay is charged to the below-the-line account where it has no effect on above-the-line budget outlays or the deficit, even though it increases the borrowing requirement.

Amounts to be paid by the government under lease-purchase agreements are treated similarly to accrued interest. When the government agrees to acquire ownership of a durable asset through a series of lease payments, the budget recognizes the present value of the lease payments with a transfer to a below-the-line lease account. Over time that account earns interest on its balance from the Treasury, so that resources in the account are just sufficient to meet all of the government's future lease payment obligations. This long-term equality between the assets of the lease account and its obligations (zero net position) illustrates the condition to be met for the creation of below-the-line accounts. The activity financed from the account should not impose any cost on the government beyond those costs recognized in payments from above-the-line accounts. This condition ensures that means of financing accounts do not provide opportunities for moving federal costs outside the budget.

Accrual recognition of the cost of lease-purchase agreements was adopted to accelerate the recognition of the cost of lease-purchases and to facilitate cost comparisons with outright cash purchases. Under a pure cash-basis of accounting, the initial cost of acquiring an asset under a lease-purchase agreement is the first-year lease payment. In contrast, the first-year cost of an outright cash purchase is the full sale price. This disparity in upfront costs created an accounting incentive to acquire assets through lease-purchase, even in cases where the present value of the lease payments were significantly higher than the upfront cash purchase price.

In the past, a similar lack of comparability confounded the choice between federal direct loans and guaranteed loans. Under pure cash-basis accounting, the outlay cost of a direct loan in the year of disbursement is the full amount of the loan. Repayments in future years, counted as offsetting collections, were recognized only in the out-year budgets when received. By contrast, federal guarantees of loans advanced by private lenders had an initial fiscal year cost of zero. Worse yet, in cases where the government collected upfront fees for its credit guarantee, the budget recorded those fees as offsetting collections. Those collections were recorded as reducing the deficit, even if the fees were less than the expected cost to the government from a default on a guaranteed loan. This budgetary accounting created bias against direct loans and in favor of loan guarantees.

The Federal Credit Reform Act of 1990 (FCRA) adopted a form of accrual budgetary accounting to increase the comparability of budget costs for direct loans, guarantees, and for grants. It also permitted the cost of credit to be shown up front by recognizing the expected long-term costs from defaults and interest subsidies when loans are disbursed. Cost recognition is accomplished in the same manner as for accrued interest and lease-purchase payables: through a payment from an above-the-line program account to a below-the-line means of financing account. Subsequent cash flows from those loans leave budget outlays unaffected because the funds are credited or charged to the financing accounts. Periodic reestimates of initial credit subsidies or costs trigger payments between the program and financing accounts to rebalance the financing accounts to a net position of zero. Those rebalancing payments are counted as either budget outlays or offsetting collections depending on the direction of the cash flows.

These examples illustrate instances in which pure cash-basis accounting is inconsistent with up front recognition of costs, but they also show how a cash-basis accounting systems can accommodate accrual measures. By monetizing the accrual with a cash outlay to a below-the-line account, cash-basis recognition is triggered. And because the means of financing is an essential component of the cash-basis budget, funds flowing into or out of the below-the-line accounts are tracked and reconciled with the borrowing requirements of the government.

No Capital Budget

US budgetary accounting does not differentiate expenditures for long-lived capital goods, such as structures or equipment, from expenditures for current period expenses. Outlays for the full amount spent in both categories are recognized when they occur. No offset is credited for the out-year value and service potential of durable assets. This is not an oversight. Both the 1967 President's Commission on Budget Concepts and the 1999 President's Commission to Study Capital Budgeting recommended against adopting a capital budget for the federal government.

Two arguments make up most of the case against capital budgeting, or deferred recognition of costs of durable assets over their expected lives. The first is that cash-basis accounting for durable investment goods is necessary to recognize costs up front when the irrevocable decision is made to incur costs. The second is that the category of durable investments is much broader than physical structures and equipment. It includes government spending for human capital such as education, training, and health; investments in public goods such as clean air and water; and enduring benefits of peace and security from military deterrence and fighting wars. The breadth of federal expenditures that might be categorized as capital investment presents the budgetary accounting system with a dilemma. Either spread the recognition of the cost of all investments, which would be a substantial share of the total budget, over their expected lives or risk creating a bias in favor of bricks and mortar and hardware over human and environmental capital. Put differently, the line separating the acquisition of structures, property, and equipment from other durable assets is so fuzzy that it would be difficult to prevent all spending from being classified as capital.

Comprehensiveness: What Should Be on Budget and Where?

A fundamental concept of the US budget is that it should be comprehensive of federal activities. Activities that are federal encompass those conducted by entities that are owned, controlled by, or are a part of the federal government; or, private entities that are performing functions of the federal government. Although this principle seems clear on its face, there are numerous different ways of including activities in the budget.

Amtrak, an intercity passenger rail line, owned by the federal government, provides a convenient example because it is currently outside the budget so that its outlays and receipts are not included in the federal budget aggregates. However, the cost of Amtrak to the government is included in budget outlays and the deficit because the government provides cash subsidies to the railroad for both capital and operating expenditures. This accounting measures the cost of federal activities, but it does not measure accurately the size of the government's role in the economy.

One alternative to the current treatment would be to bring Amtrak on budget in the same manner as federally owned electric power generation and transmission entities. In that case, Amtrak's outlays for personnel, equipment, and supplies would be included in federal gross outlays and offset by collections from sales of services. This would more accurately depict the size of the government's economic footprint, but it could diminish the visibility of the government's cost of this activity. That is because federal subsidies for Amtrak would no longer be shown as affecting budget outlays when they were paid to the rail line because the transfer would be purely intragovernmental—from one on budget account to another. The subsidies therefore would appear in budget outlays only as the funds were paid by Amtrak along with all other revenues to nonfederal suppliers.

Another alternative for bringing Amtrak into the budget would be to do so below the deficit line. In that case, federal subsidy payments would be included in budget outlays when they were paid to the railroad. But, in that case, Amtrak's outlays and collections would not be included in aggregate federal outlays and offsetting collections. During the current financial crisis, the government has taken over several failed financial institutions, and faces the possibility of becoming the controlling owner of others. Fannie Mae and Freddie Mac, formerly privately owned, federally sponsored mortgage-finance institutions, for example, have failed and been taken over by the government. The concept of budget comprehensiveness implies that these entities should be on budget. But there are at least three possibilities for doing so. The first is to follow the Amtrak example and leave them outside the budget and record the cost to the government in outlays as these are paid to protect investors in Fannie Mae and Freddie Mac securities from loss. The second is to bring them on budget above the deficit line. This would substantially increase the volume of federal gross outlays and offsetting collections because all the financial transactions of the two enterprises would be treated as federal. But, under that arrangement, federal costs of ownership would not be recognized in net outlays when those are paid to the enterprises because they would be intragovernmental transfers that cancel one another in the budget totals. The third is to bring these enterprises on budget and below-the-line. In that case, the gross cash flows of Fannie Mae and Freddie Mac would be recorded in the budget, but they would not inflate gross outlays and offsetting collections. In addition, the costs of accumulated losses of the enterprises could be recognized in outlays as paid along with the losses on new financial transactions. The Congressional Budget Office has effectively adopted option three, but the Bush administration elected the Amtrak approach. President Obama has deferred a decision pending further study.

Trust Funds

The US budget is notable for its use of "trust fund" accounts. Other countries may use functionally equivalent accounts, but use of the term "trust" is rare. A trust fund is an above-the-line budget account that is credited with taxes and intragovernmental payments earmarked for spending on designated purposes, such as Social Security (Old Age, Survivor, and Disability Insurance) benefits and federal employees' defined benefit pensions (Civil Service Retirement and Disability). Trust fund outlays to nonfederal entities are recorded as federal outlays that add to the deficit when paid.

A budget trust fund is not a genuine trust. The government is under no legal obligation to manage the assets of the fund solely in the interests of beneficiaries. Nor would beneficiaries have a legally enforceable claim to fund balances if the law that defines eligibility and benefits were changed or repealed.

Trust fund programs use the trust language and accounting to suggest owner-ship and entitlement to benefits, which make it difficult for congress to significantly reduce program benefits or to repeal the authorizing law. Thus, trust fund programs are funded with taxes or other payments that, under current law, are obligated to be spent on the earmarked purpose. Fund balances are "invested" in Treasury IOUs and earn interest. The largest trust funds have "trustees" who are responsible for issuing reports on the financial condition of the fund and its ability to pay future obligations. In the case of Social Security, the payment of earmarked payroll taxes during the working years creates an expectation of benefits to be received in retirement. In addition, the Social Security Administration periodically sends current "participants" a statement of projected future benefits based on an assumption of continued work and earnings in covered employment.

Federal civil service defined benefit pension plans are similarly financed by employee and employer contributions. The associated pension benefits are described to prospective and current employees as deferred compensation. Projected annuities are similarly reported periodically to employees, despite the well-established legal principle that employees have no enforceable claim to benefits, if the law under which benefits are paid is changed. As a counterweight to the lack of enforceable claims, political orga-nizations have formed over the years for the purpose of guarding both Social Security and federal employee retirement benefits.

The language and structure of trust funds have been used to enhance the reli-ability of benefits by making them *politically* enforceable. We leave to others whether a legally enforceable claim is more or less reliable than a politically enforceable one. Nonetheless, the current budgetary treatment of Social Security and federal civilian defined benefit pensions appears to be based on a strong assumption about the likeli-hood that future benefits will be paid. Specifically, the accounting for both programs in the budget is consistent with the assumption that no future benefits will be paid under these programs. Except for a technical distinction between on-budget receipts, outlays, and deficit and off-budget (Social Security and the US Postal Service) receipts, outlays, and deficit (which are then combined into the consolidated or unified aggregates) current accounting treats earmarked receipts as if they were general revenues whose collection imposes no obligation on the government. Accordingly, those earmarked taxes reduce the total budget deficit dollar for dollar. As shown in Figure 18-5, the current excess of earmarked Social Security receipts reduced the total budget deficit substantially. Moreover, no recognition is afforded the shortfall between projected earmarked Social Security collections and the long-term inflow required to fully fund existing benefit commitments in the current measure of the debt or the deficit.

The current budget accounting for Social Security has prompted some members of the Congress to argue that the current cash surpluses for Social Security (see Figure 18-5) are masking the true underlying federal deficit. Legislation subsequently directed that budget officials move the Social Security surpluses "off-budget." The budget agencies complied with this requirement by reporting two deficits (on budget and off budget) which they combine and report as a single unified budget deficit. It is not entirely clear that this display improves the transparency of the change in the federal fiscal position.

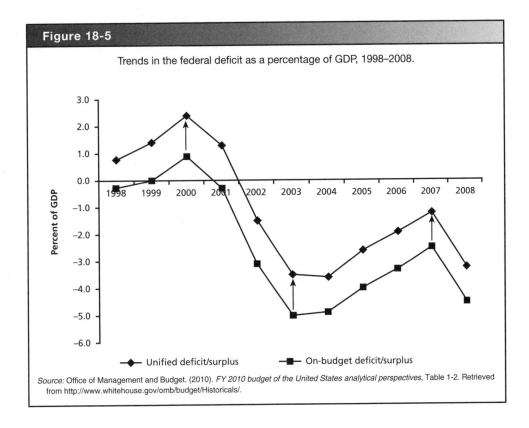

Figure 18-5

Trends in the federal deficit as a percentage of GDP, 1998–2008.

Source: Office of Management and Budget. (2010). *FY 2010 budget of the United States analytical perspectives*, Table 1-2. Retrieved from http://www.whitehouse.gov/omb/budget/Historicals/.

Performance Budgeting

For at least a century, US policy makers—including President Taft in 1912—have aimed to improve government performance by integrating information about results with budget decisions to provide resources to particular uses (Lee, Johnson, & Joyce, 2008). While the names applied to those efforts have varied and include Planning, Programming, and Budgeting (PPB); Zero-Based Budgeting; Reinventing Government; Management by Objectives; National Performance Review; Performance-Based Budgeting; and the Program Assessment Rating Tool (PART), the objective has remained the same: to increase the effectiveness and efficiency of government operations by linking the provision of budgetary resources with expected and actual results from the use of those resources. We refer to these efforts as performance budgeting.

This reform movement appeared in many countries from long-standing dissatisfaction with the process referred to pejoratively as "input budgeting" (Robinson, & Brumby, 2005). Under that approach, budgeting is regarded primarily as an exercise in providing resources to agencies and programs with little explicit attention afforded by policy makers or managers to intended objectives. Closely related concerns prompted a change in the name of the US Bureau of the Budget, Executive Office of the President to the Office of Management and Budget in 1970.

The key statutory force in ongoing US efforts to improve the operating performance of federal agencies is the Government Performance and Results Act of 1993 (GPRA). The GPRA requires agencies to identify specific and measurable goals, and to collect data on outputs and outcomes that can be used to assess their performance against those objectives.

In abstract, GPRA and the concept of performance budgeting seems elementally sound. Government programs are enacted to accomplish socially desirable purposes: reduce unemployment and poverty, improve health, raise educational achievement, assure cleaner air and water, deter crime, enforce the law, and promote peace. Efforts at achieving those objectives consume valuable resources. Matching the incremental provision of resources with the expected effects from their use is a necessary step in obtaining maximum benefit from scarce inputs.

The promise of GPRA, however, has proved elusive. One key obstacle appears to be an inability to estimate the effect of a contemplated change in budgetary resources on desired outcomes. Employment, income, education, environmental quality, antisocial behavior, and international conflict all have many causes outside the direct control of government. In order to estimate the expected contribution of government to a particular outcome, the behavior and contribution of other causal factors must be projected to estimate how the target variable would behave in the absence of the government's policy. Even with the hindsight of historical data and extensive understanding of the underlying processes, that is a tall order. To attempt to do so prospectively for a one-year budget cycle strains the limits of credibility.

The practical fallback from the impossible ideal is to use past performance to infer the future effect of incremental change in budgeted resources. Those inferences, however, lack the narrow confidence bounds necessary to persuade budget makers to move completely away from a focus on inputs.

Agency and program managers also have strong incentives to adopt objectives that are within their reach as well as their ability to measure. Thus identified performance goals often seem to be only distantly related to the high-minded goals of the underlying policy. And, where the agencies' programs have a relatively small or unknown effect on policy goals, the agency may track and report the target indicator, without adopting it as a performance objective.

As a consequence, performance budgeting in the United States has evolved into a requirement to include more information on policy goals, the related behavior of the economy and federal agencies in the budget documents. For example, the Federal Housing Administration's performance and accountability report for 2009 leads with the national goal of increasing the homeownership rate (US Department of Housing and Urban Development, 2009). In support of this objective, the agency tracks and reports home ownership rates in aggregate, as well as for minority households, households with income below the median, and central city households. Its own performance goals, however, are stated in terms of the number of households or the share of home buyers assisted by the program. It is of course impossible to determine the extent to which an agency's GPRA goals are simply a forecast of what is expected to happen in the coming fiscal year (perhaps with a downward adjustment to increase the chances of success) rather than a projection of the effects of all other forces plus a marginal increment from the agency's own efforts.

Extreme views of both input budgeting ("Here's the money; don't spend a penny more") and performance budgeting ("Another x billion dollars buys a y percent reduction in the poverty rate") are caricatures. Little evidence exists that either model has been observed in practice. Those charged with appropriating public funds have traditionally been concerned with what the public or other ruling authority was getting for its money. Performance budgeting nonetheless may have a valuable legacy. It has formalized the inclusion of information in the budget about agency activities and social conditions that motivate the use of resources.

Conclusions

Public budgeting is the process by which societies make decisions about the allocation of existing resources between public and private uses, across various public uses, and between present and future uses. At its core, federal budgeting in the United States has much in common with public budgeting in the rest of the world. In its details, however, it appears to be on the high end of the complexity spectrum.

Federal budgets and budgeting in the United States mirror the range, complexity, and dynamism of the society and the economy. Because the United States is such a large and diverse country and because budget decisions involve many policy makers addressing a variety of programs and instruments, its budget processes and documents are complex. Moreover, changes in the political, social, and economic environment mandate continuous adjustments in budgets and budgeting.

Change is also a complicating factor that US budgeting shares with other countries. This necessity manifests itself in adjustments to the current budget plan throughout the fiscal year and in changes in budget rules and processes. And periodically, budget concepts need to be revised to accommodate changes in policy instruments, information technology, and understanding of how information may be more effectively communicated to decision makers within and outside the government. Beyond the obscuring details, efforts to improve well-being by incorporating the best available information into resource allocation decisions are a unifying goal for all budget systems.

Discussion Questions

1. Are current US fiscal policies sustainable over the long term? Or do they require a shift toward reduced spending and higher taxes? What evidence would you offer in support of your conclusion? What, if anything, should the United States do about its current fiscal policies? Do you think modifying current policies can be accomplished without a crisis? How important is the existence of mandatory or direct spending programs for the aged to your answer?

2. Is the US federal budget predictable in the sense that constituents can form long-term life cycle plans with confidence that government policies will deliver on past commitments? Does that predictability reduce the ability of the government to respond to economic and political threats? How would you specify the ideal balance between predictability and flexibility of budget policy?

3. One criterion that is sometimes used in evaluating the success of a budget process is the closeness of fit between the budget numbers and the actual numbers for the budget year. Is this a useful evaluation criterion? List and discuss its advantages and disadvantages.

4. At what point is a budget final? Is that when it is most useful?

5. Under current law, accrual accounting applies to federal loans and loan guarantees. Explain the mechanics of how it might be applied to government pensions and other postemployment benefits, government provision of deposit insurance, and the purchase and use of federal office buildings.

6. Is current federal budgetary accounting for federal employee pensions consistent with the budget concept that the full cost of an activity should be recognized up front when the decision is made to incur it? Develop arguments for both possibilities.

7. Why and how might you "reform" the budgetary treatment of Social Security?

8. What is the length of the planning horizon for the US budget? Is it too short, too long, or about right? Explain.

9. What should be the role of performance measures in the US federal budget process?

References

Congressional Budget Office. (2009, August). *The budget and economic outlook: An update.* Available at: www.cbo .gov/ftpdocs/105xx/doc10521/08-25-budgetUpdate.pdf. Accessed April 21, 2010.

Congressional Budget Office. (2010). *Comparison of projected revenues, outlays, and deficits in CBO's March 2010 baseline and CBO's estimate of the president's budget.* Available at: http://www.cbo.gov/budget/budproj.shtml. Accessed May 5, 2010.

Joyce, P. G. (2008). Does more (or even better) information lead to better budgeting? *Journal of Policy Analysis and Management, 27*(4), 945–975.

Joyce, P. G. (2009, April 1). Statement before the Peterson-Pew Budget Reform Commission. Copy in possession of author.

Lee, R., Johnson, R., & Joyce, P. (2008). *Public budgeting systems* (8th ed.). Sudbury, MA: Jones and Bartlett Publishers.

Meyers, R. T. (1997). Late appropriations and government shutdowns: Frequencies, causes, consequences, and remedies. *Public Budgeting & Finance, 17,* 25–38.

Office of Management and Budget. (2010). *Analytical perspectives: Budget of the United States government: Fiscal year 2011.* Washington, DC: US Government Printing Office. Available at: http://www.whitehouse .gov/omb/budget/Analytical_Perspectives/. Accessed May 6, 2010.

Office of Management and Budget. (2009). *Analytical perspectives: Budget of the United States government: Fiscal year 2010.* Washington, DC: Author. Available at: www.gpoaccess.gov/usbudget/fy10/browse .html. Accessed April 22, 2010.

Office of Management and Budget. (2009). *Updated summary tables: Budget of the United States government: Fiscal year 2010.* Washington, DC: Author. Available at: www.gpoaccess.gov/usbudget/fy10/browse .html. Accessed April 22, 2010.

Robinson, M., & Brumby, J. (2005). *Does performance budgeting work?* International Monetary Fund Working Papers (wp/05/210). Washington, DC: IMF. Available at: www.imf.org/external/pubs/ft/wp/2005/ wp05210.pdf. Accessed April 22, 2010.

Ruben, I. (2007). The great unraveling: Federal budgeting, 1998–2006. *Public Administration Review, 67*(4), 608–617.

Schick, A. (2007). *The federal budget: Politics, policy, process* (3rd ed.). Washington, D.C.: Brookings Institution.

US Census Bureau. (2006). *Government finance and employment classification manual: Covering the activities of federal, state, and local governments.* Washington, DC: Author. Available at: http://ftp2.census.gov/govs/class06/2006_classification_manual.pdf. Accessed May 5, 2010.

US Department of Housing and Urban Development. (2009). *Performance and accountability report: Fiscal year 2009.* Washington, DC: Author. Available at: http://www.hud.gov/offices/cfo/reports/2009section2.pdf. Accessed April 21, 2010.

US Senate, Committee on the Budget. (2008, May 5). *Budget bulletin: Deeming resolutions* (Issue 6). Available at: http://www.budget.senate.gov/republican/NewBB.htm#. Accessed April 21, 2010.

WHERE TO FIND MORE INFORMATION ABOUT THE US FEDERAL BUDGET AND FINANCES

Federal Websites:

Office of Management and Budget: http://www.whitehouse.gov/omb/

Congressional Budget Office: http://cbo.gov/

Government Accountability Office: http://gao.gov/

Federal Accounting Standards Advisory Board: http://www.fasab.gov/

Financial Management Service, US Treasury: www.fms.treas.gov/frsummary/index.html

Government Printing Office: http://www.gpoaccess.gov/usbudget/

Books:

Lee, R., Johnson, R., & Joyce, P. (2008). *Public budgeting systems* (8th ed.). Sudbury, MA: Jones and Bartlett Publishers.

Myers, R. T. (1994). *Strategic budgeting.* Ann Arbor, MI: University of Michigan Press.

Schick, A.(2007). *The federal budget: Politics, policy, process* (3rd ed.). Washington, D.C.: Brookings Institution Press.

ENDNOTES

1. We thank Philip G. Joyce and the editor for their valuable comments and suggestions.
2. For a discussion of the various types of congressional committees, see Schick (2007, pp. 54–57).
3. See, for example, US Senate, Committee on the Budget (2008).

Part **6**

South America

Chapter 19

Budgeting in Brazil Under the Law of Fiscal Responsibility

Christine R. Martell

Learning Objectives

- Understand the foundation of Brazil's budget system.
- Identify the budgetary actors and their roles in Brazil.
- Identify the analytic aspects of and impacts on the budgetary process in Brazil.
- Identify budgetary reform measures in Brazil.

Introduction

The five sections of this chapter present the foundation and details of public budgeting in Brazil. Section one lays the foundation for the budget system. It identifies the federal framework that guides the budget, including the constitution, the Law of Fiscal Responsibility, and Law 4.320. The next section presents the budgetary actors and the budgetary process. The third section identifies the analytic actors and processes used in the budgetary and auditing process. Section four is a discussion of the impacts of the budget arrangements on fiscal control, planning and performance management, budget rigidity, and the budget cycle. Finally, considerations for budget reform are provided.

The Foundation of the Budget System

Brazil is a federation with three levels of government: a central union, twenty-six states and a federal district, and over 5,000 municipalities; and three spheres of government: executive, legislative, and judicial branches at each level. Although each political jurisdiction is responsible for creating its own budget through the budgetary process, the budget system in Brazil is influenced heavily by the constitution of 1988, which solidified fiscal federalist arrangements; the Law of Fiscal Responsibility of 2000, which profoundly affects the rules of the public purse; and Law 4.320, the basis for public accounting practices.

THE CONSTITUTION OF 1988

The constitution of 1988 guides the budgeting process in Brazil. It formalized fiscal power sharing among the central, state, and municipal governments by realigning revenues assignments and better defining the roles, rights, and responsibilities of state and municipal governments. It also defines various tax bases, indicates the level of government responsible for collecting each tax, and establishes a system of tax sharing among the three levels of government on the basis of generation or redistribution (Villela, 1996).

In contrast to the constitutional clarity of the post-1988 tax assignments, expenditure assignments were left implicit and remain unresolved (Nazareth & Lopes Porto, 2002; TCE, 2009b). Expenditure assignments face some federal restrictions. For example, a jurisdiction cannot spend more than 60% of its current revenue on salaries. Also, the federal government establishes minimum parameters for some decentralized policies, especially concerning education and health (Mora & Varsano, 2001).

LAW OF FISCAL RESPONSIBILITY OF 2000

The Law of Fiscal Responsibility (LFR; *Lei Complementar* no. 101) was intended to create a new pattern of medium- and long-term fiscal management and to fundamentally change the fiscal regime. A unique feature of the law is its scope, applying to three levels of government as well as to the three powers (Nunes, 2007; Nunes, 2008).

The law is far-reaching. It applies to budget processes, governs certain expenditures such as personnel, limits debt, facilitates transparency, and restricts a government from contracting out in the final months before an election. The law created new responsibilities for budget administrators, who must show that they have met expenditure limits on personnel, that revenues are available for long-term expenditures, and that they are compliant with other fiscal discipline measures (Blöndal, Chiara, & Kristensen, 2003). Penalties for noncompliance take the form of administrative, fiscal, or personal sanctions.

Another feature of the law's design connects the use of fiscal resources with goals and plans to improve long-term efficiency and accountability, laid out in increasing detail through the Multiyear Plan, the Law of Budget Directives, and the Annual Budget Law. Expenditure choices are required to be consistent with the policy direction indicated by the current administration. The LFR is complex, broad, and very detail oriented. Its implementation requires a fair amount of institutional infrastructure (de Oliveira, 2000).

LAW 4.320 OF 1964

The budgets of each governmental unit must also comply with Law 4.320 of 1964, which sets the norms for budgeting and financial control (Machado & de Costa Reis, 1998). Law 4.320 establishes accounting practices for the federal, state, and municipal governments. It guides financial accounting, budgetary accounting, real assets, and the development of financial balances. In an effort to connect planning, budgeting, and control, Law 4.320 altered the budget presentation from a line-item format to a program budget format and facilitated the use of financial data.

The Budgeting Process

The federal budget process is guided by the constitution of 1988.

> The Federal Constitution provides for three independent branches of government: an executive branch headed by the President; a legislative branch consisting of the bicameral National Congress, composed of the Chamber of Deputies and the Senate; and a judicial branch consisting of the Federal Supreme Court and lower federal and state courts. (Merrill Lynch & Co., 1996, p. 14)

The president is responsible for preparing the budget and has considerable autonomy in determining the types of programs that congress can initiate. Also, the president can unilaterally alter the budget through presidential decrees, which reduce expenditures. The president can also initiate legislation, via a law of additional credit, to increase expenditures in some policy areas such as job creation and public sector salaries or can declare bills urgent to rush them through congress.

The federal budget process is rational, whereby plans, objectives, goals, and budget details are integrated (da Cruz, Junior, Glock, Herzmann, & Barbosa, 1999). The fiscal year begins January 1st and ends December 31st. The first element is for a new executive to create a 4-year multiyear plan, the *Plano Plurianual* (PPA), which identifies the administration's priorities and the means for achieving them. The PPA sets multiyear objectives and commits both the executive and legislative branches to maintaining some form of continuity over time. The PPA is formulated by the executive branch in the first year of the administration, delivered to congress by August 31st, and must be approved by congress before the end of the extant fiscal year.

The second element is the Law of Budget Directives, the *Lei de Diretrizes Orçamentárias* (LDO), which is prepared under the direction of the Ministry of Planning, Budget, and Management (MPLAN) and the Secretary of the Federal Budget (SFB; Blöndal et al., 2003; da Cruz et al., 1999). It prioritizes the goals identified in the PPA and guides the manner in which the goals of the PPA will be attained in the following budget year. Based on review of the previous year's budget and performance, the planning secretariat advances changes to the budget and submits them to the budget secretariat. The budget secretariat incorporates the recommended changes and also determines the expenditure limits for each ministry and in the aggregate. After the expenditure limits are set, the spending ministries have three weeks to provide detailed allocations to a computerized budget system. An appeal system is in place to resolve any outstanding allocation requests. The executive branch prepares the LDO by April 15th and then advances it to the legislature for approval by June 30th. Following approval, the president signs the project into law.

Finally, based on the LDO, the SFB develops the proposed budget for the following year. Between January and May, the secretary establishes the expenditure limits for each budgetary unit based on trend data. In June, each budgetary unit presents a proposed budget detailing its planned activities and mandatory expenditures. Given revenue estimates, the next step of budget preparation is to refine the spending limits and revise the budgetary units' activities and projects, including both reductions and expansions. Finally, the formalized budget proposal is submitted to congress by August 31st.

Since 1988, congress has had the constitutional authority to amend the executive draft budget, so long as any amendments are consistent with the PPA and the LDO. Resolutions determine the rules for amendments: who can submit, how many, what defines majority support, and the scope of the amendments (Tollini, 2009). A Joint Budget Commission (CMO) evaluates proposed amendments and selects, on the basis of admissibility and value, the ones it deems worthy. Amendments can be submitted individually by a member of congress or collectively by multiple members of congress who represent either regional or cross-sectoral interests. Rapporteurs of the CMO work with the permanent sectoral committees to bring sectoral amendments under review. The CMO holds public hearings with civil society and with the executive branch authorities. Ultimately, the rapporteurs' reports and the revised draft budget are discussed and voted on by the CMO. Once the CMO plenary votes, the revised draft budget is submitted to the National Congress plenary for a vote (Tollini, 2009). Congress must approve the budget before the end of the legislative session, and finally the budget is signed by the president and turned into the annual budget law, *Lei do Orçamento Anual* (LOA).

The congress is limited in how it can revise the executive draft budget (Tollini, 2009). The congress cannot modify expenditures to "personnel and social change" and must maintain total estimated revenue and expenditures. Congress has to finance any proposed amendment by cutting other programs or increasing revenue. However, congress is prohibited from reestimating revenue and creating new revenues. To circumvent the restriction, congress employs the constitutional norm of "correction of error and omissions" in effort to estimate additional revenues.

Members of congress are assisted by two advisory units, one for the Senate and one for the Chamber of Deputies. The staff is tasked with preparing analyses, studies, and technical reports; processing the technical components of the draft PPA, LDO, and LOA; conducting analysis for amendments; preparing seminars; and being available to answer questions by members of congress (Tollini, 2009).

The central budgetary institutions in Brazil are the MPLAN, which is responsible for the development of the national budget, and the Ministry of Finance (MF), which is responsible for executing the budget. Should revenues not meet expenditures during the fiscal year, the LFR triggers an impoundment of nonmandatory expenditures that applies to each governmental branch.

The Secretary of National Treasury (STN) of the MF supervises budget execution, the operation of the Integrated System of Financial Administration (SIAFI), the administration of public debt, and the consolidation of financial information. Cash management is the responsibility of the STN. All federal revenues pass through the Unique Account of the Treasury (CUT), including governmental revenues paid through banks, and all expenditures are made from the CUT (Blöndal et al., 2003).

Budgetary and accounting classification codes are coordinated so that revenues and expenditures can be cross-listed in budgeting and accounting systems, SIAFI and the Integrated System of Budgetary Data (SIDOR) respectively. The classification system—which classifies data by organizational unit, function, subfunction, program, object of expenditure, source of revenue, and nature of transaction—also serves the Governmental Financial Statistics platform. Table 19-1 displays the federal revenue sources and expenditures by approximate share of budget.

Budgeting at the federal district, state, and municipal levels of government are determined by the Constitution and each unit's organic law. The organic laws set the budget process, cycle, and actors and delineates budgetary and taxation rights and prohibitions. A typical subnational government will follow the pattern of the federal government, whereby the PPA and LDO are developed and referenced to form the LOA. Some municipal governments, however, only require the PPA and LOA. Subnational governments must demonstrate sources of revenue, both current and capital, and budget allocations, both current and capital.

Table 19-1

Brazil Federal Revenue and Expenditures, Fiscal Year 2010 Projections

Revenue sources by share of budget		Expenditures by share of budget	
Primary revenues	**49.10**	**Mandatory expenditures**	**90.03**
Administrative revenue	31.36	Debt service	43.55
Taxes	16.44	Interest payments	6.35
Social security contributions	13.83	Contingency reserve	0.27
other	1.09	Other financial expenditures	3.95
Contributions for social security	11.75	Personnel	9.74
Revenue not administered by the MF (including concessions)	5.87	Transfers to state and local governments	8.15
Other	0.13	Social security	17.13
		Other mandatory expenditures	1.08
Financial revenues	**50.90**	**Discretionary**	**9.97**
Refinanced debt	33.88	Health	2.93
Emission of bonds	10.12	Education	1.27
Credit operations	2.66	Social, urban, and utility infrastructure	1.41
Other	4.25	Welfare	0.79
		Other discretionary expenditures	3.58

Source: Adapted from Ministerio do Planejamento, Orcamento, e Gestao Projecto de Lei 2010. Available at: http://www.planejamento .gov.br/secretaria.asp?cat=50&sub=304&sec=8. Accessed April 19, 2010.

Budgetary and Auditing Analytic Processes

The Constitution mandates that fiscal control be the domain of the executive and legislative branches, and stresses the responsibility for internal and external control. Accounting units within the executive branch serve as internal control. The legislative branches, through the Tribunal of Accounts, serve as external control. The Constitution also requires each jurisdiction to administer a unified system of internal control.

Despite the constitutional mandate, the role of accounting and auditing assumed a new level of importance following passage of the LFR (Cavaleiro, 2001). The LFR elaborates on the role of accounting with an end to control results, on the attainment of goals, and on evaluation and cost control. The focus is on control of abuses of power and efficiency. The LFR established norms of public finance regarding responsible fiscal management; risk management associated with balancing public accounts; and interaction of planning, control, transparency, and responsibility.

At the federal level, the MF and the MPLAN are responsible for internal control. The Secretary of National Treasury (STN) within the MF hosts ex post budget and financial data. MPLAN hosts the federal budget ex ante, and relevant statistics.

Under the LFR, the STN is tasked with normalizing the process of registering accounts (of budget, financial, and asset data); consolidating all the balance sheets of the union; and promoting the account integration among the spheres of government by standardizing concepts, definitions, accounting rules, and processes. The LFR mandates that each jurisdiction submit budget and financial data to the STN. The data are collected monthly at the federal level and made available to the public via the Integrated System of Financial Administration (SIAFI). The LFR stipulates that budgetary practices and plans should be transparent, and to this end the PPA, LDO, LOA, and reports by the Tribunal of Accounts of the Union (TCU) are public documents. In addition to providing raw data, the SIAFI website also hosts a series of monthly summary reports.

The STN registers in SIAFI all budgetary execution realized by public administrations. SIAFI monitors budget execution and financial control, including revenues and expenditures, expenditures of earmarked funds, the terms of payments, the cash flow, carry forwards, and financial balances. The data reported on a monthly basis include the primary and nominal balance and changes in public debt for all levels of government and for the consolidated government (Blöndal et al., 2003), capturing fiscal surplus or deficit as well as the nation's net worth.

Reports, prepared and posted by the MF on a monthly or bimonthly basis, include budget execution, attainment of fiscal goals, financial operations, revenue updates, debt position, financial transactions, and execution of the PPA. The information system is also used for financing programs; controlling budget execution; processing budgetary payments, including transfers; registering receipts; producing balance sheets; reconciling data with the CUT; providing access to data and reports; monitoring compliance with the LFR; monitoring programs of the federal PPA; and auditing financial data.

On an annual basis, the STN reports to congress on the budget, including budgeted versus actual revenues and expenditures, financial transactions, and debt position. Through SIAFI, the STN tallies the budgetary positions of all jurisdictions of the nation.

Under MPLAN, the secretary of the federal budget uses SIDOR to follow and evaluate budgetary execution, adjusting for fiscal realities when necessary (da Cruz et al., 1999). SIDOR aids the MPLAN to develop budgets and monitor their execution. SIDOR and SIAFI use the same classification system, providing consistency between budgetary and accounting information, thereby easily linking the data. Based on these databases, there is a high degree of fiscal transparency (Shand et al., 2002).

Two institutions perform federal audits (Shand et al., 2002): the Tribunal of Accounts of the Union (TCU) and the Federal Secretary of Control (SFC). The TCU, the external auditor, examines accounts of all branches of government and presents them to the congress. The TCU also reviews the president's annual budget report and verifies compliance with the LFR and constitution. The TCU also has autonomy to initiate its own inquiries about operational or performance issues. The SFC reports to the controller general of the union, which reports to the office of the president. Indirect administrations, such as authorities and state-owned companies, use internal auditors that work with the SFC, as well as private sector external auditors. The SFC evaluates compliance with the goals established in the PPA; verifies that budget activity is legal, efficient, and effective; controls debt operations; and aids the TCU in external control. The SFC follows an annual cycle, producing reports from January to May and interim financial audits from June to December.

The LRF dictates that subnational jurisdictions follow a similar auditing scheme. For subnational governments, the executive branch oversees internal control and the legislative branch of each jurisdiction is responsible for external control and for legal compliance with respect to goals presented in the LDO, debt and accounts payable limits, personnel limits, debt reduction limits, distribution of resources attained from the transfer of assets, and expenditure limits. Also, the LFR specifies that the Tribunals of Accounts will, in addition to calculating the relevant limits, intervene when they are approached or when other budgetary irregularities are determined. Each subnational jurisdiction is required to submit its budgetary and financial data to SIAFI on a monthly basis.

Efforts to improve monitoring and accounting are evident across the country. In the state of Rio de Janeiro, the State Tribunal of Accounts (TCE-RJ) created a subsecretary of Auditing and Management Control of Revenue in 2003. Data show reductions in tax evasion, inappropriate use of revenue, improved monitoring, and improved systematic controls on revenue collection (TCE, 2009a; TCE, 2009b).

Impact on Budgeting

The existing budgetary process and cycle arrangements result in a number of budgetary impacts on fiscal control, planning and performance management, budget rigidity, and the budget cycle.

FISCAL CONTROL

The LFR was largely effective at establishing fiscal control in Brazil. It rekindled the importance of planning in public management by elaborating the PPA (Rezende & Cunha, 2005) and by creating a link between legislation and financial execution. The

LDO institutionalized fiscal goals and brought to light fiscal risk, contingent liabilities, and actuarial estimates of pension obligations. The LFR regulated the use of emergency reserves by the LOA, which made programming and monitoring obligatory. The LFR created an environment of much needed fiscal control and improved the alignment of budgets and demanded compliance with fiscal goals.

The existing institutional arrangements have resulted in the mandatory establishment of public sector directives, objectives, and goals; specific norms to control costs; mandatory evaluation of results for programs financed with budgetary resources; and the necessity to establish fiscal goals and indicators to evaluate more objectively (Amaral, 2003). In turn, these have resulted in greater public participation with respect to monitoring the fiscal aspects of public administration. Efforts to incorporate evaluation in the management of government has led to organizational changes; to socioeconomic development; improvements in the transparency of government; greater access to government by citizens; and a number of programs that try to integrate planning, budgeting, and management (Nader, 2005). The financial management practices are of a high standard (Blöndal et al., 2003), especially with regard to the federal government accessing timely and accurate information about receipts and outlays, which are necessary to control debt. In terms of the quantity and quality of financial reporting, Brazil exhibits best practices.

Yet, there remain challenges to fiscal policy. First, there is conflict between the LFR and Law 4.320. In cases of conflict, the LFR supersedes the other. The macroeconomic focus of the LFR subordinated budgetary management reform. However, the law did raise awareness that budgetary planning needs more than macroeconomic controls to affect a longer term horizon, and that service outcomes are more important than service outputs.

Another shortcoming in practice is incessant inability to maintain hard budget constraints. The LFR requires bimonthly evaluation of actual-to-budgeted revenues and actual expenditures-to-authorized budgetary limits to determine if a jurisdiction will be compliant with fiscal goals. In the event that the jurisdiction shows a trend of noncompliance, allocations are frozen until adequate revenues are collected. In reaction to the inability to spend, managers create accounts payable, a dumping ground for unpaid obligations to be passed to the following fiscal year, creating debts not captured by the debt limits but leaving the legislature with some sense of participation in the budgetary process.

Afonso (2008) comments on the phenomenon of governors self-imposing fiscal austerity measures upon learning that they inherited administrations in poor fiscal health, despite the administrations showing indicators of good health. He attributes the occurrence to poor data. Even though more data are published and publicly available, their transparency is obscured by excessive amounts of information. Methodological deficiencies lead to divergence of fiscal indicators (looking good) and fiscal austerity measures by states (to reduce fiscal burden). The issue is exacerbated because the availability of data and capacity of units to analyze it vary significantly across jurisdictions, especially at the municipal level (Amaral, 2003; Nazareth & Lopes Porto, 2002).

PLANNING AND PERFORMANCE MANAGEMENT

The arrangements of the budgetary process affect the nation's ability to plan and integrate performance management ideals. Da Cruz and colleagues (1999) maintain that accounts should be used not just for legal and constitutional compliance, but to also motivate study of how to improve effective fiscal management, especially in decision making and transparency. While the intention of the constitution was to insert planning into public finance, in practice, incorporation of the PPA is used to satisfy the legal requirement and only in rare cases is used to further planning efforts. The emphasis on planning that results in fulfilling a legal requirement misplaces human energy and resources that could be used to prioritize values (Rezende & Cunha, 2005; Amaral, 2003).

The planning process breaks down for a number of reasons. First, there is lack of clarity between the PPA and annual budget, especially considering that the formal budget is based on programs, but budget execution is based on ministries where the programs do not necessarily coincide with organizational structure (Shand et al., 2002). The ability to evaluate performance results and to use accounting and auditing results for strategic policy is compromised (Cavaleiro, 2001; Nader, 2005). Second, separate organizational functions make it harder to align resources with priorities, weakening the essence of program budgeting. Budgetary control and monitoring is based on both commitments and obligations determined by the MPLAN as well as in payments determined by the MF (Shand et al., 2002).

Third, the integration of planning, budgeting, and control is limited because of the way information is used in the decision-making process, where the incorporation of performance information in the decision-making process is, at best, fragile (Rezende & Cunha, 2005). Effective use of performance information requires institutional capacity to produce good quality data and information, involvement by decision makers in the evaluation process, strategy to divulge performance information, and leaders who are committed to improving performance and decision making.

Finally, aside from poor data (TCE, 2009a; TCE, 2009b), other problems discourage the link between planning and performance: Inadequate monitoring mechanisms and the need for improvements on SIGPLAN; managers presenting data in an unclear form or exaggerating performance; punishing poor performance, but not rewarding good performance; monitoring complex multisectoral programs, where cooperation and communication can be stinted; maintaining too much distance between program managers and organizational directors; and timing lags between when information is needed and when it is produced (Rezende & Cunha, 2005).

LEGISLATIVE DISCRETION AND BUDGET RIGIDITY

The budget process is deemed inflexible, both in terms of providing managerial autonomy (Amaral 2003) and in terms of allowing legislative discretion (Shand et al., 2002). Although congress is involved, the budget process is driven largely by the executive agenda and lacks budget debate within congress (Shand et al., 2002). Congress may be further disadvantaged by having distinct congressional advisory units for each house, as the units are redundant, present conflicting interpretation to their legislators, and have a weak relationship with technical staff of the executive branch (Tollini, 2009).

Because the legislature's only legitimate way to alter the budget is through amendments, since 1988, the legislature's use of amendments has grown in terms of the number of amendments and the amounts requested. The value of amendments in recent years has reached 20% of discretionary funds. The limited discretion of the legislature has led to unrealistic revenue expectations relative to budgeted expenditure (Tollini, 2009). As the LRF requires that expenditures be frozen when revenues fall short, impoundments that were designed to be minor adjustments have reached tens of billions of *reals*. Consequently, the legislature has created a culture of impoundment whereby it can neither foresee fiscal year expenditures nor have any certainty that their expenditures will be met.

Another outcome is the use of the amendment process to disguise parochial interests as federal ones (Tollini, 2009). Rezende and Cunha (2005) criticize the budget for not accounting well for the regionalization of expenditures. Programs to overcome regional inequalities are distributed on the basis of population. Unresolved is which other criteria should be the basis of distribution, in what cases should they be applied, and how they could be applied without affecting the flexibility of resource allocation. As allocation and distribution formulas are hidden from congress, it seeks ways to support constituent interests (Tollini, 2009).

A third response to the lack of congressional discretion, and the growth in amendments, is to secure dedicated funding for a particular cause through mandates and earmarks. Even with budget shortfalls, expenditures for mandates, priorities, earmarks, and transfers are not subject to executive recision (Blöndal et al., 2003; Rezende & Cunha, 2005; Shand et al., 2002). The amount of earmarked or mandated funds is increasing, creating distortions and interfering with the conduct of public policy (Rezende & Cunha, 2005). The tax burden has been increasing, but the relative share of federal discretionary funds remains at 10%.

Basically, the reduction of budgetary space—by earmarks, requirements to meet fiscal goals, and control over how budgetary imbalances are handled—induces reactions to create additional earmarks. As a greater share of the budget becomes earmarked, the more priorities of today are passed into the future. Additionally, as more of the budget turns mandatory, there is less and less ability of the budget to manage turbulent economies.

REGULATION OF THE BUDGET CYCLE

The budget cycle is affected by the standardization of norms, definitions, and procedures. Rezende and Cunha (2005) argue that the lack of standardization impedes the ability of Brazil to attain an integrated budget cycle. Although the LFR required the establishment of standards for reports and disclosure statements, the various federal and state Tribunals of Accounts have not normalized accounting norms and interpretations. As states and municipalities are held to different interpretations depending on the entity to which they report, they must create various versions of reports to satisfy the requirements of different organizations. Also, the different norms restrict the federal government's ability to aggregate and integrate information about different jurisdictions of control. Efforts are in place for the Council on Fiscal Management to reconcile the outstanding issues.

Management of public budgets has been undermined by the lack of regulation of the budget cycle. With respect to the PPA, neither content nor form is standardized. Rezende and Cunha (2005) recommend better definitions about the specificity of the PPA, LDO, and LOA—regarding development, organization, restrictions, allowed number and frequency of revisions, and the process by which modifications can go into effect—so decision makers can respond to changes in market conditions. Also, even though the LFR applies to all governmental entities, the language is biased toward the central government, leaving uncertainty about how to operationalize and develop concepts of goals and objectives within the PPA, resulting in a variety of manifestations of the PPA.

Finally, the auditing procedures in place are criticized as weak (Shand et al., 2002). Formal reports by the TCU and SFC are inadequate to meet auditing standards and quality control, and the report format is inconsistent with generally accepted auditing standards. Also, reports are not punctual, and therefore cannot serve as the basis of up-to-date information. Reports by the SFC are not made public.

Considerations for Budgetary Reform

Considerations for budgetary reform parallel the impacts. They are elaborated with respect to fiscal control; planning, budgeting, and management; legislative discretion and budget rigidity; and regulating the budget cycle.

FISCAL CONTROL

A number of options can be considered for budgetary reform that would affect fiscal control. One recommendation promotes better integration of planning and budgeting. If the program budget is to remain the dominant format, then the recommendation is to allocate salaries by program (Shand et al., 2002; Garces & Silveira, 2002). Another recommendation for improving fiscal control is to repeal explicit elements of the Law 4.320 that have been superseded by the constitution (Nunes, 2008).

A final recommendation promotes an emphasis on performance-based budgeting (PBB) by increasing the transparency of costs and results (Rezende & Cunha, 2005). Afonso (2008) argues for better accounting of underfunded fixed investments, expenditures that reflect true costs, and debt transparency. The shift from rigidity would allow the budgetary conversation to revolve more around values and less around legal requirements. Rezende and Cunha (2005) recommend reducing macroeconomic controls on budgets, and instead, create incentives for the budget to hold a prominent place in the medium-term planning of governmental policy.

PLANNING, BUDGETING, AND MANAGEMENT

A number of authors would like to fortify the integration of planning, budgeting, and management (Amaral, 2003; Garces & Silveira, 2002; Shand et al., 2002).

> In a perspective of managing for results, it is recommended to emphasize planning and strategic management, the development of budget execution and financial orientation for program results, a continual process of organizational development that has the objective of incorporating program management into the organization's formal structures and decision-making processes. (Garces & Silveira, 2002, pp. 70–71)

Organizational performance can be improved by coordinating investment, finance, and treasury; by better coordinating planning and budgeting units within ministries and jurisdictions; and aligning programs with organizational structures (Shand et al., 2002).

Proponents of integrating a new public management (NPM) approach to budgeting encourage each executive branch to establish objectives, goals, and indicators that would allow for not only control, but also for an evaluation of program results, and would also be subject to internal and external controls (Amaral, 2003). Change requires a restructuring of internal control mechanisms, where policy goals are connected to resources, and flexibility exists to adjust resource use as plans and programs accommodate changing socioeconomic realities.

Amaral (2003) recognizes the need to not only move auditing beyond the realm of fiscal and financial control where legal compliance and efficiency are held to paramount importance, but also to open it up to accounting for outcomes with performance audits. In doing so, the evaluation emphasis would shift from financial, budgetary, and accounting to issues of management and economic and social outcomes. Based on principles of NPM, the idea is to identify performance results: Managers identify performance goals and are given the autonomy and managerial flexibility to attain them. By focusing on program incentives, cost analysis, and alternative service provision, these efforts would improve economy (controlling inputs), efficiency (optimizing return on inputs to outputs), and effectiveness (optimizing return on inputs to outcomes).

In support of a budget process that emphasizes outcomes, Amaral (2003) promotes the use of better indicators in the budgetary process. In addition to the extant focus on macroeconomic indicators, she recommends fiscal management and socioeconomic indicators that allow for identification of constituent need and performance efforts.[1] Collectively, the indicators strive to inform the general fiscal health of the entity by identifying changes in tax collection, tax effort, fiscal autonomy, degree of indebtedness, and degree of investment (Amaral, 2003). Coincidently, many of these fiscal indicators are those used by international credit rating agencies (Martell, 2003).

LEGISLATIVE DISCRETION AND BUDGET RIGIDITY

As the existing budget process sidelines congressional input and incentivizes excessive amendments that result in unrealistic expenditure expectations, increasing legislative discretion and reducing budget rigidity may improve the budget process. The first recommendation is to alter the role of the permanent sectoral committees so that they decide their own amendments that are subject to expenditure restrictions with the goals of merging technical and budget expertise and of improving expenditure and policy priority (Tollini, 2009). The sectoral committees could also incorporate performance indicators into budgetary decisions. Having the sectoral committees rather than the CMO prioritize amendments would require a constitutional change, but would enhance the legislative role in the thematic committees.

The second recommendation would be to enhance the legitimacy of congress' role in the budgetary process by creating an independent analytic arm for congress (Tollini, 2009). Tollini recommends that the two congressional advisory units be combined to create one independent, nonpartisan analytic unit to "simplify the complex budget information, promote transparency and accountability, increase the credibility of budget estimates, and quickly respond to congressmen's questions" (2009, p. 20). Combining the two units would reduce redundancy and unnecessary conflicts. Past proposals to create a unified congressional Budget Institute have failed because of fears that it would jeopardize the freedom the members of congress have in the budget process. Yet pairing technicians with budgetary expertise and sectoral policy specialists could result in better expenditure choices to achieve policy goals.

Another reform to streamline budgetary implementation is to better identify resource distribution and allocations. A measure could require the executive branch to make transparent the redistribution formulas for regional funds, so that legislative participation in the budget process would happen at a different level (Tollini, 2009). To reduce budgetary rigidity, Blöndal and colleagues (2003) recommend moving from line-item to categoric transfers.

Tollini (2009) recommends that the amendment process and congressional reliance on "errors and omissions" be reconsidered by eliminating the tactic of using "errors and omissions" to reestimate revenue and by further reducing the number of congressional amendments. In the short term, he recommends restricting the number of amendments in exchange for the executive branch committing to fund the few amendments that are approved. In the long term, he recommends creating a new public finance law that would restrict the revenue pool. That restriction could come in one of two ways: The first would require that the draft and final budget use revenue estimates in the LDO; the second would create a revenue estimating committee, comprised of executive, legislative, and private sector members who collectively decide revenue estimates. The hope is that an increased congressional role would reduce pressures for earmarking, and thus ease the budget's rigidity.

REGULATING THE BUDGET CYCLE

Finally, considerations for budget reform pertain to regulating the budget cycle with respect to accounting standards, entities that are not strictly public, normalizing the PPA, and the timing of the budget cycle. The lack of procedural integrity puts at risk the recent budgetary advancements that were made. Thus, it is important to identify the obstacles to integrating planning and the budgeting processes. "The necessity to standardize a unique norm, with clear definitions about the physical and financial dimensions, remains, therefore, evident" (Rezende & Cunha, 2005, p. 103, translated by author).

The lack of standardization of reports and disclosure statements required by the LRF and established by either the federal or state Tribunals of Accounts, impedes the federal government's ability to aggregate and integrate information about different organs of control. Although the Council on Fiscal Management has been tasked with establishing accounting norms, it is important to reevaluate its role. Another option is to consider making the Federal Accounting Council a professional association to develop more transparent accounting standards.

Regulatory reform should define how resources and expenditures for transjurisdictional entities or for entities that have both public and private elements should be accounted (Rezende & Cunha, 2005). There is a need to clarify doubts about gray areas, such as public–private partnerships, interjurisdictional consortiums, and companies that are subjected to both public and private rules (Nunes, 2008). Nunes (2008) puts forth the need to develop norms for the PPA and calls for standards on the stages of the budget process. In particular, she promotes developing standards on cooperation between powers both within entities of the federation and between levels of government, especially with respect to overlapping policy or geographic areas.

Finally, another change to be considered is to alter the time horizons for the federal, state, and local budgetary cycles so that there can be better coordination among them by sequencing the elaboration of priorities and projects (Rezende & Cunha, 2005). For example, the federal LDO would be created before the state LDOs, followed by the municipal LDOs.

Conclusions

A number of conclusions are drawn about the budgeting process in Brazil. The first is that constitutional and legislative reforms have resulted in a budget process that is driven by the executive with attempts to integrate planning and budgeting. Efforts to attain fiscal control have been largely effective. Also, analytic systems and data tracking systems are highly developed.

There is evidence, however, that there remain some areas for improvement. One pertains to the full transparency of data, and its use for decision making. Another area, related to the first, is to integrate performance management into the budgetary process by emphasizing outcomes through indicators and performance audits. An additional area of reform is the role of the congress and its relationship with budget rigidity. A final area is the regulation of the budgetary cycle, especially with respect to standardizing budgetary documents and norms.

Interestingly enough, a number of authors recommend advancing budget reforms through a Law of Public Finance (Afonso, 2008; Nunes, 2008; Rezende & Cunha, 2005; Tollini, 2009). Although the LFR of 2000 made important strides in resolving fiscal control issues, it has proven inadequate to satisfy all of the needs of a complex budgetary process, especially one that hopes to achieve outcome-based performance. There is yet to be a new basic law of public finance that better reflects the economic, political, and social transformations that have affected both the state and the citizens' expectations of it (Rezende & Cunha, 2005).

Discussion Questions

1. In addition to the constitution, which two legislative documents provide much of the framework for Brazil's federal budget process? Generally, how does each document guide the process?
2. Which of the three branches of government in Brazil is responsible for drafting the federal budget? How can the congress influence the draft budget, and how is congressional power limited with regard to changing the budget?
3. How has Brazil attempted to facilitate budget data consistency among various government powers and levels of government?
4. How have Brazil's changes to fiscal controls increased focus on budgetary outcomes?
5. Why is high quality data so important in budgeting? How has the quality of budgetary data affected Brazil's efforts to improve fiscal controls? How has data quality affected budget planning and performance management?
6. What does the author mean by "budget rigidity?" How has this affected the Brazilian governments' ability to create effective public policy?
7. Public administrators are often faced with a trade-off between efficiency and effectiveness. How does the author suggest that Brazil could improve both the efficiency *and* the effectiveness of its budgetary process?

References

Afonso, J. R. R. (2008). Conta e faz-de-conta. In D. Câmara (Ed.), *Responsabilidade na gestão pública: os desafios dos municípios* [Responsibility in public management: Challenges of the municipalities] (pp. 83–98). série avaliação de políticas públicas n. 02, organizado pelo conselho de altos estudos e avaliação tecnológica, .Brasilia: Câmara dos Deputados, Edições Câmara Available at http://apache.camara.gov .br/portal/arquivos/Camara/internet/conheca/altosestudos/pdf/Livro%20definitivo.pdf. Accessed May 4, 2010.

Amaral, R. M. (2003). *A avaliação de resultados no sector público: Teoria e aplicação prática no estado de Rio de Janeiro* [An evaluation of public sector results: Theory and applied practice in the state of Rio de Janeiro]. Rio de Janeiro: Tribunal de contas do estado do Rio de Janeiro.

Blöndal, J. R., Chiara, G., & Kristensen, J. K. (2003). Budgeting in Brazil. *OECD Journal on Budgeting, 3*(1), 97–131.

Cavaleiro, J. B. (2001). *A organização do sistema de controle interno dos municípios* [The organization of the internal control system of municipalities]. Porto Alegre: Conselho regional de contabilidade do Rio Grande do Sul.

da Cruz, F., Junior, A. V., Glock, J. O., Herzmann, N., & Barbosa, R. R. (1999). *Comentários à lei No 4.320* [Commentaries on Law No. 4.320]. São Paulo: Editora Atlas S.A.

de Oliveira, W. (2000). Lei de responsabilidade fiscal principais aspectos concernentes aos municípios, Brasília: Câmara dos Deputados, Consultoria de Orçamento e Fiscalização Financeira [Law of Fiscal Responsibility: Principal aspects concerning municipalities]. Available at: http://www.buscalegis .ufsc.br/revistas/index.php/buscalegis/article/viewFile/19171/18735. Accessed April 30, 2010.

Garces, A., & Silveira, J. P. (2002). Gestão pública orientada para resultados no Brasil [Public results-oriented management in Brazil]. *Revista do Servíco Público, 53*(4), 53–78.

Machado, J. T. Jr., & da Costa Reis, H. (1998). *A lei 4.320 comentada* [Law 4.320 Comented] (28th ed.). Rio de Janeiro: IBAM.

Martell, C. R. (2003). Municipal investment, borrowing, and pricing under decentralization: The Brazilian case. *International Journal of Public Administration, 26*(2), 173–196.

Merrill Lynch & Co. (1996, July 2). Municipality of Rio de Janeiro. Offering Memorandum, $125,000,000, 10 3/8% Notes due 1999. Copy in possession of author.

Mora, M., & Varsano, R. (2001, December). *Fiscal decentralization and subnational fiscal autonomy in Brazil: Some facts of the nineties*. Rio de Janeiro: Instituto de Pesquisa Econômica Aplicada.

Nader, R. M. (2005). *A avaliação como ferramenta para uma gestão pública orientada para resultados. O caso do Governo Federal Brasileiro* [Evaluation as a tool for results-oriented public management: The case of the Brazilian Federal Government]. CLAD. Available at: http://www.clad.org.ve. Accessed April 19, 2010.

Nazareth, P. A., & Lopes Porto, L. F. (2002, January). *As finançças dos municípios Brasileiros: O caso do Rio de Janeiro* [The finances of Brazilian municipalities: The case of Rio de Janeiro]. XIV Seminaro Regional de Política Fiscal [XIV Regional Seminar on Fiscal Policy], Santiago, Chile.

Nunes, S. P. P. (2007, November 27). *A lei de responsibilidade fiscal e a contabilidade pública: Avanços e desafios* [The Law of Fiscal Responsibility and public accountability: Advances and Challenges]. Paper presented at the Séminario Internacional de Contabilidade Pública [International Seminar of Public Accountability], Brasília, Brazil.

Nunes, S. P. P. (2008, November 28). 8 anos da LRF: A atuação dos tribunais de contas [Eight years of the Law of Fiscal Responsibility: The performance of the tribunals of accounts] Presented at the State of Ceará's Tribunal of Accounts, Fortaleza, Brazil. Available at: http://www.tce.ce.gov.br/sitetce/arq/noticias/documentos/LRF_Apresentacoes/LRF_8_Anos.ppt. Accessed May 4, 2010.

Rezende, F., & Cunha, A. (2005). *Disciplina fiscal e qualidade do gasto público, fundamentos da reforma orçamentária* [Fiscal discipline and quality of public expenditures, fundamentals of budgetary reform]. Rio de Janeiro: Editora FGV.

Shand, D., de la Fuente Hoyes, P., Mittelstaedt, C., Correa, T., Chaves, F., Macedo, J. B., Nerosky, L. C., De Moura Jr., S. C., & Araújo, L. M. (2002). Relatório sobre a avaliação do Sistema de administração e controle financeiros do Brasil [Report on the evaluation of the administrative system of financial control of Brazil]. Brasilia, Brazil: Ministry of Planejamento, Orçamento, e Gestão [Ministry of Planning, Budget, and Management. Available at: http://www.mp.gov.br/secretarias/upload/Arquivos/sof/publicacoes/relatorio_avaliacao_sacfb.pdf. Accessed May 4, 2010.

TCE. (2009a). *Municípios afrouxam a arrecadação de imposto* [Municipalities loosen tax collection]. Available at: http://tce.rj.gov.br/sitenovo/develop/noticiar/aim/no05050401.htm#arrec. Accessed April 19, 2010.

TCE. (2009b). *TCE-RJ monstra em Goiás novo controle das receitas públicas* [The TCE-RJ shows new control of public revenue in Goiás]. Available at: http://tce.rj.gov.br/sitenovo/develop/noticiar/aim/no05050501.htm. Accessed April 19, 2010.

Tollini, H. (2009). Reforming the budget formulation process in the Brazilian congress. *OECD Journal of Budgeting, 9*(1), 1–29.

Villela, L. A. (1996). *Análise comparativa das atuais propostas de reforma tributária e o impacto sobre a futura disponibilidade de recursos para Financiar o desenvolvimento urbano* [Comparative analysis of actual tax reform proposals and the impact of future resource availability to finance urban development]. Rio de Janeiro: Prefeitura de Rio de Janeiro.

ENDNOTE

1. Among the recommended fiscal indicators are GDP per capita, share of tax revenue to total revenue, share of own-source revenue, debt service per total revenue, share of personnel to total expenditure, debt service per expenditure, revenue collected to expenditures, investments per total revenue, and tax effort. Also recommended include a number of socioeconomic indicators such as rates of literacy, repeat students, poverty, access to health care, unemployment, dependence on social security, infant mortality, social development, leisure, environmental preservation, adequacy of transportation, and urban development (Amaral, 2003).

Part 7

Conclusion

Chapter 20

Learning from Others: Comparative Budgeting in the New Millennia

Charles E. Menifield and LaShonda M. Stewart

Learning Objectives

- Know and understand how to frame a comparative budgeting system.
- Know and assess how various factors affect budgeting processes.
- Know and understand the effect of reform on budget processes and procedures.
- Know and assess transparency and its impact on budget processes.

Introduction

The key question posed at the beginning of this book was: How does budgeting occur in other countries and can we learn from their successes and failures? The authors of the previous chapters addressed the question by providing a plethora of information concerning budget processes, reforms, as well as other pressing budgetary issues. When this data is aggregated however, it paints a very interesting budgeting picture around the world from a micro and macro perspective.

We begin the chapter by briefly revisiting Wildavsky's and Rubin's model. Second, we use their models as a framework to describe several factors that we examine from each of the substantive chapters. Third, we examine two other factors:

major budgeting reforms and transparency in the budgeting process. Last, we conclude the chapter by addressing the future of budgeting given the current status of the global economy.

Wildavsky's Budgeting Model and Rubin's Decision-Making Model Applied

By using Wildavsky's (1975) and Rubin's (2010) research as a framework, this research has provided much evidence to the evolutionary nature of public budgeting. We found that many factors shape and define comparative budgeting today. Before we discuss the aggregate data however, we have to digress back to the data in Chapter 1, Table 1-1 where wealth (gross domestic product [GDP] and poverty rate) was found to be highly correlated with budget predictability. Wildavsky argued that these two variables are the focal point of understanding budgeting behavior (p. 11). While we agree with his position, we also found that the role of political culture (Wildavsky refers to this as "elite culture"), as an intervening variable, is far more pervasive from a behavioral viewpoint rather than an institutional view than Wildavsky realizes. Rubin's model captures this void because it focuses more on behavior and the politics involved in the process.

Overall, when the data and information in the chapters are aggregated, it paints a different picture than expected. This picture raises several questions. First, is it feasible for one country to learn from another given differences in political culture? Second, given the economic disparities across the globe, is it possible for one country to fully implement or replicate a budget system (or parts thereof) from another country? The answers to these and other questions will ultimately determine the usefulness of this research in creating a model that can be used to compare budgeting processes around the globe, as well as demonstrate how nations handle various policy issues such as improving educational outcomes, infrastructure, health care, and other vital issues.

The data in Table 20-1 show each of the key variables in our framework along with an indicator of its use by Wildavsky and Rubin. As shown, each variable is represented in at least one of the two models employed by this research.

Table 20-1

Comparing Budget Processes Around the Globe

Factors	Wildavsky	Rubin
Form of government	✓	
Key budget officials	✓	✓ (Budget process cluster)
Revenue sources	✓	✓ (Revenue cluster)
Expenditure sources	✓	✓ (Expenditure cluster)
Subnational budget authority		✓ (Budget process cluster)
Accounting method	✓	✓ (Balanced budget cluster)
Performance budgets	✓	
Central capital budget	✓	

FORM OF GOVERNMENT

The data in Table 20-2 shows the form of government for the 18 countries examined in this analysis. Five of these countries are located in the Middle East (Iraq, Jordan, Pakistan, Saudi Arabia, and the United Arab Emirates), one in South America (Brazil), three in North America (Canada, Mexico, and the United States), six in Asia (China, Korea, Philippines, Taiwan, Thailand, and Vietnam), two in Europe (Italy and the United Kingdom), and one in Africa (Ghana). The table also shows that the majority of these countries (11) have a republic form of government indicating some form of a democratic governing process. Four countries have a constitutional monarchy and the other three function as either an absolute monarchy, a federation (of emirates), or as a socialist republic indicating a more controlled nondemocratic process.

Although the term republic is generally synonymous with democracy, it is clear that the definition varies by country. That is, participation in the budgeting process may be inclusive, but the level of involvement and the value added by each participant is not the same across the board. For example, in the United States, it is known that the president and Congress both write a budget and from these two institutions, a single document comes forth. It is also generally accepted that negotiations take place prior to the approval of the final document. Hence, both entities clearly play a key role on the revenue and expenditure side of the budgeting structure. Pakistan, on the one hand, has a republican form of government with many entities involved in the process. On the other hand,

Table 20-2	
Form of Government	
Country	**Form of government**
Brazil	Republic
Canada	Constitutional monarchy
China	Republic
Ghana	Republic
Iraq	Republic
Italy	Republic
Jordan	Constitutional monarchy
Korea	Republic
Mexico	Republic
Pakistan	Republic
Philippines	Republic
Saudi Arabia	Absolute monarchy
Taiwan	Republic
Thailand	Constitutional monarchy
United Arab Emirates	Federation (of emirates)
United Kingdom	Constitutional monarchy
United States	Republic
Vietnam	Socialist republic

it differs from that of the United States in that provincial governments play a significant role on the expenditure side, but a very limited role on the revenue side. Other differences are seen when comparing Canada, Jordan, Thailand, and the United Kingdom.

KEY CENTRAL GOVERNMENT BUDGET OFFICIALS

There appears to be a dispersion of authority amongst key central budget officials on both the executive and legislative levels for the majority of the countries. Table 20-3 shows that majority of these countries have two or more key budget officials involved in decision making on the executive level. Only two countries (China and Ghana) have one key officer on the executive level: the Ministry of Finance (MOF). On the legislative level, however, the legislative body as a whole serves as the key central budget official for eight countries (China, Ghana, Italy, Iraq, Jordan, Mexico, United Arab Emirates, United Kingdom, and Vietnam). There is a diffusion of authority among key officials for the other 10 countries. It is also noteworthy that some countries have officials that serve key roles on both the legislative and executive levels. In Saudi Arabia and Thailand, for example, the MOF is included as a key central budget official on both levels.

Several questions emanate from this table. However, for the purposes of this research, only one key question comes to the forefront: How does the number of actors involved affect the budgeting process? Although we do not have the data to conclusively answer this question, we can speculate based on the information provided in the chapters as well as some anecdotal observations in the data.

It is worth noting that an increase in the number of budget actors in some countries complicate the budgeting process. However, the political culture of the country appears to determine the level of difficulty in implementing the budget. For example, Mexico does not have a large number of key entities involved in the budget process at the federal level, but state (provincial) governments frequently usurp federal authority when implementing their budget due to the fact that revenues are limited and leave little room for state versus federal priorities (see Chapter 17). Despite the clear delineations in the power structure, some Mexican states do not seem overly concerned with ignoring federal spending mandates. Thailand has a very centralized budgeting process that is reinforced by the letter of the law (see Chapter 7). Despite the fact that cities create their own budgets, their financial autonomy is quite limited. They accept this fact as reality and make no effort to usurp federal authority. Similar comparisons can be made in the United States, as well as Jordan and Saudi Arabia to name a few countries. Quite naturally, the repercussions, or lack thereof, for not following the edicts of the national government vary by country.

MAJOR SOURCE OF CENTRAL GOVERNMENT REVENUE

Table 20-4 shows that the majority of these countries rely on income tax revenues, which include personal income and/or business taxes. These countries, however, vary in their reliance on other major revenue sources. Four countries (China, Jordan, Pakistan, and Thailand), for example, use sales tax revenue as a major source of income. Countries like Iraq, Jordan, and Pakistan rely on custom duties. The table also shows that several

Table 20-3		
Key Central Budget Official		
Country	**Executive level**	**Legislative level**
Brazil	President; Ministry of Planning; Budget and Management (MPLAN); and the Secretary of Federal Budget (SFB)	Joint Budget Commission (CMO); and Permanent Sectoral Committees
Canada	Prime minister (Prime Minister's Office and the Privy Council Office); supported by the Department of Finance	House of Commons, and the Standing Committee on Finance & Public Accounts; the Senate, and the Standing Committee on National Finance
China	Ministry of Finance	Budget Working Committee
Ghana	Ministry of Finance	Parliament
Iraq	Prime minister; Council of Ministers; and ministers of finance & planning	General Council of Representatives (COR)
Italy	Government; and Ministry of Economy and Finance	Parliament
Jordan	Prime minister; the cabinet; and the minister of finance & budget office within it	Parliament[a]
Korea	Budget Office within the Ministry of Strategy and Finance (MOSF); cabinet; and president	The National Assembly (relatively weak); the National Assembly Budget Office (NABO); and the Special Committee on Budget and Accounts
Mexico	Secretariat of Finance & Public Credit	The Chamber of Deputies
Pakistan	President; and National Finance Commission (NFC)	Parliament; and Ministry of Finance
Philippines	Department of Budget & Management (DBM); Development Budget Coordination Committee (DBCC); president; and cabinet members	The House of Representatives; Committee on Appropriations; and the Philippines' Senate Committee on Finance
Saudi Arabia	Council of Ministers; Ministry of Finance; Ministry of Economy & Planning; and the prime minister	Council of Ministers; Ministry of Finance; and the prime minister
Taiwan	Premier; Directorate-General of Budgeting Accounting and Statistics (DGBAS); Ministry of Audit; and Ministry of Finance	Legislative Yuan; and the Finance Committee
Thailand	Gang of Four: Bureau of Budget; the Office of the National Social & Economic Development Board (NSEDB); Ministry of Finance (and an independent agency); and Bank of Thailand	National Assembly; and Ministry of Finance
United Arab Emirates	Supreme Council of Rulers; Minister of Finance and Industry; and UAE Cabinet	Federal National Council
United Kingdom	Chancellor of the Exchequer	Parliament
United States	President; Office of Management and Budget (OMB)	Congressional Budget Committees; and Congressional Budget Office (CBO)
Vietnam	Ministry of Finance; Ministry of Planning and Investment (MPI); and the prime minister	National Assembly

[a] Overall, the legislature has neither been effective in utilizing its powers of appropriation, nor educated in monitoring government within a clear set of rules.

countries receive revenues from petroleum products. This includes oil extractions in Mexico, petroleum reserves in Saudi Arabia, revenue from fossil fuel reserves in the United Arab Emirates (UAE), and oil and natural gas extractions in Vietnam. Over the next few decades, it is expected that Ghana will join this group given the discovery of oil reserves. As of the date of this writing, Saudi Arabia is the only country that relies solely on petroleum

Table 20-4	
Largest Sources of Central Government Revenue	
Country	**Major Sources of Revenue**
Brazil	Income taxes; social security taxes; and industrial products tax
Canada	Personal income tax; corporate income tax; and goods and services tax
China	Value added tax (VAT); corporate income tax; and sales tax
Ghana	Direct, indirect, and international trade taxes
Iraq	Oil revenue; low levels of taxation; and customs duties and fees/charges
Italy	Income tax; corporate income tax; and VAT
Jordan	Income tax; customs duties; and excise and sales taxes
Korea	Personal income tax; corporate income tax; and consumption tax
Mexico	Personal income; VAT; and fees and royalties on oil extractions[a]
Pakistan	Personal income tax (except agriculture income); corporate income tax; customs, sales taxes on goods/excise duty (except on alcohol, narcotics); and capital value tax
Philippines	Taxes on net income and profits; taxes on property; taxes on domestic goods and services; taxes on international trade and transactions, fees and charges; and treasury income, privatization, and foreign grants
Saudi Arabia	Petroleum reserves
Taiwan	Income taxes; commodity taxes; and surpluses from state corporations
Thailand	Sales tax; income tax; and tariff tax
United Arab Emirates	Taxes on business outside of the free trade zones; and revenues from fossil fuel reserves
United Kingdom	Personal income tax; national insurance contributions; VAT; and corporate income tax
United States	Personal income tax; and payroll taxes
Vietnam	Business-related activities which include the VAT and business-related revenues that are shared between the central and subnational level; and taxes on extraction of oil and natural gas

[a] 2009 Federal Revenue Act, Mexico.

reserves as its major revenue source. The United States is the only other country that relies primarily on two major revenue sources: personal income and payroll taxes.

The overarching question from this data is: Does the revenue source or number of revenue sources affect the budgeting process? Similar to the preceding questions and data analysis, the answer appears to be contingent on a number of factors. However, a few generalizations can be made. For example, the four countries that are dependent on fossil fuels have multiple budget actors, but the evidence indicates that one or two actors/groups essentially make the budgeting decisions and have the power to enforce those decisions. On the other hand, countries that have multiple sources of revenue appear to have more actors involved in the budgeting process and behave in a more democratic fashion. There are, however, some exceptions to this statement.

For example, the United Kingdom has two major players in the budgeting process, but the House of Commons is charged with approving the appropriation of funds (see Chapter 10). In the United States, there are multiple levels of budgetary authority, but Congress approves the budget. This information suggests that the number of revenue sources do not necessarily impact budgeting in a positive or negative fashion.

MAJOR EXPENDITURE ITEMS

Table 20-5 shows that the major expenditure items vary among countries. Defense and security spending ranks as the largest expenditure for five of the countries (Iraq, Korea, Pakistan, UAE, and the United States). Three other countries (Philippines, Taiwan, and the United Kingdom) include defense and security spending as a major expenditure, but the ranking of this expenditure differs between these countries. Further analysis of other major expenditure items reveals that most of these countries (11) rank education spending as one of their largest expenditures. Six countries, however, rank health as a large expenditure, five include social welfare, and three other countries report social security as a major expenditure items. The ranking of all other expenditures (e.g., Medicare, science, transportation, debt service) differs by countries. Technology spending, for example, is included as a major expenditure for only one country, Vietnam. Medicare is another example of a major expenditure item identified in the table for only one country, the United States. With respect to the budget process, this data is useful in that it provides a snapshot of national government priorities.

Table 20-5	
Major Expenditure Items by Rank	
Country	**Largest expenditures**
Brazil	Education; transportation; and health
Canada	Elderly benefits; transfers to provinces for health and social programs; and defense programs
China	General public service; education; social security and employment
Ghana	Discretionary spending (ministries, foreign-financed investment, transfers, and repayment of domestic debt)
Iraq	Defense; public sector infrastructure (utilities); health; and education
Italy	Public debt; welfare; and education
Jordan	Nondevelopmental expenditures (e.g., salaries of military and civilian personnel, retirement benefits, and other fixed costs)
Korea	National security; social and economic development; transfers to local governments; and debt service
Mexico	Energy; education; and health
Pakistan	Defense; transfers to provinces,; and infrastructure development (education and health occur at the provincial level)
Philippines	Economic service; social service; debt service; general public service; and defense spending
Saudi Arabia	New projects; and projects under implementation
Taiwan	Education; science and culture; social welfare; and national defense
Thailand	General public service; education; economic affairs; and consuming
United Arab Emirates	Defense; education; and social services
United Kingdom	Social security; health; education; and defense
United States	National defense; social security; and Medicare
Vietnam	Recurrent expenditures and spending on tertiary education; vocation training; science; and technology

SUBNATIONAL GOVERNMENT BUDGETARY AUTHORITY

Table 20-6 shows that the majority of these countries have subnational governments with budgetary authority. Only two countries (Saudi Arabia and Thailand) do not have subnational governments with budgetary authority. What do these two countries have in common? Both have a monarchy that exercises a lot of control over the budgeting process. Three other countries in this study also have a monarchy. The difference appears to lie in the structure of government. For example, Saudi Arabia is the only country in this analysis that has an absolute monarchy, whereas Thailand has a constitutional monarchy (changed from an absolute monarchy in 1932; see Chapter 7) wherein the central government directs and supervises the country's public management. The United Kingdom, Canada, and Jordan have a constitutional monarchy. These three countries also have a prime minister, parliament, and other political bodies that are thoroughly involved in managing the budgeting process at the national level.

ACCOUNTING METHODS USED BY COUNTRY

Table 20-7 shows that some countries (e.g., China, Iraq, Jordan, and the United States) use cash-based accounting. But there appears to be a transitioning of accounting

Table 20-6

Subnational Government Budgetary Authority

Country	Budgetary authority
Brazil	Yes
Canada	Yes
China	Yes
Ghana	Yes
Iraq	Yes
Italy	Yes
Jordan	Yes
Korea	Yes
Mexico	Yes
Pakistan	Yes
Philippines	Yes
Saudi Arabia	No
Taiwan	Yes
Thailand	No
United Arab Emirates	Yes
United Kingdom	Yes
United States	Yes
Vietnam	Yes

Table 20-7	
Accounting Method Used by Country	
Country	**Method**
Brazil	Modified accrual accounting[a]
Canada	Accrual accounting for public accounts; and modified cash accounting for parliamentary spending authority
China	Cash basis
Ghana	Moving to an accrual system
Iraq	Cash basis
Italy	Cash; and obligation base and accrual base
Jordan	Cash-based accounting
Korea	Full accrual basis accounting (not fully implemented until 2011)
Mexico	Accrual accounting
Pakistan	Cash basis (transitioning to accrual)
Philippines	Fund, obligation, and cash-disbursement-ceiling accounting methods (used in government); taxes are accounted for on the cash basis; and the accrual basis is used for other revenues and expenses[b]
Saudi Arabia	Accrual basis (cash base)
Taiwan	Accrual and cash[c]
Thailand	Modified accrual accounting
United Arab Emirates	Full accrual
United Kingdom	Accrual accounting
United States	Cash basis of accounting (to measure revenues and outlays)
Vietnam	Transitioning to accrual accounting

[a] Cost or modified accrual, depending on the jurisdiction. There are plans to have a full accrual system by 2012.

[b] Pobre & Araceli, (1987, pp. 19–21 & 307–330).

[c] According to the law, the government accounting system is accrual. However, in practice, it is actually mixed. Some accounting systems are cash based due to practical reasons.

methods for other countries that are either using or planning to use some type of an accrual accounting system (modified or full). Brazil, for example, uses a modified or cost accrual accounting system, depending on the jurisdiction; there are plans, however, to have a full accrual system implemented by 2012. Pakistan uses a cash-basis method but is transitioning to an accrual approach. Ghana and Vietnam are also moving to an accrual system. Korea endorsed full accrual basis accounting, but this method will not be fully implemented until 2011.

The question that we posit is: Why are many countries shifting to an accrual system? A GAO report (US Government Accountability Office, 2000) offers some suggestions why this shift is occurring. First, accrual accounting reflects the full scope and size of a government (resources, obligations, and costs). Second, it allows for a greater focus on consumption of resources. Third, it provides a more informed link between outcomes and the use of resources to achieve them. Fourth, it allows central governments to hold agencies and subnational government more accountable for stewardship of it assets, full costs of its programs, and the ability to meet short- and long-term obligations. Fifth, it better reflects the impacts of economic events and decisions during the fiscal year. Last, it provides fuller information to the central government for improved decision making.

CENTRAL GOVERNMENT CAPITAL BUDGET

Table 20-8 shows that a majority of the countries (12) have separate capital budgets, but the level of success utilizing a capital budget differs by country. In fact, a higher level of success is perceptible for only 2 of the 12 countries (Ghana and Pakistan). Six countries (Brazil, Canada, Italy, Iraq, Taiwan, and the United Kingdom) experienced somewhat moderate success. The table also shows that in the Philippines (see Chapter 5), success is based on available funds, and reform is imminent in Saudi Arabia. There is apparently no systematic method to determine success in Jordan (see Chapter 12).

Table 20-8

Central Government Capital Budget

Country	Separate capital budget	Successful
Brazil	Yes[a]	Somewhat
Canada	Yes	Moderate
China	No	N/A
Ghana	Yes	Yes
Iraq	Yes	Moderate at best
Italy	Yes	Moderate
Jordan	Yes	No systematic method to determine
Korea	No	N/A
Mexico	Yes	Moderate
Pakistan	Yes	Yes
Philippines	Yes	Based on available funds
Saudi Arabia	Yes	Reform needed
Taiwan	Yes	Moderate
Thailand	No[b]	N/A
United Arab Emirates	No	N/A
United Kingdom	Yes	Moderate
United States	No	N/A
Vietnam	No	N/A

[a] Capital priorities are accounted for in the multiyear planning process.

[b] Capital items are included in budget agencies' proposals and in the performance-based budget.

In Chapter 18, it is argued that the United States does not utilize a capital budget because,

> cash-basis accounting for durable investment goods is necessary to recognize costs up front when the irrevocable decision is made to incur costs. The second is that the category of durable investments is much broader than physical structures and equipment. It includes government spending for human capital such as education, training, and health; investments in public goods such as clean air and water; and enduring benefits of peace and security from military deterrence and war. . . Put differently, the line separating the acquisition of structures, property, and equipment from other durable assets is so fuzzy that it would be difficult to prevent all spending from being classified as capital.

Major Budget Reforms

Given the vast array of economic, political, and social differences, we examined budget reforms separately. All of the countries examined in this study have undertaken major budgeting reform efforts in the last 20 years. Table 20-9 shows that result-based budgeting is the focus for many of these countries. It seems, however, that the focal point is more on achieving fiscal discipline and allocative and operational efficiency. China, for example, has undergone a series of reforms since the late 1990s; in 2004, its local governments started implementing performance-based budgeting (PBB), but have now recently begun participatory budgeting experiments (see Chapter 3). Korea currently implements financial management systems and techniques that include performance-based systems (see Chapter 4). In Mexico, the Governmental Accountability Act and the Fiscal Responsibility Act requires all entities receiving federal funds to participate in periodic performance assessments (see Chapter 17). The implementation of PBB is the most recent reform in Thailand and the UAE. Further analysis, however, suggests that some countries, like Jordan, experienced challenges in implementing such a reform. This country changed its

Table 20-9		
Major Reforms		
Country	**Recent reforms**	**Year of reform**
Brazil	The Law of Fiscal Responsibility (LFR); *Lei Complementar no. 101*	2000
Canada	Strategic reviews (works in progress and the government's most recent review initiative)	2007
China	China has undergone a series of reforms since late 1990s, including departmental budget reform (DBR), treasure management reform (TMR), government procurement reform (GPR), performance-based budgeting (PBB) reform, and participatory budgeting reform.	TMR in 2001; Government Procurement Law issued in 2003; 2004 China's local governments started PBB experiment; from 2005, China's local governments have begun participatory budgeting experiments

(continues)

Table 20-9 *(continued)*

Major Reforms

Country	Recent Reforms	Year of Reform
Ghana	The Public Financial Management Reform Programme	1995
Iraq	The United States introduction of Provincial Reconstruction Teams (PRTs) in late 2005–2006 focused much on the US development effort on strengthening provincial and regional government; the 2006 International Compact with Iraq represented a key role for subnational government in development planning and budgeting.	2005–2006
Italy	A new additional structure of the central government budget was defined.	2007
Jordan	In 1999, the government of Jordan decided to change its budget system from the traditional input-oriented, line-item format, to a performance-based budgeting system. Very little has been done, however, toward operational implementation of a performance budgeting process.	1999
Korea	Korea currently implements most of the advanced budgeting and financial management systems and techniques (such as top-down budgeting, performance-based systems, program budgeting, medium-year and multiyear allocation frameworks, and accrual accounting). These reforms became law in January 2007 as the National Financial Management Law. The Korean government also launched the Digital Budget & Accounting System (DBAS) in 2007.	2007
Mexico	Governmental Accountability Act and the Fiscal Responsibility Act which makes it mandatory for all entities receiving federal funds to participate in periodic performance assessments.	2006
Pakistan	Medium-Term Expenditure Frameworks have been introduced at the national and provincial level. Program budgeting has been introduced in selected sectors.	
Philippines	The Medium-Term Expenditure Framework (MTEF) and the Organizational Performance Indicator Framework (OPIF) were put in place during the formulation of the 2007 budget.	2007
Saudi Arabia	A number of structural reforms were implemented from 1999–2007 when the privatization process started to take place. The new Investment Law in 2000, the Judiciary System Law in 2007, and the Grievances Law in 2007, among other laws, are just an example of these reforms. The structure of the budget and the budget system that have been applied since 1938 has had only a minor updates and reforms.	
Taiwan	As part of Taiwan's democratization, the central government has been trying to reform the local election system and make local government more self-governing.	
Thailand	From 1959–2008, the Thai budget experienced three reforms: the line-item budget, the planning-programming-budgeting system (PPBS), and the strategic PBB. The most recent reform is PBB.	PPBS adopted in 1982; PBB in 1997; PBB was fully adopted government-wide through the public law in 2001; strategic PBB was adopted in 2001
United Arab Emirates	Adoption of PBB	2005
United Kingdom	Resource Accounting and Budgeting (RAB) introduced accruals accounting in UK public sector budgets.	1999–2000
United States	Federal Credit Reform Act of 1990 (FCRA) adopted a form of accrual budgetary accounting for federal direct loans and loan guarantees.	1990
Vietnam	The current law governing the budget process is the 2002 Law on the State Budget, which provides for decentralization.	2002

budget system in 1999, from the traditional input-oriented, line-items format, to a PBB system. But progress has been minimal at best.

Other recent reforms include attempts by Brazil to create a new pattern of medium- and long-term fiscal management process (The Law of Fiscal Responsibility [LFR]), and in the United States, there has been a movement toward reforming federal direct loans and loan guarantees (The Federal Credit Reform Act of 1990 [FCRA]).

Transparency Indices

The data in Table 20-10 examines the level of openness in government documents. The question of transparency was breached by several of the authors suggesting that it is a major concern as it relates to budgeting processes in many countries. The data in the table provides an Open Budget Initiative (OBI) score for each country examined in this analysis. The score is a product of research conducted by the Open Budget Initiative, a program that researches and advocates public access to budget information at the national level (International Budget Partnership, 2010).

Table 20-10

Transparency Score[a]	
Country	**OBI Score**
Brazil	74%
Canada	N/A
China	14%
Ghana	49%
Iraq	N/A
Italy	N/A
Jordan	52%
Korea	N/A
Mexico	54%
Pakistan	38%
Philippines	48%
Saudi Arabia	1%
Taiwan	N/A
Thailand	40%
United Arab Emirates	N/A
United Kingdom	88%
United States	82%
Vietnam	9%

[a] Data as of 2008.

The table shows that data were not available for Canada, Iraq, Italy, Korea, Taiwan, and the UAE. However, based on the information in the individual chapters, the lack of a score does not necessarily indicate the lack of transparency in the budgeting process.

Transparency in the budgeting process affords citizens the opportunity to access information at their discretion and determine what revenues are collected and how they are spent. This process gives citizens the luxury of judging whether or not government officials are good stewards of public funds. On the one hand, timely information can improve public participation in government, strengthen oversight, and improve policy choices. On the other hand, restricting information can enhance corruption, wasteful spending, and ultimately undermine the democratic process.

The data in the table shows that the United Kingdom, United States, and Brazil respectively have the greatest level of transparency in their budgeting processes. Saudi Arabia, Vietnam, and China had the lowest levels of transparency respectively (where data were available). With the exception of Mexico (54%) and Jordan (52%), no other country has an OBI score higher than 50%, as of 2008.

While there is clearly no perfect method to determining the level of transparency in a country, the data in Table 20-10 suggests that there is room for improvement in every country. However, when the level of transparency is correlated with the form of government, nations that are democratic are more likely to have a higher OBI score.

Public Budgeting in the Common Era

The data in this chapter as well as data in the preceding chapters show that the budgeting process is a difficult undertaking, and those who engage in the process have many hurdles to overcome as they continue to improve their individual systems. This information gives us much fodder to argue that Wildavsky's (1975) research remains salient today as well as the model offered by Rubin (2010). The expression, "old wine in a new bottle" seems to be quite fitting when summarizing the budgeting process around the globe. That is, many of the challenges that nations face have often been faced by other countries. As affluent countries implement cutting edge techniques, less affluent countries strive to maintain pace.

This research provided much evidence that we live in a global economy as the 1997 and 2008 financial crisis affected budgeting processes around the globe. These crises forced many nations to reexamine their budgeting and financial management practices. Hence, substantive changes were needed to minimize the effects of such events as well as to make the budgeting process more efficient and effective.

One practice is the prevalent use of accrual accounting by many countries. Premchand (2007) argues that most affluent countries and many revenue poor nations are in some stage of gravitating toward an accrual accounting system. We note that 14 of the 18 countries in our analysis use accrual accounting in some form or another, or they are moving toward implementing accrual-based accounting.

Concurrent with this shift is a movement toward PBB. This movement has also been motivated by a number of different factors including efficiency and effectiveness (in some cases, political corruption has trumped performance). The expectation by many countries is that a shift toward performance budgeting, with its outcome measures, will force government agencies to be more accountable to citizens.

However, we note that many countries have political barriers (institutional) that make change nearly impossible and these are further exasperated by limited resources. For example, identical budgeting systems can be in place in two different countries, but the implementation of the budget and the outcomes may be dramatically different due to the culture of the country. Political corruption and a lack of transparency appear to exist at unprecedented levels in many countries despite controls to limit the exercise of individual power. We note that change is very slow in some countries and many participants are tainted by the old systems and consciously make an effort to integrate old ideas into the new systems despites efforts to the contrary. This culture is partially impacted by ignorance of new systems, but in most cases it appears to be a matter of control over the process. In sum, the old process allows multiple actors to work within little fiefdoms and they simply do not want that power taken away.

More than anything, what we have taken away from this research is that political culture is one of the most pervasive factors affecting public budgeting. Both Wildavsky (1975) and Rubin (2010) highlight the need to consider it in their research. We note that there are, in fact, two rules: the rule of law and the rule of culture. In some countries, it is difficult to discern which of the two are stronger. That is, on paper, budgeting practices should occur one way, but in reality, individuals have the authority to usurp the law and implement the budget according to past customs. How often this is the case appears to vary to some extent, but as a general rule, countries that have uncertain or unpredictable budgeting patterns appear more likely to have an underlying set of rules that are contrary to the rule of law. Hence, we do not perceive that Wildavsky's model fully recognizes the salience of this variable. Rubin, however, does address this issue throughout her book. Therefore, in order for one country to truly learn and benefit from the success of another country, they must begin by understanding the unofficial rules of rules and then examine those rules in harmony with the rule of law.

Discussion Questions

1. What additional factors do you consider important in developing a comparative budgeting model? Explain why you chose those factors.
2. Based on your assessment of the information in this chapter, as well as the preceding chapters, does it appear that the type of budgeting system used by a country has a substantive impact on budget implementation? If there are exceptions, please explain.

3. Explain the correlation between budget transparency and accountability. Does budget transparency lead to greater efficiency and effectiveness? Explain your response within the context of cultural, social, political, and economic differences that exist around the globe.

4. What are the next steps in budget reform given the current state of the economy around the globe?

References

International Budget Partnership. (2010). *Open budget initiative.* Available at: http://www.openbudgetindex.org/index.cfm. Accessed April 22, 2010.

Pobre, H. P., & Araceli, B.-M. (1987). *Government accounting.* Manila. Available at: www.adb.org/documents/reports/accrual...accounting/chap04.pdf. Accessed March 26, 2010.

Premchand, A. (2007). Capital budgets: Theory and practice. In A. Shah (Ed.), *Budgeting and budgetary institutions.* Washington, DC: The World Bank.

Rubin, I. (2010). *The politics of public budgeting: Getting and spending, borrowing and balancing.* Washington, D.C.: CQ Press.

US Government Accountability Office (GAO). (2000, February 18). *Accrual budgeting: Experiences of other nations and implications for the United States.* Available at: www.gao.gov/products/AIMD-00-57. Accessed April 22, 2010.

Wildavsky, A. (1975). *Budgeting: A comparative theory of budgetary processes.* Boston: Little Brown.

Index

Page numbers followed by t or f indicate tables or figures, respectively.

Photo Credits

Chapter Openers

Chapter 1 © Mahesh Patil/ShutterStock, Inc.; **Chapter 2** © Rene Grycner/ShutterStock, Inc.; **Chapter 3** © Graphic design/ShutterStock, Inc.; **Chapter 4** © iDesign/ShutterStock, Inc.; **Chapter 5, Chapter 6** © Carsten Reisinger/ShutterStock, Inc.; **Chapter 7** © Matt Trommer/ShutterStock, Inc.; **Chapter 8** © JackF/ShutterStock, Inc.; **Chapter 9** © Fitim Bushati/ShutterStock, Inc.; **Chapter 10** © Benis Arapovic/ShutterStock, Inc.; **Chapter 11, Chapter 12** © Matt Trommer/ShutterStock, Inc.; **Chapter 13, Chapter 14** © Huebi/ShutterStock, Inc.; **Chapter 15** © Pavle Marjanovic/ShutterStock, Inc.; **Chapter 16** © Brent Walker/ShutterStock, Inc.; **Chapter 17** © Matt Trommer/ShutterStock, Inc.; **Chapter 18** © Jerry Horbert/ShutterStock, Inc.; **Chapter 19** © Graphic design/ShutterStock, Inc.; **Chapter 20** © Yakobchuk Vasyl/ShutterStock, Inc.

Unless otherwise indicated, all photographs and illustrations are under copyright of Jones & Bartlett Learning.